American Legal Thought from Premodernism to Postmodernism

American Legal Thought from Premodernism to Postmodernism

❧ *An Intellectual Voyage* ❧

Stephen M. Feldman

New York   Oxford

Oxford University Press

2000

Oxford University Press

Oxford New York

Athens   Auckland   Bangkok   Bogotá   Buenos Aires   Calcutta
Cape Town   Chennai   Dar es Salaam   Dehli   Florence   Hong Kong   Istanbul
Karachi   Kuala Lumpur   Madrid   Melbourne   Mexico City   Mumbai
Nairobi   Paris   São Paulo   Singapore   Taipei   Tokyo   Toronto   Warsaw

and associated companies in
Berlin   Ibadan

Copyright © 2000 by Oxford University Press, Inc.

Published by Oxford University Press, Inc.
198 Madison Avenue, New York, New York 10016

Oxford is a registered trademark of Oxford University Press

Library of Congress Cataloging-in-Publication Data
Feldman, Stephen M., 1931–
American legal thought from premodernism to postmodernism:
an intellectual voyage / Stephen M. Feldman.
p. cm.
Includes bibliographical references and index.
ISBN 0-19-510966-X (cl.); ISBN 0-19-510967-8 (pbk.)
1. Jurisprudence—United States.   2. Law—United States—Philosophy.
3. Postmodernism.   I. Title.
KF379.F45 2000
349.73—DC21   99-18548

1   3   5   7   9   8   6   4   2
Printed in the United States of America
on acid-free paper

To my family,
Laura,
Mollie,
and
Samuel

Acknowledgments

As I have learned over the past few years, deciding whom to thank for assistance in the writing of a book can be a daunting task. Of course, I especially thank those individuals who commented on drafts of this book: Steven D. Smith, Jay Mootz, Richard Delgado, James R. Hackney, Jr., Morris Bernstein, and Linda Lacey. A long telephone conversation with Ted White several years ago led to the idea for (greatly) expanding one of my essays into this book, and an invitation from Bernard Schwartz to participate in a conference on the Warren Court led to the writing of that original essay. All of the participants in the University of Tulsa College of Law colloquy on my book manuscript—but especially the organizer of the colloquy, Lakshman Guruswamy—were generous with their time and insights. In addition, numerous people have commented on several of my articles and essays, which partly served as the springboards for this book. Those individuals who have helped me with their insights on multiple occasions include Jack Balkin, Richard Delgado, Stanley Fish, Jay Mootz, Dennis Patterson, Mark Tushnet, Larry Catá Backer, Marty Belsky, Bill Hollingsworth, and Linda Lacey. Finally, I also benefited from the suggestions of several colleagues regarding the title of the book, including Chris Blair, Marianne Blair, Bill Hollingsworth, and Linda Lacey. In terms of financial support, the grant of a fellowship from the National Endowment for the Humanities was enormously helpful in allowing me to complete the book in a timely fashion. The Faculty Summer Research Grant Program of the University of Tulsa College of Law also provided financial assistance during this project. All of the librarians at the University of Tulsa College of Law, including Rich Ducey and Nanette Hjelm, contributed their support, but I want to express my special gratitude to Carol Arnold for facilitating my research in numerous ways.

Articles and essays that, to different degrees, served as the bases for various parts of the book were published in the following places: *Virginia Law Review, Philosophy and Social Criticism, Vanderbilt Law Review, Michigan Law Review, Minnesota Law Review, Northwestern University Law Review, Wisconsin Law Review, Iowa Law Review,* and *The Warren Court: A Retrospective* (Bernard Schwartz ed., Oxford University Press, 1996).

The science of the Law is, of all others, the most sublime and comprehensive, and in its general signification, comprises all things, human and divine.

—Professor D. T. Blake, Columbia University, 1810
(quoted in Perry Miller, *The Life of the Mind in America*)

Contents

ONE

Introduction: *On Intellectual History*, 3

TWO

Charting the Intellectual Waters: *Premodernism,
Modernism, and Postmodernism*, 11

THREE

Premodern American Legal Thought, 49

FOUR

Modern American Legal Thought, 83

FIVE

Postmodern American Legal Thought, 137

SIX

Conclusion: *A Glimpse of the Future?*, 188

Notes, 199

Index, 263

American Legal Thought from Premodernism to Postmodernism

✵ O N E ✵

Introduction

On Intellectual History

To travel from premodernism through modernism and into post-modernism might take several centuries and even millennia. American legal thought, remarkably so, has made the voyage in just over two hundred years. My purpose is to tell the story of this mercurial journey.

To narrate this story successfully, I divide the book into two parts. The first and briefer part (chapter 2 only) explores the general concepts of premodernism, modernism, and postmodernism. Drawing extensively but not solely from philosophy, I describe these concepts as a series of major intellectual stages or periods, which I then break into numerous substages. These stages and substages, as I conceptualize them, are not historical or structural necessities that somehow are fated to occur. Rather, I proffer premodernism, modernism, and postmodernism and their respective substages as heuristic devices somewhat akin to Weberian "ideal types."[1] They are interpretive constructs designed by highlighting certain recurrent and prominent (though contingent) historical phenomena, and, as such, the stages and substages can facilitate the narrative analysis of the developments in different intellectual disciplines or fields.

The second part and bulk of this book applies this interpretive framework of premodernism, modernism, and postmodernism to American legal thought, or jurisprudence. My narrative follows the movements of legal thought in America from around 1776 onward. These movements do not necessarily embody a progression—a movement upward or toward better conceptions of jurisprudence—but rather suggest a series of understandable transitions or stages of development. In short, I present American legal thought as a coherent albeit unplanned intellectual voyage over previously charted waters.

3

This narrative voyage of legal thought, moreover, has implications beyond the jurisprudential field. While some (or many) might question whether legal scholars have been intellectual leaders in America, few would deny that law always has been a central social institution in this nation. Alexis de Tocqueville proclaimed this truism as early as 1835: "[s]carcely any political question arises in the United States that is not resolved, sooner or later, into a judicial question." Over 150 years later, in 1994, Mary Ann Glendon reiterated: "Much of America's uniqueness . . . lies in the degree to which law figures in the standard accounts of where we came from, who we are, and where we are going." Partly for this reason, the story of the movement of jurisprudence from premodernism to modernism and into postmodernism depicts more than one small and insular facet of American society. Rather, the story of American jurisprudence captures much of how Americans— or at least, American intellectuals—represent themselves. For example, a crucial component of modernism is the human desire to purposefully control social relations. Modernist intellectuals, in particular, confidently profess their ability to engineer societal change and order. And frequently, this desire for control is implemented through law, as exemplified by the New Deal Congress: its repeated legislative attempts to restructure the economy can be understood as prototypical modernist efforts to reorder society. Modernism, in a sense, has "an imperative to express itself in and through the law."[2] Subsequently, in postmodernism, this instrumental use of law as well as the authoritativeness of judicial and other legal pronouncements becomes highly problematic. Hence, without overstating the point, jurisprudential theories from the various eras concerning these and other aspects of law might disclose more than initially meets the eye: they might reveal much about prevalent American perceptions and representations of social reality.

Throughout the book, I use the terms *legal thought* and *jurisprudence* interchangeably. Some current scholars prefer to define jurisprudence narrowly, as no more than a type of analytic philosophy focusing on legal concepts. Contrary to this position, my broader conception of jurisprudence—as the equivalent of legal thought—encompasses multiple perspectives of the law, including but not limited to philosophical, sociological, historical, and cultural views. Thus, I explore how jurisprudents, broadly defined, have explained, described, and theorized from a variety of perspectives the nature and practice of law in relation to judicial decision making and government in general. Indeed, during the very first stage of premodern American legal thought, most jurisprudents themselves viewed legal, political, and social thought as inextricably intertwined. Individuals such as James Wilson and Nathaniel Chipman were intellectual and political leaders of the late eighteenth century who typically wrote about law as encompassed within political and social theory. Wilson, for example, sat on the first United States Supreme Court after having been one of only six individuals who signed both the Declaration of Independence and the Constitution. In the early 1790s, he delivered to the College of Philadelphia the first lectures on American constitutional law—lectures that ranged widely in their observations and theories on human nature, morality, history, government, law, and more. To be sure, in the latter nineteenth century, the development of the professional legal academician led to more specialized jurisprudential writings—more focused on law per se, ostensibly independent from political and social thought. Yet, such a limited conception of jurisprudence, characteristic of modernism, does not adequately capture the scope of early American legal thought or, as it turns out, the rich variety of perspectives evident in postmodern legal writing.[3]

Despite the breadth of my subject matter, I otherwise limit this study in one crucial respect: I concentrate on the mandarins of American legal thought. I discuss jurisprudential leaders such as James Kent and Joseph Story in the nineteenth century and Karl Llewellyn and Henry Hart in the twentieth century. I rarely discuss the daily practice of law by the average attorney. And surely, the fully developed jurisprudential musings of someone such as Story, a Harvard professor and Supreme Court justice, would differ significantly from the average attorney's notion of law. At the same time, it is worth noting, many of the jurisprudential elites of the nineteenth century, including Kent, Story, and Oliver Wendell Holmes, Jr., were both scholars and judges, so their conceptions of law were somewhat informed by their practical experiences in deciding cases. The same is true of at least some twentieth-century elites; Benjamin Cardozo is a notable example.

Although I focus on the mandarins of American legal thought, I do not explore their ideas as pure abstractions. To the contrary, my notion of a history of ideas demands that the ideas be explicated within the social, cultural, and political contexts in which they developed. Even in chapter 2, where I tend to trace premodernism, modernism, and postmodernism as abstract heuristics, I sketch those ideas on at least some broad contextual fabrics. Most intellectual developments would be grossly distorted if presented as arising in some ethereal world, apart from their historical surroundings. The general themes of modernism, for example, cannot be understood adequately without accounting in part for the influence of the Protestant Reformation on western civilization. Thus, in the chapters focusing on American legal thought, I seek to explain (or narrate) how and why the various stages and substages emerged in jurisprudence at specific historical times. Social, political, and cultural factors always and importantly influence the development or movement of the ideas. Yet, simultaneously, from my perspective, broad ideas tend to develop in certain directions because of the content and force of the ideas themselves. Such broad ideas have, so to speak, a relatively autonomous existence. They do not solely arise from or depend on social interests or structures; the ideas are not mere superstructure in the Marxian sense. Ideas and social interests interact in a complex dialectical relationship.[4]

For example, a broad idea X might tend to develop into another idea Y, but this development might not emerge unless and until particular social, political, and cultural circumstances arise that facilitate or trigger it. As a general matter, the elements for a major intellectual change—say, from X to Y—often seem to gather over an extended time period, like clouds on the horizon, but the transition remains latent, as a mere potential, until a large social disturbance such as the Civil War or the World Wars occurs. This social upheaval then precipitates the intellectual transformation, like a sudden burst of rain. Of course, as described, the intellectual transformation is neither exactly sudden nor exactly gradual—neither revolutionary nor evolutionary. Despite final appearances, the intellectual transition should not be understood as an unexpected or unpredictable cloudburst because it has been building for years and sometimes even decades. Yet, even so, it is not truly gradual, steady, and slow because the transition does not emerge in a clearly recognizable form until the requisite social event finally triggers the ultimate transformation.[5]

When America's legal mandarins are understood in this manner within their respective historical contexts, many of them seem intelligent, erudite (and not just in law), and sometimes even brilliant. Nonetheless, all too often, legal historians and jurisprudents denigrate earlier schools of thought as insipid or downright stupid.[6] Looking backward at the legal process scholars of the 1950s, for instance, one might wonder how they could devote their careers to articulating such trite maxims as "treat like cases alike." But when understood within their distinctive historical context, including the Cold War, their efforts to defend the rule of law and legal objectivity become understandable and even compelling. Throughout this work, then, I try to make intellectual sense of the various schools of legal thought within the contexts in which they arose, although to be sure, I do not seek to justify or rejuvenate any of these earlier schools of jurisprudence.

It is worth noting, at this point, that any intellectual history of American jurisprudence that focuses on legal mandarins and that emphasizes transitions among various stages and substages might tend to overlook details and to ignore certain dissenting views that would detract from the persuasive force of the narrative. History, including intellectual history, is not carefully patterned, but a narrative that focuses on legal elites and broad periods might misleadingly suggest just such an orderliness. As a postmodernist might assert, the writing of grand narratives, meta-narratives, or meta-histories generally should be resisted because, in part, periodizations tend to flatten history. So-called stages frequently are described as if they were represented by a single voice or position. Dissenting views and oppressed voices are ignored or minimized in the rush to neatly characterize an era as illustrative of a particular idea or approach. Thus, for example, in jurisprudence, the 1920s might be presented as the age of the early American legal realists without acknowledging that many would-be realists held divergent views and that many legal scholars during that decade were not realists at all. Furthermore, one might easily fail to account for the outsiders of those years—African Americans, women, Jews, and others—who usually could not even articulate their jurisprudential views in public forums.[7]

To be perfectly candid, these potential difficulties make me pause. I have devoted much of my previous scholarship to disclosing and discussing the marginalized voices of minorities and outgroups in other contexts.[8] I do not now dismiss the importance of such voices in the history of American jurisprudence. Unfortunately, many legal elites have participated to varying degrees in racism, sexism, antisemitism, and economic classism. In this regard, despite their legal and theoretical acumen, these scholars were all too ordinary; for much of American history, it seemed that only an exceptional person could somehow escape such biases. To be sure, then, there are vital stories to be told about American jurisprudence from the perspectives of various outgroups, yet those stories are not the ones I currently wish to explore, at least not as my primary task.[9] Instead, at the outset, these potential difficulties for a jurisprudential history can serve as a caveat that helps to clarify my narrative goals.

In particular, I seek primarily to account for specific intellectual developments in jurisprudence as understood against the background of American society and through the prism of certain intellectual commonalities or tendencies that range across disciplines or fields. From my perspective, although certain broad themes and transformations are recognizable in numerous disciplines, intellectual history should not be reduced to some grand narrative of universal themes and progressions. Different intellectual fields do not develop exactly the same way or at the same pace. Consequently, I first offer a general heuristic and interpretive framework for understanding the potential transformations of intellectual history, and then I explore the application of that framework in the specific context of American legal thought. In so doing, I focus on the social, cultural, and political factors that influenced the transitions in jurisprudence. Other intellectual fields and disciplines very well may have developed in divergent manners or at different speeds. Nonetheless, over the expansive fabric of *American* intellectual thought, significant resemblances and overlaps among different areas should be expected exactly because the sundry disciplines and fields often developed in similar social, cultural, and political contexts. For that reason, my narrative of American legal thought occasionally discusses developments in other intellectual fields to help elucidate jurisprudential transitions.

To emphasize a crucial point: my general interpretive framework and more particular narrative of American jurisprudence offer, I believe, an especially fruitful and persuasive way for explicating and understanding intellectual developments. Yet, my conceptualizations of premodernism, modernism, and postmodernism, as well as the various substages within those respective eras, should not be taken to represent categorical distinctions or rigid demarcations either in intellectual history generally or in the specific instance of American jurisprudence. Without doubt, one could define premodernism, modernism, and postmodernism differently and could therefore argue that the various stages emerged at other points in American legal history. Without doubt, one could focus on different voices— dissenting jurisprudents, or regular attorneys, or state court judges, or Supreme

Court justices—and could therefore present an alternative but still persuasive history of American legal thought. And without doubt, even an intellectual history focusing on legal mandarins could instead emphasize the psychological details and idiosyncratic motivations of individual jurisprudents rather than the wide social, cultural, and political contexts for broad intellectual transitions. For example, while I stress the broad trends of the post–Civil War era as influencing Christopher Columbus Langdell's crucial deanship at Harvard Law School (during the early modernist period), an alternative approach might focus more on Langdell's life experiences, both personal and professional, as shaping his intellectual directions. What did he himself do during the Civil War? What did he do before the war? What type of legal practice did he have? Did he have a family? Who were his friends? What did he write in his letters to his friends? To his professional colleagues? One might explore these questions in detail in a more psychologically or personally oriented intellectual history.[10]

As it is, though, my purpose is to explore the movement of American legal thought over more than two centuries, and consequently, I necessarily stress broad trends and large factors. An intellectual history focusing more on personal or psychological influences, in order to be a manageable project, must concentrate on a narrow range of time or a small number of individuals, and thus is not amenable to my purposes. This is not to suggest that I ignore psychological factors, just that I do not stress them. More important, though, I also do not ignore the views of jurisprudents dissenting from the major schools of legal thought. I discuss such views when doing so seems important to the narrative flow—when such views are part of the basic story that I am telling. In fact, quite often, such critical or dissenting views help illuminate the mainstream and then lead into the next stage or substage of jurisprudential development (sometimes a dissenting view becomes the next leading school of thought). And in the latter part of the twentieth century, when members of outgroups—particularly women and racial minorities—finally secure some positions within the legal academy, their voices and views move to the forefront of the narrative. That is, in chapter 5, I highlight the critical perspectives of some outgroup members because they represent, in effect, some of the main themes of postmodern jurisprudence.

In a somewhat similar vein, I discuss judicial decisions only insofar as they fit within the narrative of my main story. Since that main story is about the mandarins of American jurisprudence and since those individuals often wrote about cases, especially Supreme Court cases, I must occasionally do likewise. For the most part, though, I discuss only those cases, such as *Lochner v. New York*, *Brown v. Board of Education*, and *Roe v. Wade*, that significantly influenced the legal scholarship of an era.[11]

Two final definitional points should be clarified. First, some writers distinguish premodern*ity* from premodern*ism*, modern*ity* from modern*ism*, and postmodern*ity* from postmodern*ism*. These writers typically characterize, for example, modernism as a cultural phenomenon and modernity as a particular social, political, and economic arrangement. Similar distinctions between the cultural and the sociological are then applied to the other eras (premodernism and postmodernism). From my perspective, though, such sharp dichotomies are problematic because cultural and social practices necessarily conjoin. As already suggested, even if intellectual developments are understood primarily as cultural manifestations, they nonetheless depend in part on social and political interests. Thus, I use the terms *premodernism, modernism,* and *postmodernism* broadly to encompass the cultural and the sociological. Most often, I will be referring to constellations of certain ideas as they occurred within particular social and historical contexts.[12]

Second, as the terms themselves suggest, premodernism, modernism, and postmodernism should be understood relationally, with modernism being the central concept both temporally and analytically, at least at this point in intellectual history. That is, premodernism is understood as pre- or before modernism, and postmodernism likewise is understood as post- or after modernism. The centrality of modernism might be due partly to an aspect of intellectual history itself: namely, that modernists were the first to periodize intellectual developments as a series of stages or broad transitions. Yet, despite this centrality of modernism, the portions of the book on postmodernism are slightly longer than those on either modernism or premodernism, at least relative to the number of years encompassed by each of the stages. For instance, the respective chapters on modern and postmodern legal thought are approximately equal in length even though modernism stretches over a century or more while postmodernism, so far, covers perhaps two decades. Although somewhat disproportionate, this space for postmodernism was nonetheless necessary. For one thing, since we are presently in the midst of the postmodern era, I lack the historical distance that would facilitate a narrower focus on what might become the most enduring threads of postmodern jurisprudential thought. Thus, in chapter 5, I discuss eight postmodern themes, but fifty years from now, a jurisprudential historian with hindsight might well conclude that, let's say, only four themes had lasting significance and deserve extensive discussion. This problem of historical distance is exacerbated by the character of postmodernism itself. In particular, postmodern intellectual thought is so strikingly interdisciplinary that a neat and brief depiction of postmodernism would be problematic; there are just too many complex and interconnected themes crisscrossing the crumbling disciplinary fences of the academic and intellectual postmodern landscape. Moreover, precisely because of this interdisciplinary complexity, the slightly disproportionate space accorded to postmodernism in this book seems worthwhile to help counter the offhand dismissals and condemnations of postmodern thought that have surfaced in some intellectual circles—dismissals and condemnations that are due most often, in my opinion, to serious misunderstandings of major postmodern themes. Admittedly, these misunderstandings occasionally arise because of the jargon-filled argot of some (but not all) postmodern writing, but regardless of the cause of the confusion—whether complexity or obfuscation—a clear presentation of postmodern themes seems vital to the main storyline of this book.

In any event, because of the relational quality among the concepts of premodernism, modernism, and postmodernism, one should not expect to grasp the entire meaning of any stage in isolation. Rather, full understanding can emerge only by comprehending the relations—the differences and similarities—among the various stages and substages. Ultimately, then, the focus on all the stages of American legal thought—premodernism, modernism, and postmodernism—distinguishes this book from other historical treatments of American jurisprudence. Many other such books ignore the pre–Civil War era and thus begin their narratives with the emergence of Langdellian legal science and Holmesian jurisprudence after the Civil War—that is, at the outset of the modernist period. I have instead included the time from the nation's inception through the Civil War as an integral part of the sweep of American jurisprudential history. This coverage of the premodern period then, it is hoped, renders the modern and even postmodern periods more vivid and intelligible.[13]

Throughout the book, the concepts of premodernism, modernism, and postmodernism structure the narrative so that it revolves around two broad interrelated themes: jurisprudential foundations, and the idea of progress. Much of the story of American jurisprudence turns on the problem of identifying (or doubting) the foundations of the American legal system and judicial decision making. Premodern jurisprudents, for example, largely agreed that natural law principles undergirded the American legal system, while modernists repudiated natural law and thus set out on a quest for some alternative foundation. The various conceptions of jurisprudential foundations that characterized the different eras, furthermore, were closely tied to shifting ideas of progress—ideas that entailed a series of different definitions of progress, different assumptions about the possibility of progress, and different hopes about how law might contribute to progress. Hence, at least for second-stage premodern jurisprudents, the natural law principles provided both a goal and a limit for social and legal progress, whereas for modernist jurisprudents, the possibilities for progress seemed endless, limited only by human ingenuity. I elaborate the general ideas of foundations and progress—as well as the general concepts of premodernism, modernism, and postmodernism—in chapter 2. For those readers interested solely in legal thought and not in the broader concepts of premodernism, modernism, and postmodernism, however, chapters 3 through 6 can be understood on their own. For that matter, chapter 2 also can stand alone as a general introduction to the broader concepts. Nonetheless, the book is an integrated whole, and all the chapters together are intended to contribute to a unified narrative.

Charting the Intellectual Waters

Premodernism, Modernism, and Postmodernism

Premodernism

Premodernism can be divided into two consecutive substages, which I call, respectively, the cyclical and the eschatological.[1] The first was marked by an abiding faith in nature or God (or the gods) as a stable and foundational source of knowledge and value. Universals were presumed to exist and to be evident in all modes of life, both physical and normative. Plato, for instance, posited the existence of Ideas (or Forms)—such as absolute beauty, goodness, and equality—that are distinct from sensible things. The Ideas are universal, unchanging, and stable, while sensible things are particular, ephemeral, and in flux. In a fashion, the particular or sensible things participate in or are imperfect manifestations of the universal Ideas.[2] More broadly, the classical Greek concept of the *kosmos* encompassed "the ordered totality of being," including universal and eternal moral and aesthetic values as well as the physical world. The Greek *kosmos* included "the *physis* of organic being, the *ethos* of personal conduct and social structures, the *nomos* of normative custom and law, and the *logos*, the rational foundation that normatively rules all aspects of the cosmic development."[3]

Because of this metaphysical unity—the integration of the normative and the physical—human access to knowledge and value (or more precisely, virtue) always remained immanent within ourselves and within the world. Individuals and societies seemed to belong to rather than to exist separately from nature and divinity. The *kosmos* was "intrinsically intelligible" and therefore accessible (or knowable) because "both mind and reality participated in the same intelligibility." Reason, as understood in classical thought, could discern the virtuous or good life. Thus, humans seemed capable of directly accessing and therefore knowing the eternal and universal principles that arose from or within the world (nature or divinity). According to Plato's doctrine of recollection, each person contains the immanent potential to achieve true knowledge of the Ideas or universal principles. "[K]nowledge and right reason," Plato contended, are already within each of us, but we have, in a sense, forgotten them. Thus, to fulfill our potential for knowledge, we must recollect the universals, or in other words, we must recover "that which we previously knew."[4]

The presumed existence of universal and eternal principles led to distinctive conceptualizations of the temporal; time or history had to harmonize with the idea of the eternal and universal. In the first stage of premodernism, time was understood to be cyclical. The Greeks observed in the physical world "the continual growth, maturity, and decline" of organisms as well as the revolutions of the planets. From these observations, they developed their understanding of the relationship between immutable principles and temporal change, which they then extended to human affairs and societal history. Civilizations would rise and fall in a type of "cyclic motion," but the eternal and universal principles remained intact. "According to the Greek view of life and the world," Karl Löwith wrote, "everything moves in recurrences, like the eternal recurrence of sunrise and sunset, of summer and winter, of generation and corruption." Thus, Thucydides assumed that his history of the Peloponnesian War revealed as much about the future as about the past: "[I]f he who desires to have before his eyes a true picture of the events which have happened, and of the like events which may be expected to happen hereafter in the order of human things, shall pronounce what I have written to be useful, then I shall be satisfied. My history is an everlasting possession, not a prize composition which is heard and forgotten."[5]

Within this integrated premodern world, the idea of the universal pervaded political thought. To Aristotle, the universal nature and ends of human life determine the best form of political society. Most important, then, one must recognize that "man is by nature a political animal" and that the *telos* or natural end of human life is *eudaimonia,* or happiness. One achieves happiness by living in accordance with virtue, and one cannot live virtuously except by acting prudently and sagaciously *within* a *polis* or political community. The good of the individual and the good of the political community are intertwined and inseparable. In "the best regime," Aristotle declared, "[the citizen] is one who is capable of and intentionally chooses being ruled and ruling with a view to the life in accordance with virtue." The government, regardless of its form or type—whether a government of the one, the few, or the many—should pursue the satisfaction of the common good and not mere private interests. For the individual, in short, virtuous participation in the political community was deemed the highest good.[6]

During the fourth century C.E., the Roman Empire established Christianity as the imperial or official religion. With this coming of the Christian era to western civilization, premodernism entered upon its second stage, the eschatological. Universal and eternal principles still were presumed to exist, though at this point, clearly, God supposedly ordained them. Yet, Christianity stressed a distinction between the spiritual and the carnal that led to a more constrained understanding of the *kosmos*. The *kosmos* (or now the cosmos) became associated more with the carnal than the spiritual and thus seemed to be more physical than normative, although it "still contained the marks of God's presence." The concept of human reason, too, became more limited. With reason alone, a person supposedly could not grasp universal and eternal truths, though one still could do so through religious faith.[7]

A key difference between the first and second stages of premodernism lay in their respective characterizations of time or history. Early in the fifth century, St. Augustine wrote *The City of God*, a tremendously influential theological, philosophical, and political treatise. Augustine argued that original sin leads to "two kinds of human society, which we may justly call two cities, according to the language of our Scriptures. The one consists of those who wish to live after the flesh, the other of those who wish to live after the spirit." The earthly city is formed by love of self, while the heavenly city—the City of God or the community of Christians—is formed by love of God. Although notoriously ambiguous, Augustine's conception of the two cities appeared to revolve around two related distinctions. According to the first distinction, the heavenly and earthly cities referred to "two communities": the saved and the damned. These two communities are "eschatological realities"—they will fulfill themselves only in their ends. One community "is predestined to reign eternally with God, and the other to suffer eternal punishment with the devil." Although unfulfilled eschatological entities, both cities nonetheless presently exist; Augustine stated that the cities have begun "to run their course." Here, then, Augustine edged over into the second distinction. He differentiated two measures of time or history: the sacred (eschatological time) and the *saeculum* (secular or temporal history). The two cities, as eschatological realities, must be understood in *sacred* history as revealed in the Scriptures. Yet, within *secular* time, the two cities currently exist together in unfulfilled (or impure) forms: "[i]n truth, these two cities are entangled together in this world, and intermixed until the last judgment effect their separation." Augustine, it seems, sought to disentangle the future of Christianity from the fate of the then crumbling Roman Empire. He therefore posited that the Christian City of God was progressing toward its fulfillment in sacred time, even though empires and kingdoms might rise and fall throughout secular (or carnal) history.[8]

Most significantly, then, Augustine incorporated an idea of progress into a world still grounded on universal and eternal principles, as ordained by God. In sacred history, progress was inherent in the very concept of a divine eschatological end or goal of two communities, the saved and the damned. In secular history, civilizations would continue to rise and fall—consistent with the first-stage premodernist conceptions—but now, under the second-stage notion, progress could be measured, in a sense, by a movement toward the fulfillment or realization of the eschatological City of God. Such progress was due not to human ingenuity or willfulness but rather to divine intervention. Moreover, such progress was not endless, not a series of continuous qualitative advancements, but rather was the realization of ultimate (divine) principles.[9]

The early Christian separation of the spiritual and the carnal threatened the metaphysical unity of the premodern world. Yet, for many centuries, this potential threat went largely unfulfilled, partly because intellectual thought remained focused on spiritual and theological affairs. Indeed, the premodern world's metaphysical unity was, in a sense, even strengthened when Aristotle's writings became widely available to Christian philosophers and theologians in the early thirteenth century. St. Thomas Aquinas explicitly attempted to synthesize the Greek and Christian worldviews, and in so doing, he revitalized human reason and renewed theoretical interest in secular poiltical affairs. According to Thomas, humans can use reason to learn certain truths about God, though other truths concerning God are accessible only by faith. And, consistent with Aristotle's emphasis on the *polis,* Thomas introduced into Christendom the idea of the political, suggesting that an individual was not merely a subject *under* a government descending from above but rather was a citizen who *participated* in government.[10]

An early sign of an approaching metaphysical rift came in the late-Renaissance thought of Niccolo Machiavelli, whose humanist political theory stressed the wellbeing of the state. Machiavelli strictly limited his Christian presuppositions: whereas medieval Christian thought maintained that divine providence determined the fate of the secular state, Machiavelli emphasized the role of sheer fortune and human nature in political affairs. Machiavelli thus presaged the development of modernist political theory, which was further spurred by the emergence of European nation-states during the sixteenth and seventeenth centuries. Nonetheless, Machiavelli retained the premodernist conception of history: civilizations were doomed ultimately to rise and fall. "Wise men say, and not without reason," wrote Machiavelli, "that whoever wishes to foresee the future must consult the past: for human events ever resemble those of preceding times." At best, then, a virtuous ruler and citizens could preserve a republic only temporarily.[11]

Indeed, for Machiavelli, the preservation and liberty of the republic are the highest values, and the citizen and ruler should do whatever is necessary to accomplish those ends—the common good—regardless of consistency or inconsistency with religious or moral values. Sheer fortune and human (sinful) nature, however, ensure the eventual collapse of all governments. The tension between, on the one hand, political order and, on the other hand, fortune and human nature—and the resultant struggle to maintain the fragile political community through secular time—was therefore a constant theme for Machiavelli. He understood *virtù* (virtue) as the (at least temporary) overcoming of fortune and human nature as one pursued the common good: citizens and rulers alike must seek to disregard their "own passions" and instead act for the good (the preservation) of the community. Machiavellian *virtù* required a successful ruler, in particular, to do whatever was necessary to preserve the political community: "A prince . . . must imitate the fox and the lion, for the lion cannot protect himself from traps, and the fox cannot defend himself from wolves." Machiavelli's overriding concern, in sum, was with how to maintain the republic despite the dire challenges that arose repeatedly through secular time.[12]

Modernism

Almost contemporaneously with the publication of Machiavelli's major writings, Martin Luther launched the Protestant Reformation in 1517 by posting his Ninety-five Theses, which denounced the Roman Catholic Church's materialistic practice of selling indulgences. Once having begun his protests, Luther continued to relentlessly criticize both the Church's widespread involvement in worldly affairs and the interrelated Thomistic concern for the political, including Thomas's Aristotelian emphasis on human reason. From Luther's perspective, he sought not to revolutionize but to purify Christianity by revitalizing the separation of the spiritual and the carnal (or secular). An individual did not need the worldly Catholic Church to explain the meaning of Christian faith; a true Christian could personally experience the primacy and the meaning of the Scriptures.[13] With regard to metaphysics, Luther and the other Protestant reformers represented the flip side of Machiavelli: both Machiavelli and the reformers undermined the metaphysical unity of the premodern world, but whereas Machiavelli focused on the secular (especially the political) at the expense of the spiritual, the reformers stressed the spiritual over the secular. In particular, Luther's most prominent follower, John Calvin, seized upon the dichotomy of the spiritual and the secular to articulate a theological position that crucially set the parameters for modernist intellectual thought.

In a manner of speaking, Calvin insisted upon the strict separation of church and state—or the spiritual and the secular—as a tenet of his Protestant reform theology. Calvin did not directly oppose the secular state to the spiritual realm, but rather he maintained that the secular and spiritual stand so absolutely apart that they cannot be antithetical. "[Secular] government is distinct from that spiritual and inward Kingdom of Christ," Calvin declared, "so we must know that they are not at variance." In other words, to Calvin, secular and spiritual government cannot be antagonistic exactly because they are completely separate: when two realms have no overlap, no point of contact, no interaction, then they cannot be antithetical. Calvin's firm support for Christian freedom of conscience illustrates the theological significance of this radical separation of the spiritual and secular. From Calvin's perspective, each individual must remain free so that his or her conscience can inwardly experience Christ and Christian faith. Neither the secular state nor even the Reformed church should attempt to coerce faith because genuine spiritual faith, quite simply, cannot be compelled. Coercion (of any type or source) belongs solely in the secular or carnal world, while conscience and faith remain entirely distinct and within the spiritual world. Somewhat ambivalently, then, Calvin and the other reformers introduced a type of proto-individualism. Reformation theology, to be sure, showed newfound respect for the individual qua individual—as the individual, in a sense, now seemed to stand alone before God—but simultaneously, the reformers stressed that, due to original sin, the individual in this world was thoroughly depraved and sinful.[14]

Overall, the Reformation contributed four crucial elements for the building of a new modernist world view. First, and most simply, the willingness of Luther, Calvin, and other Protestant leaders to challenge the Roman Catholic Church set an important social precedent. No longer were societal authorities and arrangements inviolable merely because they were traditionally accepted. If the most powerful social institution of the Middle Ages, the church, could be confronted and at least partially defeated, then no social institution was impregnable. To question, to doubt, to challenge, and to confront traditions became imaginable and even normal.[15] Second, by challenging institutional authority, by emphasizing freedom of conscience, and by insisting that individuals could directly understand the Scriptures, the reformers contributed to the eventual emergence of modernist individualism. Despite the ambivalence of the reformers' proto-individualism, modernist philosophers eventually would posit an increasingly dignified individual—an individual who, it would be assumed, could independently and autonomously choose values and goals.[16] Third, Calvin's theological dualism—his thorough disjunction of the spiritual and secular—facilitated the development of a metaphysical dualism that opposed the individual self to the objective world. This metaphysical dualism would undergird modernist thought for centuries to come. Finally, Calvin's theological dualism allowed the secular realm, in the long run, to gain increasing importance, although Calvin did not intend as much. Calvin himself sought to free the spiritual from the secular, but in doing so he simultaneously freed the secular from the spiritual. In short, Calvin's reform theology may have had the rather perverse effect of strongly contributing to the coming secularization (or disenchantment) of western society.[17]

Again, though, Calvin intended nothing of the sort. To the contrary, despite his theoretical conception of a type of separation of church and state, Calvin seemed determined to establish a Christian society, nurtured by both religious and secular authorities. He even once used his political strength in Geneva to ensure the conviction and burning of a theological opponent. Nonetheless, Calvin enforced such a rigorous division between the spiritual and secular that the secular became conceived as purely material, bereft of any worth, substance, or purpose. This ravaging of the secular realm—the complete stripping of its meaning and purpose—allowed Calvin then, somewhat paradoxically, to posit that the spiritual should, in a sense, colonize the secular. To Calvin, because the secular was purely material and devoid of meaning, the only ultimate reason for any human action in the secular world was that God had ordained it.[18] Calvin, in other words, first contrasted the spirituality of Christianity with the empty materiality of the secular world, only then to assert the right of Christianity to lay claim to the otherwise worthless secular realm. Calvin himself, thus, was certain that the spiritual should govern the secular, albeit somewhat indirectly because of the disjunction of the two realms.

Not everybody, however, shared Calvin's powerful religious convictions. His reform theology, in effect, helped propel a turn toward modernism by encouraging some individuals to focus on this-worldly activities. For these individuals, the complete separation of the spiritual and secular realms presented an opportunity: with the secular realm apparently bereft of divine meaning and purpose, humans seemed free to impose their own purposes. Humans could control the secular, including the natural or physical world, because God no longer was doing so. Furthermore, even for the most religiously devout Calvinists, the disjunction of the spiritual and secular oddly encouraged a focus on this-worldly conduct. Because of the disjunction, Calvin asserted that human activity in the secular world could not possibly lead to spiritual salvation. Humans could do absolutely nothing to change their eternal fate; they were, Calvin reasoned, not only sinful but also already predestined to salvation or damnation. With spiritual salvation therefore no longer an attainable goal (at least through secular activities or works), individuals had no choice but to focus, with all their abilities, on their respective callings in the secular world—for this must then be for the greater glory of God.[19]

This willingness to focus human energy and purposiveness on the secular world was one reason, among many, for the breakthroughs in science that steadily emerged during the sixteenth and seventeenth centuries. Even before the Reformation, the discovery or introduction of practical scientific and technological devices such as the mechanical compass and the printing press had begun to alter western society dramatically. But starting in the mid-sixteenth century, a sensational line of new scientific discoveries and theories unfolded, particularly in physics and astronomy. To mention just a few, Copernicus challenged the Aristotelian-Ptolemaic geocentric theory of the universe, arguing instead that the planets, including the earth, revolved around a stationary sun. Galileo improved the telescope, turned it toward the heavens, and gathered evidence to support the Copernican approach. Then, building on the heliocentric theory, Galileo discovered important theories of motion concerning falling bodies. By the end of the seventeenth century, Newton had discovered gravity, elaborated Galileo's theories of motion by stating the general laws of mechanics, and (along with Leibniz) invented calculus. In the midst of these breakthroughs, Francis Bacon had advocated the institutionalization of experimental research and had argued that scientific knowledge should be used to conquer nature.[20]

The scientific achievements of the sixteenth and seventeenth centuries evinced rapid qualitative advancements unprecedented in recorded human history. To some extent, the Christian eschatological idea of progress provided a ready conceptual framework for understanding these scientific advances. As early as the late twelfth century, Joachim of Flora had suggested that the Christian conception of an eschatology of sacral progress could be extended to spiritual developments within secular history. Specifically, Joachim posited three stages of human spiritual advancement based on the Father, Son, and Holy Ghost. Renaissance scholars then modified this three-stage periodization of secular history by conceiving of a movement from an ancient to a medieval (or Dark) to a modern (or Renaissance) age. Although these Renaissance scholars eventually were themselves relegated conceptually to the Dark Ages, modernists wholeheartedly adopted this periodization of history and, in so doing, posited a capacity for endless human progress. During the second stage of premodernism, the supposed metaphysical unity of the world constrained the idea of progress. Premodern progress denoted movement toward the perfect realization of eternal and universal principles; civilizations would, in this view, continue to rise and fall recurrently. But in the context of the burgeoning metaphysical dualism of the modernist world, progress became potentially limitless and a matter of human ingenuity. This modernist idea of progress, of qualitative and limitless advancements in secular affairs, harmonized with—partly arising from and partly explaining—the scientific advances of the sixteenth and seventeenth centuries.[21]

In sum, western society somewhat paradoxically underwent both secularization and sacralization. To a degree, Calvin's thorough theological disjunction of the sacred and secular freed the secular realm to grow in importance, as evidenced initially by the Scientific Revolution and later by the political and societal revolutions of the seventeenth and eighteenth centuries. Yet, despite Calvin's theology, the secular was conceptualized partly in sacral (especially eschatological) terms. Modernists, in other words, tried to shape their new visions, their new conceptions of reality, to fit the premodern eschatological mold of the world. Thus, the modernist idea of progress partially paralleled the second-stage premodern notion of progress, but simultaneously differed from it in at least three ways. First, modernist conceptions of progress focused on the secular, while the premodern focused on the sacred, eternal, and universal. Second, modernists envisioned the possibility of endless progress, while premodernists saw only the potential realization of ultimate principles. Third, modernist progress originated with and was generated by human ingenuity, while premodernist progress arose from divine intervention. In a sense, modernists substituted humans for God in the Christian salvation story. The modernist self asserted an ostensible power to control the physical world and social organization. With the modernist disposition to doubt and to challenge traditional beliefs, the social order no longer appeared predetermined or immanent. As Zygmunt Bauman observes, modernist society was like a garden: humans rationally designed and cultivated it, nurturing some plants while eliminating others (the weeds). Modernism, perhaps presumptuously, boasted "the unprecedented ability to improve human conditions by reorganizing human affairs on a rational basis." Thus, a "historicist sensibility" gradually emerged: History disclosed that the world could continually improve because of human will power and creativity.[22]

An early manifestation of these central components of modernism is found in Thomas Hobbes's political philosophy. Hobbes published his most famous book, *Leviathan*, in 1651, during the English Civil War period of the interregnum, a time of political and religious chaos.[23] In the first half of *Leviathan*, Hobbes attempted to present political theory as a science, much as Euclid had presented geometry, as a matter of axiomatic principles and demonstrable reasoning. Hobbes posited humans in a state of nature where all are roughly equal physically and mentally. In this state of nature, a "perpetuall and restlesse desire of Power after power, that ceaseth onely in Death," places each person in constant competition with and fear of all others. Hobbes, similar to the Protestant reformers, conceived of individuals as base and greedy creatures. The state of nature thus is equivalent to constant war, "such a warre, as is of every man, against every man." No one stands above the fray: there is no personal security, no societal advancement, and no cultural development. "[T]he life of man [is] solitary, poore, nasty, brutish, and short."[24]

According to Hobbes, humans would prefer to protect themselves from the dangers inherent to the state of nature, and hence their "[r]eason suggesteth" a means to achieve security. Each person must enter a covenant with all others that places all right and power in one absolute sovereign. Hobbes thus envisioned a social contract as follows: "[It is] as if every man should say to every man, I Authorise and give up my Right of Governing my selfe, to this Man, or to this Assembly of men, on this condition, that thou give up thy Right to him, and Authorise all his Actions in like manner. This done, the Multitude so united in one Person, is called a Common-Wealth, in latine *Civitas*. This is the Generation of that great Leviathan." The sovereign or Leviathan maintains civil peace and order by wielding an absolute police power: each person knows that any breach of the peace or criminal action can bring swift and legitimate punishment. Yet, the sovereign itself is above the law because the sovereign's subjects covenanted only with each other; they did not covenant directly with the sovereign itself.[25]

In the first half of *Leviathan*, therefore, Hobbes manifested two central components of modernism. He focused on the secular rather than the spiritual, and he stressed a human capacity to control, to reorder, and ultimately to improve social relations, regardless of traditional societal arrangements. In the Hobbesian world, contrary to premodern assumptions, sovereign power sprang from human minds and actions and did not descend directly from God.[26] Although people might start in a sordid state of nature, they could use their ingenuity to generate a political sovereign that immeasurably improves human prospects by maintaining civil peace and security. Indeed, unlike Machiavelli, Hobbes argued that a community of individuals not only could establish but also could sustain civil order.

Yet, Hobbes did not conclude his book on this seemingly propitious point because, from his perspective, the argument was incomplete. While Hobbes had demonstrated in the first half of *Leviathan* that reason and power could establish the commonwealth, he acknowledged in the second half that fear of any secular power pales in comparison to fear of eternal damnation. Thus, in the second half, Hobbes turned to a reading of Scripture to reinforce and complement his rational argument (of the first half). In the second half, then, the modernist tendency to apply eschatological forms to secular affairs emerged most conspicuously, although compared to later modernists, Hobbes's use of eschatological forms retained an ample dose of explicit religiosity.[27]

Significantly, the second half of *Leviathan* was imbued with Calvinist Reformed theology. According to Hobbes, "the Kingdom of God is a Civil Common-wealth, where God himself is Soveraign." This Kingdom, though, does not currently exist on earth: instead, Hobbes described an eschatological progression. Following in the Reformed tradition, Hobbes emphasized at the outset the fall of Adam, the original sin that supposedly engendered two related problems: loss of eternal life, and human pride. Continuing the story, Hobbes wrote that it nonetheless "pleased God" to covenant with the "People of Israel" (that is, Jews) through Abraham and then Moses. At this point, Hobbes unfortunately echoed traditional antisemitic sentiments by asserting that Jews were faithless and resorted to idolatry until Jesus came as the Messiah: "The End of Christ's comming was to renew the Covenant of the Kingdome of God, and to perswade the Elect to imbrace it." Thus, for Christians, at least, the coming of Christ solved one problem emanating from original sin, the loss of eternal life: eternal spiritual salvation became possible through faith in the truth of Christ.[28]

Yet, Hobbes followed a millennialist vision: even with the coming of Christ, the Kingdom of God as a sovereign entity did not arise on this secular earth. Rather, life on this earth prepares for the future second coming of Christ, the reign of God during a latter-day glory on earth. Hobbes, that is, understood the commonwealth or state as an intermediate point on the eschatological path to the eventual Kingdom of God. In J. G. A. Pocock's terms: "Hobbes had presented Leviathan's kingdom as occupying the present interval between the direct rule of God exercised in the Mosaic theocracy and the direct rule of God that would be exercised by the risen Christ." From this perspective, the political Leviathan, by compelling peace and order, solved the second and remaining problem arising from original sin, the problem of human pride.[29]

Hobbes, in effect, fully accepted Calvin's radical disjunction between the spiritual and secular, but Hobbes lacked Calvin's overarching religious convictions. Consequently, Hobbes's political philosophy demonstrated the perhaps perverse secularizing drift of Calvinist theology. For Calvin, ultimately, the final end or purpose for secular affairs was the glory of God. For Hobbes, though, the glory of God might provide the eschatological end of Christian society, but neither God nor spirituality could provide any guidance or purpose for political society in this depraved secular world. As Perez Zagorin observes, humanity is, to Hobbes, "now left solitary in a universe that is literally God-forsaken."[30]

How, then, can humanity proceed in a secular world so bereft of spiritual substance and direction? The first half of *Leviathan*, at least, can be understood as Hobbes's effort to apply the burgeoning modern scientific techniques of his era to this theological conundrum. The second half focused on Scripture to reinforce his rational conclusions concerning sovereignty. In fact, in the end, Hobbes explicitly merged together the two halves of *Leviathan* to arrive at a single conclusion: there must be but one absolute sovereign ruling over secular and spiritual affairs. That is, even though Hobbes maintained a semblance of the Calvinist freedom of conscience, he nonetheless argued for the joinder of the secular and spiritual sovereigns. Eternal salvation is so unrelated to this carnal and corruptible secular world that the notion of separate governors over the spiritual and secular appears nonsensical. Humans live only in the secular (and not the spiritual) world, and therefore only one governor or sovereign should exist. Hobbes, consequently, attacked the Roman Catholic Church because its clergy supposedly exercised authority over spiritual (not secular) affairs.[31]

Hobbes was not the only philosopher to take seriously the Calvinist disjunction of the secular and spiritual. Indeed, much of western philosophy can be understood as a series of intellectual attempts to investigate and resolve the implications of this Christian theology for secular matters. When Luther and Calvin attacked the authority of the Roman Catholic Church, they attacked the traditional Christian foundation for determining religious truth. In Catholicism, the Church claimed the prerogative of pronouncing the determinative meaning of Christianity, including the Christian Bible. Luther and Calvin's repudiation of the Church's authority, though, did not leave Protestants without a religious foundation. As already mentioned, the reformers instead proposed that the Protestant faithful could directly and personally understand the literal meaning of the Scriptures. The Bible itself provided the foundation for religious truths because, as Calvin argued, "by his Word, God rendered faith unambiguous forever."[32]

Yet, because of the Calvinist separation of the secular and spiritual, those intellectuals who focused more on the secular than the spiritual could not be fully satisfied with the Protestant theological reliance on the Scriptures. To be sure, for religious matters, the Scriptures might provide an adequate foundation (at least for some Christians), but if the secular was totally distinct from the spiritual, then the Scriptures could not ground secular truths or knowledge. This problem became especially acute given the recent spate of scientific advancements: What secular foundation could support and therefore justify humanity's rapidly progressing knowledge of scientific truths? Previously, within the metaphysical unity of the premodern world, philosophers did not need to identify or explain the foundations for knowledge; such foundations were immanent, a readily accessible aspect of intelligible reality. In a sense, premodern foundations were a given and therefore nonproblematic. But with the breakdown of the premodern metaphysical unity, with the Calvinist disjunction of the secular and spiritual, the givenness of epistemological foundations was shaken. Nevertheless, and most important, modernists retained a desire for objectivity, for solid ground, for a firm foundation for knowledge, especially scientific knowledge. Thus, for modernist philosophers in particular, the identification of epistemological foundations became a (or perhaps *the*) central issue or problem.[33]

The enormity and significance of this challenge cannot be overstated. Having repudiated religious and other traditional foundations for secular knowledge, modernist philosophers set forth on a quest for some alternative foundation or Archimedean point. To a great extent, this quest and its attendant misadventures would drive modernism from one intellectual stage to another.

In the first stage—which I call rationalism—philosophical modernists argued that pure abstract reason can firmly ground knowledge; reason can uncover or disclose truth. The prototypical rationalist, René Descartes, attempted to transform philosophy "into an epistemological investigation of the first principles of knowledge" by combining severe skepticism with rigorous deductive logic. According to the Cartesian method, the thinking subject or self turns inward to question or doubt all beliefs, and through this reasoning process, clear and distinct ideas emerge as foundational knowledge. Thus, when purified of historical and traditional prejudices, reason itself seems to yield certainty—that is, the truth. From these axiomatic truths, then, abstract reason could deduce additional truths with certitude. Descartes expressly analogized this philosophical method to the logical method of Euclidian geometry: "Those long chains of perfectly simple and easy reasonings by means of which geometers are accustomed to carry out their most difficult demonstrations had led me to fancy that everything that can fall under human knowledge forms a similar sequence; and that so long as we avoid accepting as true what is not so, and always preserve the right order for deduction of one thing from another, there can be nothing too remote to be reached in the end, or too well hidden to be discovered."[34]

Thus, Descartes, writing a little more than a century after the beginning of the Reformation, developed a philosophy that strongly resonated with Protestant theology in three important and interrelated ways. First, by articulating his skeptical method, Descartes in a sense took the Protestant reformers' confrontational attitude of doubt (which the reformers had directed against the Roman Catholic Church) and institutionalized it as an intellectual method in the secular realm. Second, as part of his skeptical method, Descartes turned sharply inward, to a reasoning self, and in so doing, he thoroughly detached the self from the external and ob-jective world. This philosophical dualism strongly resembled Calvin's theological dualism, which separated the spiritual from the secular. Third, the Cartesian iden-tification of and reliance on the individual self complemented the burgeoning theological individualism of the Protestant reformers, though the Cartesian self was largely shorn of the depravity and sinfulness that the early Protestant re-formers had stressed so forcefully.[35]

These three overlapping components of Cartesian philosophy and Protestant theology spurred the further development of modernism. A generally skeptical attitude—a willingness to doubt previously accepted beliefs and institutions—became embedded in the scientific and philosophical methods of modernist thought. Furthermore, metaphysical dualism—the acute division of subject and object—became a preeminent mark of the modernist landscape, contradistinguish-ing modernism from premodernism, with its metaphysical unity. Finally, a mod-ernist self began to emerge, asserting almost Godlike powers to choose values and goals and thus to control and remake the natural and social worlds. Indeed, the vari-ous elements of modernism began to crystallize into a coherent worldview: the indi-vidual self's ability to reason and to gain foundational knowledge facilitated human control of the secular world and thus engendered endless progress. As modernism moved forward, knowledge increasingly came to be viewed as the means for human liberation in the secular world. Descartes himself was strikingly utopian as he initi-ated the modernist philosophical project, seeking a firm epistemological foundation in a secular world effectively bereft of spiritual purpose. Contrary to the more cau-tious Renaissance humanists who previously had adopted a generally skeptical atti-tude, Descartes believed that the abstract rationality of his method of doubt could lead to indubitable truths, universal principles, and a logically ordered and all-encompassing system of secular knowledge. Later modernists would be hubristic, confident that society could progress through human ingenuity, but few would make such grandiose claims to philosophical perfection (though, of course, some would do so).[36]

In fact, the Cartesian philosophical utopia began to crumble almost immedi-ately. Significantly and ironically, Descartes's metaphysical dualism combined with his interrelated skeptical method to undermine his own claims to ground knowl-edge on abstract rationalism. Quite simply, the Cartesian skepticism or method of doubt was difficult to contain. Although Descartes primarily applied it to the secu-lar realm, Spinoza expressly extended the skeptical attitude to the religious realm, thus significantly contributing to the long-term secularization (or disenchantment) of the modernist world. Other philosophers applied the method of doubt to Descartes's own supposed proofs of secular knowledge, thus calling into question his rationalist project. Since, for the all-important purposes of science, the self must know objects of the external world with certainty, some philosophers asked: How can the self, merely by turning inward to reason, bridge the (modernist) metaphysical gap that exists between subject and object? How, in other words, can the self use abstract reason to know a priori truths about a sharply separated material world?[37]

At this point, the long-range implications of the philosophical institutionalization of the method of doubt began to emerge. Traditional beliefs had to be doubted and challenged—denigrated as mere prejudices—and often had to be discarded before truth could shine. But no sooner would one modernist philosopher sincerely invoke some epistemological foundation, such as abstract reason, than another philosopher would skeptically doubt its adequacy for firmly grounding knowledge. Modernists persistently sought foundations, but they simultaneously remained tenaciously suspicious of all such proposed foundations. Consequently, the typical modernist attitude was (and is) anxiety. And, to a great extent, this modernist anxiety, arising from the simultaneous desire for epistemological bedrock and skeptical doubting of all such footings, drove philosophical modernism toward its subsequent stages.[38]

During the second stage of modernism—which I call empiricism—the focus shifted from the reasoning self to the external world as the source of truth. Empiricists asserted that the physical objects of the external world shape human experience. Therefore, the sense experience and understanding of those objects allow the self to secure foundational knowledge directly. John Locke, the seminal empiricist of modernist philosophy, declared that "from experience . . . all our knowledge is founded." More specifically, he argued that all of our ideas arise from either sensation or reflection: that is, sensations of physical objects in the external world, or reflections on the operations of our own minds. Most important, then, our ideas of the "primary qualities" of objects, according to Locke, resemble or mirror the actual objects. Therefore, at least some of our ideas concerning objects constitute knowledge—truths known with certainty.[39]

At this stage, reason continued to perform significant functions even if it no longer remained the source of first premises and foundational knowledge. Reason could provide valuable insights about the world and could facilitate the performance of certain tasks—once empirical studies had first provided the foundational premises, the knowledge, that could adequately ground the subsequent rational processes. To a large extent, reason became instrumental: it was a vessel emptied of content, and only empirical observation could fill the void with the necessary substance about the world. David Hume, a later and extremely skeptical empiricist, went so far as to declare that "reason is, and ought only to be, the slave of the passions, and can never pretend to any other office than to serve and obey them." This reduction in the scope of reason, to an instrument for individual manipulation, underscores the continuing emergence of the independent and autonomous self of modernist individualism. In fact, Locke was perhaps the first theorist to focus explicitly on a concept of personal identity. In Locke's political theory, too, he exemplified a growing regard for the individual by teaching that all persons are "equal and independent." Contrary to Hobbes's conception of humans in the state of nature as base and greedy creatures, Locke envisioned such individuals as rational and respectful of others. And, of course, political society was legitimate only if individuals freely consented to its formation through a social contract. Individuals, in other words, had the freedom and power to construct a social order to suit their own individual purposes and to further the good of the community.[40]

This growing individualism of modernist philosophy intertwined with the development of economic capitalism. Locke himself struggled to harmonize capitalism, which was emerging in seventeenth-century England, with his posited political equality for individuals. To this end, Locke sought to justify the possession of property and the inevitable economic inequality that follows from property ownership. The crucial component in Locke's argument was respect for the individual—for the individual's labor, choices, and liberty.[41] Indeed, it was Hume's Scottish contemporary and disciple, Adam Smith, who most clearly articulated a philosophical link between individualism and capitalist society. According to Smith, each individual naturally seeks to maximize the satisfaction of one's own self-interest in the economic marketplace. This pursuit of self-interest, though, not only benefits the individual but also operates through an "invisible hand" to promote the good of society. In short, society ultimately progresses if individuals pursue their "own advantage." Thus, according to Smith, individual interest, freedom, and choice are the hallmarks of a capitalist economy, and capitalism leads to the greatest progress for society as a whole.[42]

Like the rationalism of first-stage philosophical modernism, the empiricism of the second stage also eventually succumbed to the skeptical gaze of the modernists themselves. The early empiricists had asserted confidently that experience provides foundational knowledge of the external world, but Hume himself sapped this confidence. Hume acknowledged that analytical reasoning, as in mathematics, can provide certainty, yet this form of reasoning cannot furnish information about the external world. Therefore, for knowledge of the external world to be possible, the objects of that world must somehow shape human experience or sense perceptions, as the earlier empiricists had claimed. One's sense perceptions, though, clearly are not equivalent to the worldly objects themselves; the perception of a chair, for instance, is not the same as the chair itself. At most, then, Hume reasoned, sense perceptions accurately reproduce or mirror the objects of the external world, but even if this is the case, one can never be truly certain that it is. One can only infer, not know a priori, that our perceptions accurately reflect an objective world. Consequently, Hume concluded, we cannot know with certainty the physical objects of the external world.[43]

Humean skepticism left modernist philosophy in a crisis. Metaphysical dualism—the sharp separation of the self from the objective world—was an unshakable landmark of the modernist world, but this dualism created a puzzling epistemological gap. For knowledge of the external world to be possible, the self somehow had to bridge the gap to the external world. Yet, with the pretensions of rationalism and empiricism now exposed, this mission was beginning to look hopeless: modernists might never achieve their self-imposed goal of foundational knowledge. Moreover, if neither reason nor experience could ground knowledge, then modernists might have rushed down a dead end. Yet they could not turn back because, in their eyes, the premodern world was irreparably damaged. Given the radical differences between modernist metaphysical dualism and premodernist metaphysical unity, modernists could not possibly return to the epistemological and normative foundations of premodernism. A revival of the seemingly illegitimate traditions of the earlier era was neither intellectually nor socially plausible. The modernist crisis thus threatened to become modernist despair: modernists continued unceasingly to demand foundational knowledge, even as they revealed that the tools or techniques of modernism (as well as those of premodernism) were inadequate for the task.

In a sense, the third stage of modernism—which I call transcendentalism—tried to pull the rabbit out of the hat: "Nothing up this sleeve (rationalism). Nothing up this sleeve (empiricism). But, abracadabra—and after a pass of my magic wand—I can still pull the rabbit (knowledge) out of the hat!" Just when modernism seemed to have exhausted its possible routes to knowledge, third-stage modernists desperately yet ingeniously attempted to turn back to the thinking subject and reason in order to resurrect the possibility of foundational knowledge. Second-stage modernist philosophers had argued that, for knowledge to be possible, the objects of an external world must shape human experience. But the transcendental reasoning of the third stage reversed this schema: the foremost transcendental philosopher, Immanuel Kant, argued that humans impose form and structure on the objects or phenomena of experience. Certain structures or categories, in other words, are inherent to and therefore shape all human experience and thought. Knowledge is possible, according to Kant, exactly because the categories are necessary preconditions of human experience. Kant's epistemological project then was to identify the precise categories that are a priori conditions of experience: the categories specify how humans must process their experiences of the external world. Transcendental reason, in short, provides synthetic a priori knowledge—knowledge that is prior to experience but is nonetheless informative about the objective world. Moreover, at this third stage, modernist individualism perhaps reaches its apex. Kant's entire ethical theory, for instance, revolved around respect for the dignity and autonomy of the individual. Hence, in one formulation, Kant's categorical imperative for moral conduct was to treat each rational individual "always as an end and never as a means."[44]

Transcendentalism, while unmistakably brilliant, did not eradicate the modernist crisis. Many philosophers, goaded of course by the modernist compulsion to doubt, questioned the authenticity of the transcendental solution and thus sent modernism into a fourth and final stage, which I call late crisis. These philosophers—call them critics—suggested that the third-stage modernists had looked despair in the face and were so frightened by its countenance that they immediately turned away. With eyes averted, the third-stage modernists then declared that a solution to their epistemological problems just *had* to exist. Anxiously struggling to find a last-gasp answer, they urgently thought, "We *must* have knowledge, but what conditions are necessary in order to have knowledge?" Then, presto! The modernists became transcendentalists and concluded, "We must already have satisfied those prerequisite conditions of knowledge because, after all, we so clearly have knowledge (since, of course, we *must* have knowledge)." In the words of Friedrich Nietzsche: "Kant wanted to prove in a way that would dumbfound the common man that the common man was right." To the critic, then, transcendentalism seemed to be an empty speciosity, born from desperation. In a sense, the transcendental modernist merely had described what conditions *would* exist *if* we had foundational knowledge. But describing those conditions did not make them a reality; the transcendental argument for foundational knowledge meant only that the modernist could imagine what such knowledge might be if it were a reality. Transcendental reasoning too easily and even inevitably slid into idealism. Nietzsche disparagingly referred to the "stiff and decorous Tartuffery of the old Kant" and declared that modernist philosophers were "all advocates who resent that name, and for the most part even wily spokesmen for their prejudices which they baptize 'truths.'"[45]

Significantly, though, most of the critics of the transcendental solution remained modernists. They could not envision any alternatives to modernism, and indeed, could not escape the modernist desire for foundational knowledge or the celebration of the individual self. For lack of options, then, critics often continued to use the now-conventional tools of modernism: rationalism, empiricism, and transcendentalism. The critics even used these modernist tools to demonstrate the inherent limits of modernism, to show the utter impossibility of achieving modernist goals. Consequently, critics plunged modernism into despair because while the desire for truth and knowledge remained, the hope for its fulfillment had vanished. Some modernists reacted by focusing increasingly on the individual self at the expense of epistemological certainty. These modernists became romantics—the aesthetic modernists—who celebrated the assertion of the will in art, literature, and other creative ventures.[46] Other modernists, though, still hopeful for epistemological or scientific success, reacted to the critics in one of two ways. First, some of them peremptorily declared, in effect, "If you don't have anything better to offer, just shut up!" These loyal reactionaries typically condemned the despairing critics as nihilists. Second, other more receptive yet still sanguine modernists listened to the critical arguments, were indeed troubled, and thus responded by trying to save the modernist project with some new wrinkle, some further sophistication.

Fourth-stage modernism thus was (and is) marked by swirling and inconsistent attitudes and projects: deep despair, anxiety, anger, accusatory denunciations, and increasingly intricate modernist "solutions" that pick and choose elements from rationalism, empiricism, and transcendentalism, all the while adding layers of complexity. For example, some fourth-stage modernists acknowledged that tradition or culture had proven unexpectedly persistent and difficult to overcome: to doubt previously accepted institutions and beliefs did not necessarily allow one to escape their power. Foundational knowledge seemed even more difficult to access than previously imagined. Thus, some intellectuals rejected the philosophers' monopolistic claims to provide epistemological foundations and instead began exploring other fields of inquiry. As disciplinary boundaries started to blur, various inventive strategies—including structuralism, phenomenology, Freudian psychology—were posited as penetrating into the deep regions of reality. Furthermore, the persistence of tradition or culture affected the modernist conception of the individual self: some fourth-stage modernists admitted that traditional or cultural constraints limited the options or choices for the self. The self seemed, after all, not quite as independent and autonomous as originally formulated. Ultimately, however, these modernists retained an image of the self that somehow remained in control, remained able to choose, remained an origin of power. Modernism, at this stage, might no longer boast of a totally independent and autonomous self, but a "relatively autonomous self" nonetheless endured.[47]

Postmodernism

The Holocaust was perhaps the most important social event precipitating a transition from modernism to postmodernism. In the modern worldview, the individual self's ability to reason and to gain foundational knowledge supposedly facilitated human control of the natural and social worlds and thus engendered endless progress. Human ingenuity seemed indefatigable, and confidence surged: social problems always could be solved, and the world would become better and better. The Holocaust punctured this hubris. After learning of the Nazi atrocities, few intellectuals could confidently assert that rationality and knowledge unequivocally made a better world. The Holocaust revealed most starkly that the modernist conception of rationality, embodied in the bureaucratic organization, could somehow eclipse morality to produce genocide. "It was," in the words of Zygmunt Bauman, "the rational world of modern civilization that made the Holocaust thinkable."[48]

The deflation of the modernist ego continued under the weight of the Cold War and the ever-present possibility of nuclear annihilation. Intellectual aplomb was difficult to maintain when the mere press of a button seemed to threaten human civilization as we know it. The depths of age-old traditions, the rootedness of human meaning and being, all could be destroyed in a few minutes.[49] Science itself, the apotheosis of modernist rationality, proved to be a dangerous ally. Even if nuclear war did not destroy the world suddenly, the environmental pollution produced by ostensible scientific-technological advances might do so slowly and surreptitiously. In short, the social supports for the modernist convictions in human control and endless progress were crumbling.

Other social and cultural factors contributed further to the collapse of modernism and the concomitant rise of postmodernism in the latter twentieth century. In the United States, the civil rights movement of the 1950s and 1960s and the subsequent women's movement allowed oppressed individuals and groups to compellingly articulate public viewpoints that previously had been silenced or ignored. A similar phenomenon occurred on an international scale as Third World nations began to develop. Thus, an emerging cultural pluralism confronted formerly unquestioned social and intellectual practices: modernist claims to universal truths and grand historical narratives of social progress often were denounced as manifestations of cultural imperialism.[50]

Moreover, scientific and technological discoveries continued to transform the social world despite the burgeoning concerns about the effects of such changes on the quality of human life. Most important, the advances in communication technology radically altered our lives: the introduction and development of first television and then computers generated an unprecedented information explosion. Images, sound, and data literally flash around the globe in microseconds. Meaning and knowledge now appear to have no more depth than a smiling face momentarily beaming across your television screen as you surf countless channels with the remote control. David Harvey observes that "the most startling fact about postmodernism [is] its total acceptance of the ephemerality, fragmentation, discontinuity, and the chaotic." We live by skimming along the surface, moving in hyperspeed, jumping among hyperlinks, living a hyperlife. This hyperculture, moreover, resonates with that "old worship of the new which sustains and fuels the rapid and relentless pace of commodity consumption in our late-capitalist consumer society." Postmodernism may have lost the modernist faith in control and progress, but the rate of social and cultural change nonetheless has accelerated to a dizzying pace. "Narrative has leaped from the page to the screen, music demands to be seen as well as heard, computers have jumbled our relationship to information, surveillance, and money, and television has merely changed *everything*. Now things feel like they're moving *really* fast, leaving us with the attention spans of kitties riveted by mouse-like movements."[51]

Consistent with these social and cultural changes, postmodern philosophers emerged in the second half of the twentieth century to repudiate the central modernist convictions about foundational knowledge, individual autonomy and control, and endless social progress. These postmodernists refused to continue the central modernist quest for epistemological foundations and instead began investigating our lives at the surface, so to speak. That is, if we live by skimming along at the surface, without deep foundational roots, then perhaps we ought to investigate how forces operate on that surface. It is worth noting that many of these philosophers at first neither deemed themselves to be nor were designated by others as postmodern. I am interested, though, in the development of postmodern *themes* and not merely in the use of the term, *postmodern*. Postmodern themes emerged in philosophy before they were given that label. For example, French theorists such as Jacques Derrida and Michel Foucault were initially called poststructuralists, yet I consider them to be postmodernists on the basis of their philosophical and social themes (and of course, many other commentators today would agree that Derrida and Foucault were, and are, postmodern).

An important philosopher in the story of postmodernism is Martin Heidegger. Writing before the Holocaust and other social events that shepherded in the postmodern era, the early Heidegger nevertheless challenged the tenets of modernism and opened the possibility of a postmodern philosophy. He sought to challenge the basic modernist metaphysics introduced by Descartes: a metaphysical dualism that sharply separated an autonomous subject or self from an objective world. Contrary to this metaphysical dualism, Heidegger maintained that humans must be understood to exist fully within *this* world, not as detached and autonomous spiritual minds who temporarily wander about in a material world. Heidegger attempted to connote his alternative vision of human existence as "Being-there," or *Dasein.* The essential or fundamental structure of *Dasein,* or human existence, is "Being-in-the-world," which Heidegger described as a "unitary phenomenon." That is, *Dasein* exists as an entity in the world like any other thing, like a rock or a hammer, yet *simultaneously Dasein* constitutes the world by giving meaning to things in the world. Because of this simultaneous yet dual nature of *Dasein*—as a Being that seeks to understand Being—Heidegger reasoned that human existence is characterized by practical understanding. *Dasein* cannot get behind or exist before practical understanding: one immediately experiences Being-in-the-world as the interpretation of everyday or practical activities, including activities as mundane as using a hammer or a piece of chalk.[52]

Later philosophers would elaborate Heidegger's suggested interpretive or hermeneutic turn toward human Being-in-the-world. These philosophers, particularly Hans-Georg Gadamer and Derrida, writing in the post–World War II social context, would take philosophy in a distinctly postmodern direction as they explored the conditions of human understanding.[53] Gadamer published his magnum opus, *Truth and Method*, in 1960. He articulates a philosophical hermeneutics that is most easily comprehended in opposition to modernist views of understanding and interpretation. Modernists had argued, consistent with the central tenets of modernist philosophy in general, that the meaning of a text must rest on some firm ground or foundation—such as the text itself or the author's intentions—an object that supposedly is separate and independent from yet somehow accessible to a perceiving self or subject. To understand a text correctly, according to this view, the self implements a mechanical technique or method that bridges the gap to the objective meaning of the text, or at least, mirrors in consciousness the objective content of the text. To take an example familiar to attorneys, some constitutional modernists maintain that a reader of the Constitution must somehow reconstruct in his or her own consciousness the intentions of the framers, as memorialized in the constitutional text. Otherwise, modernists insist, the textual meaning (in this case, of the Constitution) would be ungrounded and capricious: the self or interpreter, unconstrained except for personal preferences, supposedly could impose any arbitrary meaning on the text.[54]

Contrary to this modernist vision of interpretation, Gadamer's philosophical hermeneutics maintains that a text is never an object in the modernist sense: no uninterpreted or foundational source of meaning stands outside of or prior to interpretation. Instead, no matter what we do, we are always and already interpreting. In Gadamer's terms, hermeneutics is ontological. Our very being-in-the-world is interpretive, hence we can never escape or avoid interpretation and understanding. Even further, each interpretive encounter is itself ontological. Gadamer argues, for example, that when one views a painting, one does not approach it as a subject to an object; rather the painting is an "ontological event" in which "being appears, meaningfully and visibly." The hermeneutic act, then, is an ontological event in which meaning "comes into being." Gadamer's metaphysical stance thus contravenes the modernist notion of an interpretive methodology. Since a text, according to Gadamer, does not exist in an independent and uninterpreted state, its meaning cannot be derived through some mechanical technique or method: "[O]ur perception is never a simple reflection of what is presented to the senses."[55]

This rejection of modernist methodology and objectivity, however, does not mean that understanding or interpretation is purely subjective or capricious. Gadamer asserts that a reader or other interpreter is never an independent and autonomous subject who freely or arbitrarily imposes meaning on a text. Instead, an interpreter always is situated in a communal "tradition" that inculcates the individual with prejudices and interests, which then constrain and direct the understanding of any text (or text-analogue, which is any event, action, or other entity that can be understood or read as if it were a text). One's life within a community and its traditions necessarily limits one's range of vision—what one can possibly see or understand in a text. As Gadamer says, the traditions of one's community help to shape the interpreter's "horizon": "the range of vision that includes everything that can be seen from a particular vantage point."[56]

Furthermore, we are historical beings who *live* in tradition: "we are always situated within traditions . . . [which are] always part of us." Traditions are not things of the past; rather they are something that we constantly participate in. Communal traditions neither are fixed, precisely bounded entities nor are they passed on to individuals through some precise method or mechanical process. J. M. Balkin provocatively suggests that traditions are akin to "cultural software" insofar as they "become part of us and shape the way that we perceive the . . . social world." Nonetheless, traditions differ from computer software programs in two important ways: traditions cannot be reduced to a fixed quantum of data like computer software programs, and traditions cannot be *perfectly* installed or copied into each of us. To the contrary, traditions themselves take hold of us only through an interpretive process; traditions address us and must be absorbed or learned—often tacitly or unconsciously. "Tradition is not simply a permanent pre-condition," Gadamer notes; "rather, we produce it ourselves inasmuch as we understand, participate in the evolution of tradition, and hence further determine it ourselves." In short, traditions are constantly evolving, communal, social arrangements and memories that we participate in and live within.[57]

Crucially, although communal traditions and the concomitant prejudices constrain our possibilities for communication and understanding, they simultaneously *enable* us to communicate and to understand. The hermeneutic act—including understanding, interpretation, and application—is possible only *because* we participate in a communal tradition. Our traditions, prejudices, and interests actually open us to meaning, understanding, and truth: "This formulation certainly does not mean that we are enclosed within a wall of prejudices and only let through the narrow portals those things that can produce a pass saying, 'Nothing new will be said here.' Instead we welcome just that guest who promises something new to our curiosity. But how do we know the guest whom we admit is one who has something new to say to us? Is not our expectation and our readiness to hear the new also necessarily determined by the old that has already taken possession of us?"[58]

Hence, whenever we attempt to understand or interpret a text, we necessarily begin with a "fore-understanding" of that text—a fore-understanding generated from our prejudices and interests. To be clear, this fore-understanding does not subvert the interpretive process by predetermining a fixed meaning: rather, one's fore-understanding initiates a dialogical "play" between the interpreter and the text in which the meaning of the text dialectically comes into being. Interpretation requires one to question the text, probe for its meaning, ask new questions, listen to the answers, and continue in this dialogical process as if in a conversation. One's fore-understanding "is constantly revised in terms of what emerges as [the interpreter] penetrates into the meaning [of the text]." Hence, while one anticipates or fore-understands a particular meaning for a text at the outset of interpretation, the dialogical process of hermeneutics can lead one to arrive eventually at a different meaning. Regardless, though, the interpreter assumes throughout this hermeneutic process that the text is intelligible and complete, that it can communicate some "unity of meaning."[59] (In some instances, though, an interpreter might finally conclude otherwise.)

The metaphor of the hermeneutic circle illustrates the dialogical nature of interpretation. In its simplest form, the hermeneutic circle underscores the interrelationship between a text and its constituent parts: an interpreter can understand a whole text only by understanding its parts, yet an interpreter can understand the parts only by anticipating an understanding of the whole. Gadamer, however, elaborates the hermeneutic circle, bringing within its scope the complex interactions between interpreter, text, and tradition. According to Gadamer's conception of the circle, interpretation has two sides: on the one side, tradition limits the vision of the interpreter as he or she approaches the text, yet on the other side, tradition does not exist unless people constantly create and recreate it through the interpretive process itself. The latter side emphasizes that tradition is created as an ever new meaning of the text comes into being: as we participate in tradition by interpreting texts, we transform and reconstruct that tradition. Most important, the two sides of interpretation are not separate and do not function independently, rather they are simultaneous and interrelated. They resonate together as meaning "comes into being" within the hermeneutic circle.[60]

Thus, Gadamer emphasizes that the hermeneutic act is "one unified process." Modernists have insisted to the contrary—that understanding, interpretation, and application are separate events. From this modernist viewpoint, we *understand* the meaning of a text directly; we *interpret* a text only when we self-consciously reflect upon its meaning (for example, when we attempt to resolve a textual ambiguity); and we *apply* our understanding or interpretation of the meaning of the text when we attempt to transfer it to a new situation. Gadamer, however, maintains that understanding, interpretation, and application are not distinct events; rather they constitute the components of a unified hermeneutic act. We understand (or foreunderstand) a text only insofar as we open to its meaning because of our prejudices derived from communal traditions; we develop prejudices only as we simultaneously accept and reconstruct—or interpret—communal traditions; and we understand and interpret texts as well as traditions only insofar as we apply them to practical problems within our current horizon. We cannot extract any one component of this hermeneutic process, such as an understanding of a text, and treat it as an uncontested, stable, or noncontingent starting point—as a modernist foundation of sorts. Moreover, Gadamer's insistence that the unified hermeneutic act includes *application* echoes, to some extent, Heidegger's focus on *practical* understanding. To Gadamer, the element of application underscores that the hermeneutic act is always a pragmatic activity: when we approach a text, we typically do so for the practical purpose of understanding its meaning. For that reason, we anticipate the completeness of the text and assume it can communicate a "unity of meaning." Otherwise, the hermeneutic act would become merely hypothetical rather than a purposive activity in a particular or concrete context. Interpretation, most simply, does not occur in some ethereal or abstract never-never land.[61]

Jacques Derrida's deconstruction shares much in common with Gadamer's philosophical hermeneutics.[62] No less so than hermeneutics, deconstruction can be described as an attempt to identify the conditions of human understanding. Both

Gadamer and Derrida explore how we come to understand texts despite rejecting the foundationalist metaphysics of modernism. In Derridean terms, meaning is never grounded on a stable signified, rather there "is always already" a play of signifiers. Derrida writes: "[f]rom the moment that there is meaning there are nothing but signs. We *think only in signs*. Which amounts to ruining the notion of the sign. . . . One could call *play* the absence of the transcendental signified as limitlessness of play, that is to say as the destruction of . . . the metaphysics of presence."[63]

Hence, deconstruction echoes the ontological message of philosophical hermeneutics—that we are always and already interpreting. As Derrida says, there is no foundation for the "coming into being" of signs. The continual play or coming into being of signs or signifiers relates to Derrida's central concept (or "non-concept," as he sometimes says) of *différance*.

> [T]he signified concept is never present in and of itself, in a sufficient presence that would refer only to itself. Essentially and lawfully, every concept is inscribed in a chain or in a system within which it refers to the other, to other concepts, by means of the systematic play of differences. Such a play, *différance*, is thus no longer simply a concept, but rather the possibility of conceptuality, of a conceptual process and system in general. For the same reason, *différance*, which is not a concept, is not simply a word, that is, what is generally represented as the calm, present, and self-referential unity of concept and phonic material.[64]

Just as Gadamer emphasizes that our prejudices arise from communal traditions, Derrida argues that we always borrow concepts "from the text of a heritage." We can never escape our heritage or, in Gadamerian terms, step outside of our horizon. According to Derrida, we are limited to "givens belonging to the discourse of our time," hence even "deconstruction always in a certain way falls prey to its own work." That is, deconstruction always necessarily uses and reinscribes the metaphysics and linguistic structures that it seeks to deconstruct. Moreover, to Derrida, as well as to Gadamer, the givens of our heritage (our communal traditions) neither are fixed and precisely bounded entities nor are passed on to individuals through some precise method or mechanical process.[65]

If philosophical hermeneutics and deconstruction share so much in common, then what are the differences? In a sense, Gadamer pauses to celebrate moments of meaning and truth, while Derrida does not (in more mundane terms, if Gadamer and Derrida were looking at a glass of water, Gadamer probably would say it was half full, while Derrida probably would say it was half empty). Both Gadamer and Derrida stress that any text or event has many potential meanings, many possible truths; no single meaning remains fixed or stable in all contexts. Both would agree: "truth keeps happening." In Derridean terms, a text is iterable: a text, that is, can be repeated (or read) in different contexts, so its meaning can change.[66] Yet, while Gadamer therefore considers the meaning of a text to be inexhaustible, Derrida considers it to be undecidable.

To Gadamer, a determinate meaning arises in each concrete context, but because contexts can vary, the potential meaning of a text is never exhausted. Gadamer, as discussed, emphasizes that the unified hermeneutic act includes a practical component (application), so that we anticipate the completeness of the text and assume it can communicate a "unity of meaning." Because Gadamer thus focuses on the practicality of the hermeneutic act, he tends to view understanding primarily as a positive and empowering experience.[67]

Gadamer consequently downplays the deconstructive component that presents itself in the hermeneutic act, even as he implicitly suggests it. He explains that our prejudices both enable *and* constrain understanding and interpretation. Prejudices not only open us to the possibility of understanding, they also necessarily constrain and direct our understanding and communication. One's life within a community and its cultural traditions thus always limits or distorts one's range of vision—what one can possibly perceive or understand. Furthermore, Gadamer underscores that because we are historical beings who *live* in tradition, just as we live in a community, tradition is something that we constantly participate in. Thus, we constantly constitute and reconstitute our tradition, our culture, and our community as we engage in hermeneutic actions. Most important, this constant reconstitution always is simultaneously constructive *and* destructive. It is constructive in the sense that we constantly build new traditions and communities, constantly adding to our already existing traditions and communities through interpretation and understanding, thus including new concepts, interests, prejudices, and significantly, participants. Yet the reconstitution is also destructive—distortive and exclusive—insofar as we weaken or eliminate previously existing traditions and communities and exclude concepts, interests, prejudices, and participants. In short, as Gadamer articulates the hermeneutic act, interpretation and understanding implicitly are distortive and destructive in two ways: our prejudices are manifestations of power that constrain the possibilities for understanding, and the reconstitution of tradition (also a manifestation of power) necessarily destroys and excludes certain prejudices, interests, and participants. Consequently, coercion, domination, exclusion, and other distortive effects of power are always part of the hermeneutic act. The deconstructive component of hermeneutics hides within these destructive and distortive effects.[68]

Thus, Gadamer's articulation of philosophical hermeneutics contains deconstructive potential, yet he fails to pursue it. Here, then, is the crux of the distinction between Gadamer and Derrida. Whereas Gadamer focuses on the constructive and enabling power of the hermeneutic situation, Derrida focuses on its destructive and disabling component. Yet both parts are always and already present, as if there were a hermeneutic and sociological law of conservation of power: if a hermeneutic act produces meaning and empowers certain individuals and societal groups, it simultaneously represses and destroys potential meaning and disempowers other individuals and groups. Thus, for example, Gadamer describes how tradition enables us to open to the meaning of a text, but Derrida warns us that the authority of tradition is "purchased by deep violence." Tradition opens us to understanding because in part it provides an authoritative background context for the hermeneutic act. Tradition thus operates most effectively when it remains in the background, forgotten from conscious memory. But Derrida wants to re-mind us about tradition, to bring the background to the foreground, and to under-score how tradition often establishes its authority through brutality and duplicity. Deconstruction is, in a sense, "a move from within, from the radical other within"—that is, from within the confines of tradition and understanding.[69]

Because Derrida concerns himself with the disempowering and destructive quality of the hermeneutic situation, he cares little about deciding among the many potential meanings or truths of a text. Disempowerment, quite simply, is not about making decisions; rather, it is about lacking the power to decide. Thus, Der-rida is not interested in the practical component of the hermeneutic act since he does not seek to pursue or reconstruct a unified meaning for the text. To the con-trary, Derrida seeks to find and highlight the trace of the Other that always hides in the margins of our understanding. Derrida seeks to uncover the violence that necessarily exists when we understand a text—the violence that is inevitably ob-scured in the practical quest for a usable and therefore unified meaning. To Der-rida, violence manifests itself in the hermeneutic definition, exclusion, denial, and oppression of the Other—a concealed outsider—and this violence stands as an ir-reducible condition (or *limit*) of human understanding. Within the hermeneutic process of understanding, we always and already define some Other; we neces-sarily deny the potential meanings arising from some other perspective and ex-clude those potential meanings from our communal traditions. Without the Other, without the trace of denied potential meaning, "no meaning would appear" at all. Indeed, the Other is not just *on* the outside, but rather the Other *is* the outside: the location of the Other defines the outside. Thus, understanding is a political act be-cause, in announcing the meaning of the text, it normatively and substantively defines inside and outside. No preexisting border exists. Hence, Derridean de-construction also is political: it uncovers the hidden, the oppressed, the violated, the denied—the Other. Deconstruction responds to the call from the Other.[70] Gadamer may want to open to the Otherness *of* the text, but Derrida wants to re-veal the Otherness suppressed *by* our understanding of the text.

Given these similarities and differences between philosophical hermeneutics and deconstruction, an imaginary conversation between Gadamer and Derrida might go as follows:

GADAMER: "Our participation in tradition enables us to understand texts."

DERRIDA: "Yes, but what legitimates tradition? Tradition arises partly through violence and deception."

GADAMER: "Your desire for legitimacy merely reenacts modernist metaphysics. What do you want? A stable foundation?"

DERRIDA: "You are right. But you make exactly the point I am trying to stress. There is no legitimating ground for meaning other than tradition, but there is, in turn, no legitimating ground for tradition itself. Tradition is neither completely legitimate nor illegitimate. Understanding therefore is necessarily based on blindness and hypocrisy as we ignore and deny the violence and deception within tradition."

GADAMER: "Yes, but that's exactly the point. We do communicate. We do understand. These are practical activities that necessarily continue without legitimating foundations."

DERRIDA: "Yes, but the violence, the oppression, the denial . . ."

And so on. To Gadamer, this debate is inexhaustible: a new perspective constantly comes into being as our horizons shift, nonetheless we continue along in our pragmatic fashion—communicating, understanding, and interpreting. To Derrida, this tension between philosophical hermeneutics and deconstruction is undecidable: we are caught in a never-ending dialectic between the necessity and inadequacy of our linguistic forms. Both Derrida and Gadamer might agree, however, that we do not need to choose between hermeneutics and deconstruction. In fact, a choice does not even make sense: philosophical hermeneutics and deconstruction represent different planes or axes in postmodern interpretivism. They both help us to comprehend the hermeneutic act, how we come to understand a text, hence they help us understand our very being-in-the-world. Philosophical hermeneutics and deconstruction complement each other: hermeneutics illuminates the affirmative coming into being of meaning, but deconstruction stresses the limits of communication and understanding.[71]

To be sure, my renditions of philosophical hermeneutics and deconstruction are subject to dispute. Many committed deconstructionists would assert, for example, that any *summary* of deconstruction is necessarily distorted; deconstruction itself cannot be reduced to a fixed concept or commodity. Indeed, even my categorizations of Gadamer and Derrida as postmodernists are disputable. Some critics have labeled Gadamer as a conservative modernist for too readily accepting the authority of tradition and the conventional meaning of a text. Others suggest that Derrida is a poststructuralist but not a postmodernist. Going even further, some commentators declare that the very concept of postmodernism is misleading. According to some, the modern age continues unabated. From this perspective, postmodernism either has not begun or, at most, exists merely as a cultural phenomenon associated with late capitalism. Some dogmatic modernists, of course, offhandedly dismiss postmodernism as no more than "the latest fad, advertising pitch and hollow spectacle." More reactionary modernists meanwhile vehemently attack deconstruction, in particular, denouncing it either as banal drivel or as threatening the fiber of western civilization or, somehow, as both. Quite evidently, many commentators disagree about the nature and even the existence of postmodernism. Barbara Kruger observes: "To some [postmodernism is] an excuse to pile together oodles of wild and crazy decor, to others it's another example of the weakening of standards and values, to others a transgressive resistance to the sureness of categories, to others a handy way to describe a particular house, dress, car, artist, dessert, or pet, and to others it's simply already *over*."[72]

Well, to me, postmodernism certainly is *not* over. Postmodernism is best understood as an extant intellectual, cultural, and social era that, in fact, is still in its youth. The philosophies of Gadamer and Derrida denote important aspects of postmodernism, but there certainly is more to it. Partly for this reason and partly because postmodernism is so often misinterpreted or misunderstood, it is useful here to delineate eight broad overlapping themes of the era—many of which I have already introduced as components of philosophical hermeneutics, deconstruction, or both. And, to be clear, I seek to identify postmodern *themes*, rather than *defining* postmodernism, so that my discussion remains true to a postmodern ethos. A proffered definition for postmodernism would appear to reduce it to some fundamental core or essence, which would be too foundationalist, too essentialist—too modernist.

Hence, the first theme: postmodernism is anti-foundationalist and anti-essentialist, and therefore contravenes modernist epistemologies. As both Gadamer and Derrida illustrate, postmodernism is anti-foundationalist because, from their perspectives, meaning and knowledge always remain ungrounded. And postmodernism is anti-essentialist because ungrounded meanings are always unstable and shifting: meaning cannot be reduced to a static core or essence. In Derridean terms, meaning is never grounded on a stable signified, rather there always is a play of signifiers. Hence, postmodernists easily recognize that any text or event has many potential meanings, many possible truths, that can emerge in different contexts. To accentuate this point, a postmodernist often invites a reader to perform gestalt flips or paradigm moves. Just when the reader seems to have settled on an essential meaning for the text, the postmodernist insists that the reader should flip, and the reader suddenly sees a totally different meaning. In effect, the postmodernist says, "It may look like a duck now, but look again, and it's a rabbit!"[73]

This contingency of meaning relates closely to the Derridean concept of the Other. No matter how fixed or certain the meaning of a text might seem, some Other always lurks at the margins. This Other always promises the possibility of disrupting the fixity or rigidity of the text, of suggesting an alternative meaning or truth. For this reason, "different voice" scholarship, such as feminist and critical race theory, plays a prominent role in postmodernism. Whereas mainstream modernist scholars typically seek to ground knowledge on a claimed essential or core truth, different voice scholars highlight the previously oppressed voices or truths that emanate from the perspectives (or horizons) of some societal and cultural Other—a historically oppressed racial, religious, or sexual minority or outgroup. Thus, postmodernism can be understood in part as a discourse that has emerged *because* of the multiple truths that different voice scholars uncover. By uncovering multiple truths where before but one appeared, different voice scholars have helped generate and justify the anti-foundationalism and anti-essentialism charac-teristic of postmodernism. Different voice scholars repeatedly illustrate the Der-ridean play of signifiers by disclosing that seemingly stable modernist meanings are unstable and shifting. Simultaneously, exactly because postmodernism is anti-foundationalist and anti-essentialist, it explains how a minority or outgroup mem-ber can, in a sense, *live* multiple and often conflicting truths. The outgroup mem-ber frequently understands the dominant majority's truth, but also understands (perhaps more deeply and vividly) the truth of the minority or outgroup. An African-American scholar, for example, may recognize more readily than a white scholar that institutionalized religion, on the one hand, can legitimate submissive-ness in the face of grossly hierarchical social relations yet simultaneously, on the other hand, can inspire revolutionary resistance. Postmodern theory provides an explanation for this type of experience by deeming the modernist's claimed essen-tial or core truth to be no more than the socially and culturally accepted truth of a dominant majority. Postmodern theory, from this perspective, reinforces different voice scholarship and encourages outgroup members to uncover previously sup-pressed truths and meanings.[74]

More broadly, then—and this is a second theme—postmodernists tend to chal-lenge all sorts of ostensible certainties, inveteracies, edifices, and boundaries. No matter how clear, fixed, and legitimate a concept or institution might seem, it always can be disrupted. Deconstructionists, in particular, inevitably can find the hidden or oppressed Other. For this reason, postmodernists resist grand or meta-narratives or meta-theories: historical narratives or theories that claim an all-encompassing do-minion and that often depict social progress of quite heroic proportions. By seeking to reduce some field or subject area into a single neat storyline, such modernist the-ories typically obscure some Other; that is, they tend to minimize or ignore dis-senting and oppressed voices that might interfere with the narrative flow and the in-timation of endless progress. Thus, to depict more fully the pluralism of social reality—the disparate and subjugated voices—postmodernists often attempt to tell multiple "little" narratives that do not claim a universal or all-encompassing sway and that disclose change but not necessarily progress. In fact, few postmodernists claim to prove or scientifically explain social events; rather they claim no more than to narrate or interpret the events in a persuasive or fruitful manner.[75]

Because of the postmodern tendency to repudiate supposed certainties and bound-aries, postmodern scholars have subverted the walls separating well-established academic disciplines. If a scholar attempts to analyze a social issue from merely one perspective—say the sociological—she contravenes the postmodern urge to explore multiple perspectives and truths. Consequently, we see the analytical mixing of his-tory, sociology, philosophy, anthropology, literary criticism, jurisprudence, and a multitude of other subject areas. Culture, in particular, has expanded to the point where our world is, in a sense, culturally saturated. In postmodernism, culture per-vades all aspects of social and personal life, including the commercial, governmental, and psychological. Postmodern studies therefore frequently entail a significant cultural component regardless of the writer's initial perspective and academic discipline. Fredric Jameson declares that "we are *within* the culture of postmodernism to the point where its facile repudiation is as impossible as any equally facile celebration of it is complacent and corrupt."[76]

The third theme is that postmodernism revels in paradoxes. For instance, I claim now to be discussing the *themes* of postmodernism, and in the course of this discussion, I already noted that postmodernism is anti-essentialist. But the very concept of a theme, while perhaps not as reductionist as a modernist definition, seems nonetheless to suggest the existence of an essence or, at least, something like an essence. Even further, my argument that postmodernism is anti-essentialist seems to infer an essence or core for postmodernism itself: for something to be postmodern, it must be anti-essentialist. By this account, postmodernism is not postmodern. Indeed, we might paradoxically say that postmodernism includes modernism, and modernism includes postmodernism. For example, the conceptualization of postmodernism seems to assume the possibility of a grand narrative—a periodization of history that moves from premodernism, to modernism, and then to postmodernism. But such a periodization is modernist in nature: as already discussed, postmodernists consistently challenge the existence of such grand or meta-narratives. The mere idea of postmodernism as a period following modernism is, therefore, deeply modernist and in tension with the claims of postmodernism itself. Nonetheless, from a postmodern standpoint, this conclusion is unsurprising because modernism is the tradition that leads to postmodernism. Hence within modernism we find the seeds of the postmodern, and within postmodernism we find vestiges of the modern.[77]

Fourth, postmodernists are concerned broadly with manifestations of power, especially linguistic or discursive power. In the words of Michel Foucault: "[p]ower is everywhere."[78] For example, language (or more broadly, symbolism) can be understood as a means of or a technique for implementing power. In one way, language represents a technique of power because words directly and indirectly impose power. Some words, such as those constituting a promise or a threat, amount to performative acts, while other words trigger certain feelings, actions, or both in the interpreter (the person hearing or reading the words). Particular words, for instance, can trigger specific coercive and violent social actions or practices: the legal discourse denying a petition for habeas corpus can lead to a capital defendant's execution.[79]

Yet, in a second way, language looms as an even more pervasive means of implementing power. As Foucault declares: "[d]iscourse transmits and produces power." Our "distinct ways of talking about and interpreting events" constitute the shape of our very being-in-the-world. The conceptual distinctions and criteria of legitimation embedded in our discursive practices shape our understandings and perceptions of social events and reality.[80] Gadamer's philosophical hermeneutics, in particular, emphasizes this power of language. According to Gadamer, language is the "medium" of tradition and understanding: tradition exists and is handed down to us in and through language, and therefore understanding, which is possible only because of tradition, must itself be linguistic in character. Language is not simply a tool or a possession of humanity; rather one experiences the world linguistically, or in other words, one "lives in a language." In short, "[l]anguage is the fundamental mode of operation of our being-in-the-world and the all embracing form of the constitution of the world." Hence, from a Gadamerian perspective, language (as tradition) is a technique of power because it enables and constrains understanding and meaning.[81]

Yet, as already mentioned, postmodernists revel in paradoxes. So, unsurprisingly, many postmodernists maintain that, although language is a technique of power, language simultaneously drifts along remotely from power. For instance, when the Supreme Court denies the habeas petition of a capital defendant, the consequences that follow are unrelated to the niceties of legal reasoning in the Court's opinion. The reality of an execution does not turn on whether the legal doctrine or discourse mandated a particular conclusion. To the contrary, the justices on the Supreme Court exercise power over habeas petitioners not necessarily because of legal acumen or judicial expertise, but rather exactly because they are Supreme Court justices. Each justice operates from a position or role of extraordinary power within the social institution of the criminal justice system. From this perspective, then, we see that power frequently is structural. That is, power "exists in relationships—it has a primary location in the ongoing, habitual ways in which human beings relate to one another." Individuals often exercise power not because of their personal qualities, abilities, or knowledge, but because they occupy certain relatively embedded (though contingent) social roles that endure within complex social practices and institutions. To be sure, social roles do not exist in some pure or idealistic sense; they are neither self-defining nor defined solely through language (though discourse contributes to the construction of social roles). Rather, social roles are defined in part by the relations between various institutional positions, by the organizational scheme of the society.[82]

The fifth theme is that postmodernists often emphasize the social construction of the self. Contrary to the modernist notion of the independent and autonomous self, postmodernists assert that the conceptualization of one's self or identity is generated from cultural practices and societal structures. The self or human consciousness is not some ultimate foundational source of control and social progress. Derrida asserts that the self or subject is not "what it *says* it is. The subject is not some meta-linguistic substance or identity, some pure *cogito* of self-presence; it is always inscribed in language." Gadamer, likewise, emphasizes how tradition—a linguistic aspect of culture—produces personal prejudices (hence personal identity). From a more structural viewpoint, social roles do not merely empower individuals, such as Supreme Court justices, to perform certain actions; rather, social roles also help *produce* perceptions, attitudes, and actions. The very identity and being of an individual is partly constructed or constituted by the position or role that he or she holds within the organizational scheme of the society—by the set of social relations that the individual's position or role holds vis-à-vis other positions and roles. Some feminists therefore emphasize that a nurturing relationship between parent and infant can produce certain prosocial personality traits.[83] At the same time, however, this perspective underscores that cruelty, hatred, and inhumanity are also (at least partly) socially produced through the structural organization of society. An otherwise ordinary and moral person can readily perform incredible atrocities on others if placed in the appropriate social role. In one psychology experiment, for example, subjects were divided into two groups, prisoners and guards, with the guards having complete control over the prisoners. Beyond all expectations, the guards enthusiastically fulfilled their authoritarian roles by brutally mistreating the prisoners.[84]

Sixth, postmodernism is self-reflexive or self-referential. Although power is structural insofar as social roles and practices are ongoing and embedded, those roles and practices—whether modern or postmodern—always remain inherently contingent. They can and do change. Just as Gadamer noted that traditions must be recreated continually and thus tend to transform over time, social practices also must be reconstructed continually and thus tend to transform. To be sure, many social practices reconstruct themselves partly through a type of inertia, through their dead weight, yet they still must be reconstructed continually (or they will cease to exist). And within this process of reconstruction, the possibility of transformation always pulses. Thus, for instance, despite the significant similarities in the exercises of power by the current chief justice, William Rehnquist, and the first chief justice, John Jay, the institutional and social roles of Rehnquist and Jay are unmistakably distinguishable. Most obviously, among many other differences, Jay presided over a smaller Supreme Court and had the opportunity to decide far fewer cases than Rehnquist.[85]

Thus, all enduring social practices—whether modern or postmodern—tend to reconstruct (and transform) themselves, but a distinctive aspect of many *postmodern* practices is their reflexive (or reflective) self-production. That is, postmodernists realize that their (our) social practices are historically and culturally contingent and that those practices constantly reconstruct themselves through their (our) own words, thoughts, and actions. Derrida, for example, stresses how our linguistic practices reflexively reproduce themselves without the benefit of some external foundation. Postmodernists thus often turn toward their own social practices and make the cultural and theoretical awareness of those practices part of the practices themselves. In a sense, then, postmodernism transforms practices to include self-reflexive awareness. Steven Connor observes: "In trying to understand our contemporary selves in the moment of the present, there are no safely-detached observation-posts, not in 'science', 'religion', or even in 'history'. We are in and of the moment that we are attempting to analyze, in and of the structures we employ to analyse it. One might almost say that this terminal self-consciousness . . . is what characterizes our contemporary or 'postmodern' moment."[86]

Seventh, postmodernists are ironic. Whereas the postmodern threats to epistemological foundations and modernist individualism produce anxiety and despair in many modernists, in postmodernists, these threats produce . . . irony. Postmodernists and modernists display markedly different attitudes. Postmodernists know that one brilliant idea (or even two or three) cannot suddenly establish an Archimedean point or radically transform the world, but they nonetheless continue to function practically in this world, as evidenced by Gadamer's pragmatic conceptualization of hermeneutics. Consequently, postmodernists manifest irony in at least two ways. First, despite their anti-foundationalism and anti-essentialism, they frequently use modernist rhetorical devices and argumentative modes *as if* they were grounded and contained an essence. Postmodernists, however, use these modernist methods self-reflexively, always understanding their anti-foundational and anti-essential themes. In the words of Jean Baudrillard, a postmodernist "plays . . . with things that one doesn't believe in anymore." To avoid being or appearing merely modernist, then, a postmodernist often seeks to connote the irony of this use of modernist techniques—thus, the metaphorical raised eyebrow, wink, or grin. For example, a postmodernist might unexpectedly mix rhetorical styles, switching suddenly from a formal and serious scholarly style to a conversational tone. Second, a postmodernist uses modernist tools, making modernist-type arguments, while knowing that she cannot fully control those very tools and arguments. Because of the iterability of a text—its repeatability in different contexts—postmodernists ironically expect that their arguments, whether modernist or postmodernist in nature, will go in unforeseen directions and will generate unanticipated meanings.[87]

Eighth, postmodernism is, in a sense, politically ambivalent: postmodernism, especially deconstruction, has potentially radical political implications; nonetheless it can be turned to conservative ends. Many opponents of postmodernism insist that its methods lead to a "slippery slope of 'totalizing critique,'" thus undermining the possibility of critical morality and leaving us in the throes of conservative paralysis. According to this view, if postmodernists are correct, if meaning emerges from the deconstructive play of signifiers, then a text can have any meaning at all—no one meaning is better or worse than any other. If there is no ground to stand upon, these opponents add, then how can we evaluate others (or ourselves)? And if there is no way to evaluate or criticize, then why not just continue the status quo? Nevertheless, many postmodernists, including Derrida, believe that postmodernism has radical political implications. Some postmodernists seek to intervene in established social and cultural practices, not by overtly recommending alternative practices, but by disturbing and perhaps shifting the accepted structures and symbols—necessarily doing so only gradually, sometimes imperceptibly, and even surreptitiously. Derrida's deconstructive focus on the Other, for instance, can spur a drive—a potentially insatiable drive—to reveal violence and deception, to uncover exclusion and oppression. To Derrida, "[d]econstruction is justice."[88] Unsurprisingly, then, Derrida occasionally has expressed his political concern for the Other in concrete, even polemical, terms:

> Never have violence, inequality, exclusion, famine and, indeed, economic op-
> pression affected so many human beings in the history of the earth and humanity.
> Instead of extolling the advent of the ideal of liberal democracy and of the capi-
> talist market in the euphoria of the end of history, instead of celebrating the "end
> of ideologies" and the conclusion of grand emancipatory discourses, let us never
> neglect this macroscopic evidence, made of innumerable singular sufferings: no
> progress allows us to be unaware that never, in absolute numbers, never have so
> many men, women, and children been enslaved, starved, or exterminated on the
> earth.[89]

In sum, these various postmodern themes neither exhaust the meaning of post-modernism nor stand independently from each other. Unquestionably, many postmodernists would dispute my choice of themes or even my entire thematic effort. Many, for example, would challenge the very idea of social structure, denouncing it as a reified concept that contravenes the pluralism and flux of social reality. Nonetheless, to me, the thematic approach usefully elucidates postmodernism so long as one recognizes that the various themes overlap and intermingle in a pastiche of postmodern practices. Thus, for example, postmodernists self-reflexively describe or diagnose how postmodern culture manifests power by constituting a postmodern self or subject. Such studies reveal a postmodern paradox: postmodern theorists repudiate the modernist conception of the self as an independent and autonomous individual, yet the same theorists might nonetheless describe the postmodern subject as somewhat like a modernist self in hyperspeed. The culturally and socially constructed postmodern subject is one who constantly makes inane choices without firm (modernist) reasons or foundations in a quest for individual distinction. Which brand of jeans should I wear? Which type of soda should I drink? Which television channel should I jump to next? And next, and next . . . ? Which store in the mall should I shop in next, and next, and next . . . ? Which microwavable dinner should I choose? Which breakfast cereal? Which cup of South American java? Bizarrely, in the postmodern era, one seeks personal uniqueness by relentlessly choosing from a variety of mass-produced and mass-advertised products that ostensibly cater to those who are different. The postmodern subject is, most succinctly, a hyperconsumer, for whom "spending is a duty—perhaps the most important of duties." And in an epitome of self-reflexive postmodernism, the postmodern economic marketplace is itself infused with postmodern hip culture: we get the commercial that self-reflexively knows it's a commercial and tells us so with a wink and a nod—as a cartoon hero smilingly confides that he's also a toy action figure. The postmodern capitalist culture then constantly seeks to generate new (or nuanced) individual concerns that open potential market niches: maybe, after all, I *should* be concerned about the personal statement made by my choice of not merely "athletic shoes" rather than sneakers, but even further, running shoes, basketball shoes, walking shoes, tennis shoes, aerobic shoes, and when I just can't decide, cross-trainers.[90]

To conclude this chapter, I would like to suggest that postmodernism is not only in its youth but in a first stage that eventually might generate and give way to a second stage. A second-stage postmodernism, to be sure, would closely resemble the first, which I have been describing, yet what would be the distinctive characteristics of second-stage postmodernism? Before posing an answer, I must offer the obvious caveat: this discussion will be wildly conjectural and therefore should be understood as tentative and suggestive. With that said, and assuming that a second stage will in fact emerge (though it might not be called postmodernism at all because "postmodern" cultural practices change so quickly), here are some possibilities.[91]

A crucial distinction between the first and second stages of postmodernism will lie in their respective relationships to modernism. First-stage postmodernism lives in the shadow of modernism. Indeed, as mentioned, some critics of postmodernism believe that we remain in the modern age. Occasionally, even theorists more sympathetic to the postmodern forbear from discussing postmodernism per se and instead cautiously refer to a hybrid modern/postmodern era because of the uncertain border between the periods.[92] Hence, under this shadow of modernism, much postmodern writing actually tends to address modernist issues and concerns, albeit somewhat obliquely. For example, modernists focused for centuries on the epistemological problems arising from a subject/object metaphysics: What source or method could provide an objective foundation for knowledge? Postmodernists, to a great extent, remain preoccupied with these concerns, though in a radically different manner. To be certain, postmodernists repudiate modernist subject/object metaphysics and the concomitant search for an objective epistemological foundation; nonetheless they extensively detail *why* they do so. That is, postmodernists devote considerable energy to demonstrating why and how they are anti-foundationalist and anti-essentialist—why and how they are postmodernist *rather than* modernist. These theorists, in other words, reject modernist metaphysics and foundationalism, but in many instances, they do not then just move on. Rather, they elucidate their postmodern commitments largely by articulating their critical responses to modernism.

One reason for this close connection between modernism and first-stage postmodernism is evident: first-stage postmodernists are often disappointed former modernists. They were socialized and educated to believe—and they did believe—that they were independent and autonomous selves who, through the accumulation of objective knowledge, exercised extensive control over their social relations and even could contribute to important social progress. But now, for these theorists, it's over. They no longer believe. God is dead—again—and this time, they saw Him die. Imagine a radical Vietnam War protester from the 1960s who suddenly realized in the 1980s that Ronald Reagan was president, and an immensely popular president, at that. So what can such theorists do now? They no longer faithfully believe that American society will be radically transformed for the better. Yet they still know the modernist issues, the modernist moves, the modernist arguments, and perhaps most important, they retain memories of their modernist pasts. So they raise an eyebrow and smile and use the tools they have at hand—though now they use them ironically. Postmodernism, according to Baudrillard, "is a game with the vestiges of what has been destroyed."[93]

Second-stage postmodernism will arrive, in my opinion, *if* and when modernism no longer is an active or live memory. When modernism is learned as history instead of known as memory, then postmodernists will operate without the looming shadow of the modernist past. Postmodern preoccupations with modernist-tinged concerns—anti-foundationalism versus foundationalism, anti-essentialism versus essentialism, and so on—will have ended, and postmodernists will then perhaps move on. But move on to what? Many of the same postmodern themes, of course, will remain extant; but what will be different?

Some of the first-stage postmodern themes that persist into the second stage might become less vibrant. For example, anti-foundationalism and anti-essentialism seem to be requisite to postmodernism and thus will endure, but without the overbearing memory of modernist epistemologies, these postmodern commitments might seem less compelling and therefore might attract less attention from theorists. More dramatically, one aspect of postmodern irony might disappear altogether. First-stage postmodernists self-reflexively use modernist methods while knowing that the methods cannot deliver on the promise of indubitably grounded results. These first-stage postmodernists distinguish themselves from modernists, who after all frequently use similar methods, by metaphorically raising an eyebrow or otherwise connoting postmodern irony. Second-stage postmodernists presumably no longer will be overly concerned with distinguishing themselves from modernists. Hence, this form of postmodern irony very well might disappear or at least recede into desuetude, even though second-stage postmodernists probably will continue using modernist tools reflexively, thoroughly aware of their limitations. The second form of postmodern irony, it is worth noting, probably will persist. The second-stage postmodernist, that is, will continue to ironically express an expectation that her arguments, whether modernist or postmodernist in nature, will go in unforeseen directions and will generate unanticipated meanings.

Modernists constantly charge first-stage postmodernists with undermining the potential for human liberation. According to the most common modernist view, liberation can arise only from some assertion of the human will that leads to an escape from domination or alienation. Liberation, that is, revolves around the independent and autonomous (or at least relatively autonomous) self. Because first-stage postmodernists unquestionably reject this modernist conception of the self, modernist critics challenge postmodernists to otherwise explain and indeed to save the idea of human liberation. From the modernist perspective, the first-stage postmodern picture of social reality unacceptably seems to reduce humans to automatons programmed by their social and cultural surroundings. Needless to say, then, first-stage postmodernists devote considerable energy to responding to these charges. Second-stage postmodernists, though, will be largely absolved (liberated?) from these modernist charges. In fact, human liberation—or, perhaps better phrased, human freedom—might be recognized not as demanding any escape of the self but rather as requiring an understanding of the social construction of the subject. Maybe freedom can be understood as being consistent with the idea of surfing—particularly, postmodern surfing—surfing the Web, surfing the channels, and so forth. The idea of surfing suggests that I am controlled by incredible forces but that simultaneously I somehow ride them. I am not crushed, shattered, or otherwise overwhelmed—though I could be—but rather I artfully maneuver along the surface. When I surf the net, then, I move efficiently from Web site to Web site, gliding among hyperlinks, uncovering in minutes information that might otherwise have taken hours or even days to locate. Web surfing, when properly done, is a rewarding rather than a frustrating experience, even though I am confronted by more information, more power, than I can possibly handle.

Yet, a second-stage of postmodernism does not promise an inevitable utopia of human freedom. The possibility for a pathological dystopia is also evident. As mentioned, even within this vision of postmodern freedom, the chance for being forcefully overwhelmed remains present. In postmodernism, we are partly driven by a quest for the ever new, the ever original, the ever unique. We need and we get more information, more data, more knowledge—more and more and more. The quest for depth, for foundations, is dying along with modernism, so now we skim—or surf—along the surface, and all this happens at dizzying speeds, at hyperspeeds. True, we might experience an exhilarating freedom as we understand the simultaneity (or synchronicity) of our controlling and being controlled, yet we might also suffer at least three different pathological reactions. First, we might unwittingly gaze down at the surface streaking by and experience postmodern vertigo, a queasy sense of reeling out of control. Off balance, we might stumble or wobblingly settle onto our posteriors, only then to be crushed as the ongoing forces continually crash over us. We end, perhaps, sinking below the surface, like some postmodern street person, homelessly gazing at the passing blank stares.

Second, even if we keep our eyes ahead as we surf onward, we might eventually experience a type of postmodern stupor. Endless rapid change, endless information and data, can produce a numbness. There is just so much flashing by that, after awhile, it all seems so insignificant. After traveling in the closed societies of eastern Europe in the early 1980s, Philip Roth observed that, paradoxically, "[e]very word they write has endless implications, whereas in the States, one often doesn't have the sense of making an impact at all."[94] An overabundance of information apparently can drain knowledge of its importance. Within this second-stage postmodern stupor, though, we will not stumble; rather we will somehow groggily retain our balance and continue going through the motions, perhaps not surfing but nonetheless staying above the surface.

Third, perhaps the most frightening of all possible pathological conditions is suggested by the novelist Don DeLillo: "In societies reduced to blur and glut, terror is the only meaningful act. There's too much everything, more things and messages and meanings than we can use in ten thousand lifetimes. Inertia-hysteria. Is history possible? Is anyone serious? Who do we take seriously? Only the lethal believer, the person who kills and dies for faith. Everything else is absorbed. The artist is absorbed, the madman in the street is absorbed and processed and incorporated. Give him a dollar, put him in a TV commercial. Only the terrorist stands outside."[95]

This is postmodern terrorism. Instead of succumbing to the stupor that can follow from endless information and data, the postmodern terrorist attempts to stop the relentless hyperspeed of postmodern culture, if but for a moment. Through a meaningless violent act, the terrorist struggles to declare a meaning—something, anything, that will be noticed and understood despite the ongoing hyperculture. Such a terrorist, in a sense, represents a perverted postmodern reversion to modernist romanticism (recall that modernist romantics celebrated an assertion of the will in aesthetic ventures). One other related possibility should be recognized, however; namely, the idea of the postmodern terrorist might be understood allegorically: the terrorism might be imposed hermeneutically rather than physically. In other words, instead of striking out with physical violence, some postmodern terrorists might do no more than attempt to autocratically assert a meaning (for a text or text-analogue). This type of postmodern hermeneutic terrorist knows that all meaning is ungrounded, that knowledge is rushing by at dizzying speeds; she nonetheless struggles and perhaps sometimes manages, at least momentarily, to slow the pace enough to generate a text, a meaning, that seems somehow important, that seems to linger for more than a moment. Certainly such a form of terrorism would be less pathological than a physically violent terrorist act, but would it otherwise be a positive or negative move? Would such a person be brave or cowardly, smart or dull? In the abstract, I cannot say: it will all depend on the context.

ৰ্বী T H R E E ৡ

Premodern American Legal Thought

Premodern Jurisprudence: In General

Faith in the existence of natural law principles stood as one definitive feature of premodern American legal thought.[1] At the very birth of the nation, the Declaration of Independence immediately invoked "the Laws of Nature" and "Nature's God"; then, echoing John Locke, it continued with this now-familiar passage: "We hold these truths to be self-evident, that all men are created equal, that they are endowed by their Creator with certain unalienable Rights, that among these are Life, Liberty and the pursuit of Happiness." Through this natural law reasoning, Thomas Jefferson and the other signers of the Declaration attempted to establish, first and foremost, a universal right to rebel against an unjust ruler. Only then did the Americans delineate their specific grievances against Britain so as to explain why they should rebel at that particular time.[2]

The references to natural law and natural rights in the Declaration of Independence were not mere rhetorical flourish. To the contrary, natural law seemed to provide the foundation for societal values and the legal system, including especially the common law. In one of the first efforts to articulate an American conception of law, James Wilson in 1790 explained: "Nature, or, to speak more properly, the Author of nature, has done much for us; but it is his gracious appointment and will, that we should also do much for ourselves. What we do, indeed, must be founded on what he has done; and the deficiencies of our laws must be supplied by the perfections of his. Human law must rest its authority, ultimately, upon the authority of that law, which is divine."[3]

The American faith in natural law was, to a great extent, inherited from

William Blackstone, who first published his *Commentaries on the Laws of England* from 1765 to 1769.[4] Wilson and other American jurisprudents freely relied on the *Commentaries*: George Wythe, the first American law professor, based his lectures at William and Mary on Blackstone; the curriculum of the first American law school, at Litchfield, Connecticut, was structured around the *Commentaries*; and Joseph Story used Blackstone as a text throughout his tenure as a professor at Harvard. Many ordinary lawyers who learned the law by reading either on their own or in law offices did little more than read the *Commentaries*. As Nathaniel Chipman bluntly stated in 1793: "[Blackstone's] *Commentaries* are the *only* treatise of law, to which the law students, in these states, have access."[5] Furthermore, not only was Blackstone published in many American editions, but the earliest treatises to focus on American law, published during the first half of the nineteenth century, followed in the Blackstonian mold.[6]

Blackstone initially wrote the *Commentaries* to promote legal education in a university setting. In so doing, he presented law as a science, a "rational science" that necessarily included an extensive discussion of natural law. "This law of nature," Blackstone declared, "being co-eval with mankind and dictated by God himself, is of course superior in obligation to any other. It is binding over all the globe, in all countries, and at all times: no human laws are of any validity, if contrary to this; and such of them as are valid derive all their force, and all their authority, mediately or immediately, from this original." To Blackstone, that is, the principles of natural law are universal and superior to positive law, including the common law. In those fields where natural law is "indifferent," so that individuals are left at their "own liberty"—a field such "as exporting wool into foreign countries"—humans can make positive law to command or prohibit any conduct whatsoever. But in those areas where the law of nature is "not indifferent, human laws are only declaratory of, and act in subordination to [natural law principles]."[7]

Natural law, according to Blackstone, is either revealed by God or discoverable through human reason. For example, Blackstone asserted that the right of property originated in revelation: the Bible declares that God gave humankind dominion over the earth and all things upon it. Then, from the law of nature and reason, the use, possession, and occupancy of land and objects generated the concept of property. Blackstone concluded: "Property, both in land and moveables, being thus originally acquired by the first taker, which taking amounts to a declaration that he intends to appropriate the thing to his own use, it remains in him, by the principles of universal law, till such time as he does some other act which shews an intention to abandon it."[8]

American jurisprudents readily accepted Blackstone's natural law orientation for at least three reasons. First, natural law provided Americans with a convenient and useful justification for their adoption of the English common law in the various states of the burgeoning nation. Especially in the decades immediately after the Revolutionary War, if the common law had been understood merely as an English institution distinctive to Britain itself, then an American reliance on the common law would have seemed impolitic or even treasonous. If, however, the common law arose from the universal principles of the law of nature, which were revealed by God or discovered through human reason, then the common law was legitimate in America (or anywhere else, for that matter).[9]

Second, the idea that the common law was based on natural principles fit with the American social context of the late eighteenth and early nineteenth centuries. To many who thought about such matters, any society seemed to be naturally stratified or ordered. And in the United States, despite tremendous economic changes and the spread of democracy and legal equality during this period, distinct social hierarchies remained conspicuous. Consequently, many Americans readily accepted the notion that the common law imposed social obligations that arose naturally or customarily from one's status within society. Jesse Root asserted in 1798 that the common law "taught the dignity, the character, the rights and duties of man, his rank and station here and his relation to futurity [and thus] defines the obligations and duties between husbands and wives, parents and children, brothers and sisters, between the rulers and the people, and the people or citizens towards each other."[10]

Third, many Americans were so deeply committed to Protestant Christianity that they were particularly receptive to invocations of religiously rooted natural law. During the 1740s, a Protestant evangelical revival, later called the First Great Awakening, swept across the North American colonies, leading to the Christian conversion of thousands. "People from all ranks of society, of all ages, and from every section underwent the new birth. In New England virtually every congregation was touched. It was not uncommon for 10 or 20 percent of a town, having experienced grace, to join the church in a single year."[11] Partly because many of the revivalist preachers were itinerants who wandered from town to town and attracted larger and larger followings, Protestant sects began to splinter off from the main churches. Over time, then, an increasing plurality of denominations arose, and some of the already existing but smaller dissenting sects gained adherents and spread into new areas. The Baptists, for one, benefited greatly from the eighteenth-century revivalism. Yet, even though the revivals tended to splinter American Protestantism into multiple denominations, the Great Awakening ultimately was "a great unifying force that gave to 'four-fifths' of the Christians in America 'a common understanding of the Christian life and the Christian faith.'" The Awakening helped begin to forge a national consciousness across the boundaries of the various colonies. This national consciousness, which crucially continued from the late colonial era to the Revolutionary and early national periods, included a unified and vigorous commitment to sustaining multi-denominational Protestantism in "a Christian civilization." Within the confines of this pervasively Christian culture, Americans effortlessly accepted the idea of natural law, especially a natural law of divine roots.[12]

Thus, for multiple reasons, Americans readily received the Blackstonian faith in natural law as the foundation of the legal system, a faith they generally maintained until the Civil War era. For example, during the first stage of premodern legal thought—which lasted from 1776 to the early nineteenth century—Nathaniel Chipman stated in his *Sketches of the Principles of Government*, published in 1793, that "the constitutional principles of government [are] founded in the principles of natural law, in the moral and social nature of man." According to Zephaniah Swift, writing two years later, the laws of nature arise from "the Supreme Deity" and apply "to animate and inanimate matter, and rational and irrational beings." Similar views persisted during the second stage of premodern jurisprudence, which lasted roughly from 1820 to the Civil War. James Kent, in his *Commentaries on American Law*, published initially in the late 1820s, repeatedly referred to natural and universal justice, natural and unalienable rights, natural jurisprudence, and divine revelation. Even in a practically oriented work, like Francis Hilliard's *Elements of Law*, published in 1835, the author partly relied on natural law. Hilliard claimed to design his book "as a cheap manual for popular use" that "abstains from all criticism, speculation, or history; and confines itself to a plain, brief statement of principles now in force, with occasional illustrations." Nonetheless, Hilliard carefully stressed that the common law rested on principles of natural law, on "certain broad and fixed principles, which embody the essense of the system." He subsequently identified the most commonly discerned *broad* natural rights: "By the law of nature, every man has certain absolute personal rights, classed by the most approved writers into security, liberty, and property."[13]

Besides faith in natural law, a second definitive feature of premodern American legal thought was a commitment to the idea of legal science. Just as Blackstone had presented law as science, so did the American legal scholars of the late eighteenth and early nineteenth centuries. Wilson, Chipman, Swift, St. George Tucker, David Hoffman, Kent, Hilliard, and Story all consistently referred to the science of jurisprudence or legal science.[14] The specific parameters of the premodern conception of American legal science were derived from two sources: the writings of Francis Bacon and the forms of action unique to common law pleading.

Although Bacon had written his most important works in the early seventeenth century, he replaced Locke as the most prestigious English philosopher in America around the turn into the nineteenth century. Premodern American legal scholars from Wilson to Story repeatedly cited and quoted "Lord Bacon," celebrating, in Story's words, "the profoundness of his genius, and . . . the wisdom and comprehensiveness of his views."[15] The late-eighteenth- and early-nineteenth-century American understanding of Baconian science (not just legal science) emphasized a series of interrelated steps or forms of conduct: observation, generalization, and classification. A Baconian attitude was, first, grounded on faith in human sense experience such that one's careful observation could reveal truth. Then, from multi-

ple observations of the relevant phenomena, one could generalize and induce ultimate principles of nature. Finally, those principles could be classified: ordered into
a rational system. Significantly, Baconian science was Christianized in nineteenth-
century America: Christianity and science were understood not to be opposed to
each other, but rather to be complementary and mutually supportive. As Theodore
Bozeman observes: "'Truth,' in fact, pointed to an important mode of religious experience in antebellum America. To know the truth of things was to taste 'majesty
and glory,' for the massive panorama of nature was almost everywhere understood
as an unfolding of Divine creativity."[16]

In legal science, James Wilson explained the applicability of Baconianism to
jurisprudence.

> In all sciences, says my Lord Bacon, they are the soundest, that keep close to par-
> ticulars. Indeed a science appears to be best formed into a system, by a number of
> instances drawn from observation and experience, and reduced gradually into
> general rules; still subject, however, to the successive improvements, which fu-
> ture observation or experience may suggest to be proper. The natural progress of
> the human mind, in the acquisition of knowledge, is from particular facts to gen-
> eral principles. . . . In this view, common law, like natural philosophy, when
> properly studied, is a science founded on experiment. . . . Hence, in both, the
> most regular and undeviating principles will be found, on accurate investigation,
> to guide and control the most diversified and disjointed appearances.[17]

The early American treatises manifested their Baconian roots in at least three
important ways. First, although the treatises emphasized natural law and were organized loosely around broad principles—for instance, the protection of property,
liberty, and personal security—the authors tended to display a faithful acceptance
of case decisions and a bottom-up style characteristic of inductive reasoning.
They paid close attention to detail, often filling the treatises with specific low-level
rules and copious footnotes that cited and discussed numerous cases. Theophilus
Parsons's *Law of Contracts*, for instance, cited over six thousand cases.[18] Treatise
sections and subsections often reflected rather narrow factual situations in which
cases repeatedly arose. In Kent's *Commentaries*, the lecture on contracts included a
section on "passing title by delivery," which included subsections on, among other
things, payment and tender, earnest and part payment, conditions attached to delivery, delivery to agent, symbolic delivery, and place of delivery. In Kent's part on
real property, the lecture on incorporeal hereditaments included a section on easements and aquatic rights, which was subdivided as follows: of ways, riparian
rights, highways, party-walls, division-fences, and easements acquired and lost by
proscription. This last subsection was further divided into the categories of water,
light, and air.[19]

Second, Baconianism was apparent in the attention that the treatise writers gave
to classifying and systematizing American law. To American jurisprudents, law
was a science because, most important, it was a rational system of principles. Hoff-

man belittled the idea that law is "a mere collection of positive rules and institutions." Instead, "[i]f law be a science and really deserve so sublime a name, it must be founded on principle, and claim an exalted rank in the empire of reason." The lawyer, therefore, "must have entered into the principles, discovered the harmonies, and arranged with method and curiosity the innumerable topicks of the science."[20]

Third, despite their penchant for focusing on cases and low-level rules, American jurisprudents believed that legal principles, including natural law principles, existed apart from their manifestations in the decided cases. Baconianism never supported any form of nominalism, which would have suggested that nothing existed but the individual case decisions. Perhaps the best way to understand the metaphysical relationship between the cases and the principles in premodern legal science may be to compare, at the risk of mixing philosophical metaphors, American (Baconian) jurisprudence with Plato's philosophy—specifically, Plato's theory of Ideas (or Forms). "The essence of the theory of Ideas," according to David Ross, "lay in the conscious recognition of the fact that there is a class of entities, for which the best name is probably 'universals', that are entirely different from sensible things."[21] To Plato, the Ideas or Forms are real or objective entities that exist separately and distinctly from sensible things. Each sensible thing or particular instance of an object partakes of or shares in an Idea, but no particular instance perfectly exemplifies any Idea. The Ideas are universal, unchanging, and stable, while sensible things are ephemeral and in flux. For example, Plato distinguished between the many objects that are beautiful and the Idea of beauty. The myriad objects manifest or are copies of the Idea, but they are not the same as the Idea—"absolute beauty."[22]

The Platonic relationship between Ideas and particulars illuminates the relation between legal principles and case decisions in premodern legal science. While in Plato's theory, the Ideas or universals supposedly exist separately from the many sensible things, in jurisprudential theory, legal principles supposedly exist separately from the countless cases. The cases as positive law manifest the natural law principles, but the cases themselves are not equivalent to the principles. Hilliard perfectly captured this relationship between the principles and the cases in his *Elements of Law*: "[I]n law, as in other sciences, there are certain broad and fixed principles, which embody the essense of the system, and remain unchanged amidst the fluctuations of successive ages. [The] increase of the law arises, not from any change in them, but from that infinite variety of facts and circumstances, to which the transactions of mankind give rise, leaving room for doubt in each case as it occurs." Thus, the few legal principles are universal, unchanging, and stable, while the many cases imperfectly exemplify them. In the words of Joseph Story, "the decisions of Courts . . . are, at most, only evidence of what the laws are; and are not of themselves law.[23]

The degree to which American jurisprudents explicitly defined the Platonic relationship between natural law principles and case decisions should not be overstated. Although the Platonic metaphor usefully clarifies premodern legal thought, the American jurisprudents did not expressly think of themselves as Platonists. Many of them failed to precisely define natural law and natural rights, much less delineate the relations between natural law and positive law, including case decisions. "Medieval thinkers," it has been noted, "made elaborate distinctions between God's law, natural law, and human law, but Americans rarely did so." Yet, even though Americans attributed "a quite baffling comprehensiveness to the law of nature," the Platonic relationship between the natural law principles and the positive law, including judicial decisions, was widely and implicitly evident. Most American jurisprudents presumed that positive law generally comported with natural law. "[T]he law of the land is, in general, but another name for the law of nature," reported Hilliard. "Municipal rules are founded upon the basis of equity, reason, and right. If this be so, then obscurity no more belongs to the former than to the latter; upon which the instinct of conscience, the conclusions of the understanding, and the teachings of revelation pour their mingled light."[24]

Beyond such statements, Joseph Story unsurprisingly spearheaded one of the most thorough antebellum efforts to specify expressly the relations between natural law and judicial decision making. In 1837, a special Massachusetts commission consisting of Story and four other individuals reported to the governor on the possibility of codifying the common law. The commissioners discussed the proper method for deciding a case not governed by statute:

> [T]he first question is, whether there is any clear and unequivocal principle of the common law, which directly and immediately governs it, and fixes the rights of the parties. If there be no such principle, the next question is, whether there is any principle of the common law, which, by analogy, or parity of reasoning, ought to govern it. If neither of these sources furnishes a positive solution of the controversy, resort is next had (as in a case confessedly new) to the principles of natural justice which constitute the basis of much of the common law; and if these principles can be ascertained to apply in a full and determinate manner to all the circumstances, they are adopted, and decide the rights of the parties. If all these sources fail, the case is treated as remediless at the common law, and the only relief, which remains, is by some new legislation, by statute, to operate upon future cases of the like nature.[25]

According to this passage, natural law principles play two roles in common law decision making. First, natural justice (or the principles of natural law) "constitute the basis" of the common law. Natural law, that is, provides a foundation for the common law, but it is a foundation that is explicitly referred to only infrequently. Second, in rare cases, the natural law principles provide the specific source for deciding a case. These situations arise only if the common law does not already provide a source for a decision. Story and the other commissioners provided a couple of examples. If one requests and has work done for him, "a dictate of natural justice" suggests that one should pay the value of the work done. From this, the commissioners argued, an elaborate set of common law rules and pleadings follow. And according to the second example, if one borrows money, then "the common law, upon principles of natural justice, holds him liable to repay it."[26]

In addition to the Baconian view of science, the other significant source of the premodern conception of legal science lay in the forms of action unique to common law pleading. Today many legal commentators sharply distinguish legal procedure from the substance of the law, but the premodern jurisprudents rarely did so.[27] To the contrary, the writs and forms of action were entwined with the substantive rules of the common law. The links between procedure and substance were evident in Blackstone's *Commentaries*, the model for the later American treatises. When discussing the rights of persons at common law, Blackstone wrote: "I shall, first, define the several injuries cognizable by the courts of common law, with the respective remedies applicable to each particular injury: and shall, secondly, describe the method of pursuing and obtaining these remedies in the several courts." In other words, to Blackstone, discussions of rights, remedies, and the forms of action had to be inextricably intertwined: they could not be coherently understood separately and independently. For example, when discussing express contracts, Blackstone wrote:

> Express contracts include three distinct species, debts, covenants, and promises. 1. The legal acceptation of *debt* is, a sum of money due by certain and express agreement. As, by a bond for a determinate sum; a bill or note; a special bargain; or a rent reserved on a lease; where the quantity is fixed and specific, and does not depend upon any subsequent valuation to settle it. The non-payment of these is an injury, for which the proper remedy is by of *debt*, to compel the performance of the contract and recover the specifical sum due. . . . The form of the writ of *debt* is sometimes in the *debet* and *detinet*, and sometimes in the *detinet* only: that is, the writ states, either that the defendant owes and unjustly detains the debt or thing in question, or only that he unjustly detains it.[28]

Blackstone never clearly explained what came first: on the one hand, the conceptualization of an injury or a right or, on the other hand, the writ and form of action at common law. But what came first was unimportant: the key point was the close interconnection between the substantive law and the forms of action. As Blackstone stated, "wherever the common law gives a right or prohibits an injury, it also gives a remedy by action."[29]

American jurisprudents closely followed this Blackstonian understanding of the common law. In particular, the forms of action provided many of the concepts for the classification of the common law; the legal processes gave shape to the substance of the law. For example, in David Hoffman's *Course of Legal Study*, the third title or chapter offered recommended readings on personal rights and remedies. Several sections from Bacon's *Abridgment* were suggested, including on action of account, debt, covenant, detinue, trover, replevin, and so on. Likewise, in

Francis Hilliard's *Elements of Law*, the part on private wrongs included a chapter on injuries to personal property in possession, which included sections on replevin, trespass, trespass on the case, and trover. Most clearly, perhaps, James Gould and Tapping Reeve explicitly organized the curriculum of the Litchfield Law School into forty-eight titles that represented Gould and Reeve's categorization and understanding of the whole of jurisprudence. Reflecting the importance of the forms of action for classifying the common law, the titles included, among others, action for covenant broken, action for debt, action for detinue, action of account, and assumpsit.[30]

Significantly, then, common law pleading was understood to be neither arbitrary nor irrational. To the contrary, pleading itself seemed to fit neatly within the premodern conception of legal science as a rational system, as Gould explained in his *Treatise on the Principles of Pleading*. Gould deemed pleading "to be the most instructive, and therefore the most important single title in the law." Pleading is based on principles that are integrally related to the substantive law. In Gould's words, pleading owes its preeminence "not solely to the intrinsic value of its own exact and logical principles, but also, and in no small degree, to the fact, that the principles of pleading are necessarily and closely interwoven, both in theory and practice, with those of every other title of the law." Gould unequivocally depicted pleading as a "science." Consequently, he explained the purpose of his book in terms familiar to legal scientists of the early nineteenth century: "[T]he OBJECT of the present Treatise [is] to render the doctrines of Pleading more intelligible, and more easy of attainment, than many have supposed them to be, by showing them to be reasonable: In other words, by exhibiting them, not as a compilation of positive rules; but as a system of consistent and rational principles, adapted, with the utmost precision, to the administration of justice."[31]

In sum, premodern jurisprudents understood the common law as a science, a rational system of principles grounded in natural law. From this perspective, legal principles were universal yet separate from the cases themselves. The whole of jurisprudence could be rationally classified into a system that included not only the natural law principles but also a multitude of low-level legal rules that reflected the common law forms of action. While these features of American legal thought remained largely intact from the Revolutionary War to the Civil War era, jurisprudence nonetheless underwent a significant transition during this period, moving from a first to a second stage of premodernism.

First-Stage Premodern Jurisprudence: Natural Law and Republican Government

The first stage of American legal premodernism lasted from the Revolution through the early years of the nineteenth century. As would hold true during the second stage too, first-stage jurisprudents were committed to natural law and legal science. The characteristic of the first stage, though, that would distinguish it from the later second stage revolved around the political and social notion of government, including especially the idea of time or history. The new nation's governmental system, of course, arose within and was built upon the North American colonial society that preceded the Revolution. That colonial society tended to be based on traditional and hierarchical social relationships, as is typical of a premodern society, though the colonies were less stratified generally than Europe. Jonathan Edwards, an influential American Protestant preacher during the early and mid–eighteenth century, declared that all have "their appointed office, place and station, according to their several capacities and talents, and everyone keeps his place, and continues in his proper business." Significant vestiges of this premodern community remained intact in the early years of the American republic despite the changes wrought by the Revolution.[32]

The American revolutionaries' conception of government was animated in part by the so-called Opposition or Country ideology emanating from English civic republican thought. Civic republicanism could be traced back at least to Aristotelian political theory, which emphasized that individuals fulfill their nature only by living and participating in a political community. Thus, civic republicans generally stressed that virtuous citizens and leaders must deliberate about and pursue the public or common good so that, as Machiavelli had underscored, they might preserve their political community or republic as long as possible. The Opposition ideology added an especial concern that corrupt governmental officials might undermine these republican principles and political liberty. Along these lines, the American revolutionaries believed that British leaders, including the king and Parliament, were corrupt, lacked civic virtue, acted contrary to the common good, and therefore seriously violated republican principles and liberties. Hence, after the Declaration of Independence asserted a natural and universal right to rebel against corrupt government (a natural right derived also partly from Locke's more modern and liberal political theory), the Declaration then delineated a long list of republican and constitutional grievances that seemingly justified the American rebellion against Britain.[33]

Similar themes of civic republicanism, stirred together with natural law and natural rights, remained prominent in the first state constitutions. The Virginia Bill of Rights, adopted shortly before the Declaration of Independence was issued, served as a model for many subsequent state constitutions. It stressed that government should be for the common good: "government is, or ought to be instituted for the common benefit, protection, and security of the people, nation, or community." Thus, "all men, having sufficient evidence of permanent common interest with, and attachment to, the community, have the right of suffrage, and cannot be . . . bound by any law to which they have not . . . assented, for the public good." To preserve republican government and the pursuit of the common good, civic virtue must be promoted: "no free government, or the blessings of liberty, can be preserved to any people, but by a firm adherence to justice, moderation, temperance, frugality and virtue and by frequent recurrence to fundamental principles." Moreover, the Virginia Bill of Rights, as its name suggests, explicitly protected certain specified natural rights: "all men are by nature equally free and independent, and have certain inherent rights . . . namely, the enjoyment of life and liberty, with the means of acquiring and possessing property, and pursuing and obtaining happiness and safety." Hence, while the first state constitutions were not solely republican in nature—rather they relied on multiple sources, including Lockean liberalism—they nonetheless drew extensively on civic republican motifs.[34]

Despite the importance of civic republicanism, American conceptions of a republic were far from precise. While relying heavily on traditional republican themes, Americans also reformulated civic republicanism to fit their unique circumstances. Many earlier civic republicans had condoned government of the one, the few, and the many—that is, a mixed government combining elements of a monarchy, an aristocracy, and a democracy. But the Americans, from the Revolution onward, repudiated monarchies and aristocracies. Instead, they consistently conceived of their republics as being based on representative government and the idea of the sovereign people. The Virginia Bill of Rights declared, in typical fashion, "[t]hat all power is vested in, and consequently derived from the people; that magistrates are their trustees and servants, and at all times amenable to them." To be sure, the idea of "the people" was (and is) malleable, and many individuals were initially and unjustifiably excluded from this all-important political category. As Gordon Wood argues, though, the egalitarian and democratic drive triggered by the Revolution led to an ever-expanding scope of "the people." And regardless of the actual inequities of American society, many Americans nonetheless accepted the ideology of popular sovereignty as a foundation for American life.[35]

Even so, by the time that the framers wrote the new national Constitution in 1787, attitudes toward government had shifted. During the 1780s, certain problems arose under the republican constitutional governments of the states as well as under the national government organized under the Articles of Confederation. In particular, without a preexisting royalty or nobility to draw upon, Americans had to find their governmental leaders from among the ordinary people. Civic republican principles suggested that the most virtuous citizens would naturally ascend to become governmental officials and, because of their great civic commitment, would act for the public good. Indeed, in a distinctly premodern fashion, civic republicans traditionally had held a highly elitist view of the people: basically, "there were two orders of men—the talented few and the ordinary many." American leaders, to a great extent, retained this elitist vision even though they repudiated monarchies and aristocracies. Influential individuals such as George Washington and John Adams occasionally referred to the masses as "the grazing multitude" and "the common herd" and readily assumed that only independent landowners constituted "the people" entitled to participate in government in any manner. (While an egalitarian element was injected into this American type of republican elitism largely because landowning was so widespread—far more than, for example, in Europe—it should be noted that only approximately 4 percent of the population voted for the delegates who ratified the Constitution.)[36]

Hence, Americans had sought their governmental officials from among the ordinary people, with the hope that a cadre of virtuous elites would be electively chosen. Yet, from the perspective of the framers, the 1780s had unhappily revealed that too often self-interested citizens elected officials who themselves lacked a sufficiently virtuous commitment to the common good. Quite simply, if there was a virtuous elite, they were not being elected to office. John Jay wrote to George Washington on June 27, 1786: "Private rage for property suppresses public considerations, and personal rather than national interests have become the great objects of attention. Representative bodies will ever be faithful copies of their originals, and generally exhibit a checkered assemblage of virtue and vice, of abilities and weakness."[37] Popular sovereignty, democracy itself, had produced corruption and instability in the state governmental republics.

The constitutional framers sought to account and correct for these problems. Defending the newly proposed Constitution in the *Federalist Papers*, James Madison, Alexander Hamilton, and John Jay echoed Machiavelli by characterizing human nature as at least partly wicked and depraved. Based on this notion of humanity, Publius (the pseudonym adopted by Madison, Hamilton, and Jay) recognized that citizens tend to band into factions that constantly threaten the ends and security of republican government. Yet, however problematic it might be, the framers still clung to their civic republican ideals: governmental officials *should* virtuously deliberate about and pursue the common good, even if they often fail to do so. The framers retained their elitist hope that governmental officials would be "distinguished . . . by those qualities which entitle them" to be elected by their fellow citizens. This meritocratic elite—the "speculative men"—could be the "guardians" of the public good for "the mass of the citizens."[38] Indeed, it was perhaps the elitism of the framers and their Federalist colleagues that most sharply divided them from the Constitution's anti-Federalist opponents. One of the framers, Pierce Butler of South Carolina, epitomized their classically rooted republican elitism, as well as their concomitant disdain for ordinary people, when he declared at the Constitutional Convention: "[w]e must follow the example of Solon who gave the Athenians not the best Government he could devise; but the best they would receive."[39]

Following in the Machiavellian republican tradition, then, the framers sought to construct a constitutional government that would strain toward the civic republican ideals of virtue and the common good but simultaneously would protect against the self-interested political machinations of ordinary people and factional groups. The framers hoped that, under the Constitution, the virtuous elite would be elected as often as possible to governmental offices. But in the likely event that lesser individuals were elected instead, the structures of the constitutional government would nonetheless thwart their self-interested partisanship. The purpose of the Constitution, in other words, became the structuring of a stable government that would act for the public good despite the (supposed) ignobleness of human nature and the resultant fragility of the republic. James Madison captured the framers' strained conjunction of hope and cynicism in *The Federalist, Number 57*: "The aim of every political constitution is, or ought to be, first to obtain for rulers men who possess most wisdom to discern, and most virtue to pursue, the common good of the society; and in the next place, to take the most effectual precautions for keeping them virtuous whilst they continue to hold their public trust."[40]

The framers' Machiavellian concern with the fragility of the new republic actually led them to temper some of the civic republican motifs incorporated into the new constitutional government. Of course, the Constitution, claiming to speak for "We the People," still invoked popular sovereignty and representative government. But whereas little more than a decade earlier, the revolutionaries had emphasized a civic republican form of liberty that stressed citizen participation in government, the framers were more wary of potential democratic excesses and governmental corruptions. Thus, the new Constitution shifted power away from the democratic republican state governments to the new national government, but then the Constitution attempted to limit the ability of the national government to exercise its potential power. Many of the structural provisions of the Constitution— separation of powers, checks and balances, bicameralism, federalism—tended to encumber the exercise of power by the national government. The framers, in this sense, had shifted toward a more Lockean vision: they sought to protect preexisting individual rights from governmental infringement by limiting governmental power. (It is worth noting, though, that during the English Civil War and interregnum period, more than three decades before Locke had published his *Two Treatises of Government*, James Harrington had argued from within the civic republican tradition that sovereign power should be constitutionally limited.) Whereas the American revolutionaries had stressed individual liberty within the context of governmental participation, the constitutional framers tended to understand individual liberty as freedom from governmental interference.[41]

In sum, Americans had started to shift to a more Lockean and modern notion of government, but to a significant extent they remained first-stage premodernists. From the framers' perspective, governmental officials should at least strive toward the civic republican ideals of the virtuous or disinterested pursuit of the common good. Hopefully, the ordinary people would display sufficient judgment to elect those few elite individuals who possessed the requisite civic virtue to attain these republican ideals. Concomitant with their republican political motifs, the framers' idea of time or history vividly disclosed their premodern vision. For the most part, the revolutionaries and framers retained a first-stage premodernist cyclical view of history. From this viewpoint, nations, like biological organisms, had natural life cycles: they inevitably passed from a vigorous youth to a peaceful and prosperous middle age to a corrupt and failing old age. Members of the founding generation from John Adams to Thomas Jefferson repeatedly spoke, until the latter parts of their lives, of "the rise and fall of empires."[42] For example, in 1775, Benjamin Franklin distinguished "uncorrupted new states" from "corrupted old ones," while almost a quarter of a century later, in 1798, David Tappan, Hollis Professor of Divinity at Harvard College, declared:

> Experience proves that political bodies, like the animal economy, have their periods of infancy, youth, maturity, decay, and dissolution. In the early stages of their existence their members are usually industrious and frugal, simple in their manners, just and kind in their intercourse, active and hardy, united and brave. . . . The practice of these virtues gradually nourishes them to a state of manly vigor. They become mature and flourishing in wealth and population, in arts and arms, in almost every kind of national prosperity. But when they have reached a certain point of greatness, their taste and manners begin to be infected. Their prosperity inflates and debauches their minds. It betrays them into pride and avarice, luxury and dissipation, idleness and sensuality, and too often into practical and scornful impiety. These, with other kindred vices, hasten their downfall and ruin. [History shows that] virtue is the soul of republican freedom; that luxury tends to extinguish both sound morality and piety; and that the loss of these renders men incapable of estimating and relishing, of preserving or even bearing the blessings of equal liberty.[43]

Most clearly, then, the framers' overarching Machiavellian focus on the health of the seemingly fragile republic revealed their premodern attitude. Nevertheless, it is worth noting that the leaders of the founding generation, having just experienced the Revolution and the constitutional framing, might have viewed themselves as proto-modernists, seeking to purposefully reorder society to promote human progress. Nonetheless, those early Americans more readily understood themselves from a premodern vantage. True, they had sought change, yet in their minds, they had not aimed to radically reorder society in a modernist fashion. Rather, they sought to change the form of government so that they might preserve the principles and liberties of a premodern republic. In a sense, they paradoxically sought change to thwart change. That is, pursuant to the premodern cyclical view of history, change generally was associated with the decay of advancing age. Americans sought to purposefully alter their governmental arrangements when they thought it necessary to prevent or remedy such decay. Thus, the American revolutionaries had believed that the British had changed, had become corrupt, and were undermining American rights and liberties. The Americans consequently had initiated and fought the Revolution in part to reinstitute their republican rights and liberties. The Pennsylvania Constitution of 1776 illustrated this American attitude: "[A]ll government ought to be instituted and supported for the security [and] protection of the community as such, and to enable the individuals who compose it to enjoy their natural rights, and the other blessings which the Author of existence has bestowed upon man; and whenever these great ends of government are not obtained, the people have a right, by common consent to change it, and take such measures as to them may appear necessary."[44]

Similarly, the constitutional framers believed that the democratic machinations in the state governments—including, incidentally, Pennsylvania—unexpectedly but nonetheless problematically had undermined republican principles. From their own standpoint, then, the framers transformed the national governmental scheme in order to remedy the perceived problems and to preserve republican rights and liberties. The American revolutionaries and framers, in short, understood themselves not as modernist reformers but rather as protecting their most sacred and universal principles. They sought, in Zephaniah Swift's words, "to preserve the peace and good order of the community." Indeed, one should not overlook that the framers attended the Constitutional Convention and proposed the new Constitution extralegally (under the Articles of Confederation) exactly because they feared for the health of the republic. Although civilizations appeared to rise and fall—and the young American republic seemed to be prematurely yet seriously ailing—political leaders could act to delay the inevitable societal decay. The framers therefore aimed to construct a governmental scheme that first would return the republic to its rightful vigor and then would preserve the revitalized republic as long as possible. But, warned John Dickinson, cultivating "the seeds of liberty [would] demand continual attention, unceasing diligence, and frequent conflict with difficulties." (Some framers believed, though, that the apparently unending supply of land for Anglo-Americans—who were so willing to take it from the Native Americans—would allow the republic to thrive in perpetuity.)[45]

During the first decades of the nation's existence after the adoption of the Constitution, leading jurisprudents consistently displayed their premodern commitment to American republican principles. In typical fashion, St. George Tucker emphasized in 1803 that the national and state governments were republican, arising from "the PEOPLE" and their "natural, inherent, and unalienable rights."[46] Jurisprudents agreed that citizens and governmental officials should cultivate civic virtue as they deliberated about and pursued the public or common good.[47] Fearful that corruption and decay relentlessly menaced the republic, Nathaniel Chipman, Zephaniah Swift, Tucker, and others maintained the framers' Machiavellian concern that Americans follow these well-established republican principles. Once again, Tucker exemplified the contemporary American view:

> Thus while a democracy may be pronounced to be the only legitimate government, and that form of government, alone, which is compatible with the freedom of the nation, and the happiness of the individual, we may perceive that it is on every side surrounded by enemies, ready to sap the foundation, convulse the frame, and totally destroy the fabric. In such a government a sacred veneration

for the principles of the constitution, a perfect obedience to the laws, an unremitting vigilance on the part of the people over the conduct of their agents, and the strictest attention to the morals and principles of such as they elect into every office, legislative, executive, or judiciary, seem indispensably necessary to constitute, and to preserve a sufficient barrier against its numerous foes.[48]

As was true with the framers, then, the premodern sentiments of the leading jurisprudents were most evident in their expressions of republican elitism and in their ideas of time or history, correlative to their republican principles. They reasoned that the best means for securing virtuous governmental officials who would pursue the common good was to choose from a cadre of elite individuals. Swift, in particular, distinguished between pure democracies, on the one hand, and the "representative republic" of the United States, on the other hand. Drawing on the history of ancient republics, he argued that a republic based on representation was more likely to endure than one edging too near populist democracy. The people could be trusted to elect their representatives—their elite guardians of the common good—but the people would destroy a republic if they possessed excessive direct governmental power themselves. In a similar vein, Swift emphasized that, for the good of all, the senate ought to be a forum reserved for the virtuous elite:

> In every age and nation, the natural inequality of mankind, arising from superiority of ability and virtue, has laid the foundation of a natural aristocracy. In a legislature composed of a single branch, the personal influence attendant on genius, merit, and learning, might enable the possessors to form combinations, and execute plans, dangerous to the liberties of the people. Remove them to a senate, (and such will be the characters of which senates will always be composed) and they lose the opportunity of inflaming popular assemblies, by the splendor of eloquence, and of persuading them by the arts of intrigue, to adopt rash and ruinous measures. This promotion will inhance their personal dignity, and lessen their popular influence. A seat in the senate, is a proper reward for the services of those persons who are by nature endowed with talents and dispositions to do good to mankind. Such an object may divert the ardent pursuits of ambition, from schemes less praise worthy and honorable.[49]

Implicit in such an elitist vision of republicanism, of course, was a premodern understanding of history as cyclical. Because civilizations rise and fall, jurisprudential and political thinkers needed to be especially concerned with preserving the ever-threatened republic. Failure to follow republican principles presaged doom. Chipman declared: "States, kingdoms and empires, if they admit principles, which thwart the established laws of nature, like heaps of sand, opposed to the resistless force of a torrent, are inevitably swept into the gulf of dissolution." Chipman and others, though, simultaneously disclosed an incipient belief in the idea of progress, which would soon characterize the second stage of premodern American jurisprudence. Recognizing the possibility of human improvement, jurisprudents increasingly expressed the hope that the American republic somehow would escape the seemingly normal decline of old age. Montesquieu and other political theorists, Chipman argued, "join in an opinion, which has very generally prevailed, that governments, like men, from a necessity of nature, carry in themselves, from their very origin, the seeds of dissolution; that man is fatally incapable of forming any system, which shall endure without degenerating. This opinion seems to be countenanced by the experience of ages. I am apprehensive, however, that on enquiry, we shall find reason for a different opinion."[50]

Thus, in the 1790s and the early nineteenth century, legal thinkers more confidently hoped that the American republic might be of "perpetual duration." Even with this confidence, though, during the first stage, the overriding concern always was with the preservation and potential fragility of the nation. Despite the apparently unique soundness of the Constitution, if Americans personally deviated from republican principles, the country inevitably would decay—or so the first-stage jurisprudents believed. Even James Wilson—who, more than his contemporaries, favored a populist-style democracy—stressed "that few are able to trace or to estimate the great danger, in a free government, when the rights of the people are unexercised, and the still greater danger, when the rights of the people are ill exercised." Thus, unlike during second-stage premodern jurisprudence proper, first-stage legal thinkers did not associate the idea of improvement or progress with the utilitarian or instrumental use of law to promote happiness or economic prosperity. Instead, as Perry Miller writes of Chipman, first-stage jurisprudents generally viewed law as a "means by which a civilization resists its own sophistication in order to preserve, in the midst of artificiality, the eternal virtues of pristine 'Nature.'"[51]

Opposing Forces

While American legal thinkers remained largely committed to a premodern conception of law until around the Civil War, many modernist forces nonetheless pressed upon the jurisprudents. American thinkers generally derived much of their inspiration from Europeans, who at least intellectually, if not socially, were already entrenched in modernism. As discussed in chapter 2, European philosophers had entered a modernist stage during the seventeenth century. So, for example, while American jurisprudents were insistently grounding the common law on natural law principles through much of the nineteenth century, Jeremy Bentham had turned definitively toward positivism, condemning natural law as early as 1776 and, in the 1790s, denouncing natural rights as "nonsense upon stilts." Publishing in England and France, Bentham stood as the quintessential modernist when he proclaimed that the government can and should legislate instrumentally according to the "principle of utility." The government, that is, should remake society by formulating laws to promote the happiness of individuals and the community at large.[52]

Apart from this European intellectual pressure toward modernism, the American Revolution itself had unleashed a great modernizing social force: namely, the democratic and egalitarian idea of popular sovereignty. Popular sovereignty, understood broadly, connoted that an authoritative and supreme power arose from and always remained grounded in the people—a power that could be manifested in a variety of social realms, including the economic and religious as well as the political. As such, popular sovereignty resonated with a widespread drive toward a modernist-like individualism in early-nineteenth-century America; not coincidentally, Alexis de Tocqueville first coined the term *individualism* when describing America in the 1830s. If, as suggested by the idea of popular sovereignty, power emanated from the people as a whole, then power seemed to originate ultimately in each person—in the dignity and desires of the individual. According to premodern civic republican thought, private and self-interested social interactions generally had been deemed dangerous; the political community or government, consequently, had been needed to structure social relations and interactions toward the public good. But under the emerging egalitarian individualist ethos of the nineteenth century, derived partly from the ideas of Adam Smith and Bentham, the private pursuit of individual self-interest took on a more positive connotation. Indeed, quite often, government increasingly appeared to be an impediment to the individual's exercise of liberty. Virtue no longer was clearly tied to the pursuit of the common good but rather revolved around a combination of individual independence and benevolence toward others. Manifestations of this individualist ethos became evident in the religious, economic, and political spheres.[53]

Religiously, the Second Great Awakening, like the earlier First Great Awakening, was a pandemic Christian revival that spread and deepened Protestantism throughout America. Nathan Hatch argues that the "wave of popular religious movements that broke upon the United States in the half century after independence did more to Christianize American society than anything before or since." Between 1800 and 1835, church membership nearly doubled, and if one accounts for the Americans who were churchgoers but not official members, then fully 75 percent of the population was attending church. Beyond this significant quantitative influence, though, the Second Great Awakening also crucially changed the form and substance for much of American Protestantism. Before the nineteenth century, many American Protestants remained committed to the Calvinist doctrine of predestination: God supposedly had preselected a special few for salvation. During the Second Great Awakening, countless Protestants rejected the concept of predestination; instead, the ordinary individual was deemed capable of *choosing* salvation. The individualist and populist ideology of this theological transition was unmistakable: each person was empowered to choose. Protestant revivals, often at camp meetings, were directed toward the common people. At any one meeting, scores of individuals could proclaim their supposedly sudden experience of religious conversion and their newfound faith in Jesus Christ. The *Reformed Episcopal Articles of Religion*, for example, declared that the "sinner comes to Christ through no labored process of repenting and sorrowing; but he comes to Christ and repentance both at once, by means of simply believing." Salvation, so it appeared, was that easy! This religious metamorphosis in American Protestantism both supported and was reinforced by the growing American commitment to the democratic idea of the sovereign people. Indeed, by including African Americans and women, the religious revivals of the Second Great Awakening easily surpassed the egalitarian populism then present in American government.[54]

Meanwhile, economically, the United States began to change from a largely agricultural to a commercial and eventually industrial economy. The constitutional framers themselves, following John Locke, had set the stage for this transition by emphasizing the protection of an individual right to accumulate property and wealth. Consistent with this emphasis, the framers sought to prevent the enactment of extreme debtor relief laws as well as the eruption of popular economically spurred insurrections such as Shays' Rebellion. Furthermore, and of far-reaching importance, the framers hoped that the new interstate commerce clause would help spur business activity and boost the national economy. Such a promotion of commerce, incidentally, was somewhat in tension with traditional republican thought, which tended to encourage agrarian pursuits for fear that commercial activities nurtured self-interest rather than civic virtue (again, though, James Harrington earlier had argued from within the civic republican tradition to prevent supposed overreaching by the poor).[55]

For a variety of reasons, the framers' economic hopes were fulfilled, probably far beyond their wildest expectations. During the first six decades of the nineteenth century, the population of the United States grew six times over. The geographical land mass of the nation expanded just as dramatically: the Louisiana Purchase in 1803 doubled the nation's size, and when the United States won the Mexican War in 1847, the nation was able to fulfill its so-called Manifest Destiny, stretching from the Atlantic to the Pacific. This multifaceted national expansion sparked technological developments, especially in transportation and communication, as canals, railroads, steamboats, and the like were built. These changes contributed to a remarkable transformation in American economic attitudes and activities. Indeed, by the first decades of the nineteenth century, most Americans had become united in an overwhelming commitment to commerce and the rapid accumulation of personal wealth. As early as 1808, Charles Jared Ingersoll proclaimed: "[c]ommerce and liberty are correlatives. Wherever there is liberty, and no natural impediments, there will be commerce: and the American experiment has shown, that without liberty commerce cannot move with the enjoyment of its natural elasticity, or find its proper summit."[56]

This burst of self-interested economic activity coincided with the coming of the Industrial Revolution to America, chiefly to the Northeast. The War of 1812, in particular, spurred industrialization. Because of America's own restrictive trade policies and British blockades, the War of 1812 forced Americans to begin producing goods that previously had been imported. Building on this impetus, the transition in the American economy during the first part of the nineteenth century was startling: in 1800, 83 percent of the labor force was in agriculture, but by 1860, only 53 percent remained similarly occupied. Moreover, even the farmers, in a sense, became commercialized, as more and more turned from subsistence to cash-crop farming. Tocqueville declared: "what astonishes me in the United States is not so much the marvelous grandeur of some undertakings as the innumerable multitude of small ones. Almost all the farmers of the United States combine some trade with agriculture; most of them make agriculture itself a trade."[57]

All in all, the United States became a highly commercial and industrial nation, comfortable with the economic individualism championed earlier by Adam Smith in Britain. Americans generally agreed with Smith: to seek to satisfy one's own self-interest was good not only for oneself; it was good for society. Even further, to many Americans, the pursuit of one's own economic self-interest was understood to be "egalitarian and democratic." "If everyone in the society was involved in moneymaking and exchanging," Gordon Wood writes, "then to that extent they were all alike, all seeking their own individual interests and happiness." Moreover, at least for white males, there existed an abstract or formal right to pursue wealth on an equal basis with other white males. In fact, between 1800 and 1860, the standard of living of the average family meaningfully improved as the gross national product per capita more than doubled. In the industrializing states of the Northeast, for example, "the range of goods and services available to ordinary consumers increased strikingly," and the economy expanded sufficiently so that the poor had greater purchasing power in 1860 than at the turn into the nineteenth century. In the middle of the century, the ordinary white male could choose in the economic marketplace to purchase items—clothes, books, food, newspapers—that were unavailable in such variety or quality fifty years earlier.[58]

In the political realm, the scope of democratic government and political equality expanded during the early nineteenth century. Almost immediately after the adoption of the Constitution, events during the 1790s presaged a transition in the American conceptualization of government. Under the press of concrete political problems, the Federalist consensus behind George Washington crumbled: the Jeffersonian Republicans, led by James Madison as well as Thomas Jefferson, emerged to oppose the Federalists, led by Alexander Hamilton and John Adams. The Federalists preferred a stronger national government focusing on stable finances and aggressive commercial practices, while the Jeffersonian Republicans favored state governmental power and agrarian pursuits. The two sides further diverged because they accentuated different aspects of American republicanism: the Federalists stressed a premodern civic republican elitism, while the Jeffersonian Republicans advocated a more democratic popular sovereignty.[59]

The Federalists and Jeffersonian Republicans perceived such an enormous abyss between their respective positions that some contemporary observers considered the sweeping Republican victories in the elections of 1800 to be of revolutionary proportions. After 1800, in fact, the nation settled into a prolonged period of Republican rule: Jefferson, Madison, and James Monroe, all Virginians and all Republicans, held the presidency through 1825.[60] This period of Jeffersonian Republican domination contributed to and coincided with two significant changes regarding American government. First, with such internal stability, American national confidence surged during the first quarter of the nineteenth century: the nation, many now believed, would endure indefinitely. The Machiavellian concern with the fragility of the republic—related to the first-stage premodern assumption that civilizations inevitably rise and fall—faded away (or at least went into repose) as the nation generally prospered.

Second, consistent with the Jeffersonian position, the nation became more populist and less elitist in its conception and practice of government. The constitutional framers themselves had been, to a great extent, intellectual elites: "sages, scientists, men of broad cultivation, many of them apt in classical learning, who used their wide reading in history, politics, and law to solve the exigent problems of their time." But the Federalists in the election of 1800 were the last Americans to seek national elective office while professing "hierarchical values or deferential political practices."[61] Instead, a widespread anti-elitism—or in the words of Richard Hofstadter, an anti-intellectualism—gradually took hold:

> As popular democracy, gained strength and confidence, it reinforced the widespread belief in the superiority of inborn, intuitive, folkish wisdom over the cultivated oversophisticated, and self-interested knowledge of the literati and the well-to-do. Just as the evangelicals [of the Second Great Awakening] repudiated a learned religion and a formally constituted clergy in favor of the wisdom of the heart and direct access to God, so did advocates of egalitarian politics propose to dispense with trained leadership in favor of the native practical sense of the ordinary man with its direct access to truth. This preference for the wisdom of the common man flowered, in the most extreme statements of the democratic creed, into a kind of militant popular anti-intellectualism.

After the founding generation, then, intellectual elites never again would similarly predominate among the nation's political leaders. Elected officials in America, Tocqueville observed, were likely to be "inferior, in both capacity and morality, to those whom an aristocracy would raise to power," partly because democracy leads to "a general leveling" of the people. The idea of republicanism persevered, of course, but it was recast, more often emphasizing popular sovereignty or, eventually for some, union (as the sectional dispute between North and South intensified), rather than elite leadership.[62]

Hence, as elitism faded, democratic populism correspondingly flowered. At the time of the framing of the Constitution, most states allowed only white males who owned property to vote, but by 1825, every state but three extended the franchise to all white males. Equally important, the first half of the nineteenth century saw the dramatic growth of populist mass politics. In the early years of the nation, political parties had been denigrated as corrupting republican government: parties seemed to encourage partisanship or factionalism instead of the pursuit of the common good. During the 1790s, consequently, Madison and Jefferson strained uncomfortably against the perception that they represented a factional party. In the 1820s, though, Martin Van Buren championed the idea that organized political parties would be good for the nation despite their basis in self-interest. Roughly beginning with the Jacksonian Democrats in the late 1820s, then, political parties organized and developed systematic methods for appealing to the common "man"—for the purpose of turning out the vote. In fact, the participation rate of those eligible to vote increased dramatically: between 1824 and 1840, the population grew 57 percent, but the number of eligible voters casting a ballot in the presidential elections in those years increased 700 percent![63]

In sum, many modernist forces pressed upon legal thinkers during the first half of the nineteenth century. Perhaps most prominent for the development of American jurisprudence, the broad-ranging American commitment to popular sovereignty potentially transgressed the jurisprudential faith in natural law. Natural law seemed to fit most comfortably in a premodern monarchical society, based on the notion of a divine right of kings and a static social hierarchy. But the interrelated religious, economic, and political movements toward individualism and popular sovereignty in America had contributed to a restructuring of social relations. The vestiges of premodern social roles and structures withered as new social relations evolved and emerged through the nineteenth century. Compared with seventeenth- and eighteenth-century America and much of nineteenth-century Europe, societal roles in nineteenth-century America no longer seemed as rigidly hierarchical or as predetermined by one's initial status in life.[64] Moreover, at least at the level of political theory, popular sovereignty—the idea that the people are the ultimate political power and thus that the people make the law—would appear to resound with positivist jurisprudence, which is integral to modernism. That is, the idea that the people make the law could potentially conflict with the acceptance of preexisting natural law principles. As already mentioned, Americans typically deflected this potential discord by presuming that positive law comported with natural law. But conflict occasionally bubbled to the surface, especially within the crucible of slavery. For example, judges sometimes upheld the legality of slavery by declaring that law and morality are separate: even if slavery is contrary to morality and natural law, they reasoned, the positive law of the state must be supreme.[65]

In fact, the formidable modernist pressures bearing on American jurisprudents threatened to radically alter the legal system in the middle decades of the nineteenth century. Inspired partly by the modernist ideas of Jeremy Bentham, a political campaign to codify the common law started in the 1820s and received its most complete hearing at the New York State constitutional convention of 1846. Proponents of codification were motivated by a variety of factors, including particularly a concern that common law judges exercised too much discretion when deciding cases. Codifiers insisted that, consistent with the idea of the sovereignty of the people, legislators and not judges should make the law. In the end, New York resisted the pressure to codify its legal system *in toto*, but in 1848, under the leadership of David Dudley Field, the state did replace the common law writs and forms of action with a code that mandated pleading the facts giving rise to a cause of action. Most tellingly, though, in terms of the movement from premodern to modern jurisprudence, even this partial victory for the codifiers was replicated in many states only after the Civil War.[66]

Basically, despite the modernist forces pressing on American legal thinkers, opposing forces sufficiently influenced jurisprudents to delay their eventual turn to modernism until the Civil War era. Significant, for example, was the disjunction between the spreading egalitarian individualist ethos and the social reality of American life. To be sure, as already discussed, America became in some ways more populist and egalitarian during the early nineteenth century. Nonetheless, as the vestiges of premodern social strata decayed, new political and economic hierarchies began to build, starting particularly in the 1830s. Two factors somewhat unique to American society fueled this evolving social stratification: first, the entrenchment of plantation slavery in the South, and second, the ever-growing influx of immigrants. Because of legally imposed constraints on African-American slaves and deeply ingrained prejudices against immigrants (especially non-English and non-Christian immigrants), American society never was as open and fluid as the ideology of the egalitarian individualist ethos promised. Thus, for example, despite expanding suffrage, voting was still limited only to white males—no African Americans, no Native Americans, and no women. Even among white males, the right to vote did not necessarily translate into effective political power, particularly because economic inequalities were increasing. An abstract right of equal opportunity to pursue wealth did not lead to even remotely egalitarian economic consequences. As Morton Horwitz observes, legal changes promoting commercial activity did not randomly or neutrally spur economic development, but rather distributed wealth and resources in a particular and systematic manner. "[E]mergent entrepreneurial and commercial groups [won] a disproportionate share of wealth and power in American society." Somewhat predictably, then, the largest share of the burden for economic development fell upon the already disenfranchised, enslaved, and otherwise disempowered members of society—that is, on immigrants, women, African Americans, and other racial and religious minorities. Hence, although the poor gained greater wealth as the nineteenth century progressed, the gap between the rich and the poor was rapidly widening as the richest 10 percent of American society reaped a constantly increasing share of the wealth. In sum, these evolving social hierarchies—flowing from slavery, anti-immigrant prejudices, and economic developments—very well may have hampered the general movement toward modernism in America.[67]

Not only did certain factors seem to delay the advance of modernism, but also other factors seemed to nurture persistent premodern views, especially a natural law orientation among jurisprudents. Indeed, many of the developments that seemed to inject (and reflect) modernist views in American life simultaneously included elements that paradoxically reinforced premodern jurisprudential attitudes. Even the political controversies of the 1790s, so significant for introducing certain modernist notions into government, nourished premodern Machiavellian concerns, albeit temporarily so. As discussed, the Federalists and the Jeffersonian Republicans perceived an enormous gulf between their respective positions, but the actual distance between the two sides on particular issues in this multifaceted dispute was often overestimated. For instance, the Jeffersonians certainly favored popular sovereignty, yet they also still believed, to a great extent, in rule by a meritocratic elite—so long as the supposedly corrupt and aristocratic Federalists no longer held office. But from the perspectives of the Federalists and the Jeffersonians themselves, the nation seemed to be "dangerously polarized," even close to civil war. The Federalists and Jeffersonians, in other words, did not realize how much they still agreed on fundamental principles of government—how much they still shared in common. Their mutual perceptions (or misperceptions) of a wide abyss tended to sustain premodern fears of governmental corruption and fragility and led, not incidentally, to egregiously vindictive actions, such as the Alien and Sedition Acts of 1798. Thus, despite the fact that the events of the 1790s introduced some modernizing tendencies in American government, the same events simultaneously reinforced Machiavellian republican concerns about the health of the nation. Moreover, even as such Machiavellian concerns faded over the first decades of the nineteenth century and self-interested political partisanship, replete with political parties, became increasingly acceptable, remnants of premodern elitism always persisted within the American governmental system, particularly within the judiciary. Judges seemed to assume the mantle of the virtuous "umpire, standing above the marketplace of competing interests and rendering impartial and disinterested decisions." The imposition of judicially interpreted law became, in a sense, a means for controlling the partisan maneuverings of politicians.[68]

Religious developments, like those in the political realm, injected (and reflected) modernist elements in American life while, in other ways, sustaining premodern jurisprudential views. The Second Great Awakening, to be sure, transformed and spread American Protestantism and thus contributed to (and manifested) the growing individualist and populist ethos of the nineteenth century. Yet, simultaneously, the Second Awakening further Christianized American society and culture: indeed, at least throughout the nineteenth century, most Americans assumed that theirs was a Christian nation. "In the United States," Tocqueville discerned, "Christianity itself is an established and irresistible fact."

Protestantism thus provided the lens through which Americans generally saw social events and developments. Changes in American society, from this view, did
not augur a move into a positivistic and modernist world but rather bolstered a
longstanding belief in American millennial exceptionalism. Going back to the
Massachusetts Bay Puritans, many Americans had viewed themselves as establishing an earthly City of God, a "glorious kingdom of Christ on earth." For some,
the successful American Revolution and the constitutional framing served to sustain this religious conviction: America was "on a millennial course, guarded by divine Providence." With the coming of the Second Great Awakening, these views
further infused the American social body.[69]

Protestant norms and culture consequently permeated American legal thought:
the Second Great Awakening seemed to strengthen the American resolve to follow
a religiously rooted natural law. Jurisprudents and jurists typically considered
Christianity and the common law to be closely intertwined: Christianity was a
component of the common law, and the common law was based partly on Christian morality. David Hoffman, professor of law at the University of Maryland,
published his first *Course of Legal Study* in 1817 and prepared a second edition in
1836. The *Course* was intended primarily to shepherd students through the available primary and secondary works on the law; the second edition was expanded to
serve also as a resource for attorneys, judges, and statesmen. Each chapter or title
contained an extensive list of recommended readings as well as Hoffman's guiding
notes on many of those readings. Hoffman not only underscored the importance
of natural law and revelation in his definition of law, but he also began his *Course*
by focusing on the Bible. "The purity and sublimity of the morals of the Bible
have at no time been questioned; it is the foundation of the common law of every
christian nation. The christian religion is a part of the law of the land, and, as such,
should certainly receive no inconsiderable portion of the lawyer's attention." Unsurprisingly, then, state courts consistently enforced the Christian sabbath of Sun-
day and upheld prohibitions of blasphemy against Christianity. In the New York
case of *People v. Ruggles*, decided in 1811, the state's highest court upheld the
constitutionality of a common law criminal conviction of Ruggles for commit-
ting blasphemy. Ruggles had said that "Jesus Christ was a bastard, and his mother
must be a whore." James Kent, writing the opinion in the case, maintained "that we
are a christian people, and the morality of the country is deeply ingrafted upon
christianity."[70]

The fate of Thomas Paine illustrates the importance of religion to American
legal and political thinking. During the American Revolution, Paine was enormously popular as an advocate for natural rights and, more crucially, for independence from Britain. After Paine published *Common Sense* in January 1776, approximately 150,000 copies were sold during the next year. Consequently, "Paine
did more than any other individual to prepare the popular mind in America for
total separation." Yet by the early nineteenth century, Paine's popularity in

America had plunged, largely because his *Age of Reason*, published in 1794, defended the French Revolution by in part condemning all organized religious institutions, including Christian churches. "I do not believe in the creed professed by . . . any church that I know of," Paine unequivocally declared. "My own mind is my own church. All national institutions of churches . . . appear to me no other than human inventions, set up to terrify and enslave mankind, and monopolize power and profit." With such words Paine irreparably damaged his reputation in America. Regardless of Americans' political views regarding the French—and during the 1790s, once the French went to war against the British, the Jeffersonian Republicans generally supported the French, while the Federalists generally supported the British—few Americans could abide a repudiation of organized Christianity. Political and legal thinking, for Americans, had to remain consistent with their religious convictions. Thus, in Nathaniel Chipman's 1793 edition of his *Sketches of the Principles of Government*, he prominently quoted Paine on natural rights, but in Chipman's revised 1833 edition, he still discussed natural rights but had purged all mention of Paine. Ultimately, then, in a culture so infused with Christian convictions, a legal system supposedly rooted in a religiously based natural law not only was unexceptional and readily maintained but, even further, appeared to be nearly a prerequisite to general public acceptance.[71]

Seen in this light, it is unsurprising that the potential theoretical tensions between natural law and popular sovereignty did not trouble many American jurisprudents. As already discussed, although natural law and popular sovereignty might conflict, most legal thinkers tended to ignore this possibility. Even further, many jurisprudents argued that popular sovereignty was itself derived from natural law. "All men being by nature equal, in respect to their rights," St. George Tucker asserted, "no man nor set of men, can have any natural, or inherent right, to rule over the rest." According to Tucker and other jurisprudents, then, the Constitution had created a national government based on popular sovereignty that was coincident with the laws of nature. From this perspective, natural law and popular sovereignty not only failed to conflict; they supported and reinforced each other.[72]

Second-Stage Premodern Jurisprudence: Natural Law and Progress

The forces pushing jurisprudence toward modernism were opposed strongly enough to keep legal thought in a premodern stage until the Civil War era. But those same modernist pressures were adequate to precipitate a movement from a first to a second stage of premodern jurisprudence during the early nineteenth century, by approximately 1820. As already discussed, second-stage jurisprudents, like their first-stage predecessors, were committed to natural law and to the idea of legal science. Unlike the first stage, though, the second stage fully embraced a premodern idea of progress (akin to eschatological progress) that was most often manifested by an instrumental and pragmatic conception of law.

To be sure, some first-stage jurisprudents had disclosed an incipient belief in the idea of progress, but this idea bloomed in full only during the second stage. From the Americans' vantage, their experience of the first decades of national life suggested that change did not lead to societal decay, as first-stage premodernists had generally feared, but rather that change meant progress, and especially economic prosperity. Most Americans viewed the expanding population and land mass of the country to be hard evidence of progress, and the scientifically-inspired technological advances in transportation and communication only served to reinforce this impression. Hence, the idea of progress firmly took hold: through science and technology, in particular, America could push forward. Jurisprudents were fully aware of this momentous transition in America. At the constitutional convention of New York State in 1821, Kent proclaimed: "We stand at this moment on the brink of fate, on the very edge of the precipice. . . . We are no longer to remain plain and simple republics of farmers, like New-England colonists, or the Dutch settlements on the Hudson. We are fast becoming a great nation, with great commerce, manufactures, population, wealth, luxuries, and with the vices and miseries that they engender."[73]

Significantly, though, jurisprudents understood progress in premodernist or eschatological terms. They perceived progress as movement toward the realization of eternal and universal principles—principles derived from nature and Protestant Christianity. Jurisprudents, at this stage, then, did not accept a modernist idea of progress, which would posit a human capability to advance endlessly. Instead, the eternal and universal principles provided, in a sense, a goal and a limit for progress. Thus, for instance, during the second and third decades of the nineteenth century, Americans had to confront an inevitable fact: the founding generation had passed from the American scene. By the time James Monroe left the presidency in 1825, a new generation of Americans had risen to power; in fact, as if in a grand symbolic gesture, both Thomas Jefferson and John Adams died on July 4, 1826, the fiftieth anniversary of the nation. While many of the founders had viewed the Constitution as an experiment in thwarting inevitable societal decay, the new generation of political leaders more confidently began to view the Constitution within the parameters of premodern progress—the Constitution came to be seen as "a repository of first principles." The new leaders celebrated the framers as having successfully memorialized certain universal and eternal principles in the Constitution, which the new generation now would seek to perfect in practice. Joseph Story claimed that he wrote his *Commentaries on the Constitution* "with a sincere desire to commend, and to recommend the Constitution upon true, old, and elevated principles." His "principal object" in the *Commentaries* was "to present a full analysis and exposition of the Constitution [because it was] the only solid basis, on which to rest the private rights, the public liberties, and the substantial prosperity of the people composing the American Republic."[74]

Thus, in their political and legal thought, second-stage American jurisprudents came to accept fully a premodern idea of progress, which encompassed a continuing commitment to the eternal and universal principles of natural law. Kent proclaimed, therefore, that recently decided cases presumably contain "the most correct exposition of the law, and the most judicious application of abstract and eternal principles." The common law, that is, progresses as it moves increasingly closer to a perfect realization of its foundational principles. The law "must forever be in a state of progress," Story wrote, even as "the old foundations remain firm." Ideally, then, Story continued, the common law "moves onward in the path towards perfection, but never arrives at the ultimate point."[75]

The quest for progress led Americans in general to become highly instrumental and pragmatic in their attitudes. In particular, as the nation turned to commerce and the accumulation of wealth, the American notion of science changed, becoming more practical and utilitarian. Scientists became preoccupied with the pursuit of useful and profitable inventions such as the steamboat and the telegraph. Americans focused on "purely practical objects," according to Tocqueville. "[H]ardly anyone in the United States devotes himself to the essentially theoretical and abstract portion of human knowledge." Story underscored this general scientific turn in an 1829 speech given to the Boston Mechanics' Institute: "If I were called upon to state that which, upon the whole, is the most striking characteristic of our age, that which in the largest extent exemplifies its spirit, I should unhesitatingly answer, that it is the superior attachment to practical science over merely speculative science. Into whatever department of knowledge we may search, we shall find that the almost uniform tendency of the last fifty years has been to deal less and less with theory, and to confine the attention more and more to practical results."[76]

As the general concept of science altered, so too did the specific conception of legal science, as it also became increasingly focused on pragmatic concerns and the instrumental promotion of commerce. Law, jurisprudents believed, could and should be used to contribute to the progress of American society. Thus, from around 1820 onward, American legal thought was characterized not only by its continuing faith in natural law but also simultaneously by a burgeoning commitment to practical and instrumental decision making. The revered Lord Mansfield further inspired this transition to a pragmatic jurisprudence; he had demonstrated in the previous century the practical advantages of an instrumental approach to judicial decision making by, in effect, creating the commercial law of Britain. In America, Kent asserted that the question of whether to follow a rule from an earlier case "very often resolves itself into a mere question of expediency, depending upon the consideration of the importance of certainty in the rule and the extent of property to be affected by a change of it." Similarly, Francis Hilliard stated that, in common law decision making, "[g]eneral expediency,—public policy,—is often the highest measure of right."[77]

The state and federal courts thus developed policies in the form of common law rules that tended to spark commercial activity and economic development. For instance, during the first part of the nineteenth century, the courts transformed the common law concept of property to promote the release of economic "energy," while before that time, property was primarily understood to assure stability and security. Under the earlier conception of property, ownership connoted protection: the law of property allowed an owner to prevent others from harming his or her property. The courts transformed the law by developing rules that protected owners from potential liabilities for damages caused by efforts to develop their property for commercial purposes. Thus, under the later conception of property, an owner could do with his or her property whatever was desired, regardless of the effects on others.[78]

The Supreme Court's 1837 decision in Charles River Bridge v. Warren Bridge Company, when compared to the earlier Dartmouth College v. Woodward, exemplifies this transition. The Dartmouth College case, decided in 1819, arose when the state of New Hampshire enacted legislation that amended the original eleemosynary charter incorporating the college. With an opinion by Chief Justice John Marshall, the Court held, first, that the initial corporate charter constituted a contract protected under the contract clause of the Constitution and, second, that the attempted legislative amendment materially changed and unconstitutionally impaired the charter. In so holding, the Court reinforced the stability and security of vested property rights, here created under the original corporate charter.[79] By the time of the Charles River Bridge case in 1837, though, the Court was willing to conceptualize property in very different terms. In 1785, the state of Massachusetts had enacted a corporate charter for the building and operation of a toll bridge across the Charles River. In 1828 the state legislature chartered a new corporation, the Warren Bridge Company, for the purpose of building and operating a second bridge across the Charles River. Because of this second bridge, the Charles River Bridge lost much of its expected traffic and toll income. Based on the Dartmouth College holding, the Charles River Bridge Company therefore argued that its original charter had created a vested property right protected by the contract clause. The Court, now under Chief Justice Roger B. Taney, held otherwise. According to Taney's majority opinion, society was changing, and it was for the better. Law should be used to promote economic progress and prosperity, regardless of any supposed interest in the security and stability of property: "[T]he object and end of all government is to promote the happiness and prosperity of the community by which it is established. [I]n a country like ours, free, active and enterprising, continually advancing in numbers and wealth, new channels of communication are daily found necessary, both for travel and trade, and are essential to the comfort, convenience and prosperity of the people. A state ought never to be presumed to surrender this power, because, like the taxing power, the whole community have an interest in preserving it undiminished." Property, as it was now conceived, became an "institution of growth" rather than one merely of stability and security.[80]

While second-stage legal scientists became committed to a practical and instrumental approach to judicial decision making early in the nineteenth century, this pragmatic approach was understood to be entirely consistent with the concurrent natural law orientation. As Story said, when (once again) praising Lord Mansfield, specifically with regard to Mansfield's decisions in maritime and commercial law, "the general consistency with principle is as distinguishable, as their practical importance." Kent declared that the right of property not only arises from the law of nature and revelation but also spurs humanity to social and commercial progress:

> The sense of property is graciously bestowed on mankind, for the purpose of rousing them from sloth, and stimulating them to action; and so long as the right of acquisition is exercised in conformity to the social relations, and the moral obligations which spring from them, it ought to be sacredly protected. The natural and active sense of property pervades the foundations of social improvement. It leads to the cultivation of the earth, the institution of government, the establishment of justice, the acquisition of the comforts of life, the growth of the useful arts, the spirit of commerce, the productions of taste, the erections of charity, and the display of the benevolent affections.[81]

But how, precisely, could a commitment to principles, particularly natural law principles, be consistent with an instrumental approach to judicial decision making? The answer lay in the Platonic relationship between the principles and the cases. According to Plato, the Ideas exist separately from the particular instances. The Ideas are universal and unchanging, while the particular instances vary, manifesting but never perfectly exemplifying the Ideas. As already discussed, premodern jurisprudents understood the relation between legal principles and cases in a similar fashion: legal principles are universal and separate from the cases, which represent imperfect manifestations of the principles. From this perspective, natural law principles provided a metaphysical foundation for the American legal system, including the common law. Yet, the principles still had to be specifically interpreted and applied in concrete judicial disputes, and as judges did so, they were to be practical and instrumental. Indeed, as Thomas Grey has noted, jurists and jurisprudents of this time did not assume, for the most part, that they could reason deductively downward from the general principles to mechanically ascertain lower-level legal rules or the correct outcomes in concrete disputes. A knowledge of the principles might guide but could not dictate a judge's determination in any specific case. In an 1854 opinion, Lemuel Shaw captured the Platonic relation between the universal principles of natural law and his instrumental decision making in particular cases:

It is one of the great merits and advantages of the common law, that, instead of a series of detailed practical rules, established by positive provisions, and adapted to the precise circumstances of particular cases, which would become obsolete and fail, when the practice and course of business, to which they apply, should cease or change, the common law consists of a few broad and comprehensive principles founded on reason, natural justice, and enlightened public policy modified and adapted to the circumstances of all the particular cases which fall within it. [While the common law] has its foundations in the principles of equity, natural justice, and that general convenience which is public policy; although these general considerations would be too vague and uncertain for practical purposes, in the various and complicated cases, of daily occurrence, in the business of an active community; yet the rules of the common law, so far as cases have arisen and practices actually grown up, are rendered, in a good degree, precise and certain, for practical purposes, by usage and judicial precedent.[82]

Because of the instrumental approach to judicial decision making, the natural law principles faded into the juridical background in many and even most instances. Yet, although in specific cases the principles would only rarely be referred to, they always remained significant as a foundation for the legal system—a foundation of principles that could fade into the background only because so many American judges, lawyers, and jurisprudents willingly agreed on and accepted the idea of broad natural law principles. Contrary to the subsequent modernist era, the foundation (or, at least, the type of foundation) was not in dispute. Moreover, such a stable foundation was important as a means for justifying instrumental decision making in the courts. Hilliard commented on judicial lawmaking: "In one sense a court has no *legislative power*. To make any positive and general enactment would be a flagrant departure from its legitimate function. But, upon many judicial questions, the aid of authority, of analogous decided cases, is wholly wanting. It then becomes the duty of a judge, not indeed to pass an arbitrary edict, but, taking for his guide the universal law of reason and justice, to invest that law with the sanction and the imperative force of a distinct judgment, and thereby make it the law of the land, no longer open to argument and dispute."[83]

In sum, second-stage premodern jurisprudents, like their first-stage predecessors, comprehended the common law as a science, a rational system of principles grounded in natural law. Legal principles were understood to be universal yet separate from the cases themselves. The whole of jurisprudence, according to both first- and second-stage jurisprudents, could be rationally classified into a system that included not only the natural law principles but also a multitude of low-level legal rules that reflected the common law forms of action. Despite these significant commonalities between its two stages, premodern jurisprudence moved from its first to its second stage when a different notion of time and history took hold early in the nineteenth century. First-stage jurisprudents had tended to dwell upon the rise and fall of civilizations and the potential decay of the American republic.

Second-stage jurisprudents, though, fully embraced an idea of progress that assumed a human capability to constantly approach a more complete and perfect realization of the natural and universal principles. To achieve such progress, jurists and jurisprudents were to instrumentally apply the principles in a pragmatic fashion, paying particular attention to the promotion of commerce.

Nathaniel Chipman's writings strikingly illustrate the transition from the first to the second stage of premodern jurisprudence. Chipman published his *Sketches of the Principles of Government* in 1793, during the first stage. Then in 1833, during the second stage, he published his *Principles of Government,* a revised and enlarged edition of his earlier work. For the most part the 1833 edition closely resembled the 1793 edition, but one stark difference stood out: in the 1833 edition Chipman incorporated instrumental, particularly utilitarian, reasoning into his natural law outlook. Thus, in the 1793 edition, when discussing a "moral sense," Chipman wrote simply: "Man is furnished with a moral sense, by which he perceives the right, and the wrong of his actions." In 1833, though, Chipman turned to the principle of utility as a fundamental maxim of the "moral faculty" or "moral constitution": "the great end of all moral actions [is] general utility, or the general interest of society."[84] Likewise, in 1793 Chipman grounded property rights in natural law with no reference to utility at all, while in 1833 he wrote "that the right of property originates in natural principles, is confirmed by them, and finally sanctioned by the principle of utility." Moreover, consistent with Jeremy Bentham and Adam Smith, Chipman reasoned that the individual pursuit of happiness produces the greatest good for society as a whole.[85]

Indeed, Chipman posited the principle of utility as, in a sense, the ultimate law of nature. "As the end and design of all the laws of nature is general utility or the promotion of the general interest and happiness of social man, the sure test of any rule set up as a law of nature is its general tendency to promote that end." Thus, for Chipman, as for other second-stage jurisprudents, natural law and pragmatic instrumentalism (or utilitarianism) were entirely consistent. Following the Platonic relation between natural and positive law, Chipman distinguished between the immutable natural law principles and their positive applications, which varied with the circumstances: "The laws of nature and the obligations which they impose, are as immutable as the Supreme Being by whom they are ordained. When we say the laws of nature are immutable, it must be understood of the laws themselves; not of their application. The subject to which any rule of the law of nature is to applied may be changed, in which case the same laws of nature direct, a correspondent change in the application of the rule."[86]

With such an instrumental attitude firmly adopted, the later Chipman optimistically endorsed the idea of progress. The early Chipman was one of the first-stage jurisprudents who had disclosed an incipient belief in the idea of progress, hoping that the American republic might be of "perpetual duration," but during the first stage, such hope typically was held under the cloud of a Machiavellian concern for the fragility of the nation. In 1833, however, Chipman more confidently proclaimed: "[u]nder free institutions of government, the state of society will always be progressive—there will be a constant improvement in manners and knowledge." For that reason, Chipman's section on the corruption and dissolution of government was considerably shorter in 1833 than in 1793. Indeed, almost free of Machiavellian concerns, the later Chipman celebrated the American republic as measured by the principle of utility: Chipman asserted in 1833 that the end or purpose of "the science of government," in general, and the United States Constitution, in particular, was "to promote and secure the happiness of the people."[87]

The writings of Joseph Story provide a fitting final illustration of the components of second-stage premodern legal science. To Story, the science of law demanded systematization, "a scientific arrangement and harmony of principles." And, as Story described at his inauguration as Dane Professor of Law at Harvard in 1829, the science of jurisprudence is ultimately based in natural law: "the law of nature . . . lies at the foundation of all other laws, and constitutes the first step in the science of jurisprudence." Thus, in discussing contracts, for instance, Story noted: "[n]or is this obligatory force [of contracts] so much the result of the positive declarations of the municipal law, as of the general principles of natural, or, (as it is sometimes called) universal law." Finally, consistent with the dominant nineteenth-century American Protestant culture, Story elaborated the supposed ties between natural law and Christianity. He maintained that "Christianity [is] not merely an auxiliary, but a guide, to the law of nature; establishing its conclusions, removing its doubts, and elevating its precepts."[88]

While Story believed in natural law as the foundation of jurisprudence, he simultaneously emphasized that an instrumental and pragmatic approach to the law generates progress. The common law, in particular, must respond to the practical and commercial needs of the nation. "[T]he common law, as a science, must be forever in progress; and no limits can be assigned to its principles or improvements. In this respect," Story continued, "it resembles the natural sciences, where new discoveries continually lead the way to new, and sometimes to astonishing, results. To say, therefore, that the common law is never learned, is almost to utter a truism. It is no more than a declaration, that the human mind cannot compass all human transactions. It is its true glory, that it is flexible, and constantly expanding with the exigencies of society." Unsurprisingly, then, Story authored in 1842 the Supreme Court's majority opinion in *Swift v. Tyson*, holding that the federal courts should decide commercial cases based on a general federal common law that implicitly would be directed toward promoting economic activity.[89]

For Story, the principles of natural law existed separately from their imperfect exemplifications in the low-level legal rules and judicial decisions. The principles are universal, eternal, and foundational, while the rules and decisions are pragmatic and progressive. As G. Edward White suggests, Story conceived of historical "change as the progressive unfolding of first principles." Because the universal principles must be applied in a multitude of concrete contexts—in different climates, different geographies, and different economic situations—low-level legal rules and judicial decisions necessarily vary from place to place. Whereas in commercial law, according to Story, concerns shared throughout the world ought to lead to a high degree of legal uniformity on an international scale, in various other subjects, disparate interests and concerns retard uniformity, even sometimes in neighboring areas of America. The common law can be rationally systematized, but its specific rules remain forever imperfect because of "the boundless circumstances of life, which may modify, limit, or affect them." As Story succinctly summarized: "[The common law] is a system having its foundations in natural reason; but, at the same time, built up and perfected by artificial doctrines, adapted and moulded to the artificial structure of society."[90]

ᴀ F O U R ᴂ

Modern American Legal Thought

The Onset of Positivism:
The Civil War and Other Forces

As a general matter, prominent transitions in intellectual thought often seem to follow momentous social upheavals. True to form, then, the Civil War proved to be a cataclysm that triggered intellectual changes of paradigmatic proportions. Even more broadly, beyond the intellectual sphere, the war and its aftermath, including the assassination of Abraham Lincoln, ushered in momentous changes in almost every imaginable realm of American society.[1] The historian Peter J. Parish proclaims the Civil War "the central event of American history," while Eric Foner, discussing the war and the ensuing years, declares that "no aspect of life remained unaffected." The war of course began in 1861 because the states of the deep South seceded, so the Northern states initially fought to preserve the Union and only later to free the slaves. Eventually, though, many Northerners understood the struggle as one for the very progress of civilization, yet ironically, the American civilization was, in the end, thoroughly transformed. Most basically, the eradication of slavery together with the death or maiming of one-fourth of the young male population profoundly transformed the social fabric of America.[2]

Before the Civil War, America still was largely a nation of somewhat isolated small and rural "island communities." The war itself greatly destroyed the old ways of life, and afterward, during the Gilded Age of the late nineteenth century, the nation rebuilt, with new social structures arising. To be sure, antebellum America also had undergone significant changes, but from 1861 onward social change accelerated to a breathtaking pace. Between 1870 and 1900, the population grew from 40 million to 76 million, primarily because of "the largest wave of immigration in American history." Significantly, whereas during the antebellum years, most immigrants arrived from Ireland, Germany, Scandinavia, and Britain, during the postbellum period, most came from Italy, Russia, and the Balkans. This shift in immigration not only altered the makeup of America but also sparked outbreaks of nativism, racism against southern and eastern Europeans (especially Jews), and the first calls for limiting immigration. Early in the twentieth century, for instance, a United States Immigration Commission report supposedly proved that Jews, Slavs, and Italians were of lower morality and intelligence than white Anglo-Saxon Protestants. Meanwhile, the gross national product grew even faster than the increasing population would warrant, jumping more than fourfold. Technological breakthroughs brought canned goods, telephones, steel, subways, and skyscrapers. With track mileage increasing almost ninefold between the end of the war and the end of the century, railroads revolutionized transportation and led to the development of massive corporations—big business—which permanently altered all types of manufacturing and commerce in America. Most of the big factories opened in the rapidly expanding cities and typically hired large numbers of immigrant laborers. The nation became fully industrialized and urbanized, and the new corporations introduced bureaucratic organizational forms to deal with the masses of workers. Aided by the advances in transportation and communication, the corporations increasingly saw (and treated) the entire nation as a single marketplace, not as a group of discrete geographical and cultural regions. More clearly defined economic and social classes emerged, with the lower class populated greatly by immigrants and small farmers and the upper class gaining ever-increasing wealth. The "lower class became," in the words of Gordon Wood, "more conspicuous, more ethnic, more poor and more separated from the rest of society." Politics thus became riddled by class conflicts, with some of the lower classes becoming populists and some of the "old-stock" Protestant gentry becoming mugwumps as they struggled to wrest control from the new corporate and commercial powers. Finally, with the ultimate closing of the western frontier, the nation at century's end barely resembled that of 1850. According to Foner, the war and the following years prompted the "birth of the modern American state."[3]

Intellectually, the postbellum years saw the blossoming of two central tenets of modernist thought: secularism and historicism.[4] One scholarly event contributing to both of these modernist commitments was the publication of Charles Darwin's *Origin of Species* in 1859.[5] Even before this point, some American intellectuals in the wake of the Second Great Awakening had begun to wonder whether they should more sharply distinguish religion and science. Protestantism itself so sharply disjoined the spiritual from the material that it implicitly suggested the possibility of secularizing certain (material) spheres of American life, with religion supposedly placed in a separate realm. To be sure, religion remained important within this worldview (indeed, Protestantism long continued to dominate

American culture), but the secular seemingly was freed from the sacred and thus was enabled to grow in consequence—at least in the intellectual realm. Consequently, when a dispute over Darwin's theory of evolution developed during the 1870s, the pressure to secularize science, in particular, intensified. Whereas during the antebellum years most Americans had believed that science and religion were in harmony, during the early postbellum period science and religion increasingly seemed separate from and irrelevant to each other. Scientists frequently remained pious, but their religiosity was unrelated to their scientific work. Even further, many intellectuals eventually began to see science and religion as antithetical. The theory of evolution became controversial, according to Edward S. Corwin, because it challenged "the notion of special creation and [demoted] man from the kingdom of Heaven to the animal kingdom—from the status of fallen angel to the status of mere creature." From the most extreme Darwinian position, even human spirituality was understood as no more than a mere method for coping with the environment. Man's "most cherished sentiments," from this vantage, "were but the product of an evolutionary process which linked him with the other animals." Significantly, the reach of secularization was not limited solely to intellectuals. The development of mass market capitalism and improved communication had engendered mass culture: thus, intellectual trends, including secularism, could spread from high to mass culture far more rapidly than ever before. Although secularization certainly did not sweep across the entire nation, the potential conflict between secularization and piety became more visible, even celebrated.[6]

Darwin's theory of evolution also facilitated the development of a modernist idea of progress and its correlative "historicist sensibility." The "historical upheaval" of the Civil War and the Gilded Age left many American intellectuals with a deep and well-founded "sense that America had changed." Many experienced a "radical discontinuity between past and present." Darwinian theory encouraged intellectuals to understand such social change as representing a type of evolutionary advance that transcended the second-stage premodern idea of progress. Premodern progress had been constrained by the religious conviction in universal and eternal principles: premodern progress, that is, had seemed limited to a movement toward the perfect realization of such principles. But now, with secularization helping to unleash the idea of progress from religious convictions, progress could be understood to entail potentially endless improvement. Moreover, when some intellectuals coupled this emerging modernist idea of progress with the already well-developed American instrumental and utilitarian attitudes, a fully historicist sensibility arose: the endless progress of society could spring from human ingenuity.[7]

In jurisprudence, particularly, various social and cultural forces had pushed America toward modernism during much of the antebellum nineteenth century, but as discussed in chapter 3, legal thinkers had resisted these pressures.[8] The Civil War and its aftermath, though, finally precipitated a distinct jurisprudential transition from natural law to positivism—that is, from legal premodernism to modernism. Perry Miller suggests that, with the Civil War, "an era in the history of American law, as well as an era in the history of the American mind, was brought to an abrupt and violent conclusion." More precisely, perhaps no single factor influenced the general direction of postbellum jurisprudence more than the crisis over slavery: the specific antebellum arguments that proslavery and antislavery advocates formulated and, ultimately, their violent resolution in the Civil War. For much of the American legal premodern period, natural law principles provided a jurisprudential foundation that rested uncontroversially in the background of the legal system. As already mentioned, the relation between natural law and positive law occasionally became disputed within judicial cases involving slavery. But in terms of the future of American jurisprudence, the broad arguments being advanced for and against slavery might have had more long-lasting influence than specific judicial decisions. In particular, as theoretical positions evolved from the 1830s through the Civil War, the slavery dispute brought natural law from the background to the foreground of legal thought.[9]

Many members of the American revolutionary generation grew to oppose slavery partly because of their belief in a natural right to liberty, as memorialized in the Declaration of Independence. Within the first twenty-five years of the nation's existence, all states north of Delaware either abolished slavery or began gradual emancipation. Unlike the Northern states, of course, the Southern states did not similarly move to eliminate slavery. Yet, many Southerners of the revolutionary generation believed that slavery was indefensible even though it had to be temporarily tolerated as a "necessary evil." Even in the North, however, the antislavery movement slowed once the United States banned international slave trading in 1808. And regardless of any antislavery sentiments in either the North or South, racism against African Americans remained deeply ingrained in the dominant American (white) culture.[10]

During the early nineteenth century, at least three factors led many Southerners to shift their views and to defend slavery more strongly. First, the Southern economy had become increasingly dependent on the cultivation of cotton, which relied heavily on plantation slavery. Second, the almost constant geographical growth of the nation pushed the slave and free states into conflict over the status of new states and territories: Would they be slave or free? The status of new states, in particular, could determine the balance of power in the national Congress. Third, the renewal of an abolitionist movement in the North during the 1830s, led by William Lloyd Garrison and Wendell Phillips, sparked conservative reactions in both the South and the North. The Garrisonians advocated the immediate end of slavery and denounced the Constitution as, in the words of Garrison, a proslavery "covenant with death and an agreement with hell." Even many Northerners viewed the Garrisonians' immediatism as unacceptably radical, and consequently, some Northerners as well as Southerners reacted by arguing in favor of slavery (though many other Northerners advocated a more gradual end to slavery). Soon Southerners became the most prominent supporters of slavery as they repudiated their ancestors' view that slavery was no better than a necessary evil. Unsurprisingly, the emerging defenses of slavery were, in some respects, consistent with the general trend of legal thought of the time: arguments tended to be pragmatic or instrumental with natural law principles remaining mostly in the background. For example, writing in 1832, Thomas R. Dew, who was a professor at William and Mary College in Virginia, briefly mentioned natural law but then emphasized the "impracticability" of emancipation. According to Dew, in the event of emancipation, slave owners would have to be compensated for their lost "property" and the freed slaves would have to be deported, resulting in a prohibitive cost to the state.[11]

Over the next decades, though, positions increasingly came to be expressed in the stronger language of natural law and natural rights. In March 1850 Senator William H. Seward of New York spoke for three hours against the spread of slavery in the federal territories. In a brief though soon to be famous passage of his speech, Seward declared that "there is a higher law than the Constitution." The press seized upon this language and thus fully projected the question of higher or natural law into national prominence during the crucial decade preceding the Civil War. By this time, then, natural law had stepped from the background into the spotlight of American politics and jurisprudence: for both the Northern and Southern sides, much of the slavery dispute was to be articulated in the rhetoric of natural law and natural rights.[12]

In terms of the future of legal thought, this focus on natural law was critical. The divergence of Northern and Southern invocations of natural law onto separate theoretical paths eventually would lead postbellum jurisprudence in a distinct (Northerly) direction. Earlier American legal thinkers had tended to conjoin natural law and natural rights, rarely distinguishing one from the other in precise terms; natural rights were loosely understood as a component of natural law. But in the context of the antebellum slavery dispute, natural law and natural rights seemed to split: as a general matter, Northerners followed a path of natural rights, while Southerners followed one of natural law. Northern opponents of slavery often invoked the Declaration of Independence as they argued that a natural right of individual liberty contravened the legal institution of slavery. Meanwhile, Southern proponents of slavery tended to argue that natural law imposed a natural order on society, with slaves supposedly entrenched in their proper role (at the bottom); the government, according to this view, therefore justifiably enforced through legal sanctions this natural or inherent social order.[13]

The Declaration of Sentiments issued by the American Anti-Slavery Convention, meeting in Philadelphia in December of 1833, illustrates the Northern position: "The right to enjoy liberty is inalienable. To invade it is to usurp the prerogative of Jehovah. Every man has a right to his own body—to the products of his own labor—to the protection of law—and to the common advantages of society. That all those laws which are now in force, admitting the right of slavery, are therefore, before God, utterly null and void; being an usurpation of the Divine prerogative, a daring on the law of nature, a base overthrow of the very foundations of the social compact. . . . and therefore they ought instantly to be abrogated."[14] In the 1830s, such immediatist invocations of natural rights were widely deemed too radical, but by the 1850s, even moderate Northern opponents of slavery were using similar rhetoric. Charles Sumner, a Massachusetts senator from the Free Soil and then the Republican Party, maintained that the Fugitive Slave Act of 1850, which compelled Northern officials to help recapture escaped slaves, offended "against the Divine Law" and therefore should be disobeyed. Later that same year, 1852, Sumner declared that the abolition of slavery would fulfill "the great doctrines of Human Rights, as enunciated in our Declaration of Independence, and inspired by a truly Democratic sentiment."[15]

On the southern side during this period, John C. Calhoun, former vice president and long-time senator from South Carolina, most famously stated the standard Southern defenses of slavery. According to Calhoun, natural law imposed an order on society so that "nothing can be more unfounded and false" than that "all men are born free and equal." Not all people, therefore, deserve to enjoy liberty. To the contrary, bestowing liberty "on a people unfit for it, would, instead of a blessing, be a curse." From this perspective, Calhoun reasoned, the legal institution of slavery actually stood as a "positive good" for the slaves themselves: the slaves supposedly occupied their natural and appropriate position in society, and by doing so and by interacting with the white race, they were lifted to their "present comparatively civilized condition." In making this argument, Calhoun implicitly rejected Lockean liberalism in favor of an Aristotelian civic republicanism: that is, he repudiated the more modern egalitarian individualist ethos that was emerging in nineteenth-century America and instead embraced a more premodern, elitist, and ordered vision of society.[16]

Such arguments stupefied Northern antislavery activists. "Are slaveholders dunces, or do they take all the rest of the world to be, that they think to bandage our eyes with such thin gauzes?" wondered Theodore Dwight Weld in 1839. "Protecting their kind regard for those whom they hourly plunder of all they have and all they get! What! When they have seized their victims, and annihilated all their rights, still claim to be the special guardians of their happiness!"[17] Nevertheless, Southerners consistently followed and even extended Calhoun's arguments, insisting that the law of nature imposed an order upon society so that slavery was a positive good. "[T]he institution of slavery, as it exists among us at the South," declared Albert Taylor Bledsoe, a professor at the University of Virginia, "is founded in political justice, is in accordance with the will of God and the designs of his providence, and is conducive to the highest, purest, best interests of mankind."[18]

Perhaps more so than any other Southerner, George Fitzhugh was renowned for pushing the proslavery position to its extreme. Fitzhugh of course believed that "[s]lavery arises under the higher law, and is, and ever must be, coëval and coëxtensive with human nature." He explicitly endorsed Aristotle while disavowing Locke and thus questioned the existence of the (Lockean) natural rights delineated in the Declaration of Independence. Even further, Fitzhugh insisted that the idea of free labor was farcical: the free laborer in the North actually was worse off than a Southern slave. Masters and slaves, according to Fitzhugh, were "friends," while employers and laborers were "enemies." Free laborers worked all day and then still bore full responsibility for their own care, while slaves could comfortably rely on their masters.[19]

Finally, Alexander H. Stephens of Georgia, the vice president of the Confederacy, declared unequivocally in 1861 that the natural order of society provided the "corner-stone" of the new Southern government:

> The new constitution [of the Confederacy] has put at rest, *forever,* all the agitating questions relating to our peculiar institution—African slavery as it exists amongst us—the proper *status* of the negro in our form of civilization. This was the immediate cause of the late rupture and present revolution. . . . The prevailing ideas entertained by him [Jefferson] and most of the leading statesmen at the time of the formation of the old constitution, were that the enslavement of the African was . . . wrong in *principle,* socially, morally, and politically. . . . This was an error. . . . Our new government is founded upon exactly the opposite idea; its foundations are laid, its corner-stone rests upon the great truth, that the negro is not equal to the white man; that slavery—subordination to the superior race—is his natural and normal condition. This, our new government, is the first, in the history of the world, based upon this great physical, philosophical, and moral truth.[20]

Understandably, Calhoun and many other Southern defenders of slavery viewed themselves as conservatives, not radicals. They explicitly linked the idea of a naturally ordered society to the founding fathers, and the Confederate Constitution unsurprisingly resembled the original Constitution quite closely. Southerners and Northerners alike, after all, regarded Garrisonian abolitionists rather than slaveowners as radicals during the 1830s. In general terms, proslavery advocates partly conformed to the mainstream of premodern American thought by conceptualizing society in a roughly civic republican manner—as being naturally ordered with distinct elite and laboring classes.[21] Yet, the proslavery advocates simultaneously failed to recognize or accept some of the changes overtaking America during the 1800s. As already discussed in chapter 3, a wide-ranging populism was spreading across the nation, in both the North and the South. This populism, part and parcel of the idea of popular sovereignty, had eclipsed civic republican elitism at the level of national politics in the early decades of the nineteenth century. Consequently, the proslavery advocacy of an elite-led and naturally ordered society, while rooted in traditional American political thought, was running against the general sweep of national change.

Most important and most simply, though, in terms of the future of jurisprudence, the South lost the Civil War. Insofar as the victors take the spoils of war,
the North's triumph, in a sense, repudiated the Southern visions of natural law
(though the Northern invocations of natural rights were not necessarily undermined in a similar fashion). To be sure, racism remained entrenched in American
culture after the war, but few serious jurisprudential scholars would still proclaim
that the law of nature justified the legal enforcement of a supposedly inherent
order in American society. Whereas postbellum social Darwinists believed that
some persons were naturally superior and others naturally inferior, the social Darwinists tended to think of society in laissez-faire terms. They thought the superior
and inferior should be left to rise and fall on their own, without governmental assistance or interference: the legal enforcement of a natural order was considered
unnecessary and even potentially harmful.[22]

Even more broadly, the "all-or-nothing character" of natural law arguments in
general (including claims of natural rights) and the likelihood that such positions
would be inconsistent with each other and not peacefully resolvable (as demonstrated by the Civil War) tainted all declarations of natural law. In the context of the
slavery dispute before the war, assertions of natural law (and rights), according to
Peter J. Parish, had "put orthodox practical politics in jeopardy."[23] In a nation that
was becoming increasingly focused on the democratic idea of the sovereign people,
such counterpolitical arguments were problematic, to say the least. Not incidentally,
then, Lincoln and his fellow Republicans, while not averse to invoking natural
rights, most often emphasized the sovereignty of the people—"government of the
people, by the people, for the people"—which resonated with a positivist view of
the law. And from a jurisprudential standpoint, the assertion of markedly different
and opposed conceptions of natural law and natural rights engendered a thicket of
potential conjecture and confusion: legal thinkers apparently could avoid entangle-
ment in this thicket, however, by concentrating on concrete or positive manifestations of law.[24]

Other factors further contributed to the demise of natural law and the ascension of
positivism during and immediately after the Civil War. With the general postbellum trend toward secularization of intellectual matters, explicit jurisprudential invocations of natural law based on revelation began to seem unscientific and thus
unacceptable. Similarly, the emerging historicist sensibility of American intellectuals led jurisprudents to doubt the existence of eternal, universal, and unchanging
natural law principles. Meanwhile, positivism gained prestige as a theoretical position partly because of the work of the English jurisprudent John Austin. A disciple
of Jeremy Bentham, Austin first published *The Province of Jurisprudence Determined* in 1832, but his work became influential only in the 1860s when it was republished posthumously. The progenitor of analytical jurisprudence, Austin explicitly

and vigorously attacked Blackstone's conception of natural law, which had been so important in early-nineteenth-century America. Austin wrote: "Sir William Blackstone . . . says in his "Commentaries," that the laws of God are superior in obligation to all other laws; that no human laws should be suffered to contradict them; that human laws are of no validity if contrary to them; and that all valid laws derive their force from that Divine original. . . . Now, to say that human laws which conflict with the Divine law are not binding, that is to say, are not laws, is to talk stark nonsense. The most pernicious laws, and therefore those which are most opposed to the will of God, have been and are continually enforced as laws by judicial tribunals." Austin thus set forth his classic statement of legal positivism: the command theory of law. "[A] law," according to Austin, "is a command which obliges a person or persons to a course of conduct." In the postbellum years, Austin's writings strongly influenced American legal scientists as they came to grips with positivism.[25]

The interrelated decline of natural law and rise of positivism generated within jurisprudence a prototypical modernist epistemological problem: the problem of foundations. Before the Civil War, the principles of natural law had provided a theoretical foundation for the American legal system, but this foundation suddenly had crumbled. What could serve as a new foundation? To be sure, the people were sovereign, and this fact justified legislative law making. And indeed, legislation became increasingly important toward the end of the nineteenth century. But if legislation rested on the ground that it supposedly represented the sovereign will of the people, what about judicial decisions at common law? At a time when the common law still remained the most pervasive feature of the American legal landscape, what was the foundational source that guided and constrained common law judges? This metaphysical and epistemological problem provided the agenda for American legal modernism: for at least the next one hundred years, jurisprudents struggled to identify an objective foundation for judicial decision making.[26]

First-Stage Modern Jurisprudence:
Langdellian Legal Science

After the Civil War, American universities were rebuilt, as was much of the rest of the nation. Old universities reformed, young universities emerged, and universities in general ascended as a major social institution. The faculty and leaders of these "new" universities confronted a rapidly changing intellectual landscape because of the postbellum blossoming of secularism and historicism. To a great extent, American intellectuals reacted anxiously to these developments by seeking objectivity and control. Most academicians in the human sciences no longer were comfortable grounding knowledge on God—they were hesitant, that is, to attribute natural and social events to God's will—but this secularization did not diminish their desire for objectivity. Fearful of and thus unwilling to accept a world of radical subjectivity, relativism, and arbitrariness, they embarked on a modernist quest for some new source (or sources) of objectivity. This quest for objectivity provided the broad agenda for modernist research, a primary mission of the burgeoning universities. If God was dead (at least for epistemological purposes), then a God-substitute had to be found.[27] Even in the discipline of history, which would seem most likely to accept the possibility of radical historical contingency, the ideal of objectivity became "the central norm of the profession." Initially, many academic disciplines, claiming the authoritativeness of a science, sought objectivity in some type of formalism, a focus on axiomatic principles and logically coherent systems. Thus, according to George M. Marsden, secularization or, in his words, the "collapse of older theologies," led postbellum academicians to display a "passion for order, systematizing, efficiency, scientific principle, [and] personal discipline."[28]

Charles Eliot, the president of Harvard, was at the forefront of the movement to create the new type of university. In 1869, he personally selected Christopher Columbus Langdell to join the three-person faculty of Harvard's law school, leading to Langdell's appointment as dean the following year. Under Dean Langdell's leadership, the legal academic became professionalized. Before the Civil War, most attorneys had learned the law by apprenticing in law offices rather than by attending law schools. The few law professors of the antebellum period typically remained sitting judges or practicing attorneys. Langdell, however, sought to transform the law professor into a full-time teacher and scholar. From Langdell's perspective, the legal academic's position within the university would provide the time necessary for the scientific study of law. The law professor, as a professional academic, changed the study of law into a highly specialized discipline that was largely purified of external considerations. Unlike antebellum jurisprudential scholars who roamed widely in their reading and writing—David Hoffman's *Course of Legal Study,* for instance, recommended passages ranging from the Bible to Aristotle to Bacon to Bentham—the postbellum law professor instead concentrated on the study of LAW, and law only. Ethical, sociological, historical, and like concerns were simply outside the discipline. Thus, the law professor, being experienced in the scientific study of law, could in turn teach *his* students how to learn—to understand—the law. Significantly for the future of the legal academy, Langdellian law professors supposedly offered two distinctive services (or products) that were unavailable elsewhere yet needed by American society. First, the Langdellians produced scientific knowledge of the law through their legal scholarship, and second, they produced competent lawyers by rigorously training students in the now highly specialized field of scientific law. University-trained lawyers, in turn, were ostensibly enabled to offer the American public (especially well-heeled corporate clients) a distinctive and important professional service: expertise in the arcane and specialized science of law.[29]

In the realm of academics, Eliot had tapped Langdell to create a law school in the image of the rest of the new type of university. And like their colleagues in other university departments, Langdell and his disciples confronted an intellectual landscape marked by the secularizing collapse of an old theology. Specifically, in law, the old theology was natural law. Most important, then, the Langdellians were the first American jurisprudents who attempted to understand and legitimate the common law system in a now positivist world. And as a general matter, the Langdellians confronted this challenge with the intellectual tools, methods, and claims that typified the period: they wore the mantle of scientific authority, they sought objective knowledge of reality, and they logically systematized their findings.[30] In short, the Langdellians typified first-stage legal modernists. With natural law repudiated, they necessarily sought to ground the legal system elsewhere. Specifically, the Langdellians became rationalists, relying predominantly on abstract reason or logic.

Langdell rarely discussed positivism explicitly as a theory, but the Langdellians as a whole were committed positivists. Joseph Beale, a second-generation disciple of Langdell, maintained that "no principle of natural law can be regarded as law . . . until it is established as a principle of some actually living and working system of positive law." At times, Langdell himself uttered purely positivist statements. For example, he said that "[a]ll duties originate in commands of the State," and that the word *law,* as commonly used by attorneys, "means law as administered by courts of justice in suits between litigating parties." Moreover, Langdellians repudiated the natural law notions that legal principles are universal and eternal. Instead, generally consistent with a positivist outlook and a historicist (hence modernist) sensibility, Langdellians understood legal principles as developing or evolving over time. In the preface to his first casebook on contracts, published in 1871, Langdell underscored the "growth, development, [and] establishment" of legal principles—a slow growth "extending in many cases through centuries."[31]

Most clearly, though, the positivist approach of Langdellian legal scientists was exemplified in their stress on the decided cases. To Langdell, the cases (or the books containing the cases) were "the ultimate sources of all legal knowledge." By studying cases, the legal scientist could inductively discover objective legal principles or doctrines. Langdell's concept of legal science, thus, closely correlated with his case method of teaching. The case method, which he introduced, entailed a penetrating analysis of a series of cases: through a process of Socratic questioning, the professor led the students to recognize the legal principles immanent in the cases. The case method contrasted with the typical antebellum approach of presenting abstract principles and rules through lectures. According to Langdell's preface to his casebook, the case method was the best approach to teaching because the cases themselves were the "original sources." The law professor was qualified to teach the students since, as a legal scientist, he was experienced not in the practice of law but rather in the learning of law—in the discovery of the principles from the cases.[32]

Hence, two central features of Langdellian legal science were a positivist focus on the decided cases and the use of inductive reason to discover legal principles. Yet, the most salient feature of this postbellum approach was its commitment to deductive reason or logic. Indeed, Langdell's practice of legal science was remarkably Cartesian in style. Whereas the antebellum legal scientists rather faithfully accepted the multitude of cases, the Langdellian scientist applied a method of doubt or skepticism reminiscent of Descartes. Langdell explicitly turned his skeptical gaze on case precedents: "the cases which are useful and necessary for [the purpose of legal study] at the present day bear an exceedingly small proportion to all that have been reported. The vast majority are useless, and worse than useless, for any purpose of systematic study." Langdell and his colleagues then applied deductive reason with the dogged ferocity of a Cartesian in a quest to conceptualize a logically coherent and (hopefully) elegant system of legal principles and rules. "Law, considered as a science, consists of certain principles or doctrines," Langdell declared. "Moreover, the number of fundamental legal [principles or] doctrines is much less than is commonly supposed. . . . If these doctrines could be so classified and arranged that each should be found in its proper place, and nowhere else, they would cease to be formidable from their number." Stephen Toulmin tersely says of Descartes, "abstract axioms were in, concrete diversity was out." The same could be said of Langdell. Legal principles were analogous to the axioms of Euclidian geometry: they were few in number, they could be classified and arranged into a formal system, and they served as the fountainhead for the logical deduction of all other legal rules. Langdellians neatly and rationally ordered the entire legal system into a conceptual framework resembling a pyramid, with the few axiomatic and abstract principles at the apex of the pyramid and more precise and numerous rules at the base. Those case precedents that did not fit neatly into the formal and conceptual framework were deemed wrong and therefore irrelevant.[33]

The commitment to logic produced two interrelated consequences. First, analytical or logical soundness was the sole criterion for proper legal reasoning; a judge therefore was not to consider the justice or injustice likely to flow from a decision. Second, the overt pragmatic and instrumental judicial decision making characteristic of the first part of the nineteenth century was repudiated; practical (or policy) considerations supposedly would infect the logical purity that distinguished valid legal reasoning. These two consequences are well illustrated by Langdell's discussion of the mailbox rule—which specifies whether a posted acceptance of an offer for a bilateral contract is effective upon dispatch or receipt. In his *Summary of the Law of Contracts*, Langdell explained that an acceptance of an offer for a bilateral contract contains an implicit counter-offer. By analytical definition, any counter-offer must be communicated because "communication to the offeree is of the essence of every offer." Therefore, as a matter of deductive logic, an acceptance (as a counter-offer) that is mailed through the post cannot become effective until it is communicated or, in other words, received. Having concluded his syllogistic proof that a posted acceptance must be effective only upon receipt, Langdell proceeded to refute the common arguments in favor of deeming the acceptance effective upon dispatch. The final such argument confronted by Langdell was that his recommended rule—that acceptance be effective only upon receipt— would lead to injustice and practical absurdities. His response was striking: "[t]he true answer to this argument is, that it is irrelevant."[34]

To the Langdellian legal scientist, in short, legal problems were to be resolved by carefully attending to the precise analytical definitions of principles and rules and the logical consequences flowing ineluctably from those principles and rules. Although the axiomatic principles initially had to be induced from the cases, once inferred, the principles themselves were the substance of the law. As William A. Keener, one of Langdell's leading disciples, stated: "the case is simply material from which a principle is to be extracted." In postbellum legal science, then, the principles and deductive logic stood preeminent.[35]

Unsurprisingly, then, Langdellian legal science did not display the same bottom-up style of reasoning typical of antebellum legal science. Antebellum treatises usually had reflected the narrow factual situations in which cases repeatedly arose as well as the minutiae of the writs or forms of action. In contrast, postbellum legal scientists tended to display a top-down style of reasoning. As mentioned, code pleading already had replaced the common law forms of action in many states (including New York, where Langdell had practiced). Consequently, whereas antebellum legal scientists had viewed the forms of action as shaping the classification of the common law, Langdellians were freed to move to higher levels of abstraction in their classificatory systems; indeed, Langdellians were practically forced to search the cases for other organizational themes. The new organizational themes that emerged were the high-level axiomatic principles such as consideration and mutual consent (offer and acceptance) in contract law. The centrality of these principles was evident in Langdellian casebooks and treatises. For example, in Samuel Williston's treatise *The Law of Contracts,* the principles no longer merely provided a loose organizational scheme; rather they were the core of the entire project—the substantive fountainhead for the logical derivation of each chapter and section. Langdell's own *Summary of the Law of Contracts,* a short treatise-like work, focused on the analysis of contract principles; it contained remarkably few citations and discussions of cases. Indeed, in their articles and treatises, the Langdellian legal scientists tended to eschew discussing actual cases, especially avoiding factual details. Instead, to illustrate their main points, the Langdellians constructed hypothetical situations purified of irrelevant factual distractions and populated by depersonalized legal actors called A, B, and C. Langdell's disciple James Barr Ames exemplified this alphabet-soup style: "A promises C to pay him what B owes C, for C's promise to release B. If B had a defence against C, and so was not liable to him, A by the terms of his promise is not liable to C. If, on the other hand, B had no defence against C, but A had a defence against B, A must pay C. For C having given up his claim against B for A's promise to him, must be entitled to enforce it free from any equities in favor of A."[36]

If, as I suggested, the Langdellians were the first American jurisprudents to confront the metaphysical and epistemological problems of legal modernism, then their proffered solutions seem, at least on first glance, to be riddled with conundrums. The Langdellians' strong commitment to formal deductive reasoning would appear to fit best within a natural law system, where judges could, in theory, reason deductively downward from the higher law principles to properly resolve particular cases. But the Langdellians repudiated natural law. In a positivist world, where law is the command of the sovereign, judges would seem to be able to make law. Yet most Langdellians denied that judges had such power. The axiomatic principles of the common law, according to the Langdellians, were to be initially discovered by reasoning inductively upward from the cases, but the correctness or incorrectness of the cases was to be determined by reasoning deductively downward from the principles. As Thomas Grey observes, the enterprise "seems to be circular." Instead of successfully specifying the metaphysical and epistemological foundations that modernism demands, the Langdellians seemed to offer no more than a swirling cloud of dust, a circular system spinning in midair.[37]

Despite appearances, though, these tensions within Langdellian legal science can be reconciled, to some degree. To be clear, I do not intend to justify or legitimate the Langdellian approach to jurisprudence. Rather, I wish to explain how it made sense, at least to Langdellians. My explanation emerges from an analogy: if antebellum legal scientists were fruitfully compared to Plato, then postbellum legal scientists can be usefully analogized to Aristotle. Whereas Plato argued that the Ideas or Forms exist independently and separately from the particular instances, Aristotle argued that form differs from matter only in meaning. David Ross pinpoints the distinction between Plato and Aristotle: "[a]re universals, as Plato claimed in his idea theory, self-subsistent substantial entities? . . . Aristotle answers with a firm negative."[38] According to Aristotle, form and matter (or universals and particulars) are inseparable in fact: form is immanent in and exists only through concrete particulars or manifestations. The true meaning of a thing is its form, but that meaning must be embodied in matter if it is to exist. To be sure, the forms are "for Aristotle as real, as objective, as the individuals." They are not, in other words, mere mental constructs, but at the same time, they exist only as manifested in or as characteristic of the particular instances. In short, one "must not posit a separate world of universals." Hence, for example, the form of good or love does not exist apart from its particular manifestations, yet the meanings of these forms can be discussed and analyzed as universals or principles.[39]

If the metaphysical foundation, in a sense, consists of form and matter together, then how does one come to knowledge? How, that is, does one move from sense perception of matter (or particulars) to knowledge of forms (or universals)? Aristotle wrote: "these states of knowledge are neither innate in a determinate form, nor developed from other higher states of knowledge, but from sense-perception. It is like a rout in battle stopped by first one man making a stand and then another, until the original formation has been restored." To Aristotle, in other words, one initially perceives or experiences a series of particulars and then reasons inductively upward to discover the forms. Yet, despite Aristotle's stress on experience and inductive logic, he also is renowned for his passion for hierarchical classificatory schemes relying heavily on deductive logic. The highest principles or forms served as the premises (or fountainheads) for his deductively derived classificatory frameworks. Plus, Aristotle's intricate hierarchical and logical systems necessarily centered on forms rather than matter; forms could be logically related to each other and arranged conceptually, while matter contained the particular variations that would foil such logical organization.[40]

The Aristotelian relationship between form and matter illuminates the relation between cases and principles in Langdellian legal science. In contrast to antebellum legal scientists, Langdellians did not posit the existence of principles as separate and independent from case decisions. Instead, the legal principles and the cases were understood as inseparable in fact. Just as Aristotle argued that form is immanent in and exists only through concrete particulars or manifestations, Langdellians argued that principles are immanent in and exist only through cases. Keener explicitly declared that law is "a science consisting of a body of *principles* to be *found* in the adjudged *cases*." Thus, for Langdellians, legal principles are real and objective—their meanings can be discussed and analyzed—but they nonetheless exist only as they are embodied or manifested in the cases. When Keener explained the case method of teaching, he suggested this metaphysical intermingling of cases and principles: by reading cases "[i]nstead of reading principles" in treatises, the student "is studying and investigating the principles themselves." The metaphysical foundation for the common law, in other words, consists of principles and cases together.[41]

If so, then how did the legal scientist move from the cases to knowledge of the principles? Continuing with the analogy to Aristotelian philosophy, the legal scientist studied a series of cases and then reasoned inductively upward to discover the principles. But once discovered, these high-level principles served as the fountainhead for chains of deductive logic, reasoning downward to generate precisely classified and arranged formal systems. Thus, despite having its origins in the concrete cases, the intricate legal system of the Langdellians revolved around abstract principles and rules. The epistemological foundation for the common law, then, was initially the cases but primarily the axiomatic principles and deductive reason.

Four points regarding the relationship between Langdellian legal science and Aristotelian philosophy are worth elaborating. First, as was also true of antebellum jurisprudents, the postbellum legal scientists did not endorse any form of nominalism, which would have suggested that nothing existed but the individual case decisions. Despite the Langdellians' initial focus on cases—which spurred the case method of teaching—the similarity between Langdellian legal science and Aristotelian philosophy underscores the importance that the legal scientists placed on discovering the axiomatic principles, which were supposedly immanent in the multitude of cases. As Keener suggested, legal science does "not proceed on the theory that the law *consists* of an aggregation of cases." Not incidentally, the Langdellians' tendency to rationalize the law by reducing masses of cases to a few principles became especially useful to the legal profession in the latter nineteenth century. Not only had the common law forms of action ceased to provide the organizational themes for understanding the law, as already discussed, but also the West Publishing Company began its National Reporter System in the 1880s. Lawyers and judges, now flooded with an ever-growing volume of West case reports, welcomed the Langdellians' help in filtering through these cases and identifying the supposedly few important principles hidden within the deluge.[42]

Second and closely related to the first point, in Aristotelian philosophy a passion for deductive logic led to a focus on forms (or universals) rather than matter, and likewise in Langdellian legal science a passion for deductive logic led to a focus on principles and rules rather than cases. Furthermore, in a sense, the zealous commitment to deductive logic combined with the interrelated conception of legal principles as real and objective to legitimate (albeit perversely) a disregard for justice and practical considerations that otherwise might appear central to deciding cases. Langdellians realized implicitly that the relation between abstract propositions (rules and principles) and social reality (justice and practical concerns) was problematic in at least one important respect: to talk of a purely deductive logical relationship between rules and principles, on the one hand, and social reality, on the other, did not necessarily make sense. Yet, it did make sense to talk of a deductive logical relationship among different abstract propositions—that is, among different rules and principles. Therefore, when Langdellians insisted that elements of social reality such as justice and practical concerns should be irrelevant to the law, their emphasis on logical order as pivotal to understanding the legal system at least became plausible. At a minimum, we can imagine a legal system based on abstract reason if it is unconnected to social reality.[43] (Of course, the possibility of imagining such a legal system does not mean that we would want it to actually exist.)

Third, Langdellians did not consciously think of themselves as Aristotelians any more than the antebellum jurisprudents thought of themselves as Platonists. Despite the usefulness of analogizing to Aristotelianism, Langdellian jurisprudence clearly was not identical to Aristotelian philosophy; there were large and significant differences. Aristotle believed that nature was teleological and encompassed moral and aesthetic values, while the Langdellians did not. Unsurprisingly, then, Aristotle believed in natural law and justice, while the Langdellians were positivists. Aristotle had faith in the veracity of appearances and our perceptions, while Langdellians doubted and, in fact, explicitly repudiated many cases. In short, Aristotle was premodern, and the Langdellians were modern.[44]

Fourth, regardless of these important differences between the modernist Langdellian legal science and the premodernist Aristotelian philosophy, the prominent similarities between the two not only help elucidate the otherwise puzzling tensions within Langdellian jurisprudence but also signal a resemblance between antebellum (premodern) and postbellum (first-stage modern) legal science. For example, while Langdellians tended to avoid discussing actual cases in the text of their articles and treatises, sometimes they nonetheless filled their footnotes with citations, just as the antebellum treatise writers had done. Furthermore, legal scientists during both the antebellum and postbellum periods emphasized high-level principles, albeit different kinds of principles—natural law principles gave way to inductively derived positivist axioms. Most important, regardless of the distinction between the respective types of principles, both antebellum and postbellum legal scientists conceived of the common law as a rational system of principles. James Gould's statement of 1822 could easily have been made by a Langdellian in 1880: "[t]he object in some measure peculiar to my plan of instruction, is to teach the law—the common law, especially—not as a collection of insulated positive rules . . . but as a system of connected, rational principles: for, such the common law unquestionably is."[45]

The strong similarities between antebellum and postbellum legal science suggest that the Langdellians, as the first modernist American jurisprudents, failed in some ways to fully grasp the significance of the movement away from premodernism. While the Langdellians believed in progress in a modernist sense—the common law, they argued, slowly evolved—they did not completely incorporate a historicist attitude. From the Langdellian perspective, after all, judges could not just instrumentally make the law for the utility of society. In speaking of postbellum intellectual trends, in general, Dorothy Ross argues that "the mentality of the [1880s] was typically 'utopian' and in basic ways characteristic of thought earlier in the nineteenth century." This description of the postbellum period aptly fits the Langdellians: although they believed that the common law progresses, they seemed utopian in their efforts to conceive of the common law as a perfectly logical and conceptually ordered system. Perhaps, for that reason, some commentators mistakenly have assumed that the Langdellians were natural law theorists: reasoning deductively downward from axiomatic principles seems implicitly to suggest a natural law orientation. But of course, the Langdellians were positivists: the tension between their positivism and their ostensible natural law orientation—the focus on principles and logic—is reconciled, at least in part, by analogizing their jurisprudence to Aristotelian philosophy, as already explained. And it was exactly the crucial distinction between natural law and positivism that marked the antebellum period as premodern and the postbellum era as modern.[46]

Hence, regardless of the Langdellians' ambivalent grasp of historicism, they otherwise exemplified first-stage modernism. Not only were they positivists and rationalists—relying predominantly on abstract reason to disclose legal truths— but also they jurisprudentially advanced the idea of the autonomous and indepen- dent subject or self in at least two ways. First, Langdellians implicitly portrayed themselves—legal scholars—both as authoritative pronouncers of legal truth and as trusted judicial consultants. Postbellum legal science tacitly assumed that the legal scholar is an autonomous and independent self qualified to proclaim legal principles and rules and to instruct judges about the content and application of that doctrine. In other words, partly because Langdellians occupied a hybrid social role—being both university professors and lawyers—they developed legal schol- arship as a hybrid of supposedly scientific and objective research, on the one hand, and practical (lawyerly) advocacy, on the other. The Langdellians, that is, scien- tifically discovered legal truths and simultaneously advocated that judges accept and apply those truths. In their roles both as university professors and as lawyers, then, Langdellians strongly asserted their individualist selfhood, so to speak.[47]

Second, in a related vein, Langdellians helped develop legal principles and rules that gradually drew boundaries around a field or sphere of private, self-interested action. Somewhat consistent with both Adam Smith's capitalist theory and the American individualist ethos that had been advancing through the nineteenth cen- tury, the Langdellians posited the common law of property and contract as pro- tecting a preexisting economic marketplace where individuals could negotiate and trade at arms length. Within that field of economic activity, the independent and autonomous self supposedly could pursue the satisfaction of its economic and so- cial desires free of governmental interference. Not incidentally, in the late nine- teenth century, a time of rapid social change and instability, this message of laissez faire could combine with the Langdellian claims of legal certainty and scientific order to provide reassuring comfort to some of the wealthier elements in Ameri- can society (who were contributing the important funds for building the postbel- lum universities).[48]

One politically significant manifestation of Langdellian legal science was the Supreme Court's protection of liberty of contract during the *Lochner* era of the late nineteenth and early twentieth centuries. In *Lochner v. New York*, decided in 1905, the Court held as unconstitutional a state law that restricted the number of hours that employees could work in bakeries. The Court concluded that the law violated the due process clause of the Fourteenth Amendment because it infringed on liberty of contract: employees might wish to work more than sixty hours per week or ten hours per day, and the government should not stop them from doing so. The reasoning in the majority opinion reflected postbellum legal science in at least two related ways. First, the Court's substantive due process approach reso- nated with Langdellian formalism: the majority assumed that there was a preexist- ing field or sphere of private activity and that any conduct that fell within that sphere was categorically protected from governmental interference. In other words, the case turned on the Court's supposedly logical deduction of whether the prohibited activities fell within a predefined conceptual category of protected private conduct. Second, the majority's formalist conclusion itself then reinforced the ostensible boundary around the sphere of private action, where independent and autonomous selves supposedly entered freely into contractual agreements. To some extent, *Lochner* and related Supreme Court cases constitutionalized laissez-faire economics and the modern individualist ethos: supposedly to promote individual liberty or freedom of choice, the Court sought to protect the economic marketplace from undue governmental regulation or interference. During this era of laissez-faire constitutionalism and substantive due process, the *Lochner* Court invalidated in case after case social welfare legislation that ostensibly interfered with the free operation of the marketplace.[49]

The connection between Langdellian legal science and Lochnerian constitutional jurisprudence raises the question of natural rights. To be precise, if the antebellum Southern invocations of natural law were repudiated after the Civil War, as previously discussed, what of the Northern invocations of natural rights? Did some remnant of natural rights reasoning or rhetoric survive into the postbellum period? I shall examine this question from three perspectives: Congress, constitutional scholars, and Supreme Court justices.

As might be expected, regardless of intellectual trends, the politically charged institution of Congress continued most clearly to articulate positions in terms of natural rights, at least during the decade of Reconstruction immediately following the Civil War. Before and during the war, Northerners had championed the Union and natural rights against Southern invocations of state sovereignty and natural order, including slavery. For the Republican-dominated Congress of the Reconstruction era, then, assertions of federal power and natural rights confirmed the Northern victory. The protection of civil rights, specifically those rights "so essential to life, liberty, and property" as to be incidents to natural rights, became a central theme for the postbellum Republicans. Thus, Congress passed the Civil Rights Acts of 1866 and 1875 and proposed the Reconstruction constitutional amendments to validate the preeminence of federal power and individual rights to liberty and equality in the face of Southern intransigence. Of course, with widespread racism toward African Americans continuing in both the North and the South, the translation of these congressional actions into real rather than paper protections for African Americans was a totally different matter.[50]

Furthermore, while congressional politics is one thing, scholarship is another. During the postbellum period, constitutional scholars stood in a rather odd position. Most important, the Langdellian legal scientists believed that constitutional law was too political and vague to be studied scientifically. It was, in other words, not true or pure law. For that reason, Langdellians avoided teaching and researching constitutional and other public law subjects, preferring to focus instead on private law areas such as contracts, property, and torts. Constitutional law therefore was left open to other (non-Langdellian) scholars, most prominently Thomas M. Cooley and Christopher G. Tiedeman.[51] These scholars tended to be rather ambivalent on the subject of natural rights. They did not strongly repudiate natural law and natural rights, as the Langdellians had done, but neither did they rely on natural law and natural rights as a legal foundation or otherwise, as antebellum scholars had done.

To be sure, the leading constitutional treatises of Cooley and Tiedeman contained language suggestive of natural rights. More so than Cooley, Tiedeman seemed to endorse natural rights explicitly. Tiedeman began his *Treatise on the Limitations of Police Power*, published in 1886, as follows: "[t]he private rights of the individual . . . do not rest upon the mandate of municipal law as a source. They belong to man in a state of nature; they are natural rights, rights recognized and existing in the law of reason." Yet, only a few pages later, Tiedeman equivocated, as he proffered an "established principle" of constitutional law: "the courts, in the performance of their duty to confine the legislative department within the constitutional limits of its power, cannot nullify and avoid a law, simply because it conflicts with the judicial notions of natural right and morality, or abstract justice." The conception of natural rights, Tiedeman continued, might nonetheless inform judicial interpretations of the express provisions of the Constitution, such as the due process clause.[52]

Despite Tiedeman's ambiguous words in his *Treatise on the Limitations of Police Power*, when that work is understood in conjunction with his other written and spoken declarations, including his *Unwritten Constitution of the United States*, Tiedeman's position on natural rights closely resembles that of Cooley. For Tiedeman and Cooley, both, natural law and natural rights were meaningful only insofar as they had been adopted as positive law, and positive law evolved largely as a matter of the historical and cultural development of a people and nation. In a sense, then, natural rights continued to be significant only because the American people continued to support their positive enforcement and not because such rights existed in the abstract. In a speech delivered in 1887, for example, Tiedeman insisted that "[t]here is . . . no such thing, even in ethics, as an absolute, inalienable, natural right. The so-called natural rights depend upon, and vary with, the legal and ethical conceptions of the people." Finally, even with Tiedeman's and Cooley's imprecise statements concerning natural rights, one can safely conclude that neither theorist ever associated natural or civil rights with a broader natural law encompassing a natural social order as so many antebellum theorists had done (both in the first and second stages of premodernism). Partly because of the South's defeat in the Civil War and partly because of the advancing individualist ethos in American society, natural and civil rights detached from natural law. Civil rights and natural rights (to the extent that they survived the war) became individual possessions, bereft of any previously associated premodern social structures and obligations.[53]

Regardless of their stance on natural rights, Cooley and Tiedeman clearly stood as the preeminent laissez-faire constitutional theorists of the late nineteenth and early twentieth centuries. Supposedly echoing laissez-faire capitalist theory, they sought to limit the reach of permissible governmental regulations in the economic marketplace and, in so doing, to enhance individual liberty. Cooley's constitutional law treatise, first published in 1868, was the leading treatise in the field, with seven editions appearing before 1910, and was aptly referred to as Cooley's *Constitutional Limitations*. In typically ambiguous language suggestive of natural rights, Cooley struck the primary chord for laissez-faire constitutionalism:

> The doubt might also arise whether a regulation made for any one class of citizens, entirely arbitrary in its character, and restricting their rights, privileges, or legal capacities in a manner before unknown to the law, could be sustained, notwithstanding its generality. Distinctions in these respects should be based upon some reason which renders them important,—like the want of capacity in infants, and insane persons; but if the legislature should undertake to provide that persons following some specified lawful trade or employment should not have capacity to make contracts, or to receive conveyances, or to build such houses as others were allowed to erect, or in any other way to make such use of their property as was permissible to others, it can scarcely be doubted that the act would transcend the due bounds of legislative power, even if it did not come in conflict with express constitutional provisions. The man or class forbidden the acquisition or enjoyment of property in the manner permitted to the community at large would be deprived of liberty in particulars of primary importance to his or their "pursuit of happiness."[54]

Quite clearly, then, the laissez-faire constitutional scholarship of Cooley and Tiedeman was thematically linked with the Supreme Court's Lochnerian constitutional decisions: the focus for the scholars and the Court was supposedly to protect the economic marketplace from governmental interference and thus to promote individual liberty. Many critics of the Court's Lochnerian jurisprudence have disparagingly referred to it as a natural rights approach that was closely grounded on the constitutional treatises of Tiedeman and especially Cooley. Two points here should be stressed. First, the *Lochner* era Court cited Cooley and Teideman a surprisingly few number of times for the central laissez-faire proposition: that the Court has the power to strike down supposedly arbitrary governmental restrictions of the marketplace. Through 1938, the Court never cited Tiedeman's two major constitutional treatises. Meanwhile, during this period, the Court cited Cooley an enormous number of times, but rarely to support its laissez-faire viewpoint. In one of the clearest of these infrequent occasions, the Court actually relied on Cooley's treatise on torts instead of on his constitutional law treatise. Thus, the Court's Lochnerian jurisprudence may have been thematically similar to the laissez-faire constitutional scholarship, but the Court rarely invoked the leading scholars to support its controversial decisions invalidating social welfare legislation. Instead, the Court usually relied on *stare decisis,* sometimes citing long chains of its own precedents to justify yet another laissez-faire decision.[55]

Second, a close examination of the Lochnerian cases themselves reveals an ambiguous stance regarding natural rights similar to that confronted in Cooley's and Tiedeman's writings. The roots of the *Lochner* line of cases are often traced back to dissents written by Justices Stephen J. Field and Joseph P. Bradley in *The Slaughterhouse Cases,* decided in 1873, and concurrences by the same justices in *Butchers' Union Company v. Crescent City Company,* decided a decade later. Justice Field, for example, expressly argued that the Fourteenth Amendment should be understood to protect "natural and inalienable rights," including a right to enter freely into employment contracts. It bears emphasis, though, that the majority of justices in those cases neither endorsed nor rebuked Field and Bradley for their explicit invocations of natural rights. Not until 1897, in *Allgeyer v. Louisiana,* did a majority opinion mention natural rights in a case where the Court struck down a state governmental action as unconstitutional. The majority there quoted from Justice Bradley's *Butchers' Union* concurrence: "'the right to follow any of the common occupations of life is an inalienable right. It was formulated as such under the phrase "pursuit of happiness" in the Declaration of Independence.'" Even so, the *Allgeyer* Court's discussion of natural rights was not central to its conclusion that the disputed state restriction on insurance contracts violated due process. To be sure, the mere fact that the majority comfortably mentioned inalienable rights might be considered important, but in subsequent Lochnerian cases, including *Lochner* itself, the Court almost never used explicit natural rights language, much less relying strongly on natural rights to justify its decisions. The Court, though, in its heavy reliance on *stare decisis,* did cite *Allgeyer* numerous times, indeed much more often than it cited *Lochner.*[56]

In conclusion, to return to the initial question: Did some remnant of natural rights reasoning or rhetoric survive into the postbellum period? The answer is: "a little bit." The leading constitutional scholars, Cooley and Tiedeman, neither strongly repudiated nor strongly relied on natural rights. The Supreme Court in its Lochnerian decisions acted similarly, at least in its express language. Moreover, the Court almost never relied expressly on the scholars to support even the laissez-faire proposition—that the Court has the power to strike down supposedly arbitrary governmental restrictions of the marketplace—much less to support the Court's ambiguous stance regarding natural rights. Nevertheless, many later scholars, especially the critics of Lochnerian jurisprudence, reasonably presumed that laissez-faire constitutionalism *was* based on natural rights. After all, as I have discussed, the Court and the leading constitutional treatise writers used ambiguous language, never unequivocally forswearing natural rights to adopt positivism in the manner of the Langdellian legal scientists. And the justices' occasional express references to natural or inalienable rights, however rare, could reasonably justify a presumption that, in other instances, the Court at least was implicitly relying on natural rights.[57]

Finally, it is worth noting that the Court during the *Lochner* era did not strike down every challenged economic regulation. Although the Court invalidated almost two hundred such state regulations as well as additional federal statutes, it upheld many others. In an interesting study, Karen Orren has concluded that the *Lochner* Court was more likely to strike down governmental restrictions of labor or employment contracts than other governmental regulations of the economic marketplace. By means of explanation, Orren persuasively argues that the Court was implicitly protecting a vestige of the premodern master and servant relationship as embodied in the employment contract. Significantly, though, with regard to the development of jurisprudence, even if the Court's decisions had the effect of protecting such a premodern remnant, the Court never used express language even remotely suggesting that it was enforcing a natural social order, which would have been too reminiscent of the South's antebellum natural law arguments. Instead, insofar as the justices ambiguously used language invoking natural law or natural rights at all, they tended to refer to natural or inalienable rights. Moreover, as was true with Cooley and Tiedeman, the justices appeared to conceptualize natural rights as individual possessions to be wielded against others and not as otherwise related explicitly to natural law or a natural social order.[58]

Second-Stage Modern Jurisprudence: American Legal Realism

Although Langdellian legal science dominated American legal thought during the late nineteenth and early twentieth centuries, other contemporaneous jurisprudential approaches also developed. For example, the so-called historical school of jurisprudence emerged in America during the latter nineteenth century, but for various reasons, its long-term influence was limited. The leading proponents of the historical school were Europeans from an earlier generation: Friedrich Carl von Savigny, who was German and published in the early 1800s, and Henry Maine, who was English and published his most famous work, *Ancient Law*, in 1861. From their perspective, law is like language: it develops slowly as part of a national culture. In America, the clearest proponent of the historical school was James Coolidge Carter. Carter was a prominent New York attorney and leader of the bar who strongly opposed the continuing efforts to codify the law in New York in the latter nineteenth century. Consequently, except for one book published posthumously, his writing was largely "partisan and polemical" and was published as "speeches or reports in pamphlets to bar associations." To Carter, the historical approach rectified the hubris he saw in the codification movement. The common law, which Carter referred to as "custom authenticated," necessarily evolved throughout a nation's history. It could not be suddenly controlled and remade, as the codifiers supposedly sought, without leading to "mischief" and "confusion." In fact, earlier in the century, Savigny himself similarly had drawn on his historical approach to oppose codification in Germany.[59]

At any rate, Carter's ideas did not flourish in American legal thought. He may have weakened his own jurisprudential position when he extended his opposition to codification into a general antagonism toward legislation; he insisted that legislation was actually inconsistent with democracy. Even Langdell did not display such aversion to legislation: he believed that statutes were important and deserved careful study, just not in American law schools, which were to focus on pure law (that is, the common law).[60] Carter's more hostile viewpoint obviously ran against the grain of American political thought with its ever-increasing emphasis on the sovereignty of the people. In the end, then, the historical school was only of secondary importance in American jurisprudence. Its main themes resonated somewhat with other late-nineteenth-century thinkers, such as Cooley and Tiedeman in constitutional theory, as well as with political defenders of laissez-faire who opposed social welfare legislation. In the long run, though, the historical school was not sufficiently historicist: it viewed history as generating and conservatively imposing normative values or customs. The more modern historicist view, which took firm hold at the turn of the century, was to view history as disclosing the potential for endless progress inspired by human ingenuity. Modernists sought to control and reorder society for the general welfare. Thus, ironically, the greatest long-term significance of the historical school for American legal thought may have been its encouragement of a general historical awareness— an awareness that ultimately was embodied more fully in the modernist strains of historicism.[61]

Whereas the long-term influence of the historical school was minimal, the same cannot be said for the jurisprudence of Oliver Wendell Holmes, Jr. Holmes too was Langdell's contemporary and often is considered his first great critic, yet in many ways the early Holmes was strongly aligned with his Langdellian peers. Most important, perhaps, Holmes was a committed positivist. He declared that natural law jurists were "naïve," and as early as 1872, when explicitly discussing Austin's positivist jurisprudence, Holmes wrote that "sovereignty is a form of power, and the will of the sovereign is law, because he has power to compel obedience or to punish disobedience, and for no other reason."[62] As a positivist, Holmes was fully engulfed in the modernist wave of postbellum jurisprudence. Hence, lacking the antebellum legal scientists' faith in case precedents, Holmes (like Langdell) doubted and questioned cases, as revealed in the magnum opus of his early thought, *The Common Law,* where he attempted to reconceptualize the system of the common law. Holmes exhibited remarkable skepticism concerning judicial opinions, arguing that they often obscure or deny the actual bases for decision. Moreover, his effort to reconstruct the common law revealed a typical modernist quest to establish foundations.

Indeed, Holmes claimed to rest the entire common law on one basic principle. At the beginning of his two chapters on torts, Holmes wrote: "my object . . . is to discover whether there is any common ground at the bottom of all liability in tort, and if so, what that ground is. Supposing the attempt to succeed, it will reveal the general principle of civil liability at common law." Holmes believed that he successfully concluded his study by finding an ultimate foundational principle: a (supposedly) objective standard of reasonableness best exemplified by "the average man, the man of ordinary intelligence and reasonable prudence."[63] In a sense, then, *The Common Law* was deeply reductionist—attempting to condense the entire common law into one principle—and for that reason, it was highly abstract, formal, and conceptual. In short, in many ways, it strongly resembled a work of Langdellian jurisprudence. Indeed, Holmes elsewhere acknowledged his admiration for writers, including Langdell, who brought logical and conceptual order to the common law.[64]

Despite the similarities between Holmes and the Langdellians, Holmes sat uncomfortably within their group. To Langdellians, on the one hand, once the axiomatic principles of the common law had been induced from the cases, then the principles and deductive logic became preeminent as the legal scientist conceptualized a logically ordered system. To Holmes, on the other hand, while logic was important, it never overshadowed pragmatic concerns. In 1870, Holmes asserted that "although the general arrangement [of the common law] should be philosophical [or logical], compromises with practical convenience are highly proper." In *The Common Law*, Holmes declared: "in substance the growth of the law is legislative. . . . The very considerations which judges most rarely mention, and always with an apology, are the secret root from which the law draws all the juices of life. I mean, of course, considerations of what is expedient for the community concerned."[65]

If the Langdellians failed in some ways to grasp the complete importance of the movement away from premodernism, as already discussed, then perhaps Holmes more thoroughly understood this transition. Holmes might even be considered the first American jurisprudent to shift fully to a modern historicist sensibility, which he suggested in his most famous aphorism, "The life of the law has not been logic: it has been experience." He initially wrote this phrase in a critical review of Langdell's *Summary of Contracts* and then repeated it on the first page of *The Common Law*. Holmes continued in *The Common Law*:

> The felt necessities of the time, the prevalent moral and political theories, intuitions of public policy, avowed or unconscious, even the prejudices which judges share with their fellow-men, have had a good deal more to do than the syllogism in determining the rules by which men should be governed. The law embodies the story of a nation's development through many centuries, and it cannot be dealt with as if it contained only the axioms and corollaries of a book of mathematics. In order to know what it is, we must know what it has been, and what it tends to become. We must alternately consult history and existing theories of legislation.[66]

Even further, then, in stark contrast to Langdellian jurisprudence, Holmes recommended that judges openly acknowledge their lawmaking (or legislative) power and more consciously attempt to make law for the good of society. In discussing the mailbox rule, for instance, while Langdell had focused on a syllogistic proof, Holmes emphasized practical considerations: "[in the mailbox situation] the doubt [is] whether the contract is complete at the moment when the return promise is put into the post or at the moment when it is received. If convenience preponderates in favor of either view, that is a sufficient reason for its adoption."[67]

Thus, consistent with a modern historicist attitude, Holmes believed history revealed that society progresses and that humans can control and direct societal change. While this modern attitude might be hubristic, it is not necessarily utopian. Unlike the Langdellians, Holmes never conceived of the common law as a perfectly logical and conceptually ordered system. "The truth is," Holmes asserted, "that the law is always approaching, and never reaching, consistency. It is forever adopting new principles from life at one end, and it always retains old ones from history at the other, which have not yet been absorbed or sloughed off." In fact, Holmes, if anything, was more cynical than utopian and hopeful. Later in his career, he ruefully observed: "I believe that the world would be just as well off if it lived under laws that differed from ours in many ways, and . . . that the claim of our especial code to respect is simply that it exists, that it is the one to which we have become accustomed, and not that it represents an eternal principle."[68]

In sum, while Langdellians conformed neatly to first-stage modernism, Holmes fit only uneasily. Langdellians sought to ground the common law by focusing chiefly on axiomatic principles and deductive reason. Holmes willingly considered principles and logic, but not at the expense of practical experience. Holmes's pragmatic historicism, in effect, presaged the second stage of legal modernism—empiricism—when jurisprudents would focus primarily on experience as an objective source of knowledge. This Holmesian anticipation of second-stage modernism emerged most clearly, though, in his later jurisprudential writing, particularly *The Path of the Law*, published in 1897. In that essay, Holmes argued that legal studies should aim to predict "the incidence of the public force through the instrumentality of the courts." To predict the use of the public force, Holmes reasoned, a legal scholar should place himself in the position of the "bad man." The bad man concerns himself only with knowing when the courts will inflict punishment; he remains indifferent to logical consistency and abstract principles. Holmes thus suggested the advantage of an external or behavioristic view of the law: the legal scholar, similar to a bad man standing outside of the judicial process, can observe that certain stimuli produce predictable judicial responses and legal consequences.[69]

Although second-stage legal modernism still would not fully crystallize until the 1920s and 1930s with the development of American legal realism, rudimentary elements of the second stage also marked the early-twentieth-century writings of the sociological jurisprudents, such as Roscoe Pound and Benjamin Cardozo. Like Holmes, these jurisprudents expressed inconsistent (or ambivalent) sentiments about Langdellianism. As were the Langdellians as well as Holmes, the sociological jurisprudents were committed positivists, and they retained a significant concern for legal principles, rational order, and systemic organization. Yet, the sociological jurisprudents attacked the Langdellians' overly formalistic legal reasoning, disparagingly dubbed by Pound "mechanical jurisprudence." Legal truths and correct judicial decisions, in many instances, could not be merely discovered. The "administration of justice," they reasoned, instead sometimes demanded that common law judges should *make* law for the good of society.[70]

In many ways, Pound and his colleagues jurisprudentially echoed the contemporary politics of the moderate Progressives, who aimed generally to remedy hardships arising from laissez-faire capitalism and mass industrialization. Progressivism emerged with a political and intellectual perception of American society as a multitude of conflicting vested interests, including those of laborers and capitalists. Even so, most Progressive intellectuals still believed that Americans ultimately agreed (or at least should agree) on certain supposedly traditional American values, such as honesty, hard work, and temperance. Progressives consequently tended to support governmental restrictions on trusts and child labor, while they simultaneously moralized about sins such as drinking and prostitution and occasionally voiced nativist sentiments. Thus, the sociological jurisprudents, as Progressives, accentuated politically moderate legislative as well as judicial law making, insisting that the law should change sufficiently to meet changing social conditions. Unsurprisingly, then, Pound initiated a long-running scholarly critique of the *Lochner* Court's laissez-faire constitutionalism, which he denounced for, among other reasons, being a manifestation of natural rights reasoning.[71]

Even though the Progressive political movement faded around World War I, the second stage of legal modernism fully bloomed in the 1920s and 1930s with the advent of American legal realism.[72] At least three factors combined to spark the growth of realism after the war. First, the work of first-stage legal modernism seemed nearly exhausted. After the Civil War, Langdellian legal scholars faced the challenge of conceptualizing the American legal system shorn of both natural law principles and the organization previously imposed by the common law forms of action. Langdellians, for the most part, had readily mastered and even completed their task, at least as they perceived it: the abstract rationalization and conceptual ordering of the now modernist legal system. Many young legal scholars in the next generation therefore faced the frustrating prospect of mundanely repeating the past, rationalizing and re-rationalizing the law over and over again. Legal scholarship had become, as the realist Fred Rodell phrased it, "qualitatively moribund."[73]

Second, some of these young legal scholars recognized the significance and the potential of the burgeoning social sciences, which were rapidly developing in other parts of the universities. As the social sciences ascended, the Langdellian emphasis on pure law—isolated from history, economics, psychology, and other disciplines—seemed especially problematic to law professors swept up in the excitement of contemporary intellectual trends. Both Walter Wheeler Cook and Underhill Moore heard a lecture in 1922 in which the philosopher John Dewey asserted "that law was best seen as an empirical science." For Cook and Moore, this lecture transformed their jurisprudence, inspiring them toward a more empirical or "experimental" method. Indeed, Cook, along with Herman Oliphant, Hessel Yntema, and Leon Marshall, helped create in 1929 the Institute of Law at Johns Hopkins University, which was devoted to the empirical study of law and made no pretense of training students to become attorneys.[74]

Third, political pressure began to mount, especially with the coming of the New Deal in the 1930s, to reject the *Lochner* Court's laissez-faire constitutionalism in order to clear a path for liberal economic legislation. The New Deal, widely supported by immigrants and other political outgroups, was far more liberal than the earlier Progressive movement, which tended to sermonize about traditional American values. "The New Deal," in Laura Kalman's words, "became Progressivism without moralism." Through legislation, including the creation and expansion of administrative agencies, Franklin Roosevelt and other New Dealers openly and affirmatively attempted to change the American economy so as to end the Great Depression. While laissez-faire capitalism apparently had produced economic collapse, privation, and injustice, the increasingly bureaucratic national government sought to control and indeed to resuscitate capitalism. The New Dealers enacted numerous statutes, such as the National Industrial Recovery Act, the Social Security Act, and the National Labor Relations Act, that aimed "to make the industrial system more humane and to protect workers and their families from exploitation." As many realists became politically aligned with the New Deal, they supported exactly the type of liberal economic legislation that the *Lochner* Court had repeatedly invalidated. A large number of leading realists, including Jerome Frank, Thurman Arnold, Abe Fortas, and Felix Cohen, eventually moved into important official positions in the New Deal. Moreover, apart from politics, realists generally followed Roscoe Pound's reasonable (if not necessarily correct) initial categorization of Lochnerian constitutionalism as being based on natural rights. From the realists' perspective, then, the *Lochner* Court was propagating antiquated and premodern prejudices that dangerously impeded modern progress.[75]

In terms of the transition from first-stage to second-stage modernism, two components of the realist movement bear emphasis: first, the rejection of the abstract rationalism of first-stage modernism, and second, the turn to empiricism as a source of foundational knowledge. Realists denounced the abstract and decontextualized rationalism of Langdellian legal science as unrelated to meaningful social reality, unrelated to human experiences of the external world. Whereas Langdellian scholars claimed that their abstract reasoning enabled them to discover objective legal truths—the rules and principles of the common law—realists such as Felix Cohen belittled the Langdellian rules and principles as "transcendental non-sense." For instance, to determine whether a court has jurisdiction over a corporation, a Langdellian would ask, "Where is the corporation?" The Langdellian then ostensibly would turn to abstract rules and principles to resolve this question—concluding, let's say, that the corporation is in New York. But Cohen argued that, despite the Langdellians' pretensions, their rules and principles could not produce a determinative outcome in this case. "Clearly the question of where a corporation is, when it incorporates in one state and has agents transacting corporate business in another state, is not a question that can be answered by empirical observation," Cohen wrote. "It is, in fact, a question identical in metaphysical status with the question . . . 'How many angels can stand on the point of a needle?'" Langdellian-style reasoning merely provided a label for a conclusion somehow reached through other means or methods. The result in this instance—that the corporation is in New York—connotes that, for unarticulated reasons, the court has decided that the corporation ought to be subject to suit in New York.[76]

Karl Llewellyn, writing in *The Bramble Bush*, trumpeted the realists' iconoclastic stance toward abstract rationalism and their concomitant focus on the resolution of actual disputes: "[G]eneral propositions are empty. . . . [R]ules alone . . . are worthless. [The] doing of something about disputes, [the] doing of it reasonably, is the business of law. And the people who have the doing in charge, whether they be judges or sheriffs or clerks or jailers or lawyers, are officials of the law. What these officials do about disputes is, to my mind, the law itself."[77] According to the most radical realists, abstract rules and principles not only failed to determine judicial outcomes, but even further, they were either obscurant or totally irrelevant. The Langdellian image of legal science was therefore a myth, perhaps a dangerous and misleading one at that. In a remarkable confession, a realist federal district court judge, Joseph Hutcheson, claimed to decide cases based on "intuitive" hunches. Rules and principles served at most as post hoc justifications—as "fancy rationalizations of legal action"—cleverly constructed to obfuscate while appearing to justify the judge's intuitive conclusion. When the realist Abe Fortas became a Supreme Court justice, he occasionally wrote draft opinions bereft of legal citations and then instructed his clerks to "decorate" them with appropriate doctrines and precedents. It is worth noting, though, that even when the realists were most voraciously irreverent and destructive, during the late 1920s and early 1930s, Langdellian rationalism did not completely disappear from the jurisprudential scene. The contemporaneous formation of the American Law Institute and its commencement of the Restatement movement can be understood as a Langdellian reactionary response to realism. In the face of realist criticisms, the Restaters (many of whom were aging Langdellians) largely aimed to clarify common law fields, such as contracts and torts, by presenting them in an abstract, conceptually ordered, and formal fashion.[78]

Regardless of the Restatement movement, the realists' attack on abstract ratio-nalism was propelled forward, in part, by their political opposition to the *Lochner* Court's laissez-faire constitutionalism. The realists correctly viewed the *Lochner* Court's judicial formalism as closely related to the Langdellians' jurisprudential formalism. Consequently, an attack on one was an attack on the other. Apart from the realists' repugnance toward the apparent natural rights orientation of Lochner-ian constitutionalism, the realist critiques took typically one of two forms, only the first of which focused on abstract formalist reasoning. The *Lochner* case had turned on the Court's supposedly logical deduction that the legislatively prohibited em-ployment activities—working excessive hours in a bakery—fell within a prede-fined conceptual category or sphere of private conduct, purified of governmental interference. The realists asserted that this abstract rationalism not only had failed to peel away traditional cultural prejudices, but actually had reflected and rein-forced them, thus further obscuring the truth. In other words, according to the re-alists, the *Lochner* Court had relied upon the assumed existence of a preexisting sphere of private conduct that protected individual freedom, but that reliance had not been grounded on the experience of social reality. Rather, the assumed sphere of private conduct had been an illusion generated by cultural prejudices. In the words of Robert Hale, systems of *"laissez-faire* are in reality permeated with coer-cive restrictions of individual freedom." Individuals could enter into employment contracts, which were supposedly within the private sphere, only because the gov-ernment already had created and continued to sanction the body of contract law. The so-called private sphere could not exist purified of governmental action: to the contrary, the private sphere existed only *because* of governmental action. More-over, despite the Court's assumptions, individuals within the private sphere were not necessarily free: the absence of governmental interference was not equivalent to freedom since various individuals and groups within the private sphere con-stantly coerced each other. Indeed, in many instances, governmental action could increase individual freedom.[79]

The second realist critique of laissez-faire constitutionalism originated with Holmes's dissent in the *Lochner* case itself. Holmes had argued strongly that the Court should have deferred to the legislative decision to restrict the hours of em-ployees. The Court, failing to exercise the appropriate degree of judicial restraint, had intruded into the institutional role of the legislature. Although Holmes's dissent initially went relatively unnoticed, within five years sociological jurisprudents and other Progressives were celebrating it. Following in this path, the realists then seized on Holmes's position to emphasize the ability of individual governmental ex-perts other than judges—that is, experts in *legislatures* and *administrative agencies*—to use instrumental reason to reorder society for the promotion of the economic and social well-being of a broad spectrum of citizens. Thus, Holmes's call for judicial restraint in constitutional cases resonated strongly with the realists' eventual New Deal politics, which manifested a strong modernist belief in human ingenuity and social progress.[80]

Despite the realists' attacks on abstract rationalism, most realists did not reject the modernist commitment to foundational knowledge; they merely denied that abstract reason could disclose legal truths. To the realists, the rationalism of Langdellian legal science as well as Lochnerian constitutionalism had proven inadequate to strip away culturally produced traditions and prejudices. "[M]any of the axioms of legal thinking," Jerome Frank asserted, "do not appear on the surface but are concealed and must be dug out for inspection." So in a move typical of second-stage modernism, realists turned to experience as the source of objectivity. Perhaps abstract legal rules and principles did not constrain judicial decisions, realists asserted, but concrete facts of the external (and social) world did influence or even determine such decisions. Furthermore, consistent with the development of second-stage modernism, the relevant facts increasingly seemed to revolve around the actions of individuals. The facts that might sway a particular judge could be as seemingly idiosyncratic and arbitrary as the hair color of a witness, the nasal twang of an attorney, or the breakfast the judge happened to eat that morning. According to Frank, "[t]he human element in the administration of justice by judges is irrepressible."[81]

Consequently, realists argued that empirical studies carefully attending to the observable behavior of legal actors could reveal the stimuli that caused predictable judicial responses. "Only empirical observation," Walter Wheeler Cook declared, "can give one postulates useful in any particular science, including legal science." For these realists, then, the methods of the emerging social sciences of the 1920s promised to produce objective knowledge of the legal system. The newer social sciences stressed "quantitative methods and behaviorist psychology" as they became "more and more committed to objectivity, empiricism, and inductivism." Many realists, such as Cook, Underhill Moore, and Charles Clark, either recommended or actually adopted (or attempted to adopt) the methods of the social sciences. Moore, for instance, instituted an empirical study of Connecticut banking practices, focusing on the legal issue of maturing time notes. Instead of analyzing this issue by examining doctrine and cases, as a Langdellian might do, Moore sent questionnaires consisting of twenty-seven inquiries to all the commercial banks in Connecticut, gathered the answers, and sought to identify the actual banking practices regarding time notes. Another realist, William O. Douglas, performed a similar empirical investigation into the causes of bankruptcy. Using social scientific methods, such as control groups and extensive questionnaires, Douglas generated a "statistical study," which served as the basis for his numerous recommended improvements of the Bankruptcy Act.[82]

Consistent with second-stage modernism, then, the realists were full-fledged historicists: their awareness of rapid historical change led them to believe that society could progress endlessly because of human ingenuity. Empirical studies, from this viewpoint, would provide the knowledge necessary for the instrumental control and reordering of society. The philosophical pragmatists, such as Dewey and William James, influenced many realists to conceptualize their empiricism in relation to "the practical need to solve real problems." Douglas, for example, confidently concluded his empirical studies of the bankruptcy system as follows: "it is apparent that if a system were provided which took cognizance of the many economic and social problems antecedent to bankruptcy, it would be possible to integrate the bankruptcy power into programs of social planning in many fields and to effectuate different policies for different problems." Thus, most ambitiously, realists who became New Dealers assumed that they could purposefully craft legislation to remedy the worst societal ills, particularly the Great Depression. Abe Fortas typified this modernist hubris: "[we] could see the new world and feel it taking form under our hands. It was one of those periods of flux when there was practically no obstacle between thinking up an idea and putting it into effect."[83]

Only slightly more modestly, other realists maintained that they could remake the common law for the good of society. Although all realists rejected the abstract and formal rules of Langdellian legal science, some realists suggested that a new type of legal rule could be formulated based on the realist/empirical approach to the law. According to this view, judges and scholars would reshape the law by studying "concrete instance" after "concrete instance," thus discovering the real-world consequences of legal rules and judicial decisions. Felix Cohen called this method the functional approach. Scholars would describe and recommend legal doctrine that was empirically built, in a sense, from the ground up. Thus, instead of having abstract principles that were overly broad and general in their compass, legal rules would reflect the narrow factual categories that arose in real-world situations. For example, instead of having contractual doctrine that applied similarly to all individuals, no matter how situated, contract law should account for the important differences between merchants and nonmerchants. Narrower rules could reflect the reality that merchants and nonmerchants entered into contracts in significantly different ways. Furthermore, insofar as the legal system contained broader principles, the realists argued that such principles or standards should be understood to invite judicial discretion in their particular applications. Concepts such as "unconscionability" and "reasonableness" should not be rigidly defined but rather applied in a flexible and intuitive fashion, turning on the specific facts in each case. In a related vein, these realists argued that *judges* should *make* law to function so as to promote certain ethical values and substantive goals. Judges primarily were responsible for resolving concrete disputes, but in so doing, they were to perform "social engineering." For example, Cohen argued that in answering the question "Is there a contract?" a judge should not focus on abstract and formal legal principles such as consideration. Instead, the judge should concentrate on whether one party or the other should be liable for certain actions. What real-world consequences would follow, what values and goals would be promoted, by the various possible decisions? Of course, the realists' argument that judges should do social engineering was somewhat in tension with their Holmesian-inspired criticism of the *Lochner* Court's judicial activism. For the most part, though, this tension was avoided by emphasizing judicial social engineering in the common law fields, such as contracts and property, and insisting on judicial restraint in constitutional law.[84]

Third-Stage Modern Jurisprudence: Legal Process

American legal realism eventually encountered a form of the epistemological crisis that typifies the conclusion of second-stage modernism: the recognition that foundational knowledge might be unattainable because, regardless of the pretensions of rationalism and empiricism, the subject might never bridge the chasm between itself and the external world. More specifically, legal realism encountered this crisis in the area of substantive or ethical values. The realist/empiricist critique of first-stage rationalism meant that values no longer could be derived from abstract reasoning, and of course, the earlier rejection of premodernism meant that realists could not locate values in some preexisting natural order. To the realists and other second-stage modernists, quite simply, empirical studies provided the only means to foundational knowledge. Yet, unlike knowledge of the physical world, ethical values apparently could not be discovered from or grounded clearly on empirical evidence. Values, in other words, seemed to be merely relative, arising out of the concrete and particular vagaries of human experiences. Consequently, a mounting ethical and cultural relativism accompanied the rise of realism and the interrelated empirical social sciences. By the 1930s, intellectuals found it difficult to justify any set of moral values or cultural tenets over any others. All values and cultures had equal claims to validity (and invalidity).[85]

This rise of ethical and cultural relativism presented a serious challenge to legal and political theorists in the 1930s. How could political decision makers—judges, legislators, and administrators—legitimately determine substantive values and goals? Even more broadly, how could citizens in a republican democracy rationally discuss and decide political issues, especially if the citizens were swayed by cultural prejudices and demagogic symbols? Indeed, to many theorists, politics seemed to be no more than a matter of raw power, with political decisions spewing irrationally from the interplay of interests in each particular and concrete circumstance. By 1940, in fact, most realists had abandoned their attempts at pure empirical research. Such research might uncover value-free truths for social scientists, but for legal and political theorists who hoped to articulate and justify substantive values and goals, empirical research simply could not provide the necessary foundational knowledge. As William O. Douglas confessed: "[a]ll the facts which we worked so hard to get don't seem to help a hell of a lot." Finally, political events toward the end of the 1930s intensified this challenge to legal and political theory. Specifically, for many American intellectuals, the international ascent of totalitarianism, especially Nazism, rendered a firm belief in democracy and the rule of law a necessity. Yet the rise of ethical relativism forced intellectuals to contemplate a disconcerting question: If all values are relative, then why is American democratic government better than totalitarianism?[86]

Thus, the conjunction of intellectual currents and international events thrust the theoretical justification of democracy to the forefront of American thought. Interestingly, a focus on democratic theory per se was somewhat unusual in intellectual circles. Because of the nation's republican ideology and populist tendencies, as well as other causes, America gradually had grown more democratic through its history. At least as a formal matter (and not necessarily as a social reality), the Fifteenth Amendment, ratified during Reconstruction in 1870, extended the right to vote to African Americans, and the Nineteenth Amendment, ratified in 1920, extended suffrage to women. Moreover, to be sure, the nature of *republicanism* (including its democratic component) had been exhaustively debated in the past—for example, during the founding and Civil War eras. Yet, to a degree, it was in the 1930s that *democracy*, as a theory of government, became a predominant intellectual concern in America. In fact, after World War II, democracy not only remained paramount for American intellectuals but also became a central judicial and political issue. Before the 1940s, the Supreme Court rarely even mentioned democracy, but from that point forward, the Court gave increasing attention to it. Besides continually referring to democracy in its opinions, the Court decided a number of cases that were explicitly intended to promote democratic participation—striking down, for example, some of the mechanisms that different states had designed to impede African-American participation in the democratic process (despite the Fifteenth Amendment). The Court, for example, struck down as unconstitutional both racially discriminatory gerrymandering and poll taxes in state elections. More broadly, the Court held that no person's vote should be worth more or less than another's: one person, one vote. Meanwhile, Congress enacted legislation—the Voting Rights Act of 1965 and parts of the Civil Rights Act of 1964—designed to guarantee the right to vote by eradicating literacy, educational, and character tests that had been used to discourage minority participation. Also in 1964, the Twenty-fourth Amendment was ratified, prohibiting poll taxes in federal elections, and in 1971 the Twenty-sixth Amendment guaranteed the right to vote to anyone eighteen years of age or older.[87]

This now longstanding political and judicial emphasis on democratic participation, though, emerged with the intellectual turn toward democratic theory during the mid- to late 1930s. As the Second World War threatened, political thinkers struggled to answer the intellectual puzzle presented to American democratic government by the conjunction of ethical relativism and international totalitarianism. In a sense, Americans mobilized not only materially but also intellectually for the war (a mobilization that continued with the Cold War in the 1950s). In a presidential address delivered to the American Political Science Association in 1938, Clarence Dykstra threw down the gauntlet for political and legal thinkers: "[a] paramount question which the world faces is whether responsibility can be achieved and maintained through the democratic process." As Dykstra unequivocally declared, "Nazis, Fascists, [and] Communists . . . have challenged us to find a solution within the orbit of the representative system."[88]

Just before World War II, then, some imaginative theorists responded to this challenge by taking the transcendental turn to third-stage modernism. To initiate this intellectual move, these theorists presumed that, quite simply, American government was better than totalitarianism just because it was democratic: the commitment to democracy was unshakable. So, just as Kant had asked what conditions are necessary to explain human experience, political theorists now asked what conditions are necessary for democracy. For example, in 1939, John Dewey asked what type of culture promotes the political freedoms of democracy. To Dewey, democracy had flourished in America because the culture had produced "a basic consensus and community of beliefs"—that is, a commitment to democracy. Yet, Dewey queried, how can we insure that democracy would not degenerate into totalitarianism, as it had in other parts of the world? He concluded that the political methods or procedures of democracy—such as consultation, persuasion, negotiation, and communication—need to be extended into the cultural realm in order to assure the development and preservation of a culture that would, in turn, promote political democracy. In short, for Dewey, the key to democracy lay in democratic procedures: "democratic ends demand democratic methods for their realization."[89]

Two of Dewey's themes—the commitment to procedures or processes and the belief in an American social consensus—became central components in the development after World War II of a relativist theory of democracy. While just a few years earlier the relativity of values had threatened to disarm American governmental theory, the same relativism now became the theoretical foundation for democracy. According to relativist democratic theory, a society must constantly choose what substantive values to endorse and thus what ends to pursue, but since values are relative, the only legitimate means for choosing among disparate values is the democratic process. In a totalitarian state, the government autocratically chooses and enforces certain values and goals, but democracy is different. In a democracy, each individual supposedly brings his or her preexisting values to the political arena, and then through the democratic process, the community chooses to promote and pursue particular values and goals. At the communal level, the democratic process itself provides the only criterion for validating normative choices; there is no standard of validity higher than acceptance by the people in the political arena. Democracy thus resembles capitalism: the marketplace (democracy) provides a forum for the expression of individual preferences and values, and then production (the government) responds accordingly.[90]

The most important formulation of this relativist theory of democracy was called pluralism. Pluralists viewed the political process as a legitimate battle among competing interest groups, all of whom bring preexisting and largely irrational (or arational) values to the political arena. Interest groups attempt to form coalitions, to compromise, and otherwise to gather political support in an unprincipled struggle to satisfy their own desires by influencing or controlling legislators. Individuals, interest groups, and legislators never consider a community interest or common good. Robert Dahl typified this perspective when he wrote: "[i]f unrestrained by external checks, any given individual or group of individuals will tyrannize over others." The results of political battles therefore matter less than the process itself: the process legitimates the results. Values are relative, but democracy must continue.[91]

Moreover, many political theorists believed that American culture produced a needed consensus regarding democratic processes. Although various individuals and interest groups might clash in political struggles, they shared certain elementary cultural norms that prevented the society from splintering into embittered fragments. Once again, Dahl captured this spirit: "[t]o assume that this country has remained democratic because of its Constitution seems to me an obvious reversal of the relation; it is much more plausible to suppose that the Constitution has remained because our society is essentially democratic." American society, according to this view, stood fundamentally and harmoniously joined in a cultural consensus celebrating the processes of democracy: individuals freely express diverse viewpoints, they negotiate, they disagree, and they compromise. As Edward Purcell has since noted, postwar theorists saw Americans as committed to a process of "unreflective practicality."[92]

The perception of social consensus developed for at least three reasons: television, coercion, and postwar prosperity. First, while seven thousand television sets had been produced in 1947, 7.3 million were produced only three years later. By the mid- to late 1950s, television had become a major media force and, simultaneously, had entered an "age of bland": advertisers and sponsors had pressured networks to eliminate controversial programming, and vacuous quiz shows were now among the most popular programs. Furthermore, as network television spread into so many households, the commercials led to "the dramatic expansion of mass consumer culture." Across the nation, viewers were encouraged to use the same cereals, the same toothpastes, the same headache pills, the same detergents, the same everything. Television, in other words, induced consensus both explicitly and implicitly. Second, during the 1950's Red Scare, with Senator Joseph McCarthy and the House Un-American Activities Committee coercively hounding alleged subversives and Communists, the number of avowed radicals dwindled, in the academy as elsewhere. In fact, hundreds of faculty were dismissed, and "a climate of caution and self-censorship" clouded university life for years thereafter. Third, despite this repressive atmosphere, a sense of economic, military, and political superiority formed throughout America. The United States was the only major nation to emerge from World War II "immeasurably stronger, both absolutely and relatively. . . . In a new balance of power it was a colossus on the international stage." Indeed, a postwar economic boom transformed America into "the affluent society." After the war the nation enjoyed a "quarter century of sustained growth at the highest rate in recorded history." Such power and success, many Americans smugly assumed, was deserved: the nation stood for noble values of equality, liberty, and democracy. Hence, by the early 1960s, many Americans shared the view "that the businessman and the unskilled laborer, the writer and the housewife, Harvard University and the Strategic Air Command, International Business Machines and the labor movement, all had their parts to play in one harmonious political, intellectual, and economic system." Americans, at this point, generously aimed to share the benefits of their democratic and capitalistic institutions with the rest of the world—though, of course, the rest of the world did not always appreciate this American largess.[93]

Jurisprudents, meanwhile, readily endorsed the intellectual emphasis on democracy that arose around World War II. In an influential article published in 1952, for example, Yale Law School professor and soon-to-be-dean Eugene V. Rostow proclaimed that the "Constitution should guarantee the democratic legitimacy of political decisions." Moreover, for the most part, legal theorists accepted the relativist theory of democracy, but they still needed to address specific questions concerning the rule of law in a democracy. If judicial decision making were merely a matter of fiat, of cadi justice, then the rule of law was no more than a myth, and the balloon of democratic government would rapidly deflate. Since the political commitment to democracy was steadfast, so too was the legal commitment to the rule of law. Although legal realism was not completely dead, most scholars now condemned the realists as nihilists: they had, after all, rejected legal rules and rationality as significant determinants in judicial decision making. Legal reasoning and the rule of law must be an undeniable given, despite realist claims. Thus, like the political theorists, legal theorists took a transcendental turn. Just as the political theorists had asked what conditions are necessary for democracy, legal theorists asked what conditions are necessary for the rule of law. If these conditions for the rule of law could be specified, they would provide the desired foundational source for objective judicial decision making. In their quest for these essential conditions, the legal theorists, again like the political theorists, focused primarily on process, supported by an assumed social consensus about the acceptability of the American legal system. It is worth noting that these "legal process" professors shared easily in the idea of a social consensus partly because of a lack of diversity among themselves. During the 1940s and 1950s, the overwhelming majority were white males. While this fact obviously did not guarantee their agreement on all issues, the homogeneity did reduce the likelihood that sharp disagreements on basic premises and broad outlooks would crystallize.[94]

Although the legal process school of thought blossomed after the Second World War, its jurisprudential roots were evident in contemporaneous prewar criticisms of the realists. For example, Lon Fuller argued that the realists focused too heavily on the observable behavior of judges and other legal officials. Consequently, the realists undermined democracy by assuming that the law is simply what judges do and that legal rules and judicial reasoning are meaningless. Furthermore, according to Fuller, the realists' haste to reject legal reasoning prompted them to make a positivist error by impugning a necessary connection between fact and value—between the law as it is and the law as it ought to be. As Fuller eventually elaborated his theory, this connection between fact and value becomes manifest in an inner morality of law. Fuller specified the components of this inner morality of law by asking the transcendental question characteristic of third-stage modernism: What are the conditions that make law possible? He concluded that these conditions consist of eight *procedural* desiderata, such as the requirements that laws should be clear, well publicized, and prospective. In short, according to Fuller, the processes of the inner morality of law constitute "an essential condition" for the presence and power of law.[95]

Third-stage legal modernism, then, in the form of the legal process school of thought, had emerged clearly by the 1950s. Legal process theorists were thoroughly committed to explaining the rule of law and justifying judicial decision making in the American democracy. As early as 1951, Henry M. Hart already had articulated the central theme of legal process: the "principle of institutional settlement." As restated by Hart and Albert Sacks in their well-known though long-unpublished course materials *The Legal Process: Basic Problems in the Making and Application of Law,* "[t]he principle of institutional settlement expresses the judgment that decisions which are the duly arrived at result of duly established procedures . . . ought to be accepted as binding upon the whole society unless and until they are duly changed." The legal process principle of institutional settlement developed the realists' institutional critique of laissez-faire constitutionalism: according to the realists (following Holmes), the *Lochner* Court had been guilty of judicial activism because it had intruded into the institutional role of the legislature. Legal process theorists, though, pushed this institutional critique to its extreme limit: the concept of the institution became paramount. According to legal process, society creates and designates different legal institutions to resolve different kinds of societal problems. Courts are, quite simply, different from legislatures. Consequently, judges are not free to make law in the same way that legislators are free to do so. At the same time, courts perform certain activities or "essential" functions that legislatures should not infringe upon, as Hart emphasized in his famous 1953 *Harvard Law Review* dialogue on the limits of congressional power over federal court jurisdiction.[96]

The legal process theorists not only pushed the realists' institutional critique of *Lochner* to its extreme, they further elaborated it through transcendental analysis: if courts, legislatures, and other governmental entities have different institutional roles, what are the processes that define those roles or make them possible? The various governmental institutions, from this perspective, are largely defined by the different procedures or processes that are integral to them, and individuals working within different governmental institutions are therefore constrained by the respective processes. Hence, legal process theorists devoted substantial scholarly and pedagogical resources to the development of fields such as administrative law and federal jurisdiction, subjects where they focused on separation of powers and federalism—that is, on the institutional and process-based relationships among the legislative, executive, and judicial branches, as well as those between the state and federal governments. Indeed, the central legal process themes were featured perhaps nowhere more clearly than in *The Federal Courts and the Federal System*, by Hart and Herbert Wechsler; the casebook that has (seemingly forevermore) defined the subject matter of federal courts courses. In the preface to the first edition of that book, the authors wrote:

> The book deals mainly with . . . problems of federal-state relationships but it also has two secondary themes. In varying contexts we pose the issue of what courts are good for—and are not good for—seeking thus to open up the whole range of questions as to the appropriate relationship between the federal courts and other organs of federal and state government. We also pose throughout problems of the organization and management of the federal courts, wishing to promote understanding of the task of federal judicial administration and of the means available for its improvement.[97]

According to legal process theory, the process that defines judicial decision making, in particular, is called "reasoned elaboration." Reasoned elaboration requires a judge always to give reasons for a decision, to articulate those reasons in a detailed and coherent manner, and to assume that "like cases should be treated alike." The judge must relate the decision to the relevant rule of law and must apply the rule of law in a manner logically consistent with precedent. This "striving for consistency is a matter of necessity," Hart and Sacks declare in a distinctly transcendental tone, "if legal arrangements are to be workable at all." Furthermore, in the context of common law cases and statutory interpretation, reasoned elaboration requires a judge to apply the law "in the way which best serves the principles and policies it expresses." In a sense, then, the process of reasoned elaboration acknowledges a limited amount of judicial activism in certain specified contexts. Nevertheless, the central message of legal process theory is opposed to legal realism: legal rules and judicial opinions matter. According to legal process, the requirements of reasoned elaboration meaningfully constrain judges in ways that executive officers, legislators, and administrators are not constrained. Reasoned elaboration specifies the conditions or processes that engender the rule of law in a democracy, and those processes provide an objective foundation for neutral and apolitical judicial decision making.[98]

During this third stage of legal modernism, the commitment to the independent and autonomous self who uses instrumental reason to control and reorder society continued unabated. This commitment was evident in at least three ways. First, political and legal theorists typically claimed that the relativist theory of democracy was rooted in a modern individualist tradition, which supposedly arose from John Locke's political philosophy and undergirded the American constitutional framework. Louis Hartz, for example, argued that American constitutionalism shared a fundamental assumption with Lockean theory: legitimate government arises when free and atomistic individuals join together to create a political community that protects liberty and property. Because of this tradition of individualism, Hartz proclaimed, "Burke equaled Locke in America." Second, specifically in legal process theory, Hart and Sacks's definition of law resounded with modernist individualism: "Law is a doing of something, a purposive activity, a continuous striving to solve the basic problems of social living." In a similar vein, the legal process principle of institutional settlement asked the fundamental question: Who decides? That is, what governmental institution or actor should appropriately decide specific issues (and then, of course, what processes should guide or constrain those decisions)? Quite clearly, experts within certain governmental institutions— legislatures and administrative agencies—were deemed qualified to use instrumental reason to direct or control society. Indeed, as already discussed, even judges occasionally could make law to help achieve the principles and policies of statutes and the common law. Third, the legal process scholars firmly believed that they were themselves important actors in the legal system. They were convinced that they should instruct Supreme Court justices about the law, that the justices would listen, and that the Court's decisions (hence the scholars' instructions) changed American society. For many years, the prestigious *Harvard Law Review Forewords,* which began in 1951, were the special preserve of legal process scholars as they sought to enlighten the Court. Evidence even suggests that at least one justice, former Harvard professor Felix Frankfurter, pondered scholars' suggestions, though of course he did not necessarily follow them. And as late as 1968, a somewhat pessimistic *Foreword* writer still hoped that scholarship could influence the Court: "Even in a day when the law reviews are much cited but not often heeded, it may still serve a purpose to hold up to the Court a mirror that emphasizes its warts."[99]

From one perspective, legal process theorists merely identified, albeit carefully and precisely, the craft norms for legal institutions, particularly judicial decision making.[100] If a judge wants to be good, the theorists insisted, then he or she should just do what we say. Indeed, looking backward at legal process scholars, they often seem so arrogant, yet prosaic, as to be puzzling: why would intelligent scholars devote their careers to articulating such trite maxims as "treat like cases alike"? But when legal process is viewed as third-stage modernism, the dedication and even zeal of its devotees becomes understandable. After World War II, legal foundationalism seemed endangered: the rule of law and the objectivity of judicial decision making were under intellectual siege. The realists had irremediably discredited the abstract rationalism of Langdellianism, and now the realists' own empiricism was likewise disparaged. And in the midst of this intellectual crisis and impending despair, the legal process theorists believed that they had discovered the solution. They somehow had pulled the rabbit out of the hat! With transcendental reasoning, they explained how America had democracy and the rule of law. They justified America during the Cold War. They described the structures, the conditions, the *processes* of the American legal system that produced the objective foundations necessary for judicial decision making.

Fourth-Stage Modern Jurisprudence: Late Crisis

A variety of seemingly unconnected factors contributed to the Supreme Court's most important decision of the post–World War II era, *Brown v. Board of Education*. The rise of totalitarianism in Europe during the 1930s led not only to an American intellectual focus on democratic theory, as already discussed, but also applied social pressure on Americans to live up to their professed democratic ideals. Overt racism and antisemitism had been socially respectable and quite common in America before World War II. In fact, Jews who fled Germany for America during the 1930s thought that antisemitism (as a form of racism) was worse in America than in pre-Nazi Germany! After the War, however, overt racism and antisemitism resounded too closely with the violence of the Holocaust and thus became socially embarrassing; for their own emotional well-being, Americans needed to differentiate themselves sharply from the Germans. In the words of Jerome A. Chanes, "Adolf Hitler gave antisemitism a bad name." The same can be said of Hitler and racism. The Germans were racist monsters, but Americans were different: Americans were exceptional. Americans were committed to equality and liberty for all, or so, at least, many Americans now wanted to believe.[101]

Of course, the continued existence of Jim Crow laws in the South called into question such egalitarian beliefs and declarations. The enforcement by state governments of laws that explicitly segregated and discriminated against African Americans was difficult to square with the American ideals of (or pretensions to) democracy and equality. In the early postwar years, though, many white Americans continued to ignore the dissonance between the social reality and the ideals. Such indifference became more difficult to harbor as the civil rights movement spread in the late 1950s. By the early 1960s, television had become the primary source of news for most Americans, and flickering images of southern atrocities inflicted on civil rights protesters generated unprecedented national support for legal and social changes (leading, for example, to the Civil Rights Act of 1964). Eventually, then, *overt* racism (including antisemitism) became a social faux pas: racism went underground and became secretive, tacit, and unconscious. To be sure, and quite obviously, overt racism and antisemitism never disappeared completely in America, but they became far less common—far less part of the normal and natural experience of daily life.[102]

Meanwhile, with regard to Supreme Court jurisprudence, from the late nineteenth century through the mid-1930s, the Court largely followed the laissez-faire constitutionalism exemplified in the *Lochner* decision. But political and intellectual pressure led to the transformation of the Court in 1937: a commitment to judicial restraint replaced the *Lochner* Court's activism in cases involving economic regulations. For the most part, the Court accepted the realists' institutional critique of *Lochner,* and at least temporarily, a majority of justices consistently deferred to Congress and the state legislatures. Nonetheless, a crack in this judicial consensus quickly appeared with Justice Harlan F. Stone's footnote 4 in *United States v. Carolene Products,* decided in 1938. Stone suggested that although judicial restraint was appropriate in cases involving economic regulations, some degree of judicial activism might be appropriate in cases involving certain personal rights and liberties. Soon the previously aligned Progressives and New Deal liberals on the Court divided into two groups. One group of justices, led by Hugo Black and William O. Douglas, seized on Stone's insight and insisted that there were "preferred freedoms," such as freedom of speech and freedom of religion, that merited special judicial protection. The second group of justices, led by Felix Frankfurter and Robert H. Jackson, insisted on (almost) strict adherence to a philosophy of judicial restraint. According to this latter group, if the Court were to pick and choose among various rights, designating some as preferred and others as not, then it would be as guilty as the *Lochner* Court of unconstrained activism. This dispute was never merely a matter of constitutional theory; the political and social pressures of the World War II era also bore on the justices. For example, in 1940, the Court upheld the expulsion of two public school students, who were Jehovah's Witnesses, for their religiously motivated refusal to salute the flag. Subsequently, religious bigotry surged across the nation, sometimes erupting in violence. Hence, in an abrupt about-face, the Court overruled itself, holding in 1943 that compulsory flag salutes were unconstitutional; in the midst of World War II, violent religious persecution seemed a bit too totalitarian for the judiciary to disregard.[103]

In this social and judicial context—with a nation struggling to deal with its own racism, and with a divided and volatile set of Supreme Court justices—*Brown v. Board of Education* arrived at the high Court in 1952, challenging the constitutionality of racial segregation in public schools. Unsurprisingly, after the justices' post–oral argument conference in December 1952, the result in the case was unclear. At best, the justices might hold segregation unconstitutional by a mere five-to-four vote. Significantly, though, Justice Frankfurter already had decided to vote that racial segregation should be held unconstitutional, regardless of his otherwise staunch advocacy of judicial deference to legislative actions. At the conference, Frankfurter convinced the other justices to order reargument for the next Court term, supposedly to answer specific questions drafted by him and his clerk, Alexander Bickel. The questions focused on the history of the Fourteenth Amendment and the problems related to a decree if segregation were held unconstitutional. Frankfurter's true motivations in seeking reargument are now subject to scholarly dispute. Historians initially argued that he had assumed a position of leadership on the Court and, in that role, was seeking to delay a decision so that a stronger majority might form. More recently, scholars have relied on newly un-covered evidence to argue that Frankfurter merely was seeking some principled basis for harmonizing his usual judicial restraint with the decision that he already had settled on—that school segregation was unconstitutional. Regardless of Frankfurter's motivations, the effect of reargument was to delay the decision until the following term. Then, in a remarkable turn of events, Chief Justice Fred M. Vinson died in September 1953. When *Brown* was reargued in December 1953, Earl Warren was the new chief justice.[104]

As chief justice, Warren unquestionably played a crucial role in securing the final unanimous decision in *Brown*. Among other strategic maneuverings, Warren facilitated unity by convincing the justices to split the case into two parts, treating the question of the decree (*Brown II*) separately from the merits of the constitu-tional claim (*Brown I*). With regard to the individual justices, a desire to do the right thing, morally and constitutionally, surely motivated some of them. Some of the justices undoubtedly shared the growing postwar American sentiment that overt racism no longer was socially or morally acceptable. Several other consider-ations, though, also bore down on the justices, influencing their direction. The Na-tional Association for the Advancement of Colored People (NAACP) had orches-trated a sustained (though perhaps unsystematic) legal campaign that built slowly but steadily on the already existing tradition of equal protection until the "separate but equal" doctrine of *Plessy v. Ferguson* appeared facially indefensible. In addi-tion, the perpetuation of overt racism in the Jim Crow laws hampered the eco-nomic development of the nation, especially in the South. Internationally, such racism hindered the nation's efforts to woo Third World countries during the Cold War. In short, for much of the nation, legally enforced segregation had become a distasteful obstacle to progress.[105]

In any event, *Brown v. Board of Education* finally held that racial segregation of public school children violated the equal protection clause of the Fourteenth Amendment. Warren's opinion for the Court was uncommonly brief. He began by stating that the history of the adoption of the Fourteenth Amendment did not pro-vide any clear guidance to the Court; hence, he reasoned, the Constitution must be interpreted in light of the current social context surrounding racially segregated public education. Warren then emphasized two points. First, segregation had detri-mental psychological effects on African-American children. Second, public educa-tion was immensely important in America:

> Today, education is perhaps the most important function of state and local gov-ernments. Compulsory school attendance laws and the great expenditures for ed-ucation both demonstrate our recognition of the importance of education to our democratic society. It is required in the performance of our most basic public re-

sponsibilities, even service in the armed forces. It is the very foundation of good citizenship. Today it is a principal instrument in awakening the child to cultural values, in preparing him for later professional training, and in helping him to adjust normally to his environment. In these days, it is doubtful that any child may reasonably be expected to succeed in life if he is denied the opportunity of an education. Such an opportunity, where the state has undertaken to provide it, is a right which must be made available to all on equal terms.

Therefore, Warren concluded, "[s]eparate educational facilities are inherently unequal."[106]

The decision and opinion in *Brown* helped catapult American legal thought into the fourth stage of modernism, late crisis, characterized by deeply inconsistent attitudes and projects—anxiety, despair, anger, denunciations, and increasingly complex modernist solutions that seized upon combinations of rationalism, empiricism, and transcendentalism. *Brown* not only generated social furor, it also engendered academic uproar. The early legal process materials had not focused on the question of judicial review in the context of constitutional decision making. *Brown* brought this problem to the forefront and in so doing almost immediately uncovered the inherent weaknesses within the transcendental reasoning of legal process theory.[107]

Interestingly, in the first *Harvard Law Review Foreword* after *Brown*, Albert Sacks effusively praised the decision and the Court. He wrote that *Brown* "illustrates the functioning of the judicial process at its best" and that Warren's brief opinion represented "judicial statesmanship" because, in part, of "[i]ts style of straightforward simplicity." Nonetheless, Sacks initiated the legal process assault on the Warren Court by criticizing its excessive use of per curiam summary opinions. Here, then, a basic tension between legal process scholars and the Warren Court immediately crystallized. Legal process theorists emphasized the importance of rules and legal reasoning in judicial opinions, but the Warren Court was deciding cases without adequately explaining its reasoning process. By the next *Foreword*, the relationship between the legal process scholars and the Court had already deteriorated. In a rebuke partially aimed at Sacks, Robert Braucher caustically noted that he would *not* be praising the Warren Court's "judicial statesmanship."[108]

The tension between the legal process scholars and the Warren Court continued to simmer over the next few years. The legal process theorists, consequently, elaborated their basic theoretical points in the course of criticizing the Court. For example, Alexander Bickel and Harry Wellington condemned not only the Warren Court's excessive use of unexplained per curiam decisions (as Sacks had done), but also its issuance of vacuous opinions, resembling negotiated agreements, instead of "rationally articulated grounds of decision." Ernest Brown criticized the Court for summarily disposing of too many cases without the benefit of full briefing and oral argument. The Court, in other words, was failing to follow the procedures that were necessary for reaching properly reasoned conclusions. Henry Hart argued that the mounting caseload of the Court prevented it from fulfilling its institutional role—to write opinions with clearly articulated reasons and principles. The Court must exemplify the rule of law: "Only opinions which are grounded in reason and not on mere fiat or precedent can do the job which the Supreme Court of the United States has to do." In presenting this argument, Hart elaborated the process of reasoned elaboration at the appellate level. According to Hart, a group of judges who reason together through a case should experience a "maturing of collective thought," a rationalizing process that allows the tribunal to transcend the idiosyncrasies of the individual judges.[109]

The heated dispute between legal process theorists and the Warren Court finally boiled over in 1958, when Herbert Wechsler issued the ultimate challenge to the Court and its defenders. In his article *Toward Neutral Principles of Constitutional Law,* Wechsler argued that because of institutional differences, only courts (not legislatures and executives) must give reasoned explanations for their decisions. These explanations must not be ad hoc, instrumental, or unprincipled. To the contrary, a court must justify each decision with a "neutral principle": a ground or reason that attains "adequate neutrality and generality" by transcending the immediate result of the particular case. Most important, Wechsler then tested *Brown,* the Warren Court's flagship decision, against this standard of neutral principles. His effort to identify a neutral principle to support the decision led to the conclusion that freedom of association was the only possibility. Wechsler acknowledged that segregation contravenes the freedom of association of those who want to integrate (the plaintiffs in *Brown*), but he questioned whether the application of this principle in *Brown* was truly a neutral or reasoned application. Wechsler strikingly concluded that forced integration also *contravenes* freedom of association—particularly, the freedom of association of those who wish to remain segregated. Consequently, Wechsler charged that the principle or rule of *Brown* was not neutral, and therefore the decision was objectively wrong.[110]

Wechsler's denunciation of *Brown* sparked an immediate flurry of scholarship. On the one hand, Wechsler's attack seemed almost inevitable. After Sacks's initial praise of *Brown,* legal process scholars had become increasingly hostile toward the Warren Court. Their primary complaint revolved around the Court's supposedly inadequate opinions, which repeatedly failed to satisfy the requirements of reasoned elaboration. From the legal process standpoint, the Warren Court often seemed to be little more than a wayward realist, refusing to recognize the importance of the rule of law as expressed in well-reasoned judicial opinions. Thus, if not Wechsler, some other legal process theorist was sure to return eventually to *Brown,* the Warren Court's preeminent decision. Moreover, such a re-examination of the remarkably brief *Brown* opinion was likely to conclude that it had not satisfied the demands of legal process (since Warren apparently made no effort to do so). As Wechsler had resolved, "[t]he problem [in *Brown*] inheres strictly in the reasoning of the opinion." Yet, on the other hand, many scholars saw Wechsler's attack and conclusion as categorically unacceptable. If nothing more, *Brown* symbolized American equality and thus stood invulnerable, even if its acceptance somehow undermined the legal process defense of the rule of law.[111]

Consequently, many scholars struggled to vindicate the decision in *Brown*, though often without offering any broader defense of the Warren Court. Louis Pollak offered an alternative opinion for the *Brown* decision that, he claimed, satisfied Wechsler's demand for a neutral principle. Charles Black likewise offered a neutral principle in defense of *Brown*, but more important, he also angrily denounced Wechsler and legal process. To Black, racial segregation was a tragic social relationship in a concrete historical reality, and the demand for a neutral principle tended to dangerously abstract the human pain of this calamity. Thus, according to Black, the substantive result in *Brown* was so compelling that it should endure regardless of whether it could be justified with a neutral principle. If legal process could not defend *Brown*, then by necessity, legal process must be wrong. *Brown* must stand.[112]

By around 1960, then, *Brown* and the Warren Court had helped precipitate the late crisis of fourth-stage legal modernism. During the third stage, legal process theorists had used transcendental reasoning to describe the conditions needed for the rule of law and objective judicial decision making in a democracy. But the Warren Court, and *Brown* in particular, presented an intransigent reality. Warren Court opinions suggested that, at best, legal process theory described an imaginary world, not reality. Moses Lasky lamented that the concepts of reasoned elaboration and neutral principles were merely theoretical, unrelated to the actuality of judicial decision making. Other jurisprudents were far harsher. In 1960, Addison Mueller and Murray L. Schwartz flatly condemned the concept of neutral principles as untenable. They argued that any principle, when logically extended, eventually would conflict with some other competing principle. No principle was truly neutral, and therefore, the legal process theory of neutral principles could not provide an objective foundation for constitutional decision making.[113]

Although legal process would remain the primary jurisprudential approach for many more years, its hegemonic hold on the academy already had loosened and slipped considerably. In the words of the hoary Karl Llewellyn, writing in 1960, jurisprudents were experiencing "a crisis in confidence." This crisis had "come to lay a pall and palsy on heart and hand because it goes to whether there is any reckonability in the work of our appellate courts, any real stability of footing for the lawyer." Soon, scholars began turning every which way as they struggled to satisfy the foundational demands of the modernist worldview. Different writers drew on rationalism, empiricism, transcendentalism, or whatever intellectual tools were at hand. Many theorists seized upon philosophical or social scientific methods in their quest for objective footings. Ronald Dworkin integrated legal process with the English tradition of analytical jurisprudence, which ran from John Austin to H. L. A. Hart. In so doing, Dworkin attempted to explain how the process of judicial reasoning enables judges to correctly decide cases on a principled basis. Some legal theorists strove to incorporate John Rawls's political philosophy into jurisprudence. For instance, Frank Michelman, in defending later Warren Court decisions that protected indigents' receipt of governmental assistance, argued from a Rawlsian perspective that the state should have a duty to protect the poor "against certain hazards which are endemic in an unequal society." In the mid-1960s, an empirically oriented law and society movement emerged; some sociologists and law professors combined to form in 1964 the Law and Society Association. Many of these scholars used empirical methods to study whether Supreme Court decisions effectively changed American society: for example, did Court orders to end prayers in the public schools cause school boards actually to eliminate such religious practices? These so-called gap studies generally concluded that the judicial decisions did not achieve their desired goals, but in typical modernist fashion, the scholars then suggested that these studies might themselves lead to more effective means of social control and change. Significantly, then, unlike earlier stages of modernist jurisprudence, leading scholars during this late crisis period failed to agree widely on the worth of any overarching jurisprudential approach.[114]

Two of the leading emergent jurisprudential developments of this period were the law and economics movement and critical legal studies. Law and economics scholars sought to use the methods of economic analysis to discover objective truths about the legal system, particularly in the common law fields of contracts, torts, and property. As with economic analyses in general, a fundamental modernist assumption provided the starting point for the law and economics approach: all individuals seek to maximize the satisfaction of their own self-interest. If individuals are left free to rationally pursue their self-interest, then society itself supposedly will achieve its highest good, which is the distribution of resources and goods in the most economically efficient manner. Basically, economic efficiency increased as the total production for the society correspondingly increased. Indeed, working largely from these assumptions, the economist Ronald Coase had published an article in 1960 that eventually served as the wellspring for the law and economics movement. The Coase Theorem asserted that in a world without transaction costs, the assignment of legal rights would not affect the distribution of resources, which naturally would move to the most efficient allocation.[115]

Building on the Coase Theorem and the underlying economic assumptions, law and economics scholars suggested that their methods had both descriptive and prescriptive implications. Descriptively, they claimed that economic analyses accurately portrayed the historical development of the common law—a development that had led to greater economic efficiency—regardless of what judges themselves thought they had been doing over the years. In a sense, then, the law and economics scholars followed the realists by repudiating the value of judicial opinions, but like the legal process scholars, the law and economics writers nonetheless saw a distinct logic in the process of judicial decision making. Other law and economics scholars pushed the analysis further to make prescriptive recommendations for the legal system. Most prominently, Richard Posner argued that common law judges ought to shape the law to mimic the economic marketplace. If a supposedly unregulated marketplace would lead to the distribution of goods in such and such a manner, then common law judges ought to aim for the same distribution of goods. For what mattered, according to Posner and his colleagues, was not the equitable distribution of goods—that all persons are dealt with fairly—but rather that goods are distributed so as to increase the efficiency of the overall system. And supposedly, an unregulated marketplace produced the most efficient results. A law and economics approach, in sum, aimed to increase the total production of the society regardless of the equities or inequities that ensued.[116]

For many, the appeal of an economic approach to law was its ostensible scientific rigor. In the first volume of the *Journal of Legal Studies,* a journal founded in 1972 and dedicated to publishing law and economics articles, Posner declared: "The aim of the *Journal* is to encourage the application of scientific methods to the study of the legal system. As biology is to living organisms, astronomy to the stars, or economics to the price system, so should legal studies be to the legal system: an endeavor to make precise, objective, and systematic observations of how the legal system operates in fact and to discover and explain the recurrent patterns in the observations—the 'laws' of the system." To be sure, the law and economics movement has evolved. Today, for instance, the most vital element of the movement is perhaps public choice theory, which applies economic analysis to political activity, such as legislative decision making. Nevertheless, law and economics retains its distinctly modernist orientation, epitomized by its claim to scientific objectivity.[117]

The critical legal studies (CLS) movement emerged in the early to middle 1970s. Many of the "crits" were former student protestors of the Vietnam War who had become disenchanted during law school with the legal process depiction of a fair and neutral American legal system and a moderate liberal political consensus. As the crits entered the legal academy, they challenged mainstream jurisprudence, particularly of the legal process ilk (and eventually law and economics too), as they focused their attention on class-based economic divisions within American society—divisions that flowed from the unequal distribution of wealth among different groups. Whereas the legal process scholars had sought to show the inherent rationality of law, the crits sought to demonstrate how law serves as an ideology that unjustifiably legitimates disparities of wealth and power in American society. Contrary to legal process assertions, CLS scholars argued that judicial decision making is not a neutral process, but rather is political through and through. Not only is law political, it is political with a tilt: it favors those persons and groups who already are well favored in America. In the legal system, the "haves" consistently (though not always) come out ahead. Yet, the crits contended, the law is ideological because it tends to obscure or mask this political tilt: the law claims to be neutral and just, even as it simultaneously and consistently favors certain powerful groups. The crits therefore rejected the possibility of improving the legal system with liberal piecemeal reforms. Such reforms inevitably would be absorbed and co-opted into the ideology of the law, leaving the system virtually intact. Instead, the crits insisted, the only escape lay in the total or revolutionary transformation of the system.[118]

The crits, it is worth emphasizing, were modernists. Without doubt, the disciplinary boundaries among different academic fields were starting to show cracks at this time, as was evident in other contemporaneous cross-disciplinary jurisprudential movements, such as law and economics. But perhaps more than the scholars in any other current movement—and certainly more than previous modernist scholars, including the realists—the crits were eclectics. They began citing sources from all over the map, including many continental thinkers. Their footnotes referred to Weber, Marx, Husserl, Heidegger, Habermas, Merleau-Ponty, Arendt, Durkheim, Sartre, Feuerbach, Levi-Strauss, and others—certainly not traditional American legal authorities. Yet, despite the crits' willingness to move beyond the realm of the ordinary citation, they largely remained committed to basic modernist assumptions, as was true of many of the continental thinkers they cited. Most important, one of the central features of CLS writing was the so-called fundamental contradiction. Duncan Kennedy provided its seminal statement:

> [T]he goal of individual freedom is at the same time dependent on and incompatible with the communal coercive action that is necessary to achieve it. Others (family, friends, bureaucrats, cultural figures, the state) are necessary if we are to become persons at all—they provide us the stuff of our selves and protect us in crucial ways against destruction. . . . But at the same time that it forms and protects us, the universe of others (family, friendship, bureaucracy, culture, the state) threatens us with annihilation and urges upon us forms of fusion that are quite plainly bad rather than good. A friend can reduce me to misery with a single look. Numberless conformities, large and small abandonments of self to others, are the price of what freedom we experience in society.[119]

As presented by Kennedy, the fundamental contradiction was a structural phenomenon characterized by the bipolar opposition of two extremes: individual freedom and communal coercion. Robert W. Gordon called it "one of the most threatening aspects of social existence: the danger posed by other people, whose cooperation is indispensable to us (we cannot even have an individual identity without them to help define it socially), but who may kill us or enslave us." Because the fundamental contradiction was a deep structure, crits argued, it was not readily apparent at the surface level of everyday life, but if one dug below the surface, it tended to reappear over and over in different contexts and different guises. Consequently, CLS writers devoted considerable time to explaining how various realms of the legal system arose from the underlying structure of the fundamental contradiction. Gerald E. Frug partially attributed the powerlessness of modern cities to it, while Frances E. Olsen related a dichotomy between the family and the economic marketplace to this basic structure.[120]

The crits' devotion to the fundamental contradiction marked them as modernists in two important ways. First, they believed that social life could be reduced to this basic or foundational building block, which then could be used to explain all manner of diverse societal developments. As Kennedy phrased it, all legal issues reduced to the "single dilemma of the degree of collective as opposed to individual self-determination that is appropriate." The fundamental contradiction became, in effect, the objective source of truth for the crits. Second, despite their scholarly commitment to this underlying structure, the crits simultaneously believed that somehow, someway, they could overcome the constraints of the fundamental contradiction to usher in a new social life of true freedom. In the end, then, the crits believed that they could help remake society for the good of humankind. Modernist progress could march onward.[121]

Critical legal studies is perhaps best understood as a generational movement. From this vantage, the crits were those critical or radical thinkers who entered the legal academy in the 1970s and dominated left legal thought for fifteen years or so. To be sure, other critical thinkers followed the crits, but for a variety of reasons, these more recent critical writers are best not categorized within the CLS movement (most important, many of the more recent critical thinkers are postmodern rather than modern). The crits themselves were motivated greatly by their experiences as war protestors as well as by their profound disappointment with their own law school experiences. Consequently, at times, the crits seemed almost obsessed with demonstrating the utter failure of their law school professors, who had labored arduously to elucidate the basic legal process themes. For example, Paul Brest and Mark Tushnet argued that the aim of constitutional theory, which eventually became a wellspring of legal process writing, was logically impossible. From the legal process perspective, a valid constitutional theory would need to ground constitutional decisions on some objective foundation while simultaneously remaining politically neutral. As Brest and Tushnet concluded, these legal process goals for constitutional theory were inherently inconsistent. Legal process thinking was, in other words, self-contradictory, and those legal process scholars who had devoted entire careers to constitutional theory had, in effect, wasted their professional lives. Regardless of such broadsided attacks on their academic predecessors, critical legal scholars seemed to draw the movement to a close sometime during the 1980s. Duncan Kennedy, deservedly, symbolically concluded the brief era of the crits when he explicitly repudiated the concept of the fundamental contradiction, declaring in 1984 that "it must be utterly extirpated and rooted out." Then, as the crits matured, many of them moved into more mainstream endeavors. Tushnet, for example, became a leading constitutional historian, while Brest became dean of the Stanford Law School (even though only a few years earlier, Paul

D. Carrington, then the dean of Duke Law School, had barked that crits ought to be banished from law school teaching).[122]

Meanwhile, despite the multifarious paths that legal thought had taken, legal process theory had not totally disappeared—far from it. Some loyal legal process scholars, their anxiety climbing, had pushed onward in their battle against the Warren Court. From their perspective, the Court consistently had ignored and thus had weakened the rule of law; cries of nihilism were heard once again. Other more hopeful legal process scholars struggled to defend *both* legal process and the Warren Court by developing increasingly complex theories. Indeed, over time, Wechsler's challenge to *Brown* generated some of the most imaginative and sophisticated writing of the legal process genre. Richard Wasserstrom, for example, most eloquently articulated the legal process response to the realist-like rule-skepticism that appeared to debase many Warren Court opinions. According to Wasserstrom, the realists had confused two distinct processes: the process of discovery and the process of justification. The process of discovery describes how a court reaches a conclusion in a case, while the process of justification describes how the court justifies or legitimates its conclusion. As applied to the process of discovery, the realist critique of legal reasoning and judicial opinions was correct: judicial opinions often do not accurately describe how judges reach their conclusions. As applied to the process of justification, however, the realists were mistaken: judicial opinions accurately describe (or *should* accurately describe) how judges justify their conclusions. That is, the realists failed to recognize that the purpose of the judicial opinion should be to describe the justification and not the discovery of the conclusion. Whereas the process of discovery might not be rational, the process of justification can and should be strictly rational. For ultimately, according to legal process, this requirement of strict rationality in the process of justification meaningfully (and objectively) constrains judicial decision making. Hence, the Warren Court's consistent failure to adequately justify its decisions improperly and dangerously freed the justices from the institutional restraints of reasoned elaboration.[123]

If Wasserstrom most eloquently articulated the legal process argument for well-reasoned judicial opinions, then Alexander Bickel most eloquently stated the institutional critique of judicial activism in constitutional decision making. Bickel, echoing pluralistic political theory, argued that the legislative process is a wide-open clash of interests, open to everyone and controlled by shifting majorities. Legislative actions are largely unprincipled and, at best, reflect the most expedient means for solving problems and attaining goals. Nonetheless, to Bickel, the central commitment of our constitutional government is the democratic process, and legislative actions are therefore legitimate exactly because they are democratic—they supposedly represent the will of the majority of the people. Thus, when the Supreme Court strikes down a legislative act as unconstitutional, the Court supposedly defeats the democratic will. If the institutional role of the legislature is to allow the free play of democracy, then the institutional role of the Court in judicial review forces it to act contrary to the spirit of democracy. The Court's role, in short, creates a "counter-majoritarian difficulty."[124]

Bickel himself presented one possible solution to this countermajoritarian difficulty. According to Bickel, judicial review can be justified only if it adds something significant to government that is otherwise lacking. Because Bickel believed that the legislative process allows an unprincipled clash of interests, he argued that judicial review should inject principles or ethical values into our governmental system. Since, consistent with pluralistic political theory, Bickel saw an American society agreeing on basic cultural norms, he concluded that the Supreme Court's institutional function must be to enunciate and to apply those "enduring values of our society"—Wechsler's neutral principles. Bickel explained: "[T]he root idea is that the process [of judicial review] is justified only if it injects into representative government something that is not already there; and that is principle, standards of action that derive their worth from a long view of society's spiritual as well as material needs and that command adherence whether or not the immediate outcome is expedient or agreeable."[125]

Even so, Bickel insisted, the Court should act prudently, exercising self-restraint, so as to minimize its conflicts with the democratic process of the legislature. The "passive virtues"—doctrines such as standing, mootness, and ripeness—allow the Court carefully to bide its time. By relying on these passive virtues, the Court can avoid deciding many constitutional cases on the merits, thus deferring to the legislative judgments, but the Court can still seize those rare cases where a decision on the merits fosters the articulation of enduring values. The Court thus maintains its precarious yet crucial countermajoritarian function in our democratic system.[126]

As American legal thought already was entrenched in fourth-stage modernism, Bickel's solution to the countermajoritarian difficulty was immediately suspect, despite its sophistication and ingenuity. Gerald Gunther accused Bickel of undermining the rule of law because his passive virtues did not provide objective foundations for judicial decision making. To Gunther, the passive virtues were "hollow formula" that provided "virtually unlimited choice [to the Court] in deciding whether to decide." As such, they were "law-debasing" and ultimately inconsistent with legal process theory. More significant, Bickel himself eventually questioned whether the Court could ever articulate truly neutral principles. If all substantive values were relative—as the relativist theory of democracy suggested—then the Court could articulate neither neutral nor objective values. To the later Bickel, the modernist quest for foundations purified of cultural traditions was tragically absurd: reason, standing alone, was empty of content, and values necessarily arose from tradition itself. Consequently, the entire legal process defense of the rule of law in the American democracy seemed doomed, and legal scholars confronted the deep despair of fourth-stage modernism.[127]

This despair, however, drove some legal process scholars to even higher levels of sophistication. Indeed, legal process theory may have reached its apex with John Hart Ely's constitutional theory of representation-reinforcement, which attempted to harmonize legal process and *Brown*. Accepting Bickel's skeptical conclusion about neutral principles, Ely vowed to intensify the commitment to process. The only solution to the problem of value relativism, according to Ely, was to develop a pure process-based approach to constitutional adjudication. The Court should never even attempt to articulate substantive values or goals, neutral or otherwise; all substantive value decisions must issue from the democratic process. Yet, Ely realized, the democratic process is not always fair and open, so the Court should not automatically defer to legislative judgments. Instead, the Court should police the processes of democratic representation: a legislative action should be overturned as unconstitutional if and only if it resulted from a malfunctioning or defective democratic process. In Ely's view, process alone provides the foundation for objective judicial decision making. Furthermore, representation-reinforcement actually dissolves the countermajoritarian difficulty because judicial review supports and promotes the democratic process.[128]

Ely elaborated his theory by arguing that the Court can police the democratic process in two ways. First, the Court should clear the channels of political change. To do so, the Court prevents the political "ins" from insuring their continued political power by choking the channels of political change and permanently excluding the political "outs." For example, denying or diluting the right to vote through legislative malapportionment is a "quintessential stoppage" in the democratic process and therefore must be prevented by the Court. Second, and most important for the defense of *Brown*, the Court should facilitate the representation of minorities. That is, the Court must prevent representatives from systematically disadvantaging minorities because of hostility or prejudice. The democratic process is malfunctioning if everyone is not "actually or virtually represented." Minorities that technically participate in the democratic process by voting are nonetheless excluded if their elected representatives ignore their interests merely because they are minorities. Hence, for example, when a legislature intentionally discriminates against a minority for an improper motive, such as racial hostility, the Court should find the legislative action unconstitutional. For this reason, then, representation-reinforcement theory supposedly justified *Brown* and its condemnation of racial segregation in the public schools. Legislatures that had mandated racial segregation had not adequately represented the interests of African-American constituents. Moreover, the segregated education of African-American children eventually inhibited their ability as adults to fully participate in the democratic process.[129]

Ely's theory of representation-reinforcement was elegant in its simplicity. Even so, critics swarmed immediately and devastatingly to the attack. For example, Ely had argued that the Court should police the democratic process by facilitating the representation of minorities, but as critics quickly noted, the *Court* itself had to differentiate among the various societal groups who had been losers in the unprincipled battles of pluralistic democracy. The Court designated some such groups as (discrete and insular) minorities entitled to special judicial protection while deeming other groups *mere* losers in the democratic process. These *mere* losers were, in effect, left to fend for themselves in the legislative arena, unprotected by the courts. From the perspective of legal process theory, though, the Court's necessary differentiation between societal groups was problematic: it required the Court to engage in exactly those unconstrained substantive value choices that representation-reinforcement theory was supposed to forbid. Perhaps, the critics concluded, representation-reinforcement offered a defense of *Brown,* but it did so (if at all) only by sacrificing the central goal of legal process, neutral and objective judicial decision making. As Paul Brest sardonically observed, Ely had articulated process-based constitutional theory so artfully that his failure unwittingly demonstrated the impossibility of ever achieving a successful theory: "John Hart Ely has come as close as anyone could to proving that it can't be done." The same could have been said at that point for modernist jurisprudence in general: despite over a century of effort, the self-imposed goals of modernist jurisprudence seemed inherently unachievable.[130]

✦ F I V E ✦

Postmodern American Legal Thought

Across a Shadowy Border:
From Modern to Postmodern Jurisprudence

America of the 1950s and early 1960s was a nation characterized by consensus and confidence.[1] Many Americans, including most legal process scholars and political theorists, had believed throughout the 1950s that the nation was joined in a consensus celebrating democracy and the rule of law. Moreover, they were confident that because of American knowhow, prosperity, and power, these noble principles could not only suffuse the lives of all Americans but also could beneficently shape the entire world. Yet, this period of consensus was, perhaps, "a fool's paradise . . . a time of false complacency and of hubristic and dangerous illusions." The early civil rights movement suggested the flaws in the idea of consensus, but then widespread support for the movement itself became part of the consensus—reflecting ostensibly the American commitments to liberty and equality. And the successes of the early movement only fueled American confidence: most Americans believed that Southern racism could be defeated so that all citizens would have an equal chance to share in the American dream. This was indeed a time of "grand expectations." According to James T. Patterson, "[p]eople talked confidently about winning 'wars' against contemporary problems, ranging from poverty to cancer to unrest in Vietnam." Ultimately, however, events from the early 1960s through the early 1970s would defeat these expectations, dramatically shattering American perceptions of harmony and success. The transformation of the civil rights movement, the assassinations of President John F. Kennedy, his brother Senator Robert F. Kennedy, and Martin Luther King, Jr.; the Vietnam War and its concomitant protests; and the Watergate Affair left Americans shaken with self-doubt and "tore consensus to shreds."[2]

Perhaps more than any of the other events, the Vietnam War epitomizes the dissolution of American confidence. Americans' prosperity combined with their modernist hubris to convince them that they could engineer social progress throughout the world. During the Cold War, the American idea of progress was equated with stopping Communism. In Vietnam, this vision translated into the interrelated objectives of defeating the Communists of North Vietnam and assuring supposedly free economies and governments throughout southeast Asia. Yet, starting with the commitment of United States military troops in 1964 and 1965, America seriously underestimated the resolve of the North Vietnamese. The pursuit of the United States' goals therefore required the nation persistently to escalate its efforts in the war. Nevertheless, with each escalation, with each new bombing offensive and each shipment of yet more troops, the United States somehow failed to make significant headway toward its ends. In fact, during the war, the United States dropped seven million tons of bombs on Vietnam, more than twice the amount that the Allies had dropped during World War II in Europe and Asia. With escalation abroad came frustration at home, as America polarized between those for and against the War: in 1965 a strong majority of Americans supported the country's involvement in Vietnam, but by 1969 a majority of Americans opposed it. Many of the opponents candidly voiced their dissatisfaction by participating in the renowned protest demonstrations of that era.[3]

The United States finally withdrew its troops from Vietnam in 1973, with President Richard Nixon's administration proclaiming a negotiated "peace with honor." Nevertheless, in early 1975, the North Vietnamese entered South Vietnam's capital, Saigon, and defeated the South Vietnamese government. Even though America had spent $350 billion in the war, and 58,000 Americans, over 415,000 Vietnamese civilians, and approximately one million North Vietnamese soldiers had been killed, the United States had failed miserably to achieve its goals. Such a military fiasco of course had international ramifications, but it also had far-reaching domestic implications, one of which was that the American people no longer believed in themselves as they had at the dawn of the 1960s. Americans had to accept the fact that, despite their nation's vast economic and military resources, the United States had been unable to defeat a tiny, relatively undeveloped country in southeast Asia. The war had disclosed limitations and shortcomings even in "the best and the brightest" of America, who supposedly had orchestrated the nation's efforts. The same year South Vietnam fell, Senator John C. Culver of Iowa lamented "that Vietnam had taken a mighty toll on the national will of the American people."[4]

If the Vietnam War epitomizes the Americans' loss of confidence, the fate of the civil rights movement perhaps best exemplifies the vanishing of consensus (as well as further illustrating the loss of confidence). For several years, starting with

Rosa Parks's refusal on December 1, 1955, to move to the back of a bus in Montgomery, Alabama, the key organization in the movement was the Southern Christian Leadership Conference (SCLC), led by the ministers Martin Luther King, Jr., Ralph Abernathy, and Fred Shuttlesworth. The writings of King, in particular, reveal the optimistic attitudes of the SCLC leaders, the sense that African Americans could become successfully integrated into a cohesive and egalitarian American community. Even though King was, in his own words, "aware of the complexity of human motives" and cognizant of "the glaring reality of collective evil," his unwavering commitment to nonviolent resistance demonstrated his conviction in the potential for communal progress. "[O]ur aim is to persuade," King proclaimed. "We adopt the means of nonviolence because our end is a community at peace with itself. . . . We will always be willing to talk and seek fair compromise, but we are ready to suffer when necessary . . . to become witnesses to the truth as we see it."5

By the early 1960s, the Student Nonviolent Coordinating Committee (SNCC) had emerged as another key organization in the evolving civil rights movement. SNCC was constituted primarily of young people, including many college students, who initially had participated in sit-ins at lunch counters. Most SNCC members "began as believers in the liberal creed," yet they "ended up rejecting the system." As Godfrey Hodgson explains: "[SNCC leaders] started out convinced of the relevance of the Christian gospel, of the promise of America, and of the righteousness of the federal government. Fear, pain, disappointment and betrayal changed them. They became more pessimistic, more skeptical, more scoffing— and more separatist. They lost faith in the political paradise." Ironically, by the time that King made his famed *I Have A Dream* speech at the March on Washington in the summer of 1963, the dream already was fading. King spoke of "a dream deeply rooted in the American dream that one day this nation will rise up and live out the true meaning of its creed—we hold these truths to be self-evident, that all men are created equal." But Malcolm X retorted with a very different vision: "I don't see any American dream, I see an American nightmare." To him, the March on Washington should have been called "the farce on Washington" because, during the planning stages, the Kennedy Administration had clandestinely but successfully worked to de-radicalize it; partly because of Administration pressure, the March focused on the enactment of civil rights legislation rather than more incendiary issues, such as economic injustice. Then, in the two years after the March, the civil rights movement was transformed "from a protest movement into a rebellion." Starting in Watts, Los Angeles, in 1965, a series of violent race riots swept through American cities. By the summer of 1966, King's integrationist proclamations of "We Shall Overcome" were increasingly drowned out by the voices of SNCC's Stokely Carmichael and others demanding "Black Power," which connoted, for some, the exclusion of whites from the civil rights movement. More and more African Americans, instead of seeking merely equality of opportunity, now demanded an equality in substantive results that would have entailed real and extensive social and economic changes—changes that many white Americans were unwilling or unable (or both) to deliver.[6]

In short, America of the 1960s and early 1970s experienced a series of events that radically altered the citizens' perceptions, expectations, and hopes. The consensus and confidence of the 1950s had dissolved: "The real crisis of the sixties was that, for the first time since the Civil War and Reconstruction, a generation of Americans were compelled to ask not, as people asked in the Depression, how to solve their problems, but whether problems could be solved. That is why the great conflicts of the age of Kennedy and Nixon challenged the central promise of American life as it was not challenged by a shortage of jobs in the 1930s, or by war in the 1940s and Cold War in the 1950s."[7] Putting this in different words, modernism seemed to have reached an impasse. Instead of Americans coming together and healing wounds, the polarization of the 1960s became fragmentation in the 1970s. A type of rights-consciousness had emerged, echoing the civil rights movement, but now with more numerous and varied interest groups seeking to have rights vindicated and past wrongs remedied. The National Organization for Women had formed in 1966, and the women's movement stepped to the forefront of the national scene. Environmental organizations and other public interest groups materialized. Even the major league baseball players organized their own Association. In sum, American society appeared to have splintered irreparably into diverse and opposed groups (or perhaps, more precisely, many Americans had only first become aware of certain societal divisions that had long existed). These disjunctures then "dominated American life for decades after the 1960s." Even within a rights-conscious society, the existence of so many groups simultaneously demanding justice for their causes meant that chances for success, for real social change, were minimal. American social structures resisted demands for rapid (and sometimes even incremental) changes—however legitimate such demands might be, and quite often, they seemed eminently reasonable. Hope for social transformation thus typically was brief and rapidly gave way to frustration, pessimism, and cynicism.[8]

These paradigmatic changes in American society were reflected in Supreme Court cases—or more precisely, in assertions of rights before the Court as well as in public reactions, both wildly positive and wildly negative, to those Court decisions that recognized and protected such rights. Even in the early to mid-1960s, these societal changes were beginning to emerge, as illustrated by the case of *Engel v. Vitale*. During the 1950s—the period of ostensible consensus—the Board of Regents of the state of New York had recommended that local school boards have children recite a prayer each day in school in order to promote religious commitment and moral and spiritual values. The Regents recommended the use of a supposedly "nondenominational" prayer: "[a]lmighty God, we acknowledge our dependence upon Thee, and we beg Thy blessings upon us, our parents, our teachers and our Country." In 1958, when the school board in the town of New Hyde Park, Long Island, adopted this prayer for use in the classrooms, several parents decided to challenge its constitutionality. Early reactions to this litigation were ominous, as the plaintiffs received numerous hate letters. One letter, for example, stated: "[t]his looks like Jews trying to grab America as Jews grab everything they want in any nation. America is a Christian nation." Another letter declared: "[i]f you don't like our God, then go behind the Iron Curtain where you belong, Kike, Hebe, Filth." Quite evidently, cracks in the supposed American consensus were beginning to show.[9]

When the Supreme Court under Chief Justice Warren decided the case in 1962, *Engel v. Vitale* held that the daily recitation of the Regents' prayer in the public schools violated the establishment clause. The Court drew upon Protestant history to interpret the establishment clause: the Puritans, the Court recalled, had fled England for America in the seventeenth century to avoid following the government-imposed use of the *Book of Common Prayer* for the Church of England. Daily recitation of the Regents' prayer, according to the Court, resounded too closely with the official imposition of a prayer book. The Court reasoned further that the First Amendment prohibited any law that established an "official religion," even if the law did not coerce religious practices. Regardless, the Court recognized that coercion in fact existed in this particular context, although the students were allowed to remain silent or to leave the room when their classmates recited the prayer. "When the power, prestige and financial support of government is placed behind a particular religious belief, the indirect coercive pressure upon religious minorities to conform to the prevailing officially approved religion is plain." As was soon noted in the *New Republic*, *Engel* sparked a "savage controversy." Although some commentators celebrated the decision for establishing a high wall of separation between church and state, many others scorned the Court for betraying "the American way of life." For example, a *Wall Street Journal* editorial lamented the feared implications of the decision: "[p]oor kids, if they can't even sing Christmas carols." Unsurprisingly, in light of American history, *Engel* produced a spurt of proposals to add a Christian amendment to the Constitution; indeed, the 1964 platform of the Republican Party called for such an amendment.[10]

Even with the importance of *Engel,* the most significantly controversial Supreme Court cases of the 1960s and 1970s—hence the most influential for the transition from modernist to postmodernist jurisprudence—were undoubtedly *Griswold v. Connecticut* and *Roe v. Wade,* decided in 1965 and 1973, respectively. The decision in *Griswold* arose after a prolonged political and legal battle over the anti-contraception statute of Connecticut.[11] The statute already had been challenged in a declaratory judgment action before the Supreme Court four years earlier. In *Poe v. Ullman,* the Court held, by a slim five-to-four majority, that the case was not ripe for adjudication. Justice Felix Frankfurter, one of the strongest advocates of judicial restraint on the Court, wrote a plurality opinion celebrating the passive virtues. By the time that *Griswold* reached the Court, however, Frankfurter and another member of the *Poe* majority had retired. Thus, Estelle Griswold, the director of the Planned Parenthood League of Connecticut, and most of her colleagues were confident of finally achieving victory.[12]

In *Griswold,* Justice William O. Douglas wrote a rather disjointed majority opinion holding that the anti-contraception statute violated a constitutional right of privacy. Douglas seldom revised his opinions extensively, but in this case, he substantially modified his first draft in reaction to a letter from Justice William J. Brennan. Douglas's first draft relied primarily on the First Amendment right of association, but Brennan's letter, drafted largely by one of his clerks, suggested that even though Douglas did not rely on substantive due process, his reasoning "may come back to haunt us just as *Lochner* did." In the revised opinion, Douglas took two steps to deflect the likely accusation that the Warren Court was, in effect, reenacting the misguided and now condemned constitutional wanderings of the *Lochner*-era Court. First, Douglas claimed that, contrary to *Lochner,* the Court in *Griswold* would not move beyond the bounds of its institutional role: "We do not sit as a super-legislature to determine the wisdom, need, and propriety of laws that touch economic problems, business affairs, or social conditions. This law, however, operates directly on an intimate relation of husband and wife and their physician's role in one aspect of that relation."[13]

Second, Douglas significantly modified his line of reasoning. Although he began his analysis of the merits by retaining his original emphasis on the right of association, Douglas abruptly declared in the midst of this discussion that the First Amendment has a penumbra that protects privacy. He then shifted his focus from the right of association to several other guarantees in the Bill of Rights. Each of these guarantees, he reasoned, produces or emanates penumbras of privacy. Douglas then recast his initial discussion of the right of association as merely illustrative:

> [S]pecific guarantees in the Bill of Rights have penumbras, formed by emanations from those guarantees that help give them life and substance. Various guarantees create zones of privacy. The right of association contained in the penumbra of the First Amendment is one, as we have seen. The Third Amendment in its prohibition against the quartering of soldiers "in any house" in time of peace without the consent of the owner is another facet of that privacy. The Fourth Amendment explicitly affirms the "right of the people to be secure in their persons, houses, papers, and effects, against unreasonable searches and seizures." The Fifth Amendment in its Self-Incrimination Clause enables the citizen to create a zone of privacy which government may not force him to surrender to his detriment. The Ninth Amendment provides: "The enumeration in the Constitution, of certain rights, shall not be construed to deny or disparage others retained by the people."[14]

Then, after briefly discussing some specific protections of privacy, Douglas found that these various penumbras combine to generate a *zone* of privacy—a whole greater than the sum of its parts (the respective penumbras). Rather abruptly again, though, Douglas shifted his focus, now to the marital relationship, and then he quickly concluded that the anti-contraception law infringed the protected zone of privacy. "The present case, then, concerns a relationship lying within the zone of privacy created by several fundamental constitutional guarantees. And it concerns a law which, in forbidding the use of contraceptives rather than regulating their manufacture or sale, seeks to achieve its goals by means having a maximum destructive impact upon that relationship. . . . Would we allow the police to search the sacred precincts of marital bedrooms for telltale signs of the use of contraceptives? The very idea is repulsive to the notions of privacy surrounding the marriage relationship." Douglas finished the majority opinion with a broad rhetorical flourish, suggesting that the right of privacy was natural law: "[w]e deal with a right of privacy older than the Bill of Rights—older than our political parties, older than our school system."[15]

The other justices themselves blatantly revealed their considerable concern about the reasoning in *Griswold*. During oral argument and at the postargument conference, Chief Justice Warren and Justices Hugo L. Black and Byron R. White were troubled by the possible justifications for overturning the statute and the potential reach of those justifications. In particular, they wondered about the implications for abortion. Furthermore, although the vote to hold the statute unconstitutional was seven to two, only four other justices joined Justice Douglas's opinion. Justices John M. Harlan and White each concurred only in the judgment and wrote his own opinion. Even Justice Arthur J. Goldberg, who joined Douglas's opinion, nonetheless wrote a separate concurrence, and Chief Justice Warren and Justice Brennan joined Goldberg's concurrence as well as Douglas's majority opinion. Justices Black and Potter Stewart wrote dissents.[16]

As did Douglas, all the other justices wrote their concurring and dissenting opinions in the shadow of *Lochner*. Of course, the dissents of both Black and Stewart most vigorously accused the Court of overstepping its institutional constraints and of therefore acting like the *Lochner* Court. At times, Black sounded remarkably like a legal process theorist: "My point is that there is no provision of the Constitution which either expressly or impliedly vests power in this Court to sit as a supervisory agency over acts of duly constituted legislative bodies and set aside their laws because of the Court's belief that the legislative policies adopted are unreasonable, unwise, arbitrary, capricious or irrational. The adoption of such a loose, flexible, uncontrolled standard for holding laws unconstitutional, if ever it is finally achieved, will amount to a great unconstitutional shift of power to the courts which I believe and am constrained to say will be bad for the courts and worse for the country."[17] Unsurprisingly, the justices were not alone in voicing their concerns about the reasoning in *Griswold*. Legal process theorists, joined by other scholars, continued their assault on the Warren Court with two typical and related criticisms: first, the legal reasoning in the opinion was inadequate, and second, the Court had moved beyond its proper institutional role (it was *Lochner* all over again). Paul Kauper, for instance, castigated Douglas's opinion as a lame attempt to appear objective when it was truly based on substantive due process. Hyman Gross maintained that Douglas had distorted the meaning of "privacy," while Alfred Kelly criticized Goldberg's use of constitutional history, suggesting that it obscured the Court's return to "an open-ended concept of substantive due process after *Lochner*." Raoul Berger insisted that *Griswold* "exemplifies the readiness of the Justices to act as a 'super-legislature' when their own emotions are engaged." Even Thomas Emerson, who had represented Griswold before the Supreme Court, acknowledged that scholars could easily criticize the opinion.[18]

Robert Bork was perhaps the most outspoken critic of *Griswold*. Bork agreed with Herbert Wechsler that all constitutional decisions must be based on neutral principles, but Bork then argued that the *Court* cannot legitimately *choose* any fundamental values for judicial protection. Any such choice by the Court would not be neutral—the value would not be a neutral principle. To Bork, the Court should decide constitutional issues based on values chosen solely by "the Founding Fathers." The Court can identify these values through only two methods: first, by finding rights "specified" in the constitutional text or intent of the framers, or second, by recognizing rights, such as in the free speech area, that are necessary to preserve our governmental processes. Otherwise, the justices necessarily impose their own values on the rest of American society: "[w]hen the Constitution has not spoken, the Court will be able to find no scale, other than its own value preferences, upon which to weigh the respective claims." Finally, Bork concluded that *Griswold* was "a typical decision of the Warren Court": it perfectly illustrated how unprincipled judicial decision making can undermine the democratic process.[19]

Regardless of the scholarly attacks on *Griswold*, it served as the springboard for the most important and controversial Supreme Court decision of the latter twentieth century: *Roe v. Wade*. *Roe* of course challenged the constitutionality of the state of Texas's anti-abortion laws, which prohibited abortions except "for the purpose of saving the life of the mother." When the case first was argued before the Court in December 1971, two appointees of President Richard Nixon, Lewis F. Powell and William H. Rehnquist, had recently been confirmed by the Senate but had not yet joined the Court, now presided over by a previous Nixon appointee, Chief Justice Warren Burger. After this initial oral argument in *Roe*, there appeared to be a five-to-two majority in favor of striking down the Texas statute on the narrow ground that it was unconstitutionally void for vagueness. In fact, Justice Harry Blackmun circulated a draft opinion that focused on this procedural point and that did not reach the merits of the underlying substantive constitutional claim. After some uncertainty, though, the justices finally voted to have the case reargued the following term before a full Court. Significantly, Blackmun used the summer to study the issue raised by the substantive constitutional claim; he returned to his home in Minnesota—he had been an attorney for the Mayo Clinic there—and further researched abortion and anti-abortion laws.[20]

After *Roe* was reargued early the following term, Blackmun clearly had a strong majority that favored striking down the anti-abortion laws on the merits. He rewrote his opinion based on his summer research and distributed a draft to the Court on November 22, 1972. In this draft, Blackmun concluded that states should be allowed to prohibit abortions after the first trimester of a woman's pregnancy. Justice Thurgood Marshall, however, sent Blackmun a letter—a letter drafted almost entirely by Marshall's clerk, Mark Tushnet—suggesting that the focus should be on viability: states should be allowed to regulate for the health and safety of the mother after the first trimester, but states should not be allowed to prohibit abortions until viability, after the second trimester. In personal conversations with Blackmun, Justice Brennan had recommended similar changes for the draft opinion. Consequently, on December 21, 1972, Blackmun distributed a nearly final draft opinion that closely followed the suggestions of Brennan and Marshall (and Tushnet).[21]

The final decision and opinion, issued January 22, 1973, held that the Texas anti-abortion laws violated the due process clause of the Fourteenth Amendment. Once again, as in *Griswold*, the justices were thoroughly aware of the potential connections between *Roe* and *Lochner*. Indeed, to say that *Lochner* floated like a ghost in the shadows would be to understate its significance. If *Lochner* were a ghost, it was whispering "Boo!" in the ears of the justices to see if they would flinch. Blackmun therefore commenced the majority opinion by admitting "the sensitive and emotional nature of the abortion controversy." He then sought to distinguish *Roe* from *Lochner*, expressly invoking Holmes's *Lochner* dissent in his support:

> Our task, of course, is to resolve the issue by constitutional measurement, free of emotion and of predilection. We seek earnestly to do this, and, because we do, we have inquired into, and in this opinion place some emphasis upon, medical and medical-legal history and what that history reveals about man's attitudes toward the abortion procedure over the centuries. We bear in mind, too, Mr. Justice Holmes' admonition in his now-vindicated dissent in *Lochner v. New York:* "[The Constitution] is made for people of fundamentally differing views, and the accident of our finding certain opinions natural and familiar, or novel, and even shocking, ought not to conclude our judgment upon the question whether statutes embodying them conflict with the Constitution of the United States."[22]

Hence, Blackmun's method in this albeit brief and oblique introductory passage was to establish the *Roe* Court's legitimacy. Unlike the *Lochner* Court, the *Roe* Court would decide objectively—or in Blackmun's words again, the decision would be resolved "by constitutional measurement, free of emotion and of predilection." One pillar supporting this objective decision would be a thorough and correct understanding of the history surrounding abortion. Blackmun thus devoted a substantial chunk of the opinion to tracing the history of anti-abortion laws, starting as early as ancient Greek and Roman times. In so doing, Blackmun aimed to refute the claim that anti-abortion laws were firmly embedded in American traditions: to the contrary, he reasoned, anti-abortion laws were an anomaly introduced mostly in the latter part of the nineteenth century.[23] After exploring why states had begun enacting anti-abortion laws at that point, Blackmun turned to the heart of the opinion: the right of privacy.

Blackmun began by acknowledging that the "Constitution does not explicitly mention any right of privacy," but he immediately added that "[i]n a line of decisions . . . the Court has recognized that a right of personal privacy, or a guarantee of certain areas or zones of privacy, does exist under the Constitution." Of the decisions that the Court then cited, *Griswold* clearly was a crucial precedent. Blackmun then explained, most significantly, that the right of privacy included a woman's interest in choosing whether or not to have an abortion:

> This right of privacy, whether it be founded in the Fourteenth Amendment's concept of personal liberty and restrictions upon state action, as we feel it is, or, as the District Court determined, in the Ninth Amendment's reservation of rights to the people, is broad enough to encompass a woman's decision whether or not to terminate her pregnancy. The detriment that the State would impose upon the pregnant woman by denying this choice altogether is apparent. Specific and direct harm medically diagnosable even in early pregnancy may be involved. Maternity, or additional offspring, may force upon the woman a distressful life and future. Psychological harm may be imminent. Mental and physical health may be taxed by child care. There is also the distress, for all concerned, associated with the unwanted child, and there is the problem of bringing a child into a family already unable, psychologically and otherwise, to care for it. In other cases, as in this one, the additional difficulties and continuing stigma of unwed motherhood may be involved. All these are factors the woman and her responsible physician necessarily will consider in consultation.[24]

Blackmun continued, however, by adding "that this right is not unqualified and must be considered against important state interests in regulation." The remainder of the opinion therefore focused on precisely when state interests would sufficiently outweigh a woman's interest in choosing so as to justify state interference with the abortion decision. State restrictions on abortion, the Court reasoned, would be allowed only if necessary to achieve a "compelling state interest." Blackmun's subsequent analysis of the asserted state interests thus led to the Court's trimester framework. During the first trimester of a pregnancy, the state is prohibited from restricting abortions in any manner. During the second trimester, the state's interest in protecting the health of pregnant women justified state regulations of abortions but solely for the purpose of protecting pregnant women. Finally, after viability and during the third trimester, the state's "interest in protecting the potentiality of human life" is so strong as to justify state prohibitions of abortions, unless "necessary to preserve the life or health" of the pregnant woman.[25]

Unsurprisingly, with *Lochner*'s ghost whispering in their ears, all the concurring and dissenting opinions, except for Chief Justice Burger's brief concurrence, dealt with *Lochner* in one way or another. Justice Stewart's concurrence reasoned that in light of *Griswold*, *Roe* should be properly understood as a substantive due process decision even though it then would echo more closely with *Lochner*. Justice Douglas, also concurring, retorted that neither *Griswold* nor *Roe* should be characterized as relying on substantive due process. And as one might expect, the dissents of Justices Rehnquist and White dismissed Blackmun's assertion that the majority had exercised objective "constitutional measurement." They charged that *Roe* was a substantive due process decision, that the Court was exceeding its institutional bounds, and that the decision was therefore *Lochner* all over again.[26]

Of course, as with *Griswold*, *Roe* sparked a flurry of scholarly criticism. After the outburst of *Griswold* critiques, the criticisms of *Roe* were rather predictable, though they were infused with a new energy that reflected the passions generated on all sides by the abortion issue. One of the most important attacks came from one of Earl Warren's former clerks, John Hart Ely, who at the time was a Yale Law School professor. Apart from his elegant and powerful writing style, the force of Ely's critique derived from his declaration that most Warren Court decisions, including *Brown v. Board of Education*, were defensible from a legal process perspective (as I discussed at the end of chapter 4). Ely, in other words, was not attacking every activist decision coming down from either the Warren or Burger Courts, but rather was designating *Roe* for atypical condemnation. Ely articulated five criticisms of *Roe* that many other commentators later would repeat or elaborate. First, he declared that the Constitution "simply says nothing, clear or fuzzy, about abortion." Second, he asserted that even if *Griswold* correctly had recognized a constitutional right of privacy, such a right would not encompass a woman's interest in choosing whether or not to have an abortion. Privacy might include keeping the government out of marital bedrooms, as in *Griswold*, but that was a far cry from procuring an abortion. Third, Ely maintained that the *Roe* Court had exceeded its institutional limitations by balancing interests in a legislative manner. Fourth, he argued that even though many controversial Supreme Court decisions could be defended pursuant to representation-reinforcement theory (a term he only coined subsequently), *Roe* could not be similarly justified. "Compared with men," Ely commented, "very few women sit in our legislatures, a fact I believe should bear some relevance . . . to the appropriate standard of review for legislation that favors men over women. But *no* fetuses sit in our legislatures. Of course they have their champions, but so have women." Thus, when "[c]ompared with men, women may constitute" a discrete and insular minority deserving special judicial protection, but when "compared with the unborn, they do not." Fifth (last but certainly not least), Ely proclaimed that the *Roe* Court had followed "the philosophy of *Lochner*." In fact, Ely argued that *Roe* and *Lochner* were "twins to be sure," but of the two, "*Roe* may turn out to be the more dangerous precedent."[27]

Many other prominent scholars attacked *Roe*. Archibald Cox went so far as to vindicate natural law but nonetheless concluded that no "precept of sufficient abstractness [could] lift the [*Roe*] ruling above the level of a political judgment." And as with *Griswold,* one of the most outspoken critics of *Roe* was Robert Bork. He reiterated the common criticisms—the *Roe* Court had exceeded its institutional limitations by acting like a legislature, and by doing so, the Court had repeated the sins of the *Lochner* Court—but Bork distinguished himself with his mordancy. Writing in 1990, he sneered: "The discovery this late in our history that the question [of abortion] was not one for democratic decision but one of constitutional law was so implausible that it certainly deserved a fifty-one-page explanation. Unfortunately, in the entire [*Roe*] opinion there is not one line of explanation, not one sentence that qualifies as legal argument. Nor has the Court in the sixteen years since ever provided the explanation lacking in 1973. It is unlikely that it ever will, because the right to abort, whatever one thinks of it, is not to be found in the Constitution."[28]

Despite the numerous and harsh critics, *Roe* (and *Griswold*) did not lack for defenders. Yet, even those who praised the result in *Roe*—a constitutionally protected right to choose whether or not to have an abortion—often criticized the majority opinion. For example, Sylvia Law suggested that a woman's interest in choosing should have been protected as a matter of sexual equality rather than as a matter of privacy. Indeed, because American legal thought already had plunged into fourth-stage (late crisis) modernism, there was no shortage of diverse and imaginative proposed defenses of the right to choose an abortion, the right to privacy, and other controversial constitutional (or would-be constitutional) rights. Simultaneously, though, exactly because this was fourth-stage modernism, few scholars convinced any others to follow their respective proposals, and many scholars viewed the proposed theories of others as patently inadequate.[29]

Legal thought thus swirled into a maelstrom of despair. The 1950s jurisprudential stalwart, legal process, already had lost its hegemonic hold on the legal academy, but now it seemed to be losing its grasp altogether. Legal process theorists struggled along with a multitude of other scholars as they all desperately tried just to hang onto their modernist goals and methods. Legal modernism demanded that judicial decision making—including constitutional adjudication—be based on some objective foundation. Yet, despite yeoman (sometimes even heroic) efforts for over one hundred years—despite sundry attempts at rationalism, empiricism, and transcendentalism—legal theorists were unable to discover any such ground for the rule of law. Supreme Court decisions such as *Brown, Griswold,* and *Roe* highlighted this failure and magnified the scholarly desperation. While these landmark decisions apparently could not be defended successfully within the parameters of modernist legal thought, many scholars nonetheless viewed the cases as substantively right—almost too right to dispute.

Ultimately, these cases forced modernism to confront the possibility of its own demise because its self-imposed demands now seemed plainly unachievable. As early as 1966, Archibald Cox's *Foreword* to the *Harvard Law Review* epitomized the dilemma that many Warren Court decisions had engendered for legal scholars. Cox unabashedly praised "the magnificent accomplishments of the Warren Court," yet simultaneously, he lamented that "when all this is said, ability to rationalize a constitutional judgment in terms of principles referable to accepted sources of law is an essential, major element of constitutional adjudication." By the late 1970s, after *Roe,* some scholars even expressly renounced their modernist quest for foundations. Arthur Allen Leff recognized that in premodernism, normative questions supposedly were resolved religiously: "God's will is binding because it is His will that it be." But at the end of modernism, normative values ultimately seemed ungrounded, despite the innumerable efforts to discover foundations: "[u]nder what other circumstances can the unexamined will of anyone else [than God] withstand the cosmic 'says who' and come out similarly dispositive? *There are no such circumstances.*" As Roberto Unger quipped, law professors seemed to be "a priesthood that had lost their faith and kept their jobs."[30]

As scholars searched futilely for some theory that could justify decisions such as *Brown, Griswold,* and *Roe* without sacrificing an objective rule of law, two opposed general modernist approaches to the specific problem of constitutional interpretation had emerged by the late 1970s: interpretivism and noninterpretivism. Interpretivists (sometimes called originalists) argued that only the constitutional text and the intent of the framers could legitimately ground constitutional decisions; the Court could strike a legislative act as unconstitutional only if it is inconsistent with "norms that are stated or clearly implicit in the written Constitution." Noninterpretivists (sometimes called nonoriginalists), on the other hand, argued that the text and the intent of the framers are hopelessly ambiguous and incomplete and must therefore be supplemented by some other source or sources. Since these theoretical debates arose during the late crisis of fourth-stage legal modernism, different noninterpretivist theorists proffered wildly diverse sources of meaning and value, including tradition, societal consensus, and even natural law. According to a natural law proponent, for example, the Court could hold a legislative act unconstitutional if the act were inconsistent with natural rights or justice. Interpretivists responded by arguing that noninterpretivism merely provides a pretext for bypassing the Constitution. Constitutional objectivity could come only from the text and the intent of the framers: if we go beyond those sources, constitutional adjudication lacks standards and hence cannot be critically evaluated. Noninterpretivists replied that their respective approaches were at least as objective as interpretivism: from their vantage, their favored sources of meaning and value—tradition, societal consensus, or whatever—provided a firm foundation for decision.[31]

The problem for both interpretivists and noninterpretivists, as John Hart Ely suggested, was ethical relativism, which had spawned the pluralistic political theory so widely accepted during the post–World War II era. Ethical relativism undermined any vision of judicial review grounded on a supposedly objective source, whether it be the written text, natural law, or anything else. Ely persuasively argued that interpretivism as well as the most commonly accepted forms of noninterpretivism are all indeterminate: they fail to satisfy their self-imposed mission of providing an objective source to ground judicial review. Ely's pointed criticism of natural law seemed to apply equally to other noninterpretivist as well as interpretivist approaches: "The advantage of [natural law] is that you can invoke it to support anything you want. The disadvantage is that everybody understands that." Interpretivism and noninterpretivism, in Ely's hands, always sank into a maelstrom of relativistic subjectivity: the Supreme Court justices inevitably seemed to impose their personal values on society. As discussed at the end of chapter 4, Ely of course offered his own theory of representation reinforcement as an objective method for resolving constitutional disputes, but his critics immediately responded that this approach was no more determinate than any of the others.[32]

At this point, facing the apparent indeterminacy of all theories, some constitutional scholars, such as Thomas C. Grey and Paul Brest, swung around and took a different tack. They began to argue that the initial distinction between interpretivism and noninterpretivism may have been misleading; even supposed noninterpretivists, after all, always claimed to be interpreting the Constitution. Perhaps, the argument continued, constitutional adjudication—indeed, all other adjudication as well—is *always* a matter of interpretation. And if adjudication is always an interpretive enterprise, then the most promising path for constitutional and other legal theorists was to investigate the process of interpretation itself.[33]

Once legal theorists began to take this "interpretive turn" in the 1980s, at least three factors influenced them to seek ideas and inspiration extensively from writers outside the legal academy. First, fourth-stage modernist legal scholars already had set a recent precedent of sorts in legal scholarship by relying on nonlegal thinkers such as the philosopher John Rawls and the economist Ronald Coase (and of course, decades earlier, the American legal realists had built on the work of empirical social scientists). During the fourth stage, the critical legal studies scholars were especially influential in this regard because of their heavy use of European continental thinkers. Furthermore, already by the mid-1970s, James Boyd White, a professor of law and English at the University of Michigan, had begun to focus on the relations between law and literature. To White, the linguistic or interpretive practices of law, no less so than those of literature, help constitute our culture and community.[34]

Second, during the late 1960s and 1970s, a severe job shortage developed in the humanities and social sciences. Peter Novick describes the situation in history: "[a]t the 1970 meeting of the American Historical Association there were 2,481 applicants for 188 listed positions, and competition was so fierce that security measures had to be introduced to keep those seeking jobs from destroying invitations to interviews addressed to their competitors." Yet, during those same years of the 1960s and 1970s, law schools were booming, with many faculties expanding. Numerous individuals consequently chose to become law professors even though they were inclined more toward the humanities and social sciences. When given the opportunity or excuse, then, such law professors readily turned to nonlegal resources.[35]

Third, as the intellectual culture of postmodernism spread, disciplinary boundaries started to crumble in many American academic fields. Legal thought was just one of them. A critical early event in the transformation of the American academy came in 1966, when Johns Hopkins University hosted a conference entitled "The Languages of Criticism and the Sciences of Man." "This intergenerational, international, and interdisciplinary conference, which eventually included one thousand humanists and social scientists in a two-year series of follow-up colloquia and seminars, established a broad interdisciplinary base for the introduction of French theory into the American academy." While initially this conference influenced mainly literary studies, anthropology, and, to a lesser extent, history, its effects rippled outward, combining with other factors. By 1980, the interpretive cultural anthropologist Clifford Geertz, who himself strongly influenced jurisprudence, commented about disciplinary boundaries in general: "what we are seeing is not just another redrawing of the cultural map—the moving of a few disputed borders, the marking of some picturesque mountain lakes—but an alteration of the principles of mapping. Something is happening to the way we think about the way we think."[36]

Perhaps no factor was more significant to the breakdown of disciplinary fences than the widespread dissemination of Thomas Kuhn's book *The Structure of Scientific Revolutions,* published initially in 1962 and republished in 1970. For at least a century of university life in America, the natural sciences had provided the ideal of objectivity, of modernist foundationalism—an ideal to which nearly all disciplines aspired. Kuhn's importance thus stemmed from his apparent attack on that ideal, insofar as he challenged a traditional view of natural science. According to the traditional view, science is objective and mechanistic, and progresses in a linear fashion: scientists supposedly progress in their knowledge of nature as they develop theories based on the neutral observation of brute objective data. Kuhn persuasively repudiated this traditional view. Instead, he argued that scientists understand or interpret the world in accordance with or through a "paradigm"—a broad vision or map of reality, a worldview, accepted by a community of scientists. The scientific community's paradigm shapes the questions that scientists find interesting and appropriate for research, and even more important, the paradigm shapes the scientists' perceptions of data. A paradigm, Kuhn asserted, was a "prerequisite to perception itself."[37]

Kuhn's notion of revolutionary science underscored the pervasive influence of an accepted or dominant paradigm. Scientific communities, according to Kuhn, are occasionally rocked by revolutions where one dominant paradigm is replaced by another. A prototypical example of a scientific revolution was the transition from the Aristotelian-Ptolemaic geocentric theory of the universe to the Copernican heliocentric theory. Such a paradigmatic revolution is indeed momentous: "Led by a new paradigm, scientists adopt new instruments and look in new places. Even more important, during revolutions scientists see new and different things when looking with familiar instruments in places they have looked before. It is rather as if the professional community had been suddenly transported to another planet where familiar objects are seen in a different light and are joined by unfamiliar ones as well." Kuhn therefore suggested that science progresses by becoming more complex and specialized as it moves from one paradigm to another, but contrary to the traditional view, science does not necessarily move closer and closer to some objective truth.[38]

Despite the conclusions of some readers, Kuhn did not intend to show that science is impossible, but rather to explain exactly the opposite: how science is possible. He sought to explain how individuals successfully learn to operate or to do science within a scientific community. Regardless of Kuhn's purposes, his ideas gradually seemed to free scholars in multifarious disciplines from aspiring toward a traditional and modernist view of scientific objectivity. Novick observed that "[t]he work of Thomas Kuhn was inescapable in practically every realm." Scholars began to draw on an ever-widening variety of sources and disciplines as they reconceptualized the goals and methods of research in their respective though now more amorphous fields. Many such scholars, of course, tended to reiterate Kuhn's concept of the paradigm as they struggled to articulate more postmodern and interpretivist notions of understanding and knowledge. Nowhere, though, was Kuhn's influence more evident than in jurisprudence, where discussions of paradigms and revolutionary transformations became commonplace. In an influential early article on legal hermeneutics, for example, Robert M. Cover cited Kuhn and described "legal tradition [as] part and parcel of a complex normative world [that helps] establish the paradigms for behavior." Similarly, in a 1986 article, Suzanna Sherry argued for "a paradigm shift in moral, political, and constitutional theory." In fact, Laura Kalman reports that, as of 1995, Kuhn's *Structure of Scientific Revolutions* had been cited in 521 law review pieces (and even in five federal cases).[39]

Consequently, like scholars in many other fields, legal theorists began to roam more freely beyond their disciplinary borders. Those jurisprudents who embarked on the interpretive turn in the 1980s thus quickly discovered writers from other disciplines who had previously developed sophisticated approaches to interpretation. Besides Kuhn, Stanley Fish (a literary critic), Richard Rorty (an American philosopher), and Hans-Georg Gadamer (a German philosopher, discussed in chapter 2) were among those especially influential in jurisprudential circles. Under the influence of such thinkers, some constitutional theorists finally stopped asking the inveterate modernist question: What foundations can objectively constrain or ground constitutional interpretation and adjudication? Instead, these constitutional scholars began asking a *postmodern* question: How does (constitutional) interpretation occur?[40]

Stanley Fish provides a fitting illustration of the turn toward postmodern interpretivism in jurisprudence. In his early work in English literary criticism and as a Milton scholar, Fish had been renowned as following reader-response theory, which emphasized the reader's experience of a text as determining the textual meaning. In his later writings, however, Fish significantly modified his approach to interpretation. Indeed, the later Fish articulated an approach that resonated closely with Gadamer's philosophical hermeneutics. This later and more postmodern interpretivist Fish started to attract the attention of jurisprudents in the early 1980s. Eventually, in a prototypical postmodern move, Fish himself became so embroiled in the jurisprudential disputes concerning legal interpretation that he literally crossed disciplines, going from literary criticism to legal scholarship; he ultimately became a professor of law as well as of English at Duke University.[41]

As Fish shifted to jurisprudential studies, he imported a complex and intellectually polished approach to interpretation, including legal interpretation. For years, modernist constitutional scholars had been stuck on the horns of an *either/or* dilemma: *either* we have objectivity, *or* we have unconstrained subjectivity. Modernist notions of judicial review demanded that constitutional interpretation be based on some firm foundation—such as a supposedly objective constitutional text or the framers' intentions—yet every proposed foundational theory appeared to degenerate into a subjective relativism that left constitutional interpretation apparently unconstrained, merely a matter of whimsical personal preferences. Fish claimed to resolve this dilemma by, in effect, eliminating both of its horns. According to Fish, objectivity is impossible because we always are already interpreting. Neither the text, the author's (or the framers') intentions, nor anything else is accessible as brute data or, in other words, as an uninterpreted source of meaning. "[T]here is no such thing as literal meaning, if by literal meaning one means a meaning that is perspicuous no matter what the context and no matter what is in the speaker's or hearer's mind, a meaning that because it is prior to interpretation can serve as a constraint on interpretation."[42]

Simultaneously, though, Fish asserted that the individual interpreter or reader is never unconstrained—never free merely to impose her personally preferred meanings on the text. Rather, the interpreter always is limited by the practices of her interpretive community, which impart "assumed distinctions, categories of understanding, and stipulations of relevance and irrelevance." Thus, for the same reason that objectivity is impossible—because we always are already interpreting—unconstrained subjectivity likewise is impossible. No interpreter ever stands prior to or outside of interpretive practices, which always and necessarily limit one's interpretation of any text, including for example the Constitution. As Fish stated, "there has never been nor ever will be anyone who could survey interpretive possibilities from a vantage point that was not itself already interpretive."[43]

For Fish, then, the concepts of an interpretive community and practice fulfill the same hermeneutic functions as Gadamer's notions of tradition and prejudices as well as Kuhn's notions of a scientific community and paradigms. Using Fish's terms, an interpretive community shapes the practices of its members, and those practices "at once enable and limit the operations" of interpretation and perception. Indeed, in a thought to which both Gadamer and Kuhn surely would assent, Fish declared that "already-in-place interpretive constructs are a condition of consciousness." By belonging to and participating in an interpretive community—which everyone always does—one necessarily internalizes the "'know how' or knowledge of 'the ropes'" of that community's practices, which provide "a sense of relevancies, obligation, directions for action, criteria, etc." Fish then specifically applied his conception of interpretation to judicial decision making: "The very ability to formulate a [judicial] decision in terms that would be recognizably legal depends on one's having internalized the norms, categorical distinctions, and evidentiary criteria that make up one's understanding of what the law is. That understanding is developed in the course of an educational experience whose materials are the unfolding succession of cases, holdings, dissents, legislative actions, etc., that are the stuff of law school instruction and of the later instruction one receives in a clerkship or as a junior associate."[44]

Quite clearly, Fish's notion of interpretation, legal or otherwise, is thoroughly postmodern. He repudiated foundationalism, but unlike a modernist, he did not then see himself relegated to nihilism or relativism. Rather, by invoking his enriched notion of interpretive practices, Fish insisted that textual meaning always is determinate, albeit in an odd manner. A text, according to Fish, can have a plurality of meanings only if we take the text out of context, only if we imagine the text in the abstract. But, as Fish reminds us repeatedly, we always are situated in a context: we never interpret a text in the abstract or in some never-never land. Whenever we turn to a text, we already have certain purposes in mind, certain presuppositions, certain values, and so on. And situated in a concrete context within a specific interpretive community, the interpreter always understands a particular meaning in a text. Yet, Fish added, that meaning can change as the context changes. "Paradoxically," Fish explained, words cannot mean anything one likes, "but . . . they always and only mean one thing, although that one thing is not always the same."[45]

Finally, Fish often closed his writings with an inimitable postmodern flourish by proclaiming that his insights into interpretation are acutely irrelevant. From Fish's standpoint, theoretical discussions of an interpretive practice cannot directly modify that practice; in other words, an awareness of the workings of an interpretive practice cannot liberate us from the practice itself. We always remain embedded within the interpretive constraints of the practice, regardless of our clever theories and sagacious perceptions. Liberation or freedom is impossible because we always must be limited by our "preconceptions, biases, or personal preferences"; that is the nature of our being-in-the-world. This interpretive truth, according to Fish, is as valid for the practices of lawyers and judges as for other practices. Thus, "judging or doing judging is one thing," Fish concluded, "and giving accounts or theories of judging is another."[46]

In sum, Fish brought postmodern theorizing into jurisprudence in a manner that resonated closely with the continental philosophy of Gadamer, even though Fish rarely even cited him. Many other legal thinkers walked (or swam) with Fish along this same path, though they often more explicitly invoked the ideas of Gadamer, Jacques Derrida, Michel Foucault, Jacques Lacan, and other postmodern European thinkers. Meanwhile, other jurisprudents likewise turned in a postmodern direction, but they chose different paths to travel. A few of these other jurisprudents approached postmodernism from the perspective of analytical philosophy, often drawing inspiration from thinkers such as Ludwig Wittgenstein and Willard van Orman Quine. Dennis Patterson, for one, argued that Quine had repudiated the modernist correspondence theory of truth. According to the correspondence theory, a proposition or belief is true if it accurately reflects or corresponds with an independent and objective reality. According to Patterson, "Quine's point—a postmodernist one—is that no sense can be made of the idea of something making our beliefs true other than other beliefs." Thus, turning away from modernist conceptions of truth, Patterson attempted to build on Wittgensteinian philosophy to develop a postmodern jurisprudence—a "new conception of legal justification." Patterson elaborated: "Instead of producing theories of truth and meaning, philosophy now takes as its task the perspicuous description of linguistic practices. In law, this means describing legal practices of justification [or] "forms of argument." Nothing—not the word, not morality, not economy—makes a proposition of law true. We use forms of legal argument (such as arguments from text, history, structure and doctrine) to justify our assertion of the truth of legal propositions. The forms of argument are the grammar of legal justification. They are the way in which a proposition of law is shown to be true."[47] The theorizing of such philosophically inspired jurisprudents mixed with other factors in the burgeoning production of postmodern legal scholarship in the 1980s and 1990s. For instance, the introduction in the 1970s and further development in the 1980s and 1990s of computer-assisted legal research has transformed legal culture, including scholarship as well as legal and judicial practice. Richard Delgado and Jean Stefancic have noted that the traditional methods of organizing published judicial decisions and law libraries, such as the West Publishing Company's key number and Digest system, tend to structure and constrain legal research. These organizational "devices function like DNA; they enable the current system to replicate itself endlessly, easily, and painlessly. Their categories mirror precedent and existing law; they both facilitate traditional legal thought and constrain novel approaches to the law." Computer-assisted legal research, however, has begun to break the chains of the traditional organizational technologies. Attorneys today are less likely to begin their research by identifying a pre-existing West key number and then following that number to the already catalogued cases in the Digests. Instead, researchers can initiate searches for a wide variety of legal materials, cases or otherwise, by choosing to combine words and phrases in personally generated Boolean-type inquiries (which combine search terms with connectors such as "and," "or," and "not"). As Delgado and Stefancic recognize, "[f]ree text searching allows the searcher a wider range of choice in subject searching, freeing him or her from former reliance on fixed subject headings." The West key number system thus should no longer directly limit computer literate researchers (who still might be constrained by a variety of other factors, such as limited imagination).[48]

Yet, in prototypical postmodern fashion, the technology of computer-assisted research seems paradoxically to yield inconsistent effects—simultaneously generating both fragmentation and synthesis. On the one hand, in conjunction with the seemingly unlimited supply of published cases, computer-assisted research has in a sense fragmented or shattered legal rules and principles. A decade ago, West already had published approximately two and a half million cases and was publishing around sixty thousand new cases each year. Assuming arguendo that, earlier in the twentieth century, the doctrine of *stare decisis* had constrained legal and judicial practice to an appreciable degree (which is of course disputable), the doctrine nonetheless would seem no longer to be able to fulfill this function. Too many cases are too readily accessible through computer-assisted research. At this point, it might be reasonable to assume that a competent attorney sitting in front of a computer would be capable of finding in a matter of minutes a precedent to support just about any desired proposition of law. Moreover, the existence of hyperlinks within legal databases facilitates moving rapidly from one source to another to another to another, ad infinitum. All it takes is a click of the mouse. A researcher now can maneuver across a database, jumping from position to position, flitting from case to case until she finds a decision satisfactorily supporting her point of view. Even a Supreme Court decision might now seem to have roots no deeper than the screen of your computer monitor. "Hypertext [makes] assumptions of centrality fundamentally problematic," writes George P. Landow. "In fact, hypertext thrives on marginality. In hypertext, any linked text can serve as annotation, commentary, or appended text; and each linked text exists as the *other* text, which leads to a conception (and experience) of text as Other."[49]

On the other hand, computer-assisted research can perform a synthetic function for scholars, attorneys, and judges. With literally millions of cases ready to hand, the researcher needs some type of filtering tool to avoid being overwhelmed with unmanageable data. While the West key number system could fulfill this need, computer-assisted research provides a more flexible and expandable technology that better fits the ever-increasing volumes of cases. In computer terminology, the graphical user interface (GUI) of current legal research software programs allows researchers to identify and grasp useful quanta of information despite the seemingly unlimited data floating in the infosphere. The GUI is a "half unveiling and half disappearing act," according to Steven Johnson in *Interface Culture*. "It makes information sensible to you by keeping most of it from view—for the simple reason that 'most of it' is far too multitudinous to imagine in a single thought." In sum, computer-assisted research might fragment legal doctrine by providing access to a boundless supply of cases, but the GUI is simultaneously a symbolic form "designed precisely . . . to battle fragmentation and overload with synthesis and sense-making."[50]

Perhaps even more important than computer-assisted research, though, the broad changes that rippled through American society in the 1960s and early 1970s—the losses of confidence and consensus—were eventually manifested as strongly in the legal academy as in the rest of the nation. These losses are evident today in the diverse and uncertain attitudes that currently prevail in the legal academy regarding the effectiveness of law to change and control society. For example, most scholars for years assumed that the decision in *Brown v. Board of Education* was a landmark that significantly aided the civil rights movement. Recently, though, some scholars have argued to the contrary, that *Brown* actually impeded the movement by inflaming Southern white resistance to social and political change. Still other scholars have replied that while *Brown* initially inflamed resistance and thus slowed the movement, the long-term effect of *Brown* was positive. According to this view, the media coverage of the Southern white resistance—particularly the atrocities inflicted on peaceful civil rights protestors—eventually generated widespread political support for change, leading to the Civil Rights Act of 1964 and similar legislation that was enacted as part of the Great Society program. Still other commentators insist that the Great Society legislation has failed miserably to effect real and lasting change in America. With such sharp disagreement over *Brown,* one of the most important decisions in Supreme Court history, it is unsurprising that Richard Posner recently observed that lawyers (including law professors) seem to have lost confidence in their own abilities to ameliorate even distinctly legal problems. "Some of the supposed triumphs of the 1930s through 1950s have been revalued and no longer seem so triumphant; this is true, for example, of the Federal Rules of Civil Procedure and of the Administrative Procedure Act (and of the trial and administrative processes generally)." Likewise, Posner sees that consensus has given way to fragmentation: "[t]he spectrum of political opinion in law schools, which in 1960 occupied a narrow band between mild liberalism and mild conservatism, today runs from Marxism, feminism, and left-wing nihilism and anarchism on the left to economic and political libertarianism and Christian fundamentalism on the right." Even those legal scholars deemed somewhat centrist in their political beliefs often appear to be ideologically isolated from their colleagues.[51]

To a great extent, the breakdown of consensus among law professors resulted from the transformation of the demographic makeup of the legal academy. Because of the successes of the civil rights and women's movements, starting in the 1960s and 1970s (however limited those successes might in fact be), an increasing number of women and persons of color entered not only the legal profession but the legal professoriate during the latter twentieth century. This diversification of the legal academy was spurred greatly by the boomtown atmosphere prevalent in many law schools during the 1960s and 1970s. For example, in 1973–1974, following in the wake of Watergate, "[o]ver 135,000 Law School Admission Tests were administered . . . nearly 14,000 more than the previous year and almost twice as many as those given in any year of the 1960s. The more than 125,000 enrolled law students in 1976 paid more than $275 million in tuition." With so many students and so much tuition flowing in, many law faculties expanded at a frenzied pace. Between 1967 and 1975, for example, "the number of tenure track law teachers at the nation's accredited law schools increased by 80 percent." During this halcyon era, law schools could hire members of previously excluded outgroups—primarily women and racial minorities—without threatening the security of white males. Indeed, as their faculties frantically expanded, the law schools could continue to hire substantial numbers of white males even as outgroup members were simultaneously joining the faculties. To illustrate, in 1960, only 11 of the 1,645 tenure track law faculty were women—that is, just over half of 1 percent of the full-time law professors—while by 1979, the number of women had increased to 516, which constituted 10.5 percent of a total that had risen to almost 5,000.[52]

The infusion of appreciable numbers of women and people of color to law faculties led to the emergence of a type of "outsider jurisprudence." The writings of outgroup or minority scholars often revealed a vision of the legal system that differed radically from that of the legal process and other mainstream scholars. The legal system, from the perspective of some outgroup scholars, did not deal equally with different societal groups. Rather, the manipulation of the rule of law itself was a means for propagating social, economic, and political inequities. In situations where legal process scholars saw the neutral and objective application of legal rules—treating like cases alike—some women and minority writers instead saw the subjugation of outgroups. In other words, mainstream and outgroup scholars both seemed to observe the same social and legal events, but each group saw and experienced them in strikingly different ways. Mainstream modernist scholars, when confronted with a significant legal event such as the decision in *Brown v. Board of Education,* typically believed that the event embodied an essential truth about the law, a truth with a stable and fixed core. Outgroup scholars, when confronted with the same event, were more likely to recognize the existence of multiple truths. For instance, an African-American constitutional scholar might recognize more readily than a white scholar that the Constitution is a tool of both oppression and liberation: the Constitution appeared to legitimate slavery and Jim

Crow as legal institutions, yet supported the civil rights movement and desegregation. Thus, a person who lives (or perhaps empathizes with) the truths of a minority or an outgroup stands poised to recognize that the modernist's claimed essential or core truth is actually the accepted truth of a dominant cultural majority.[53]

For this reason, the emergence of outsider jurisprudence fueled the development of postmodern legal thought. Outgroup jurisprudents have urged other scholars, in effect, to hear a "different voice," to acknowledge the legitimacy of an unusual or alternative view of the legal system. Indeed, when one recognizes the emergence of *multiple* different voices—including at least feminist, critical race, and more recently, gay and lesbian theorists—then modernist claims to identify essential truths and to ground knowledge on firm foundations become highly problematic. The multiple voices of outsider jurisprudents uncover multiple truths where before but one truth was evident. Outgroup scholars consequently have helped generate and justify the anti-foundationalism and anti-essentialism characteristic of postmodernism. In a sense, outgroup legal scholars repeatedly illustrate the Derridean play of signifiers by disclosing that seemingly stable modernist meanings are unstable and shifting. In the words of the critical race and feminist scholar Patricia J. Williams, "it really is possible to see things—even the most concrete things—simultaneously yet differently."[54]

Unsurprisingly, then, some outsider scholarship can fairly be characterized as prototypical postmodernism. For example, scholars such as Richard Delgado and Derrick Bell in critical race theory and William Eskridge and Marc A. Fajer in gay and lesbian studies often use narratives or storytelling instead of analytical methods in their scholarship. Such storytelling ranges from the often mystical tales of Bell to intense first-person accounts of an author's own experiences, such as Eskridge's description of his denial of tenure because of his sexual preference. Whatever the particular style, all forms of storytelling—though especially a *Rashomon*-like telling of multiple stories—not only resonate with postmodern anti-foundationalism but also suggest that a currently accepted truth is, perhaps, no more than a story itself. To be sure, if enough people accept a certain story, then it can become so pervasive that most do not recognize it as a story per se; instead, they see it as objective truth—as politically and culturally neutral. But outsider narratives aim to disclose such truths as cultural and therefore contingent norms. In his article *Gaylegal Narratives,* Eskridge argues that traditional modernist legal scholarship is itself a form of storytelling:

> Legal scholarship is inevitably narrative. Traditional scholarship tells stories about the parties to a lawsuit and their experiences in appellate court; the way in which judicial opinions interrelate with one another; the creation and implementation of statutes; the tug-of-war among interest groups, administrators, and legislators accompanying agency adjudications and rulemaking; the history of various legal institutions and their respective leaders; and the history of legal

scholarship itself. The stories told in traditional scholarship focus on issues important to legal elites and are told from their point of view, which is often presented as the consensus or neutral perspective. Since these elites have been overwhelmingly white, male, affluent, and ostensibly heterosexual, one might wonder whether their stories really reflect social consensus or neutral values.[55]

Despite the close and apparent ties between outsider jurisprudence and postmodern scholarship, many writers also have recognized a tension between the two. Early outgroup scholars—especially feminists (who came first) and, to a lesser extent, critical race theorists—were modernists rather than postmodernists. Unsurprisingly, then, leading feminists such as Martha Minow have worried "that postmodernism risks a relativism that conflicts with feminist commitments to political engagement, and with a continuing ability to name, authoritatively, and to fight, effectively, what is oppressive." A quick summary of the recent history of feminist jurisprudence underscores this potential tension between feminism and postmodernism. Feminist jurisprudence can be understood as having developed through four overlapping and rapidly evolving stages or types: liberal, cultural, radical, and postmodern. First, liberal feminists such as Sylvia Law and Wendy Williams argued that, before the law, women should be treated the same as men. To a great extent, these liberal feminists elaborated legal process theory in the particular area of gender equality. They asserted that when women and men were similarly situated, they should be treated equally—that is, treat like cases alike. Second, cultural or different voice feminists such as Robin West largely explored the ramifications for jurisprudence of Carol Gilligan's influential book *In a Different Voice*. Gilligan, a psychologist, had argued that women and men tend to develop distinctive sets of ethical values, perhaps because of cultural influences. Most basically, the feminine ethic emphasizes caring for others, while the masculine ethic stresses following abstract rules. Gilligan showed further that the feminine ethic of care largely had been ignored in earlier psychological theories of ethical development, and as a corrective remedy, she suggested that the feminine ethic should be not only recognized but also embraced. Gilligan, that is, sought to celebrate difference (or a different voice). Following Gilligan's cue, cultural feminist jurisprudents argued that the legal system favored and manifested the masculine ethic, and that therefore a jurisprudential application of the feminine ethic of care would transform and indeed improve American law. Third, radical feminists, most prominently Catharine A. MacKinnon, argued that gender relations always are about power—about men dominating and subjugating women. To some extent, radical feminist theory overlapped with critical legal studies insofar as both groups drew from Marxist and other European critical social theories.[56]

Most important, in terms of the tension between modernist and postmodernist positions, these first three types of feminists—liberal, cultural, and radical—often seemed to reduce all women to WOMAN: defined (albeit sometimes only implicitly) by a preconceived and limited set of abstract characteristics, perspectives, or interests. According to cultural feminists, for example, all women tended to interact with others in certain ways that manifested an ethic of care. From such a modernist perspective, all women seemed to share a universal essence—an essence that outgroup feminists such as Angela P. Harris subsequently challenged as looking suspiciously white, heterosexual, and upper middle class. Harris argued that because of such "gender essentialism," even when the existence of women of color, lesbians, and poor women was recognized in the early feminist jurisprudence, such women would at most be discussed only as they differed from a norm or standard derived from the white, heterosexual, and upper-middle-class WOMAN.[57]

Furthermore, the early feminists as well as the early critical race scholars were unabashedly normative: they explicitly recommended various means for transforming the American legal system so as to improve the lives of women and people of color. For instance, MacKinnon was renowned for championing the enactment of legal restrictions on pornography, while in a highly influential 1987 article, Charles R. Lawrence advocated that the Supreme Court change its equal protection doctrine based on his sophisticated depiction of racism, which accounted for unconscious as well as conscious biases. This type of normative scholarship—a type of glorified advocacy—contrasted sharply with the essays issuing from postmodern legal theorists, who decried such blatant displays of normativeness, at least when they appeared in the writings of legal process and other mainstream scholars. From the postmodern perspective, the overt advocacy, which marked such normative legal scholarship, misleadingly suggested that the reader (as well as the writer) was an autonomous and independent individual who could choose to change the legal system and could successfully implement any such desired changes—as if it were that easy. As these postmodern theorists repudiated such manifestations of modernist individualism, they in turn drew the ire of many outgroup scholars, who effectively posed the following question to postmodernists: "Why do you question the ability of individuals to choose and pursue normative goals and values through the legal system just when historically oppressed and excluded subjects have gained sufficient social power and recognition so that they too might pursue their own goals and values?" Indeed, some outgroup scholars excoriated postmodern theory as little more than an ideology that suited the needs of "white, privileged men of the industrialized West."[58]

Nonetheless, in more recent years, an increasing number of outgroup jurisprudents—including feminist, critical race, and gay and lesbian theorists—have begun to explore the connections between and possible integrations of outgroup and postmodern themes. As already suggested, outgroup scholars partly can be understood as prototypical postmodernists insofar as they repeatedly demonstrate the existence of multiple truths and therefore undermine modernist claims to foundationalism and essentialism. Even further, though, some outgroup scholars have explicitly embraced postmodernism. These postmodern outgroup scholars are developing approaches that incorporate the critical theoretical perspectives of postmodernism with the radical political orientations that typified earlier forms of outsider jurisprudence. For instance, postmodern feminists such as Joan Williams have argued that feminists can recognize that women differ from men yet can still avoid assuming the existence of either an essential WOMAN or some stable set of essential differences between the sexes. According to Mary Joe Frug, postmodern insights suggest that differences between women and men are indeed contingent and therefore are subject to "political struggle," including contests within the realm of legal discourse. The "continuous interpretive struggles over the meaning of sex differences," Frug insisted, "can have an impact on patriarchal legal power." And in an erudite though somewhat abstruse book focused on the relation between postmodernism and feminist jurisprudence, Drucilla Cornell sought "to free 'feminine' writing and the evocation of the feminine . . . from the charge of essentialism." To do so, Cornell suggested that the feminine should be understood not as an object or essence, but rather as a contingent position in relation to other persons—a position from which one can open to and identify with those others. For Cornell, the postmodern emphasis on the instability of meaning can be invoked to support the feminist political aim of undermining gender hierarchy. "Writing from the position of the feminine involves an explicit, ethical affirmation which in itself is a performative challenge to the devaluation of the feminine. We affirm the feminine . . . even as we recognize that the feminine cannot be reduced or identified with the lives of actual women."[59]

Postmodern Themes in Legal Thought

Because of a combination of diverse causes, American legal thought has twisted over a shadowy border from modernism to postmodernism. In the previous section of this chapter, I discussed several dialectically interrelated factors as spurring the movement from modern to postmodern jurisprudence: the breakdown of consensus and confidence among Americans in general, including the legal professoriate; the Supreme Court's highly controversial decisions in *Griswold v. Connecticut* and *Roe v. Wade* and the subsequent scholarly reactions to those cases; the flourishing of interdisciplinary work in many fields, including law, and the subsequent influence on jurisprudents of postmodern ideas from other disciplines such as philosophy, literary criticism, and cultural anthropology; the emergence of an interpretive turn in legal thought, particularly in constitutional theory; the development of computer-assisted legal research with a graphical user interface; and the changing demographic makeup of the legal academy, which contributed to the development of outsider jurisprudence. The degree and manner in which these causal factors have combined is anything but clear; as the novelist Cormac McCarthy observes: "[i]n history there are no control groups." Regardless of this uncertainty about the causes, though, the movement from modernism to postmodernism represents a broad cultural, social, and political transformation that itself transcends disciplinary boundaries, touching most if not all academic fields, including jurisprudence.[60]

The postmodern interpretive strategies of writers such as Stanley Fish and the innovative approaches of postmodern outsider jurisprudents, which I discussed in the previous section, denote important aspects of postmodern legal thought. Yet, to present a more complete picture, I will explicate the manifestation of each of the eight general postmodern themes that I introduced in chapter 2, though now I will focus on the interrelated themes in the specific area of jurisprudence. To be sure, postmodern legal scholars do not present a unified front.[61] Indeed, some of the most interesting postmodern legal scholarship amounts to "postmodern policing": when one postmodernist criticizes another postmodernist for, in effect, not being postmodern enough. Even so, despite the disagreements among various postmodern jurisprudents, the interrelationships and integration of the various postmodern themes in legal writing are striking. When viewed as a whole, postmodern legal scholars do, indeed, seem to be articulating a paradigmatic worldview corresponding to those of premodernism and modernism. And just as premodern and modern legal thought fit closely with the broader culture of each respective era, postmodern jurisprudence resonates with the cultural times in which we live. Here, then, are the eight themes of postmodern legal thought.[62]

First, postmodern legal thinkers reject the interrelated modernist commitments to foundationalism and essentialism. For over one hundred years, American legal modernists have sought a foundation for law and judicial decision making; in so doing, they have ranged from rationalism to empiricism to transcendentalism. Postmodernists, on the other hand, maintain that knowledge and meaning always remain ungrounded, and that ungrounded meanings always are unstable and shifting. According to Douglas E. Litowitz's *Postmodern Philosophy and Law*, which approaches postmodern jurisprudence from an analytical vantage, postmodern anti-foundationalism reflects "a deep distrust and skepticism of the metaphysical and/or epistemic foundations which have historically been offered by lawyers and philosophers in support of particular arrangements of the legal system." Consequently, postmodern legal theorists constantly question the ostensible stability of particular words as well as entire legal texts; Fish's postmodern interpretivism, discussed in the previous section, represents but one manifestation of this phenomenon. Consistent with this anti-foundationalist theme, for example, postmodern feminists now proclaim that "'[w]oman' is a troublesome term, in feminism and in law. The category is neither consistently nor coherently constituted in linguistic, historical, or legal contexts."[63]

To underscore the pervasive and potentially radical reach of anti-foundationalism and anti-essentialism, some postmodernists insist that, contrary to modernist claims, there exists no such thing as an easy case in the law. Even the constitutional provision requiring the president to be at least thirty-five years old is open to multiple interpretations. Arguing along these lines, the postmodern deconstructionist Anthony D'Amato emphasizes that textual meaning varies with context. Hence, "because contexts can change, there can be no such thing as a single interpretation of any text that is absolute and unchanging for all time." Modernists who insist that there are easy cases in constitutional law—such as an eighteen-year-old being ineligible for the presidency—overlook this basic postmodern insight into the importance of context. As an abstract hypothetical, the issue of an eighteen-year-old president might be ridiculous, but if it were to arise in the context of a real case, the issue would look very different. The modernist's "so-called easy case of the eighteen-year-old President is itself outrageous," D'Amato concludes. "[I]t will not come up—and if it does, in some future context, then it will no longer be outrageous." Putting the importance of context in slightly different terms, modernists see easy cases only because they implicitly accept the stability of some background context or assumptions that seem to ground objective textual interpretations. Postmodernists, however, stress that such background assumptions always can be brought to the foreground and displaced, and by doing so, postmodernists deconstruct textual meanings that had previously appeared to be uncontroversial.[64]

Pierre Schlag, one of the leading postmodern jurisprudents, suggests why modernists believe (mistakenly) that law is ontologically grounded on a firm foundation. Certain distinctive methods of legal education, according to Schlag, induce students to develop an abiding faith in the firm substantive existence of law. The abstruseness of Socratic questioning, in particular, often leads law students to suspect that their professors are "hiding the ball"—where the ball metaphorically represents the law. Professors adeptly move the ball around, flipping it from one hand to the other, sliding it behind the back, and always keeping it just out of the anxious sight of the (sometimes) attentive students. Watching this deft display, the students believe that the professors must be *hiding* the ball, since they never quite see it. Thus, the students implicitly assume that some solid ball actually exists: How could (and why would) professors perform such tricks if there were no such ball? In this way, future attorneys, judges, and law professors develop "a pious faith in the ontological and epistemic character of law." They deeply believe in the ball, in a "stabilized preinterpretive" law.[65]

But Schlag then raises the postmodern deconstructive point: regardless of the faith or belief of modernist attorneys and scholars, there just is no stabilized preinterpretive law. Modernist legal scholars may have written endlessly about legal doctrines as if the doctrines actually existed as "robust object-forms with stabilized identities"; nevertheless, legal rules and principles are not grounded on "any robust or stabilized referent." Moreover, the ontological vacuousness of the law enables modernist jurisprudents to devote lengthy articles, books, and even multivolume treatises to the construction of increasingly elaborate doctrinal frameworks, neatly and logically relating the many ostensible legal principles and rules to each other. From Schlag's postmodern viewpoint, though, modernist scholars could say just about anything they want about the principles and rules because they do not actually exist as stabilized referents. It is quite easy to construct a most imaginative and even elegant doctrinal edifice if one is working with those most pliant of materials—nonexistent rules and principles.[66]

Other postmodern jurisprudents have connected anti-foundationalism and anti-essentialism with a concern for the Derridean Other. According to Derrida, the hermeneutic process of understanding always and already defines some Other. Whenever we understand a text from within our own horizon—which is the only way to understand a text—we necessarily deny potential meanings that might arise from some other perspective or horizon. In an article on deconstruction and legal interpretation, Michel Rosenfeld writes: "[A]ll texts (whether oral or written) are writings that refer to other writings. A text is not a pure presence that immediately and transparently reveals a distinct meaning intended by its author. Instead, from the standpoint of deconstruction, every writing embodies a failed attempt at reconciling identity and difference, unity and diversity and self and other. A writing may give the impression of having achieved the desired reconciliation, but such impression can only be the product of ideological distortion, suppression of difference or subordination of the other."[67]

To be clear, then, the Other refers not only to suppressed textual meanings but also to marginalized and subjugated individuals and groups (or outgroups)—those individuals and groups whose meanings (or voices) are obscured or ignored. Postmodernists thus argue, in the particular realm of feminist jurisprudence for example, that modernists have relied on "gender essentialism"—the assumption that all women share some universal essence. This modernist essentialism has tended to silence certain voices—particularly those of women of color, lesbians, and poor women—"in order to privilege others." More broadly, postmodern jurisprudence "throws into question the categories and classifications upon which law has uncritically supported exercises of power that have silenced and opposed in the name of nature or in the name of practical necessity." Derrida himself has equated deconstruction with justice, suggesting that the deconstructive focus on the Other nourishes an unquenchable political desire to reveal violence and deception, to uncover denial, exclusion, and oppression. From this perspective, the law always constructs and suppresses some Other, and deconstructive justice (or "deconjustice") seeks to disclose this suppression. As Larry Catá Backer explains, "[i]t is the nature of all groups—it is the defining characteristic of all social systems—to define a zone of deviance and to sanction those within its bounds." Thus the deconstruction of legal concepts, according to J. M. Balkin, is a call "to remember aspects of human life that were pushed into the background." Contrary to common modernist misconceptions, "[d]econstruction is not a denial of the legitimacy of rules and principles; it is an affirmation of human possibilities that have been overlooked or forgotten in the privileging of particular legal ideas."[68]

To illustrate, the significance of laissez-faire theory for American law can be deconstructed. Laissez faire arises from certain background assumptions that generally remain unexamined or unquestioned. Most important, laissez-faire theorists assume that all humans are naturally and solely motivated by their own self-interest. From this as well as other premises, the laissez-faire advocate reasons that, in the economic sphere, "unregulated market transactions are the best way to realize human goals," and governmental regulation of the economic marketplace therefore should be minimized. But the deconstructionist seeks to question the background assumptions: "our social vision and system of laws are not based upon human nature as it really is, but rather upon an interpretation of human nature, a metaphor, a privileging." In particular, when one begins to doubt the validity of the key assumption of laissez faire—the purely self-interested person—this economic being begins to look suspiciously like "a social moron." The economist Amartya Sen, himself no overt deconstructionist, colorfully illustrates the absurdities that would follow if people truly acted wholly from self-interest: "[T]he assumption [is] that when asked a question, the individual gives that answer which will maximize his personal gain. How good is this assumption? I doubt that in general it is very good. ('Where is the railway station?' he asks me. 'There,' I say, pointing at the post office, 'and would you please post this letter for me on the way?' 'Yes,' he says, determined to open the envelope and check whether it contains something valuable.)"[69]

Significantly, from the deconstructive vantage, when privileged assumptions are questioned, then other possibilities emerge from the margins. We can recognize, for example, that many considerations other than self-interest motivate people to act. These motivations can be noble or base, ranging from altruism and justice to racism and antisemitism. The simple and common act of voting, for instance, apparently does not flow from the rational pursuit of self-interest: the costs in time and effort clearly outweigh any potential benefits that are likely to flow from one's single vote, yet many people choose to make this economically futile gesture. Indeed, even the very pursuit of economic self-interest "ultimately depends upon social cooperation and the sharing of values." To be sure, though, the deconstructive aim is not necessarily to privilege some other motivation over self-interest; human actions in most instances cannot be reduced to any single motivation, whether self-interest or otherwise. Rather, the deconstructionist seeks to disrupt our initial assumptions and to disclose how they suppress alternative visions of people as social beings. In the end, the deconstruction of laissez faire suggests that the ideal of a marketplace unburdened by governmental regulation seems to be based on a cramped and tenuous interpretation of human existence.[70]

Closely related to the first postmodern theme, then, is the second: postmodernists tend to defy all sorts of ostensible certainties, inveteracies, edifices, and boundaries, including the borders of academic disciplines. Postmodernism, that is, "forces us to entertain the possible non-necessity of our customary categories." This postmodern propensity leads to constant challenges to the traditional categories of legal doctrine. Gregory S. Alexander, for instance, repudiates a conceptualization of property grounded singularly on modernist individualism. Under this modernist notion, "[t]he purpose of property and its constitutional protection [was] nothing more or less than to create a wall between the individual and the collective that [would] guarantee the individual the space, literally as well as figuratively, to satisfy his own desires." Alexander declares that this "single privileged understanding" of property is outmoded, and he instead proffers a postmodern conception of property. In particular, Alexander sees an irresolvable dialectical conflict between the individualist and a more communitarian notion of property that emphasizes public responsibility.[71]

More broadly, William L. F. Felstiner and Austin Sarat challenge the traditional conception of the lawyer-client relationship. According to Felstiner and Sarat, the lawyer-client relation traditionally has been understood and analyzed from one of two opposed modernist perspectives: either as rigidly structured by predefined social roles or as arising from the actions of autonomous individuals. Felstiner and Sarat reject this dichotomous vision as too closely circumscribed by modernist notions of society and the individual. The lawyer and the client neither are imprisoned by fixed preexisting social structures nor are they free and independent individuals. Felstiner and Sarat instead propose a postmodern view that understands the lawyer-client relationship as always constrained yet contingent—as limited yet subject to constant transformation through negotiation.[72]

Postmodern irreverence also has led many jurisprudents to defy the modernist idea of legal scholarship itself as narrowly focused on doctrine (and after the realists, public policy). Interdisciplinary legal studies drawing on Foucault, Rorty, Gadamer, Wittgenstein, Kuhn, Nietzsche, Derrida, Heidegger, Lacan, and a host of others are commonplace. Frequently, because of the cultural saturation of American society—indeed, culture seems to pervade all aspects of social and personal life—postmodern scholars tend to understand law from the perspective of cultural and social studies. This tendency is especially pronounced in postmodern outsider jurisprudence, where scholars strive to understand how the symbols and structures of American culture and society, including legal culture and relations, obscure and suppress outgroup voices—the Derridean Other. Many outsider jurisprudents, for example, repudiate the modernist conception of racism as constituted solely by individual intentional acts of discrimination. Racism, instead, is conceived as a cultural and societal phenomenon manifested in unintentional as well as intentional actions and unconscious as well as conscious attitudes. "Racism is woven into the warp and woof of the way we see and organize the world," Richard Delgado and Jean Stefancic explain. "[I]t is one of the many preconceptions we bring to experience and use to construct and make sense of our social world. Racism forms part of the dominant narrative, the group of received understandings and basic principles that form the baseline from which we reason."[73]

While such cultural and social emphases predominate in outsider jurisprudence, other postmodern scholars also use similar methods. Balkin, for instance, explicates postmodern constitutionalism by exploring "how postmodern culture and technology have affected law as an institution."

> What effect have the rise of mass media and the industrialization of symbolic forms had on the way that the public understands their legal rights and their ability to participate in the legal system? One might well invent, by analogy to the phenomenon of "sound bites," the concept of "law bites," or symbols of the legal system that have become the common cultural coin of the general public. A classic example of the law bite in operation are reports of motorists arrested by Canadian police who repeatedly insisted that their *Miranda* rights be read to them. Mass broadcast of American police shows (and later *L. A. Law*) has apparently altered the public's perception of the criminal and civil justice system, and not only in America. These symbolic representations of law become the common forms of discourse and benchmarks of expectation about law among the lay public.[74]

To be sure, some legal modernists—frequently, individuals with degrees and professional credentials in both law and another discipline—harshly criticize these postmodern interdisciplinary scholars as dilettantes. Most often, though, such modernist critics sound rather shrill as they struggle to protect their professional and disciplinary turf. Certainly modernists, no less than postmodernists, should criticize the substance of others' work, but they should not criticize the work merely because the wrong person (or a person in the wrong discipline) wrote it. Such ad hominem criticism misses a crucial point of interdisciplinary postmodern scholarship. Postmodernists recognize that legal problems, issues, and events do not necessarily fit neatly within disciplinary boundaries. Professional and academic disciplines have developed for a variety of reasons, including the accumulation of wealth, prestige, and power—not merely for their comprehensive explanatory potential. No single discipline provides sufficient purchase for an adequate understanding of social events, including law. If one remains locked within a predefined discipline, one's understanding of an event may be skewed to fit within those disciplinary borders and may ignore alternative truths about that event. For that reason, postmodern legal scholars frequently ignore modernist fences as they jump from place to place, from discipline to discipline, as if they were following a contingent and evolving path of hypertext links on the World Wide Web. Without doubt, though, following links on the Web sometimes leaves one exhausted and frustrated, with little achieved other than eye strain and a headache. Similarly, interdisciplinary scholarship occasionally stalls in jargon-filled banality and fails to successfully integrate its multiple perspectives. Yet, the interdisciplinary nature of postmodern legal scholarship often spurs innovative and provocative approaches and portrayals of the American legal system; approaches and portrayals that are suppressed when scholars are limited to a single discipline.[75]

The third theme is that postmodern jurisprudents tend to recognize, explore, and even celebrate paradoxes. Modernist scholars, searching for foundations and essential truths, tend to view paradoxes suspiciously, as denoting problematic inconsistencies. Postmodernists, being anti-foundationalists and anti-essentialists, do not find paradoxes troubling. To the contrary, postmodernists expect paradoxes. Unsurprisingly, then, Peter Schanck concludes his article on the implications of postmodernism for statutory interpretation with a paradox: "postmodern ideas can and do exert a powerful influence on contemporary theories of statutory interpretation. Paradoxically, however, I also contend that any attempt to develop a postmodern theory of statutory construction or to justify an interpretive theory on postmodern grounds is *anti*postmodern." Schanck, here, follows Stanley Fish's lead by suggesting that postmodern theoretical insights into an interpretive practice, such as statutory construction, cannot be applied directly to transform that practice.[76]

From a postmodern vantage, paradoxes can reflect social and hermeneutic realities. Since any text or social event contains multiple truths and voices, some likely will stand in paradoxical relation to each other. Delgado, for instance, argues that, because of the racism embodied in American culture and society, hate speech constitutes "words that wound." Racist and other hate speech is forceful—it makes a difference. It can seriously harm a victim in recognizable ways. Yet, simultaneously and paradoxically, Delgado and Stefancic maintain that free speech exchanged in a so-called marketplace of ideas is unlikely to successfully combat or substantially reduce racism. Speech is, in this context, ineffective or lacking in force. From Delgado and Stefancic's perspective, these paradoxical theses concerning speech do not illustrate a fatal inconsistency in their reasoning but rather reflect the social reality of living in a racist culture and society. Hate speech is effective because it aligns itself consistently with other powerful racist forces in American society, while arguments against hate speech are neutralized by the same racist forces. Racism impels hate speech forward with extraordinary and injurious speed, yet racism simultaneously deflects even the most eloquent entreaties against hate speech.[77]

This paradox involving speech leads into the fourth postmodern theme: a focus on power and its manifold manifestations. Modernists tend to locate power in a discrete and conscious center, such as an individual, a group of individuals, or a sovereign. Power, from this modernist vantage, often is understood as "a 'thing' possessed" by a person or institution, as if it were a tool to be wielded over others. Thus, in constitutional theory, Kendall Thomas observes that too often "we speak of Congress 'having' the power to regulate interstate commerce, of the President 'having' the power to appoint members of the Supreme Court, of the Supreme Court 'having' the power to hear cases arising under the Constitution." Contrary to this modernist conception of power, postmodern legal scholars follow Foucault in maintaining "that 'power is everywhere and in everyone.'" In the words of Felstiner and Sarat: "[Power] is not like a tool sitting on a shelf, waiting to be picked up and applied to the task at hand. Power, rather, is enacted and constituted moment-by-moment. It is seen in indirect moves and sleights-of-hand, in ruptures and ellipses, and in what is left unsaid and unacknowledged as well as in forceful, continuous and overt assertion. Power is continuously produced in the regular and apparently uneventful routines and practices that comprise most social interactions."[78]

Thus, "[p]ower has many dimensions and is enacted in many domains," but one of the most pervasive—and one frequently emphasized by postmodern legal theorists—is the linguistic or discursive domain. Postmodernists from Dennis Patterson, who follows Wittgensteinian pragmatism, to Francis J. Mootz, who follows Gadamerian hermeneutics, agree that "[a]ll understanding occurs in language," while deconstructionists assert similarly that "[t]here is nothing outside of the text." Thus, postmodern legal scholars tend to explore the implications of conceptualizing law as a manifestation of linguistic power. Sanford Levinson and J. M. Balkin, for instance, stress the performative power of legal language—that many legal utterances, like a subpoena or a contract, directly impose power. Levinson and Balkin add, though, that legal language is not "exceptional in its complicity with power." Rather, the "legal act of interpretation . . . is the normal, paradigmatic act of interpretation, while an imagined quiet 'powerless' lecture on Keats is the exception." More broadly, other postmodern legal scholars explore how the language of law contributes to the construction of social reality. The postmodern feminist Tracy E. Higgins explains:

> [P]ostmodernism emphasizes the regulatory role of language and the interpretive process itself. Beyond the direct regulatory [or performative] implications of its decisions in particular cases, the [Supreme] Court's construction of the legal discourse surrounding gender affects the structure of arguments raised on women's behalf, the kinds of harms that may be translated into legal claims, and even the degree to which those harms are experienced or acknowledged as violations by the individual. Similarly, feminist legal theorists' critique of and engagement with this legal discourse regulates the scope of feminist reinterpretations of women's experience. Thus, for the Court and its feminist critics, to choose among competing accounts of womanhood is not merely to reinforce exclusions but to alter the way women experience and express their lives.[79]

The postmodern concern with linguistic power relates closely to anti-foundationalism and anti-essentialism. "Because language is socially and culturally constituted, it is inherently incapable of representing or corresponding to reality; hence all propositions and all interpretations, even texts, are themselves social constructions."[80] Of course, this anti-foundationalist and anti-essentialist conceptualization of language and interpretation has prompted many modernists to charge that postmodernists are dangerous nihilists or relativists. Yet, fears of nihilism and relativism are modernist hobgoblins that fail to spook most postmodernists. Instead, postmodernists look through these hobgoblins to see how language works—how language generates meaning and understanding. Just as Thomas Kuhn claimed to explain how scientists work successfully—and not how science was impossible—postmodern legal scholars claim to explain how textual understanding arises rather than how it fails. Stanley Fish, to be sure, was a leader in this regard, but many others have further explored legal language and understanding.

Some postmodernists, for instance, explicitly turn for support to Gadamer's philosophical hermeneutics. As discussed in chapter 2, Gadamer has argued that communal traditions inculcate us with prejudices and interests that simultaneously enable yet constrain interpretation and understanding. We never can step outside the horizon of our prejudices and interests to find some firmer foundation for understanding: we are, in other words, always and already interpreting. Yet, even though we never can escape our prejudices and interests—derived from tradition—tradition constantly changes because the process of interpretation itself continually questions and reconstructs tradition, thus transforming our prejudices and interests. When imported into the context of constitutional interpretation,

> [p]hilosophical hermeneutics [suggests] that the meaning of the Constitution comes into being through the interpretive encounter between the reader and the text. The horizon of the interpreter, arising from prejudices and tradition, must fuse with the horizon of the text through the dialectical play and dialogue of the hermeneutic circle. Thus, as the horizon of the present shifts over time, the meaning of the Constitution is always potentially new and different. An objective meaning, in other words, is not simply waiting to be discovered, yet meaning is not imposed by unconstrained individuals or societal conventions. Instead, constitutional interpretation is an ontological event in which meaning comes into existence. The two sides of understanding resonate within the hermeneutic circle. Tradition, embedded in one's horizon, always limits one's vision of the Constitution and thus directs and constrains understanding and interpretation. Yet, tradition is constantly being created and recreated as the meaning of the Constitution comes into being.[81]

Dennis Patterson, meanwhile, turns to Wittgensteinian pragmatism to explain the understanding of legal texts. According to Patterson, understanding arises from knowing how to participate in a practice. "[W]e have a world in concert with others because we understand the manifold activities that constitute that world. Catching on to and participating in these activities—knowing how to act—is the essence of understanding." Understanding, then, amounts to "acting appropriately" in response to an utterance. "For example, one evinces understanding of the request 'Please pass the salt' by passing the salt or by explaining why it is impossible to do so. Understanding is made manifest in the act of passing the salt, and the act is a criterion for having understood the utterance."[82]

For Patterson, understanding a legal text is no different from understanding another text insofar as it is an "interpretive enterprise" or practice. "[L]aw is an activity and not a thing. Its 'being' is in the 'doing' of the participants within the practice." Consequently, "[a] claim that some proposition of law is true is vindicated if one can show that on any particular occasion one is correctly using the words in question." Yet, because there is a "special language of law," legal practice has in a sense a distinct grammar: a set of systemic or organizational "rules" for playing the "game," for participating in the practice of law. Patterson thus unsurprisingly has applauded Philip Bobbitt's attempt to describe a specific grammar for the practice of constitutional law. In Bobbitt's terminology, constitutional law consists of the manipulation of six "modalities of argument": "historical (relying on the intentions of the framers and ratifiers of the Constitution); textual (looking to the meaning of the words of the Constitution alone, as they would be interpreted by the average contemporary 'man on the street'); structural (inferring rules from the relationships that the Constitution mandates among the structures it sets up); doctrinal (applying rules generated by precedent); ethical (deriving rules from those moral commitments of the American ethos that are reflected in the Constitution); and prudential (seeking to balance the costs and benefits of a particular rule)." Bobbitt has explained that these "modalities of argument are no more than instrumental, rhetorical devices to be deployed in behalf of various political ideologies. The modalities of constitutional argument are the ways in which law statements in constitutional matters are assessed."[83]

Despite the postmodern quality of such Wittgensteinian approaches, their reductionist tendencies also have provoked postmodern policing. Whenever a theorist claims to reduce an entire practice to a limited and well-defined set of argumentative strategies or modalities, postmodern critics are sure to launch a deconstructive attack proclaiming, in effect, that the theorist is not being postmodern enough. After all, remember (the second identified postmodern theme) that many postmodernists tend to defy all sorts of ostensible certainties, inveteracies, edifices, and boundaries. Hence, Bobbitt has been criticized for attempting "to preserve a certain purity within the language game of constitutional argument." This attempt is "doomed to failure" because constitutional argument, like all "[l]iving language games," is "motley and variegated, often chaotic, and always jerry-rigged." Likewise, Patterson's notion of jurisprudence—as no more than "the accurate description of the forms of argument used by lawyers to show the truth of propositions of law"—has been faulted for its politically conservative "uncritical acceptance of the normal or conventional."[84] All of which is to say, perhaps, that postmodernists disagree about even the most important issues. Of course, considering that the postmodern world view tends to question unity and to accept fragmentation—to encompass deconstructive forays into the Derridean abyss—such disagreement is hardly surprising.

Despite the unquestioned centrality of linguistic power in postmodern analyses of the American legal system, many postmodern jurisprudents nonetheless insist that "language simultaneously floats or plays at distance from power." These post-modernists tend to emphasize the structural component of power. In their article on the lawyer-client relationship, Felstiner and Sarat elaborate the postmodern conceptualization of social structures as habituated patterns of behavior:

> While people work out the terms of their interactions daily, they do not begin with a clean slate each day or in each situation; within any setting there is a limited number of available moves. Consider the situation of teacher and student or employer and employee at the beginning of any ordinary day. Hierarchical relationships, routine divisions of labor, and parochial practices will generally dictate who exercises what kinds of authority over what kinds of matters, who will do what and how each of the participants will feel about the day's tasks. The student will not question the lesson plan or the teacher's prerogative to evaluate student performance; the employee will not openly resist the day's assignment or the employer's prerogative to say when a job is ready for delivery to a customer.[85]

Kendall Thomas draws on the concept of social structures to argue that laws prohibiting homosexual sodomy should be unconstitutional. Such laws, according to Thomas, contribute to the widespread acceptance of homophobic violence, which is structurally produced: "Homophobic violence is a social activity 'structured by rules that define roles and positions, powers and opportunities, thereby distributing responsibility for consequences.' Viewed systemically, the objective and outcome of violence against lesbians and gays is the social control of human sexuality." From this perspective, social structures help construct who we are, for better or worse. They simultaneously enable and limit our possibilities, though Thomas and other outsider jurisprudents tend to stress the constraints that emanate from such structures: "[t]he combined force of homosexual sodomy law and homophobic violence is to impose invisibility on gays and lesbians, to make it as difficult as possible for gays and lesbians to enter 'the common political life of the community,' and to restrict as much as possible their access to political power."[86]

Postmodern jurisprudents, though, do not assert that social structures are rigid or fixed mechanisms. A primary difference between, on the one hand, social and legal theorists who are true structuralists and therefore modernists and, on the other hand, theorists who are poststructuralists and therefore postmodernists is that, unlike their modernist predecessors, the postmodernists always recognize the contingency and plasticity of social structures. Structures are not stable but rather are constantly being negotiated and reconstructed in everyday social relations. They exist only in the habituated and repeated daily interactions of everyday life, and thus they can and do change. In particular, cultural symbols and social structures exist in a dialectical and dynamic relationship. Culture, including legal culture, helps produce and reinforce social roles and structures, and consequently, cultural transformations sometimes lead to structural changes.[87]

Yet, even though postmodernist jurisprudents maintain that social structures always are contingent, words alone cannot readily transform such structures. Our social roles typically are too well habituated and unquestioned for words to have substantial transformative power vis-à-vis the ingrained structures of our society. This recognition helps explain Delgado and Stefancic's argument about the limitations of free speech as a means to social transformation. Free speech exchanged in the marketplace of ideas is unlikely to reduce racism significantly because, in part, racism is structurally entrenched in American society. For that reason, free speech might be "a powerful asset to the dominant group, but [it is] a much less helpful one to subordinate groups." Racism, from this perspective, cannot be diminished merely by talking about it. Instead, a substantial reduction in racism could follow only from the broad alteration of American societal structures—a feat not easily accomplished after more than two centuries of slavery and almost another century of the legally enforced apartheid of Jim Crow laws.[88]

The deficiency of free speech as a mechanism for producing significant social change relates to the fifth postmodern theme: the social construction of the self or subject. As already mentioned, modernists tend to locate power in a discrete and conscious center, frequently in an individual self. Modernists thus argue that the individual self can exercise power and control over social and natural developments. The self, from this perspective, is the source of the modernist idea of progress—the notion that society can endlessly improve. Postmodern jurisprudents such as Pierre Schlag insist that even those modernists who acknowledge that cultural and societal factors impinge on the individual self's autonomy and independence nonetheless retain a belief in an at least relatively autonomous self: "a constructed self that concedes that it is socially and rhetorically constituted yet maintains its own autonomy to decide just how autonomous it may or may not be."[89]

Postmodernists reject the modernist conception of the individual self and the concomitant idea of progress. Instead, postmodernists declare that the self is decentered. The self or subject no longer is viewed as a sovereign center of power and control that can purposefully direct society toward a boundless advance. From the postmodern standpoint, the self or subject is socially constructed, generated by social structures and cultural symbols. Balkin, for instance, asserts that the self "is not fully in control of what she sees; she is part of a larger legal and political culture that shapes the very forms of her understanding. She does not choose the terms of her ideology or social construction. Rather she chooses through them; they form the framework within which her choices are understood and made." For this reason, leading critical race scholars such as Derrick Bell and Richard Delgado have turned toward a type of "racial realism." From their perspective, racism is so deeply embedded in American society and culture and hence embodied in our socially constructed selves that we cannot simply *choose* to eradicate or even to substantially reduce racism—in society or in ourselves. We just do not have sufficient power and control over either social relations or our own psychological makeup to accomplish directly such a difficult undertaking.[90]

Exactly because the self is socially constructed, postmodernists maintain that the self does not have an essence or core. The self is, in a second sense, then, de-centered. This aspect of the decentering of the self closely relates to the themes of anti-foundationalism and anti-essentialism: the self, one might say, lacks the foundation or essence that could center it. In the postmodern era, cultural symbols and social structures are so pervasive yet diverse and mutable that the self seems to consist of a multiplicity of intersecting and contingent voices and identities. Like postmodern society, the self is fragmented. Thus, many feminists reformulate the "self as a site constituted and fragmented, at least partially, by the intersections of various categories of domination/oppression such as race, gender, and sexual orientation. [One's identity, then] is made up of the various discourses and structures that shape society and one's experience within it." James Boyle pushes the postmodern notion of a multiplicitous and intersectional self even further: "the determinants of class and race and age and group and religion and sexual orientation and role and mood and context constitute us in a changing pattern from moment to moment. From their varied intersection springs up a postmodern self. 'I' am merely the place where these things happen." This postmodern understanding of the self has implications for the law. For instance, john a. powell suggests that "[t]he theory of the intersectional self presumes that identity is marked by many intersecting traits and that the implication of this cannot be understood by simply adding these traits together. For example, an African American female's experience is not adequately captured by adding the traits of a (White) female with that of a Black (male). Thus, in terms of the law, rules that prohibit racial and gender discrimination by addressing them as discrete phenomena do not adequately extend protection to a person marked by both subordinate gender and racial status."[91]

Significantly, although postmodernists insist that the self is socially constructed, most postmodernists attempt to avoid reducing the self to a socially determined automaton. These postmodernists stress that social structures and cultural symbols do not exist apart from the daily and mundane individual actions that constitute them. According to Patricia Ewick and Susan S. Silbey, consciousness is "part of a reciprocal process in which the meanings given by individuals to their world, and law and legal institutions as part of that world, become repeated, patterned and stabilized, and those institutionalized structures become part of the meaning systems employed by individuals." From this perspective, Ewick and Silbey continue, "consciousness is neither fixed, stable, unitary, nor consistent. Instead, we see legal consciousness as something local, contextual, pluralistic, filled with conflict and contradiction." To be sure, then, social and cultural inputs make us who we are, but those inputs simultaneously constrain and enable us. That is, social structures and cultural symbols imbue or empower us with certain abilities and outlooks even as those structures and symbols also severely limit our possibilities. We may not have direct control over social relations, but we all always participate in the constant construction and reconstruction of society and culture. For many postmodern legal scholars, especially members of outgroups and minorities, this dialectical conception of the self—as simultaneously constructing yet constituted by social structures and cultural symbols—seems crucial to retaining their critical political stance. From this perspective, we may be unable to control directly and to transform purposefully oppressive social and cultural constructs, but we nonetheless might be able to disturb and therefore alter the processes of their reconstruction. Deconstructionists, as already discussed, often aim to disclose the marginalized Other and, in so doing, to possibly disrupt unjust oppression and subjugation.[92]

The social construction of the self often is discussed in the context of the sixth postmodern theme: the self-reflexivity of postmodern practices. Postmodernists often turn toward their own social practices and make the cultural and theoretical awareness of those practices part of the practices themselves. Postmodernism, in a sense, transforms practices to include self-reflexive awareness. This self-reflexivity has led many postmodern jurisprudents to dwell somewhat narcissistically on the practice of legal scholarship itself. During the postmodern era, the amount of meta-scholarship—scholarship about scholarship (instead of scholarship about legal or judicial practice)—has surged. Several postmodern scholars, for instance, have pilloried modernist legal scholarship for being consistently and overtly normative. Modernist scholars, that is, typically respond to some specified legal and social problem by explicitly advocating that the Supreme Court adopt some doctrinal framework or that Congress enact some proposed statute. Yet, as postmodernists chide, such an explicit normative recommendation addresses the reader as if she were an autonomous and independent self who could choose to effectuate any desirable doctrinal or statutory improvement in the law. Modernist legal scholarship, in other words, tends to reinscribe the modernist self—the self as the sovereign center of power and control who can purposefully and effectively transform social relations, including the legal system. For this reason, many postmodern jurisprudents rather glaringly refrain from concluding their scholarship with a modernist-style recommendation to implement some overt legal change.[93]

Most prominently, Pierre Schlag has relentlessly criticized modernist scholarship for its normativeness and its interrelated reinscription of the modernist self. For example, in an article entitled *The Problem of the Subject*, Schlag analyzes how modernist legal scholars ranging from the Langdellian legal scientists to the critical legal scholars have monotonously constructed and reconstructed our (supposed) existence as relatively autonomous selves while simultaneously avoiding any investigation into the actual existence or functioning of these modernist selves or subjects. "American legal thought," Schlag maintains, "has been conceptually, rhetorically, and socially constituted to avoid confronting the question of who or what thinks or produces law." In prototypical postmodern fashion, Schlag seeks to reverse this systematic evasion—to bring the background to the foreground—by confronting precisely that question or problem: the problem of the subject.

> Each and every social, legal, and political event is immediately represented as an event calling for a value-based choice. You are free to choose between this and that. But, of course, you are not free. You are not free because you are constantly required to reenact the motions of the prescripted, already organized configuration of the individual being as chooser. You have to, you already are constructed and channeled as a choosing being. Not only is this social construction of the self extraordinarily oppressive—but it often turns out to be absurd as well. Much of its absurdity can be seen in the normative visions that routinely issue from the legal academy urging us to adopt this utopian program or that one—as if somehow our choices (I like decentralized socialism, you like conservative pastoral politics, she likes liberal cultural pluralism) had any direct, self-identical effect on the construction of our social or political scene. The critical insistence on making political value choices is utterly captive to a conventional and nostalgic description of the political field—a description and definition of the field that is guaranteed to yield political disablement and disempowerment. To tell people that they are already empowered to make political value choices is, in effect, to bolster the dominant culture's representation that we are free-choosing beings and to strengthen the forces that lead to our own repeated, compelled affirmation of (meaningless) choices.[94]

Why do modernist legal scholars continue to advocate ineffectively for legal changes and to reinscribe the relatively autonomous self? For one reason, modernist scholars themselves have been acculturated to believe that they are relatively autonomous selves that should and do make recommendations or choices. Furthermore, they are, according to Schlag, trapped like mice "in a maze." This metaphor vividly depicts the constraints imposed on modernist scholars by their structural roles in the university, the legal profession, and society in general. Before joining the academy, many law professors were judicial clerks, frequently working for appellate judges. As such, they quickly adopted a self-identified role consistent with the judicial position, distanced from the actual practice of law. In this societal role or position, law professors posit a romanticized vision of law that denies the true violence of the American legal system—and they do so over and over and over again, as they can see nowhere else to go, nothing else to do. "[T]he discipline of law is, in some sense, constantly driven to try to escape from or deny its own violent ontology," Schlag explains. "This is why in the 'law' of the academy we get so much happy talk jurisprudence—promises of law as 'a grand conversation,' promises of law as subservient to 'progressive legal thought,' promises of law as responsive to the imperatives of 'efficiency,' promises of a law that is always already one way or another becoming the very best it can be." Most modernist scholars cannot escape from this maze of happy talk because doing so would require them to relinquish their self-identified roles as modernist scholars. That is, they would need to give up doing or understanding law in the manner that they have been disciplined or socialized to follow for most of their professional lives.[95]

On the one hand, then, the overtly normative discourse or language of modernist legal scholarship unwittingly stands at a distance from the application of power through the legal system. Modernist scholars believe that their normative recommendations influence legal and political decision makers as they implement power, but in reality, such writing has little or no effect on legal actors. In particular, as Schlag and others have underscored, judges largely do not listen to or even care about what legal scholars write. Modernist scholarship thus often amounts to little more than the author's mere proclamation that she likes or dislikes an imagined normative framework. Schlag caustically quips that "the acid simplicity of the 'that's cool'/'that sucks' dichotomy on Beavis and Butt-head might be a lucid insight into the vacant character of contemporary popular culture [but as] an insight into the normative structure of the vast bulk of American legal thought, the contribution is, of course, unimpeachable."[96]

On the other hand, though, Schlag's analysis suggests that such normative legal discourse constantly reconstructs a vision or understanding of reality centered on the relatively autonomous self. By telling us that we must choose this or that path, normative discourse consistently and repetitively reminds us that we are free to choose whichever path is most appealing. Moreover, according to Schlag, this insistent reconstruction of the modernist self engenders political conservatism. Instead of generating, seeking, and pursuing paths of genuine political empowerment and transformation, we are duped into passivity, meekly pretending that we are relatively autonomous selves who freely discuss, choose, and change our worlds. In short, normative legal thought may not achieve what it claims to do, but paradoxically, it nevertheless accomplishes a lot.[97]

Some postmodernist jurisprudents extend this self-reflexive turn on legal scholarship by criticizing not only modernist scholars but other postmodernists as well. We find that Mootz criticizes Schlag, who criticizes Fish, who criticizes Patterson, and so on. That is, as already mentioned, postmodernists sometimes adopt the guise of the postmodern police, reproaching other postmodernists for not being postmodern enough. Fish, for instance, has accused Patterson of portraying readers in a far too modernist fashion—with too much choice, individuality, and freedom. Meanwhile, Schlag has devoted an entire article to showing how Fish himself ultimately and unknowingly reinscribes the relatively autonomous self of modernism. Mootz, though, faults Schlag's critique of normative legal scholarship for being too simplistic. "The central problem for contemporary jurisprudence is not the maze of normative legal discourse," Mootz asserts, "but the failure to recognize the maze as an unavoidable condition that is productive of knowledge." Indeed, consistent with Mootz's position, many postmodern outsider jurisprudents insist that some degree or form of normativeness is not only unavoidable but is a sine qua non of worthwhile scholarship. Such postmodern normativeness does not lead necessarily to modernist-style recommendations for doctrinal or statutory change but nonetheless accentuates the potential for self-reflexive participation in the constant construction and reconstruction of our contingent and therefore transformable culture.[98]

Finally, some postmodern jurisprudents push the self-reflexive turn toward scholarship even further by focusing on postmodernism in general, including their *own* postmodern orientation. As mentioned, postmodernists have stressed how modernist scholars are constrained by their roles or positions within the social structures of the university, the legal profession, and society in general. But the same is equally true of postmodernists. All scholars, postmodernists as well as modernists, are professors who must teach and publish (at least until they receive tenure). As professors, then, postmodernists and modernists must constantly be expressing a point of view on a host of issues—whether to their students or to their (hoped-for) readers. The substantive viewpoints of modernist writers may be more obvious since they often expressly recommend a normative goal or value, but postmodernists too try to communicate some idea or critical theme that necessarily arises from a distinctive vantage or standpoint. Even the most steadfast postmodernist who successfully conveys an unmodern sense of openness or tentativeness—for example, by explicitly narrating instead of arguing, or by interpreting instead of describing—always has at least an implicit point of view. And from a postmodern perspective, any such point of view necessarily rests on certain background assumptions—a background context. Hence, one sure-fire way for a postmodern jurisprudent to critique another scholar, whether modernist or postmodernist, is simply to point out how that scholar has certain unexamined background assumptions. Of course, from a postmodern standpoint, having unexamined background assumptions (or prejudices derived from tradition) is unavoidable; nonetheless, this recognition does not in any way help fortify those assumptions. Thus, the postmodernist always can bring somebody else's background assumptions to the forefront and subject them to critique. "Any text, even a postmodern deconstructive text, can be deconstructed."[99]

Significantly, then, a postmodernist can even deconstruct her own postmodern position. As with everyone else, the postmodern deconstructionist always "has a particular ax to grind"—that is, some goal or point of view dependent on certain background assumptions. Hence the postmodern deconstructionist always can attempt to bring her own background assumptions to the foreground and to subject them to deconstructive critique—but of course, other background assumptions then would stand behind that critique, and so on, ad infinitum. Regardless of how postmodern a jurisprudent seeks to be, if she authors an article or book or, for that matter, communicates in any manner at all, then she must in effect domesticate or limit her postmodernism. If one doggedly tried to follow postmodern insights to their furthest reaches, then everything would be deconstructed, including those postmodern insights; imagine traveling continually outward until being caught suddenly in the gravitational field of an interstellar black hole that was sucking everything, including yourself, into its abyss. So, to avoid such a deconstructive implosion, we always at some point manage to stop: to talk, to communicate, to write, to whatever.[100]

A postmodern legal scholar's self-reflexive awareness of her own practices often is communicated through the use of irony, the seventh postmodern theme. Because the postmodernist continues to work and live in a structured role as a law professor, she constantly expresses viewpoints on various issues to her students and readers. The postmodern legal scholar, that is, constantly constructs narratives and arguments that draw upon the available rhetorical tools or modes of discourse— namely, the postmodernist must use modernist as well as postmodernist concepts to present her views. But whereas modernist scholars use similar tools with earnestness, postmodern scholars use these tools with irony. To some extent, post-modernists continue to perform in modernist-like practices, including legal scholarship, but with a significantly different attitude. Postmodern jurisprudents thus use modernist tools despite knowing that they cannot perform as promised—the tools cannot deliver any objectively grounded results. Yet for these postmodernists, no other options exist. There are no other rhetorical or discursive devices that can be grasped. In this sense, then, postmodern scholarship amounts to "playing with the pieces"—including the fallen pieces that remain from deconstructed modernist positions. To be sure, though, while postmodernists might be said to be playing with scholarly tools or pieces, such play is not necessarily frivolous (though sometimes it can be); as the previous discussion of deconstruction and justice should suggest, much postmodern scholarship is politically and morally charged.[101]

Through irony, then, the postmodern scholar signals that even though she might use modernist methods, tools, and sources, she uses them with the self-reflexive awareness that they cannot deliver modernist objectivity. A common postmodern technique for connoting such irony is pastiche: the juxtaposition in one text of different styles, sources, and traditions. Pastiche allows the postmodernist to suggest the contingency of each of the various styles, sources, and traditions—to communicate the idea of anti-foundationalism—even as the postmodernist uses the modernist-like methods and sources. Put in a different way, a scholar's use of unconventional and unexpected sources and styles can represent a wink or a nod to the reader that signifies postmodern irony.[102]

Among postmodern jurisprudents, Balkin and Schlag have used pastiche to evoke irony. Both have relied, for example, on that rich source of postmodern culture, television. In an article on tradition, deconstruction, and law, Balkin playfully (or sarcastically) questions the importance of various American traditions because they were not featured on *I Love Lucy*. Schlag, meanwhile, juxtaposes serious (modernist) legal philosophy with television: he asks the reader to consider what role the renowned jurisprudent Ronald Dworkin might play on the television show *L. A. Law.* Elsewhere, Schlag mixes styles in a different manner. In *The Problem of the Subject,* he largely follows the strict decorum of formal legal writing (that is, modernist legal thought); nonetheless he manages to poke fun at the vapid rigidity of such formal writing by referring to Dean Langdell as "Chris." This playful mix of styles marks the metaphorical arched eyebrow, suggesting Schlag's self-reflexive and ironic use of the more formal style. Schlag writes: "One can imagine, for instance, Chris Langdell waking up one day, forgetting to use the imperial declarative mode, and writing not, 'The law is . . .' but instead, 'I *think* the law is. . . .' By writing that sentence, Chris might have recognized that he (the 'I'), far from passively receiving the commands of law, was actively engaged in *thinking* (*i.e.,* constructing) the law."[103]

The eighth postmodern theme is that postmodernism appears to be, in a sense, politically ambivalent. Many postmodern legal theorists stress, and rightly so, that postmodernism, especially deconstruction, has potentially radical political implications. Balkin explains an initial connection between deconstruction and political justice: "[D]econstruction has a goal; its goal is not destruction but rectification. The deconstructor critiques for the purpose of betterment; she seeks out unjust or inappropriate conceptual hierarchies in order to assert a better ordering. Hence, her argument is always premised on the possibility of an alternative to existing norms that is not simply different, but also more just." For that reason, then, Derridean deconstruction supports the pursuit of justice, but paradoxically—and moving beyond Balkin's point—deconstruction simultaneously and radically disrupts any claim to justice. Deconstruction urges us to remain always wary of and to refrain from final declarations of justice, and in so doing, deconstruction compels us to quest tirelessly after justice. "[W]henever we label an event or action as just, there is necessarily the trace of the Other hiding in the margins of our understanding. Within each hermeneutic act in which the meaning of justice comes into being, there is injustice. Each act of justice violently and duplicitously excludes, denies, and oppresses some Other. Hence, justice cannot be fulfilled; it is always displaced." Derrida, as already noted, goes so far as to declare that "[d]econstruction is justice."[104]

Unsurprisingly, then, most postmodern legal scholars appear to be progressive or left-leaning in their politics. As such, they often seek to intervene in established social and cultural practices through deconstruction, by disturbing and shifting the accepted social structures and cultural symbols. Schlag's tenacious deconstructive critique of modernist legal scholarship illustrates this point. He seeks to disorient the typical practice of legal scholarship so that law professors become more politically cognizant of their complicity in the violence of the legal system. Yet, the radical political potential of postmodernism emerges perhaps most conspicuously in the writings of postmodern outsider jurisprudents, as they overtly struggle to disclose and transform the oppressive cultural assumptions embedded in American law. For these postmodernists, deconstruction can provide a theoretical technique and justification that supports their political struggles. The deconstructive emphasis on the instability and plasticity of textual meanings resonates with the outsider insistence that there always exist multiple voices and multiple truths—even if the dominant cultural perspective appears to deny that very point. Deconstruction thus fits neatly with the goals of outsider scholarship, which, in the words of William N. Eskridge, "seeks to challenge the law's agenda, its assumptions, and its biases."[105]

At the same time, though, postmodernism can seem to support political conservatism in certain contexts. Indeed, it is worth reiterating that many outsider jurisprudents remain suspicious of postmodernism; they fear that postmodern deconstructive views might undermine the conviction needed to support radical political movements. Beyond these suspicions and fears of political insouciance, moreover, there is a far more concrete and striking exemplification of postmodern political conservatism. Namely, politically conservative manifestations of postmodernism have surfaced in the forum of the United States Supreme Court under Chief Justice William H. Rehnquist. To be clear, I do not argue that the justices have become avowed or overt postmodern theorists such as we find in the legal academy, but rather that the justices, like others in America, live within a postmodern culture. Consequently, postmodernism has in a sense infused their judicial practice; some of the justices, including some of the most politically conservative ones, occasionally seem to allude to or draw on postmodern themes in their opinions.

For example, the joint opinion in *Planned Parenthood v. Casey,* authored by Justices O'Connor, Kennedy, and Souter, displays the postmodern themes of self-reflexivity and anti-foundationalism. *Casey* reexamined the issue of whether the Constitution protects a woman's interest in choosing whether or not to have an abortion. *Roe v. Wade,* of course, had held initially in 1973 that the constitutional right of privacy encompasses this interest: states therefore could not prohibit abortions until viability or the last trimester of a pregnancy. Justice Blackmun, as discussed earlier in this chapter, had begun the majority opinion in *Roe* by suggesting that, despite "the sensitive and emotional nature of the abortion controversy," the Court's decision would be legitimate because it would be objective. As Blackmun phrased it, the Court would "earnestly" resolve the case "by constitutional measurement, free of emotion and of predilection." By the time that the Rehnquist Court decided *Casey* in 1992, after twenty years of post-*Roe* anti-abortion and pro-choice litigation, rhetoric, protests, and violence, the justices did not even hint that the decision was objective. To the contrary, the Court claimed to decide in accordance with "reasoned judgment," which, the joint opinion explained, does not have boundaries "susceptible of expression as a simple rule."[106]

In an important part of the joint opinion, the Court extensively discussed the doctrine of *stare decisis* and the possibility of overruling *Roe.* Ultimately, the *Casey*

Court reaffirmed *Roe* and its main holding, that there is a constitutional right to choose whether to have an abortion before viability. Most interestingly, though, in the course of this discussion, the joint opinion self-reflexively pondered how over-ruling *Roe* might undermine the Court's own legitimacy. Unlike in *Roe,* the *Casey* Court did not proclaim that its legitimacy was grounded on being objective. Instead, the *Casey* Court suggested that its legitimacy arose from public perceptions of the Court and its decisions. For the Court to retain its power, the joint opinion reasoned, the American people must believe that the Court's decisions are based on constitutional principles. If the Court were to overrule *Roe,* however, the *Casey* decision would seem too political, injudicious, and unprincipled. The Court specu-lated that it could not even "pretend" to overrule *Roe* on a principled basis. There-fore, a decision to overrule, the joint opinion concluded, would seriously under-mine the Court's power and legitimacy.[107]

Now, how does the *Casey* opinion manifest postmodernism, at least to some de-gree? For one thing, the Court's extended self-reflexive turn upon its own prac-tices resonates with postmodernism. Beyond this point, and in clear opposition to the more modernist pretensions of *Roe,* the *Casey* Court did not claim that its deci-sion was objective or based on some firm foundation. Yet, according to the Court, the lack of a foundation is not overly important because what really matters is not objectivity but rather public perceptions. The Court's legitimacy depends on noth-ing deeper than perceptions and beliefs. The Court seemed to acknowledge that it operates in a hall of mirrors. The justices then must be concerned not to change di-rections too abruptly for fear that they might strike and shatter a mirror. And if that were to happen, then all perceptions of legitimacy would go awry.

Paradoxically, though, the mere fact that the *Casey* Court turned to gaze upon itself and to self-reflexively contemplate its own practices suggests that traditional or modernist notions of legitimacy are no longer relevant. For, of course, if the Court's power were truly threatened, the Court would not save itself by expressly announcing that it was deciding a case for the benefit of *public perceptions.* The Court, if it were truly threatened, would not suggest that it might decide the in-stant case differently if only it could *pretend* to decide on a principled basis. To the contrary, a purely modernist Court, like the Court in *Roe v. Wade,* would briefly and forcefully assert that its conclusions were objectively grounded on a firm foun-dation. Yet, by openly examining its own legitimacy, the *Casey* Court instead con-notes the possibility that, at least in most cases, it could actually say anything in an opinion because the Court's power and legitimacy no longer arise from or depend on its opinions. So few people still take the Court's opinions seriously that the jus-tices could, let's say, quote poetry, in their opinions, and few people would notice, and even fewer would care.

In fact, that is exactly what Chief Justice Rehnquist has done: quoted poetry—at length. In the first flag desecration case, *Texas v. Johnson,* decided in 1989, the Court held that the burning of an American flag in political protest was symbolic conduct protected under the free speech clause of the First Amendment. The Court's decision effectively invalidated statutes of forty-eight states and the federal government that had prohibited desecration of the flag. Chief Justice Rehnquist dissented. He commenced his opinion by suggesting that American history constitutionally justified flag desecration statutes. He thus proceeded into a rendition of that history based primarily on poetry. He began with Ralph Waldo Emerson's "Concord Hymn":

> By the rude bridge that arched the flood
> Their flag to April's breeze unfurled,
> Here once the embattled farmers stood
> And fired the shot heard round the world.[108]

The Chief Justice then turned to the story of Francis Scott Key and "The Star-Spangled Banner," from which Rehnquist quoted several lines. Finally, he turned to John Greenleaf Whittier's Civil War poem "Barbara Frietchie," which recounts a tale of a ninety-year-old woman flying the Union flag as Confederate troops, led by Stonewall Jackson, marched through her Maryland town. Rehnquist did not merely quote a passage of the poem, he inserted the entire composition, all sixty lines. Here is a sample. By way of background, when Jackson first saw the flag, he had his men shoot it down. Barbara Frietchic, though, snatched up the flag and waved it back at the Confederate troops, challenging them to shoot again. Whittier wrote:

> "Shoot, if you must, this old gray head,
> But spare your country's flag," she said.
> A shade of sadness, a blush of shame,
> Over the face of the leader came;
> The nobler nature within him stirred
> To life at that woman's deed and word;
> "Who touches a hair of yon gray head
> Dies like a dog! March on!" he said.[109]

Rehnquist's somewhat bohemian conception of authoritative sources in *Johnson* contrasts strikingly with another one of his dissents, written fifteen years earlier in a case that also involved flag desecration. In *Smith v. Goguen,* decided in 1974, the Court held that a Massachusetts state flag desecration statute was unconstitutionally void for vagueness. Unsurprisingly, Rehnquist, then an associate justice, dissented. As in the later case of *Johnson,* Rehnquist referred to poems (and also songs) in his dissenting opinion. He even quoted the identical passage from Emerson. Beyond Emerson, though, Rehnquist quoted from none of the other poems or songs except for two words from "Barbara Frietchie." His legal reasoning was far more conventional or modernist; his discussion of verse was brief and intended merely to underscore the importance of the flag in American life.[110]

So despite the similarities between the cases of *Johnson* and *Smith v. Goguen,* Rehnquist changed during the interval of fifteen years—becoming, we might say, more avant-garde (or postmodern). He is not alone in this group either. In fact, his leading partner is probably Justice Antonin Scalia. An excellent example is in the case of *County of Sacramento v. Lewis*, decided in 1998. *Lewis* involved a police officer who allegedly had been deliberately or recklessly indifferent to life during the apprehension of a suspected offender. The Court held that the officer, under the circumstances, had not violated the Fourteenth Amendment's guarantee of substantive due process. Scalia agreed with the Court's conclusion but refused to join Justice Souter's majority opinion. In his concurrence, Scalia criticized Souter's standard for determining a violation of substantive due process. The Souter majority opinion pronounced that an executive action violates substantive due process only if it is so "arbitrary" that it "shocks the conscience."[111] Scalia maintained that this standard not only was overly subjective but also had been rejected by the Court only a year earlier, in the case of *Washington v. Glucksberg*. According to Scalia, Souter's concurrence in *Glucksberg* had proposed a similar standard of arbitrariness, and the *Glucksberg* majority had repudiated it. To make his point, Scalia relied on the famed songwriter (and now, perhaps, legal authority), Cole Porter. Specifically, Scalia paraphrased a passage from Porter's song "You're the Top," in order to suggest that Souter's substantive due process standard was the ultimate in subjectivity: "[I]f anything, today's opinion is even more of a throw-back to highly subjective substantive-due-process methodologies than [Souter's] concurrence in *Glucksberg* was. Whereas the latter said merely that substantive due process prevents 'arbitrary impositions' and 'purposeless restraints' (without any objective criterion as to what is arbitrary or purposeless), today's opinion resuscitates the ne plus ultra, the Napoleon Brandy, the Mahatma Ghandi [*sic*], the Celophane [*sic*] of subjectivity, th' ol' 'shocks-the-conscience' test."[112]

How do Rehnquist's and Scalia's invocations of poets and songwriters relate to postmodernism? Rehnquist and Scalia appear to suggest that they are not writing their opinions with the earnestness that had characterized more modernist justices and times. By including in their opinions somewhat bizarre passages and references—bizarre, that is, from a modernist perspective—the justices seem to use pastiche to evoke a postmodern ironic attitude. The justices, in other words, are juxtaposing different styles, sources, and traditions in a manner that implicitly connotes the contingency of each. The justices' quotation and citation of poets and songwriters represents a wink or a nod to the reader. The reader is warned that even though the justices also continue to use ostensible modernist tools and sources, they use them with the self-reflexive awareness that they cannot deliver modernist objectivity. The justices thus are, in a sense, playing with the pieces, as they use modernist sources and tools without earnestly believing in their efficacy. Unsurprisingly, then, in *James B. Beam Distilling Co. v. Georgia*, Scalia suggested that even if judges make law, they must *pretend* to discover it.

"[T]he judicial Power of the United States" conferred upon this Court . . . must be deemed to be the judicial power as understood by our common-law tradition. That is the power "to say what the law is," not the power to change it. I am not so naive (nor do I think our forebears were) as to be unaware that judges in a real sense "make" law. But *they make it as judges make it,* which is to say *as though* they were "finding" it—discerning what the law is, rather than decreeing what it is today changed to, or what it will tomorrow be.[113]

Thus, even as Rehnquist and Scalia play with the pieces, they still most often use the traditional modernist tools of judicial decision making, such as the doctrine of *stare decisis*. They parse the supposedly precise meanings of various case precedents and weave elaborate webs of rationally consistent legal propositions. But the justices seem to know that these types of legal arguments are just the tattered remnants of their modernist beliefs. They know that their decisions are not objective and do not rest on firm foundations. They know, in the words of Scalia, that "the Court is entitled to call a 'central holding' whatever it wants to call a 'central holding.'" They know—better than anyone else knows—that they rarely even write the opinions that bear their names. Their clerks do most of the writing; indeed, the clerks even largely determine which cases the Court will decide. Yet the justices know that it all does not really matter. The structures of the Court's power are too well entrenched in American society: the content of the Court's opinions thus neither legitimate nor undermine its position and power. The Court will continue to decide cases, and the justices will continue to write—or at least, to sign—their opinions. The Court will continue to deal life and death—for, to be sure, the justices may be playing with the pieces, but they play seriously. In sum, the Supreme Court's brand of postmodern jurisprudence illustrates that despite the potentially radical political implications of postmodern theory, postmodernism can be turned to politically conservative ends.[114]

Without doubt, many postmodern legal scholars would dispute my characterization of postmodern jurisprudence. Among other criticisms, they might disagree with my designation of the eight main postmodern themes; they might criticize my specification of the content of any or all of the themes; or they might reject my thematic approach to postmodernism altogether, suggesting that such an approach resonates too closely with modernist attempts to reduce complex concepts (or eras) to precise definitions. Simultaneously, though, I obviously believe that many postmodernists will find much to agree with in my portrayal of postmodern jurisprudence. Moreover, postmodernists would unite widely in their opposition to a common modernist retort to postmodern scholarship. In particular, many modernist jurisprudents (somewhat predictably) recommend that we should choose to stave off postmodernism. From this modernist perspective, postmodernism is no more than a theoretical or ideological viewpoint that can be evaluated and rejected if found inadequate. And, of course, modernists conclude that postmodernism is, in fact, inadequate. Modernists unsurprisingly depict postmodernism by forcing it to fit within modernist dichotomies: hence, because postmodernists do not claim to establish foundations for objective knowledge, modernists conclude that postmodernism must be nihilistic, solipsistic, and relativistic. As such, postmodernism is dangerous and irresponsible and must be repudiated in favor of modernism. Yet, from a *postmodern* viewpoint, we do not have such a *choice* between modernism and postmodernism; the movement from modernism to postmodernism is, in part, a contingent cultural and social transformation. "Individuals and societal groups might influence this transition, but they do not control it. Only in a modernist dream can we consider the options, choose the best one, and then effectively implement it."[115]

Conclusion

A Glimpse of the Future?

The voyage of American legal thought has here been traced from one stage to another, from one substage to another. Much of this story has turned on the interrelated ideas of foundations and progress. In the premodern era, natural law principles seemed to undergird the legal system. During the earliest decades of the nation's history, legal and political thinkers were largely concerned with preserving the republic and its commitment to eternal and universal principles. From approximately 1820 through the Civil War, though, jurisprudents combined their conviction in the existence of natural law principles with a belief in a premodern idea of progress. Natural law still provided the foundation for the legal system, but America apparently could progress by instrumentally and pragmatically implementing those principles. As such, natural law seemingly provided both the goals and the limits for American jurisprudents and jurists as they sought to perfectly realize the eternal and universal principles. After the Civil War, American legal thought entered its modernist period with the onset of positivism: for the most part, jurisprudents repudiated natural law. Consequently, the idea of progress was unleashed from the natural law limits that inhered during the premodern era. Progress came to be seen as potentially endless, dependent solely on human ingenuity. Even with the rejection of natural law principles, though, modernist jurisprudents retained a desire for grounding the legal system on a firm foundation. Without such a foundation, modernists feared, the law would be overly subjective and relative—even nihilistic. Yet, because natural law principles seemingly could no longer provide the needed foundation, the modernist quest for an alternative foundation began. Jurisprudents turned to rationalism, empiricism, and then transcendentalism as they struggled to identify an objective ground for the law. During the latter part of the twentieth century, American legal modernism entered its final substage, late crisis, which was marked by confusion, despair, and creative complexity. Legal scholars retained their strong desire to locate a jurisprudential foundation, yet they feared that this goal was unachievable. Finally, in the last decades of the century, American legal thought began its postmodern period. Many jurisprudents rejected the modernist quest for foundations yet refused to succumb to the modernist hobgoblins of subjectivism, relativism, and nihilism. Postmodernists thus began to explore the ramifications of anti-foundationalism for our understanding of law. Many postmodernists also denounced the modernist idea of endless progress. Humans were not the sovereign centers of control posited by modernists. We might influence social changes, but our efforts at control were likely to be met by frustration and surprise as they led in unexpected and sometimes harmful directions.

To be sure, the stages of premodernism, modernism, and postmodernism and their respective substages are not clearly demarcated in intellectual history. Stages and substages neither appear magically out of thin air nor just stop and disappear. New stages and substages always develop in part out of what preceded them, while vestiges from one stage (or substage) always remain evident in the next one, and even the next after that, and so on. For instance, natural law and natural rights reasoning, so prominent in premodernism, faded during the modernist period, but remnants lingered in constitutional scholarship and constitutional decision making during the late nineteenth and early twentieth centuries. Indeed, references to natural law still occasionally surface today. Langdellian legal science, definitive of first-stage modernist jurisprudence, has been denounced by subsequent modernists and postmodernists alike, yet the effects of Langdellianism are vibrant in legal scholarship and legal education even now; postmodernists would not bother to discuss and decry Langdellianism but for its lasting and current significance. Likewise, the second-stage modernist era of American legal realism may have passed long ago, but realism nonetheless lives on in its effects on casebooks as well as scholarship, particularly those scholarly approaches that focus on the social sciences, prominent for example among members of the Law and Society Association.[1]

Consequently, it is unsurprising that the border between modernist and postmodernist legal scholarship remains cloudy. While the transition from modern to postmodern jurisprudence is, in my opinion, not only discernible but also momentous, this transition is neither undisputed nor all-pervasive. Many legal scholars still consider themselves to be modernists, and rightly so. Moreover, many of these modernist jurisprudents expressly castigate postmodernists. Indeed, at least for some modernists, any hint of a postmodern perspective by another writer automatically provokes a welter of opprobrium—with accusations of nihilism, relativism, irresponsibility, and the like spewing forth. Even the distinction between modernism and postmodernism is contested. While some scholars fully embrace the idea that we live today in a postmodern age, others prefer to talk of the current age as modern/postmodern—and still others of course insist that we either currently remain in or should choose to return to modernism.[2] Yet, one paradox of the postmodern age is that even avowed modernists sometimes seem to be strongly influenced by postmodern culture. This phenomenon is evident from the discussion of postmodernism and the Supreme Court at the end of the previous chapter. The Supreme Court justices, as mentioned, have not become overt or avowed postmodernists. If you were to ask Chief Justice Rehnquist, for instance, whether he is a postmodernist, I am confident that he would either say "No" or laugh in your face. But that is not the point. Rather, the justices, like other Americans, live in a postmodern culture, and as such, they are influenced occasionally to act in a postmodern way and to have a postmodern attitude. And the justices do so regardless of whether or not they would identify themselves as postmodernists.

More important in the context of this study is that postmodern culture seems to be infusing the scholarship of even avowed modernist jurisprudents. As a general matter, we might say that modernist lawyers and scholars carry a toolbox containing devices such as *stare decisis,* logical consistency, the plain meaning of the text, the intentions of the framers or the parties, policy arguments, and balancing tests. Modernists reach in and pull out the tools they need to suit their particular instrumental purposes, to construct arguments for or against certain substantive positions. Learning to choose the right tools and to use them well is part of learning to think like a lawyer. Recently, though, some modernist scholars have recognized that certain postmodern insights might be useful for constructing their modernist arguments.[3]

In particular, these modernist scholars usually have seized on one oft-discussed aspect of postmodern theory and have tossed it into their toolbox. Many postmodernists, as discussed in chapter 5, maintain that the traditions and culture of a community simultaneously enable and constrain all communication and understanding. Thus, for the individual within the community, one's current horizon of sociocultural prejudices and interests *always* shapes understanding, communication, and perception in general, including normative values and goals. Although this postmodern insight can have radical implications, modernists have appropriated it, domesticated it, and used it as a tool—a new doodad that can be wielded when constructing legal arguments. These modernists have put this postmodern insight into their lawyer's toolbox, storing it securely and taking it out only as needed. And for these modernists, this insight (or tool) can be most fruitfully exploited to criticize the normative positions of other modernists. But then, once the values and goals of others have been neatly deconstructed and swept away, the modernist writer typically begins to articulate his or her own normative position. Quickly, the tool must be returned to its box—otherwise it might threaten the coherence of the writer's own express objectives.

Steven D. Smith is a modernist legal scholar who uses this postmodern tool. In his book on the separation of church and state, *Foreordained Failure*, published in 1995, he argues that the Constitution does not embody a principle of religious freedom. Of course, judges and constitutional scholars have long been asking "something like the following question: 'What is the meaning and scope of the principle of religious freedom embodied in the Constitution?'" If, as Smith maintains, no such principle exists, then this question becomes unanswerable.[4]

Smith argues that many constitutional scholars use some type of *theory* to explicate a supposed principle of religious freedom in the First Amendment. To refute such theoretical approaches, Smith reaches into his toolbox and pulls out his postmodern doohickey. He contends that a general theory of religious freedom is impossible: any such theory inevitably founders on a logical conundrum.

> The function of a theory of religious freedom is to mediate among a variety of competing religious and secular positions and interests, or to explain how government ought to deal with these competing positions and interests. To perform that function, however, the theory will tacitly but inevitably privilege, or prefer in advance, one of those positions while rejecting or discounting others. But a theory that privileges one of the competing positions and rejects others a priori is not truly a theory of religious freedom at all—or, at least, it is not the sort of theory that modern proponents of religious freedom have sought to develop.[5]

In other words, Smith here draws upon the postmodern assertion that all normative values or positions are culturally and socially contingent. To postmodernists, all theory—indeed, all communication and understanding—arises from one's current horizon of sociocultural prejudices and interests. Hence, Smith readily argues that any theory of religious freedom—as a distinctive normative position—necessarily rests upon certain (often tacit) background beliefs or assumptions. Those background beliefs or assumptions always remain controversial and are exactly the types of assertions that the theory itself supposedly reconciles neutrally with other competing beliefs. But of course, the theory cannot neutrally reconcile its own assumptions with other competing beliefs exactly because the theory rests on those very assumptions. Smith concludes: "[t]he problem, simply put, is that theories of religious freedom seek to reconcile or to mediate among competing religious and secular positions within a society, but those competing positions disagree about the very background beliefs on which a theory of religious freedom must rest."[6]

At this point, though, Smith tosses his postmodern gizmo back into the toolbox. He wants to critique the jurisprudence of the religion clauses but not to become embroiled in larger jurisprudential controversies regarding theory. "I do not want to deny in any universal way that 'theory' may be possible and desirable in the law; my challenge here is directed only to theories of religious freedom." Smith's reluctance to follow the extended implications of his postmodern insight enables him to conclude with a normative recommendation for the Supreme Court. Although he qualifies this recommendation, he nonetheless suggests that the Court should consider refusing to enforce a principle of religious freedom, leaving the protection of religious liberty and equality to the "political process." Smith thus manages to sidestep the potentially radical political implications of postmodernism for constitutional jurisprudence in general and instead reaches a politically conservative conclusion.[7]

In sum, even though many modernist legal scholars excoriate postmodernism, some simultaneously domesticate postmodern insights to construct and defend their modernist positions.[8] Doing so, without doubt, can seriously skew a writer's conclusions. Smith applied his postmodern doohickey and found that a constitutional principle of religious liberty does not exist. *If* it were the case that *other* constitutional principles truly exist (which Smith seems to assume but does not address), then perhaps Smith's normative suggestion that the Court should consider not enforcing a principle of religious liberty might be sensible. After all, one might reasonably conclude that the Court can enforce only existent constitutional principles. Yet, if Smith's postmodern-like argument were expanded to suggest that *no* constitutional principles at all truly exist—at least not in the traditional modernist sense—then Smith's normative suggestion becomes highly questionable. Religious liberty would be on no weaker footing than any other liberty or right. Thus for instance, unlike Smith, one might suggest that the concept of constitutional principles needs to be completely rethought or that a coherent abstract constitutional principle is unnecessary to the practical or pragmatic enforcement of general norms. But the selective use of postmodernism as a critical tool—wielded against the views of other writers—still ostensibly allows the creative modernist author (and Smith is a good one) either to recommend a desired normative goal or to ground some preferred governmental process or normative value on an ostensibly firm foundation.

Hence, postmodern views have seeped into modernist scholarship, but at the same time, postmodern jurisprudents continue to write under a cloud of modernism. Many postmodernists tend to be preoccupied with modernist concerns—such as anti-foundationalism versus foundationalism, anti-essentialism versus essentialism, and so forth. Postmodern jurisprudents continue to stress exactly those aspects of their scholarship that distinguish them most clearly from their modernist colleagues and predecessors. As suggested in chapter 2, then, postmodernism might enter a second stage when it moves out from under this cloud, when postmodernists no longer dwell on modernist concerns. Thus, without reiterating the general suggestions offered at the end of chapter 2 concerning the possible metamorphosis of postmodernism, the specific question to be addressed here is as follows: How might a potential second stage of postmodernism be manifested in the realm of American legal thought? Before attempting to answer this question, though, the caveat from chapter 2 should be repeated: this discussion of second-stage postmodernism will be tentative and suggestive. Certainly, if the border between modern and postmodern legal scholarship still remains cloudy, as I ac-

knowledge, then any discussion of a potential second-stage postmodern jurisprudence must be understood as, at best, wildly conjectural.

In any event, I initially will approach second-stage postmodern legal thought
from a perhaps counterintuitive perspective: the vantage of the Supreme Court. I
already have contended that postmodern culture has partly infused Supreme Court
decision making, but now I would like to add a paradoxical supplement to this assertion. Rather than contemplating Supreme Court postmodernism secondarily or
as derivative from postmodern legal scholarship, I want to consider the possibility
that the Court offers at least a partial glimpse of the future by presaging aspects of
second-stage postmodern legal thought. How can this be? The Court's structural
role in American society is crucial: the Court's role pushes the justices to approach
postmodern insights from a direction that differs radically from that of postmodern scholars. And from the Court's direction, postmodernism has materialized in
strange ways that, arguably, might foreshadow second-stage postmodernism.

To understand the Court's brand of postmodernism more fully, it is first necessary to recognize how the justices' situation epitomizes the current postmodern
cultural condition in at least one important fashion. Postmodern cultural studies, as
noted in chapter 2, often describe the postmodern subject or agent as somewhat
like a modernist self in hyperspeed: the culturally and socially constructed postmodern subject is one who constantly makes inane decisions or choices without
firm (modernist) reasons or foundations in a quest for individual distinction. The
fragmentation of American culture has mixed with capitalist commercialism to
commodify radicalism. The postmodern subject is a hyperconsumer who seeks to
buy radical individuality or uniqueness by repeatedly choosing from a variety of
mass-produced and mass-advertised products. From this perspective, Supreme
Court justices can be seen as typical postmodern subjects. The justices (qua justices) may not be hyperconsumers precisely, but they are hyper–decision makers.
Like their modernist predecessors on the Court, the current justices must decide
and decide and decide some more—that is their role in American society, to decide
cases as well as deciding whether to grant certiorari for numerous other cases; the
Court, for instance, disposed of nearly 7,000 cases during the 1977 term. Yet unlike their modernist Supreme Court forerunners, at least some of the justices now
seem to make their decisions without the benefit of belief in a firm modernist foundation, without the reassuring comfort of ostensible objectivity. To decide without
foundations, that is the current justices' role in a postmodern world.

As such, Supreme Court justices differ from postmodern legal scholars in an important fashion. Still dwelling under the shadow of modernist concerns, postmodern scholars or theorists tend to stress the instability of textual meanings. Many
postmodern scholars, in their efforts to refute modernism, seem to enjoy few things
more than deconstructing a widely accepted and dominant reading of an important
text, whether that text be law, literature, philosophy, or otherwise. Such a deconstruction of a dominant reading inevitably discloses previously suppressed alterna-

tive meanings or truths for the text. These postmodern deconstructionists, then, are clearly hostile to any authoritative pronouncement of a single meaning for a text. Yet, such authoritative pronouncements routinely issue from the Supreme Court. After all, one role of the Supreme Court is to decide cases, and in so doing, they must proclaim *the* law. Whereas many postmodern scholars celebrate the multiplicity of textual meanings and truths, the Supreme Court's authoritative pronouncements instead, in effect, suppress or kill alternative meanings. Jacques Derrida and his jurisprudential disciples might declare that a text's meaning is undecidable, but the Supreme Court justices must decide. Law professors can revel in textual ambiguities—in fact, such ambiguities helpfully generate a plethora of scholarly publications—but Supreme Court justices must pronounce the law.[9]

Hence, because of the Court's position as an authoritative pronouncer of law, the justices—at least in their roles as justices—are unlikely to be postmodern in the same way that law professors are postmodern. Instead of becoming avowed and overt postmodern theorists who celebrate multiple textual meanings—as has happened with many professors—the justices will continue to hand down decisions. The justices thus are more apt to use postmodern insights, like anti-foundationalism, as if they were modernist tools, like *stare decisis,* that can facilitate the satisfactory resolution of cases. To be sure, this instrumental use of postmodern insights can lead to accusations that the justices are being merely disingenuous or inauthentic rather than truly postmodern.[10] Indeed, from this perspective, one might go further to conclude that there is an inherent tension between postmodern theory and judicial decision making; there must be, accordingly, an insuperable limit to the idea of postmodern jurisprudence. Perhaps the practice of legal scholarship can become postmodern, but the practices of law and judicial decision making cannot do the same. To some extent, this observation might partially explain the apparently growing gap between legal scholars and judges. In fact, if their respective structural roles in American society lead them in opposite directions, particularly in reaction to postmodern culture, then this gap is likely to become a long-lasting and unbridgeable abyss. Unlike their modernist predecessors who dwelled on judicial opinions, postmodern jurisprudents will continue to pay less and less attention to judges and their opinions, while judges, including Supreme Court justices, will react by continuing either to ignore or disdain the outpourings of legal scholars.[11] Yet, simultaneously, one should not overlook the possibility of an alternative and more postmodern understanding of the Supreme Court. If one views postmodernism at least partly as a matter of culture, then as suggested, certain Supreme Court actions can be understood precisely as manifestations of postmodern culture in judicial practice. But because the justices are apt to appropriate postmodern insights in an instrumental manner, as tools, the justices will paint a rather odd picture of postmodernism—odd at least from a first-stage postmodern position.

Perhaps, though, the Supreme Court's angle on postmodernism presages an aspect of second-stage postmodern legal thought. In particular, the Court's form of postmodernism might anticipate the pathological condition of postmodern terrorism. As described in chapter 2, postmodern terrorism can take two different forms: physical or hermeneutic. The postmodern terrorist recognizes that meaning is ungrounded and that, in postmodern culture, knowledge is rushing by at dizzying speeds. Yet, instead of either being crushed by this hyperculture or succumbing to a type of stupor, the postmodern terrorist attempts to stop the relentless hyperspeed of postmodern culture, if only for a moment. The terrorist might do so through a physically violent act or, in a less harmful manner, by attempting a hermeneutic action that autocratically asserts a meaning (for a text or text-analogue).

The Supreme Court can be understood as foreshadowing both physical and hermeneutic postmodern terrorism. From a hermeneutic outlook, few postmodern scholars would maintain that deconstruction implies a textual free-for-all where "anything goes"—even though modernist critics consistently charge postmodernists with this position. From a postmodern standpoint, deconstruction explicates how one comes to understand a text and how that process entails certain conditions or limits. Yet, from the Supreme Court's vantage—arising in part from their structural position—postmodernism might look precisely like a license for unconstrained textual interpretation. The justices (or at least some of them) recognize that their judicial decisions cannot be objectively grounded on firm foundations, yet they still must decide the cases. The justices must, therefore, autocratically pronounce the law. They must proclaim meaning—meaning that they realize is ultimately ungrounded, ephemeral, and shifting, yet is declared in the most authoritative fashion. The justices might be playing with the judicial pieces in a postmodern fashion, but they will continue to act, in many instances, as if they were discovering objectively based rules of law or even deducing uncontroversial conclusions from eternal principles. And the justices can do so without modernist anxiety. They no longer dread the possibility that their decisions are not objectively grounded. Rather, the justices know not only that their decisions are ungrounded but also that such groundlessness does not truly matter. The justices can play with the tools of modernist judicial practice and decision making with impunity. Thus, for conservative justices such as William Rehnquist and Antonin Scalia, the lack of foundations seems to do little more than to justify following their conservative political inclinations. And what else should they do, they might ask, if there are no modernist foundations and rules to force them to go in different political and legal directions? Unlike their estranged associates in legal academe, the justices cannot celebrate the undecidability of textual meaning because, as the justices might sneer, they are just too busy deciding real cases. And what of physical postmodern terrorism? It follows from the justices' hermeneutic terrorism. For when the justices autocratically proclaim the law, the Court's decisions often have material consequences, sometimes as extreme as life and death. When the Court denies a habeas corpus petition for a capital defendant, for instance, the petitioner faces almost certain death, regardless of whether the Court's pronouncement is objectively grounded or not.[12]

Finally, what do these observations suggest about a potential second stage of postmodern legal scholarship? Postmodern terrorism is one possibility here, but not the only one. As discussed in chapter 5, a significant component of postmodern jurisprudence is meta-scholarship—scholarship about scholarship. Yet, the idea of such meta-scholarship becomes problematic in a projected second-stage post-modernism where the cloud of modernism has dissipated. Most frequently, meta-scholarship is not merely scholarship about scholarship, but more precisely, it is *postmodern* scholarship deconstructing *modernist* legal scholarship. Hence, if mod-ernist legal scholarship were no longer being produced—if the cloud of mod-ernism had lifted—then postmodern legal scholars no longer could write meta-scholarship deconstructing current modernist scholarship. What then? I am reminded of a quotation from a Website commenting on postmodern American culture: "[we Americans are] actually being colonized on a cultural level. How else to explain the sudden spectacular popularity of absurdly un-American products like 'handcrafted' beer and boutique bread? Since when are Budweiser and Won-derbread not good enough for Americans?"[13] This passage suggests, however obliquely, at least four possible futures for postmodern legal scholarship.

In the first possibility, postmodern jurisprudents themselves, like the Supreme Court justices, might engage in a type of hermeneutic postmodern terrorism. If buying Budweiser and Wonderbread always have been good enough for Ameri-cans, then in jurisprudential terms, writing about legal rules and principles and ju-dicial decisions always has been good enough for American legal scholars. Follow-ing this sentiment, some second-stage postmodern jurisprudents actually might return to writing doctrinal scholarship—writing about legal rules and principles and judicial decisions—though without modernist pretensions. These postmodern jurisprudents might recognize that judicial decision making will continue regard-less of postmodern culture, and that judges (and justices) therefore will continue to enunciate modernist-like justifications for their decisions—whether or not the judges still believe that such justifications and decisions are objectively grounded. Thus, second-stage postmodern scholars might write doctrinal scholarship that closely resembles modernist doctrinal scholarship, but the postmodernists will do so with a different attitude and a different purpose. Modernists wrote (and still write, for that matter) doctrinal scholarship with an anxious conviction in founda-tions: they earnestly invoked modernist tools of judicial reasoning and decision making in an effort to purposefully direct courts to objective answers. Postmod-ernists might instead write doctrinal scholarship playfully and ironically rather than earnestly and anxiously. Knowing that their doctrinal recommendations can-not seriously constrain judicial decision making, postmodern scholars nonetheless might proffer doctrinal frameworks that playfully parody judicial opinions and that simultaneously model a playful and ironic mix of modernist judicial tools in conjunction with postmodern insights. Yet, ultimately, second-stage postmodern jurisprudents might write such doctrinal scholarship merely because they are in the postmodern condition, and as such, they might feel an urge to do little more than assert some meaning as forcefully or terroristically as possible. Put in different words, second-stage postmodern jurisprudents might start using Budweiser and Wonderbread with an attitude.

Yet, and this is a second possibility, second-stage postmodern jurisprudents actually might relinquish and then stop talking about Bud and Wonderbread altogether. Meta-scholarship—postmodern scholarship about modernist scholarship—can be understood as the postmodern deconstructive critique of the use of Bud and Wonderbread. But if we all stop using Bud and Wonderbread, then postmodernists no longer need to deconstruct their current use. If postmodern culture sufficiently permeates legal and jurisprudential practices so that everybody starts using handcrafted beer and boutique bread, then who would care about Bud and Wonderbread? This possibility presents perhaps the most uncertain future for postmodern legal scholarship. What would postmodern jurisprudents talk about if they were not criticizing modernist scholars (and were not writing playful parodies of judicial decision making)? At best, I can offer some tentative possibilities. Postmodern scholars might write more about the phenomenon of law in a postmodern society. How does law arise? How does law operate within postmodern culture? Then again, postmodern scholars might continue to dwell narcissistically on legal scholarship—though now focusing on postmodern scholarship itself, or in other words, on the question of what exactly postmodern scholars should write about.

In a third possibility, the future of postmodern legal scholarship might be little different from its present: a distinct second stage of postmodern jurisprudence might not emerge at all. Why not? Maybe Bud and Wonderbread always will be there. After all, economics matters. Some Americans cannot afford to buy anything but Bud and Wonderbread; in fact, some people cannot afford even those standards. Indeed, isn't any postmodern critique that analogizes to the use of Bud and Wonderbread just a bit too upper-middle-class and pretentious? And while this criticism of postmodernism might be somewhat typical, isn't it nonetheless disturbing? From this perspective, postmodernists often appear to be white academicians, standing to the side of real social struggles—those of the poor, people of color, and other outgroups—and theorizing about what it's all about, colonizing the words and actions of the outgroups and minorities. And just as there always will be poor Americans who might need to buy Bud and Wonderbread, or similar nearly generic brands, there also always will be average attorneys who are just trying to get by—drawing up wills, handling car accidents, helping with workers' compensation claims, whatever. Many of these attorneys just do not have time for highfalutin theory; they need to make a living. For that, they want some basic rules, a few precedents, and some good form books. Moreover, these attorneys will continue to practice in state and local courts where judges also will continue to hand down the decisions of mundane judicial practice. Indeed, as already discussed, even at the highest levels of the federal judiciary, the structural role of the courts in American society demands decision after decision after decision. And if so, one might reasonably assume that some legal scholars will write about such judicial decision making, recommending decision after decision after decision. Modernist legal scholarship, in other words, is unlikely to disappear for the foreseeable future exactly because there always will be American jurisprudents who insist upon writing about Bud and Wonderbread—about decisions supposedly determined by objective rules and principles. Consequently, it follows, there also always will be a significant role for postmodern jurisprudents who seek to write meta-scholarship—postmodern scholarship deconstructing modernist scholarship, deconstructing the Buds and Wonderbreads of the American jurisprudential scene, even if such postmodern writing can itself be deconstructed as a form of class-based elitism.

The fourth possibility is that second-stage postmodernism will not be postmodern at all; rather second-stage postmodernism will be no more than a return to modernism. Perhaps, though, by that time, many jurisprudents will follow current modernists such as Steven D. Smith by domesticating one or two postmodern themes and tossing them into the lawyer's toolbox (probably without acknowledging or, for some jurisprudents, even recognizing their postmodern origins). When it is helpful, these jurisprudents will pull out their postmodern doodads, use them to their advantage, and then put them safely away. The potentially radical quality of postmodernism, in other words, will have been subdued, with just a few postmodern remnants occasionally being dragged out of the toolbox like sophisticated policy arguments. Of course, to a great extent, this is the modernist's dream: modernist jurisprudence will triumph over the current postmodern vogue. After all, from this perspective, what *is* postmodern legal thought, or in other words, what is handcrafted beer and boutique bread? In the end, it is still just beer and bread. And when the fad passes, Bud and Wonderbread will remain—or so the modernist hopes. Yet, how probable is this turn? Once one tries the handcrafted beer and boutique bread, the old Budweiser and Wonderbread never quite seem the same. Can we really turn around and go back to the past? Even if we tried, the old Bud and Wonderbread might not be waiting for our return; they might not remain as they once were. After all, while economics matters, it is hard to predict. Instead of just Wonderbread, for instance, we might have Wheat Wonderbread, Rye Wonderbread, Multigrain Wonderbread, Raisin Wonderbread, Health Nut Wonderbread, High-Fiber Wonderbread, and Wonderbread Original. Wonderbread itself will have become boutique bread. So, then, where would we be, in the modern or the postmodern?

Notes

1. Introduction

1. See Max Weber, Economy and Society 20–22 (Gunther Roth and Claus Wittich eds., 1978); Max Weber, The Methodology of the Social Sciences 90, 100 (Edward A. Shils and Henry A. Finch eds., 1949); Stephen M. Feldman, *An Interpretation of Max Weber's Theory of Law: Metaphysics, Economics, and the Iron Cage of Constitutional Law,* 16 L. & Soc. Inquiry 205, 212 n. 31 (1991).

2. Alexis de Tocqueville, 1 Democracy in America 280 (Henry Reeve text, revised by Francis Bowen, Phillips Bradley ed., Vintage Books 1990) (first published in 2 volumes in French in 1835 and 1840); Mary Ann Glendon, A Nation under Lawyers 259 (1994); David Theo Goldberg, *The Prison-House of Modern Law,* 29 Law & Soc'y Rev. 541, 544 (1995) ("an imperative").

3. On James Wilson, see James Wilson, The Works of James Wilson 59–710 (1967; first published 1804); Mark David Hall, The Political and Legal Philosophy of James Wilson, 1742–1798, at 1, 20–22 (1997). Dennis Patterson is an example of a current scholar who defines jurisprudence more narrowly. He writes: "The task of jurisprudence is the accurate description of the forms of argument used by lawyers to show the truth of propositions of law." Dennis Patterson, *The Poverty of Interpretive Universalism: Toward the Reconstruction of Legal Theory,* 72 Tex. L. Rev. 1, 56 (1993).

4. See Robert W. Gordon, *New Developments in Legal Theory,* in The Politics of Law 281, 286 (David Kairys ed., 1982) (describing how the legal system must operate somewhat independently or with relative autonomy "from concrete economic interests or social classes").

5. See Thomas S. Kuhn, The Structure of Scientific Revolutions (2d ed., 1970) (explaining paradigm changes in science).

6. See, e.g., Grant Gilmore, The Ages of American Law 42 (1977) (referring to C. C. Langdell as "essentially stupid").

7. Rita Felski, The Gender of Modernity 171–72 (1995); Jean-Francois Lyotard, The Postmodern Condition: A Report on Knowledge xxiv (G. Bennington and B. Massumi trans., 1984); Saul Cornell, *Moving beyond the Canon of Traditional Constitutional History: Anti-Federalists, the Bill of Rights, and the Promise of Post-Modern Historiography*, 12 L. & Hist. Rev. 1, 6–7 (1994).

8. See, e.g., Stephen M. Feldman, Please Don't Wish Me a Merry Christmas: A Critical History of the Separation of Church and State (1997); Stephen M. Feldman, *Whose Common Good? Racism in the Political Community*, 80 Geo. L. J. 1835 (1992).

9. See Jerold S. Auerbach, Unequal Justice: Lawyers and Social Change in Modern America (1976) (emphasizing the ethnic prejudices of elite attorneys in the early twentieth century, and the consequences of such prejudices for the legal profession and American society); Morton J. Horwitz, The Transformation of American Law, 1780–1860 (1977) (emphasizing economic interests as structuring the story of American law of the early nineteenth century).

10. On different types of intellectual histories, see Stephen M. Feldman, *Intellectual History in Detail*, 26 Reviews in Amn. Hist. 737 (1998). For an excellent example of a more psychologically detailed type of intellecual history, see N. E. H. Hull, Roscoe Pound and Karl Llewellyn: Searching for an American Jurisprudence (1997).

11. *Roe v. Wade,* 410 US 113 (1973); *Brown v. Board of Education,* 347 US 483 (1954); *Lochner v. New York,* 198 US 45 (1905).

12. Compare Robert Hollinger, Postmodernism and the Social Sciences xiii, 21, 40–42 (1994) (suggesting that modernity is often deemed more sociological and modernism more cultural); Stephen Toulmin, Cosmopolis: The Hidden Agenda of Modernity 6 (1990) (distinguishing modernity from modernism) with Marshall Berman, All That Is Solid Melts into Air 131–32 (1988 ed.) (arguing against separating the cultural—modernism—from the political, economic, and social—modernization); Steven Connor, Postmodernist Culture 44–51 (1989) (focusing on postmodernity and postmodernism); David A. Hollinger, *The Knower and the Artificer, with Postcript 1993,* in Modernist Impulses in the Human Sciences, 1870–1930, at 26 (Dorothy Ross ed., 1994) (focusing on the ambiguity of the term *modernism*).

13. See Andreas Huyssen, *Mapping the Postmodern*, 33 New German Critique 5, 10 (1984) (discussing how postmodernism is relational to modernism). Grant Gilmore's *The Ages of American Law* is one jurisprudential history that includes a discussion of the antebellum period—albeit a brief one. Gilmore, *supra* note 6, at 19–40.

2. *Charting the Intellectual Waters*

1. Some sources that helpfully discuss either premodernism, modernism, or both include the following: Zygmunt Bauman, Modernity and the Holocaust (1989) (hereafter Bauman, Modernity); Isaiah Berlin, The Crooked Timber of Humanity (1990); Richard J. Bernstein, Beyond Objectivism and Relativism: Science, Hermeneutics, and Praxis (1983); Hans Blumenberg, The Legitimacy of the Modern Age (Robert M. Wallace trans., 1983) (first published in German in 1966); Louis Dupré, Passage to Modernity (1993); Stephen M. Feldman, Please Don't Wish Me a Merry Christmas: A Critical History of the Separation of Church and State (1997); Rita Felski, The Gender of Modernity (1995); D. W. Hamlyn, A History of Western Philosophy (1987); Karl Löwith, Meaning in History (1949); Ted V. McAllister, Revolt against Modernity (1996); Stephen A. McKnight,

Voegelin's New Science of History, in Eric Voegelin's Significance for the Modern Mind 46 (Ellis Sandoz ed., 1991); Joshua Mitchell, Not by Reason Alone (1993); J. G. A. Pocock, The Machiavellian Moment (1975); Richard H. Popkin, The History of Skepticism from Erasmus to Spinoza (1979); Richard Rorty, Philosophy and the Mirror of Nature (1979); Quentin Skinner, 1 The Foundations of Modern Political Thought: The Renaissance (1978) (hereafter Skinner 1); Quentin Skinner, 2 The Foundations of Modern Political Thought: The Age of Reformation (1978) (hereafter Skinner 2); Richard Tarnas, The Passion of the Western Mind (1991); Leslie Paul Thiele, Thinking Politics: Perspectives in Ancient, Modern, and Postmodern Political Theory (1997); Stephen Toulmin, Cosmopolis: The Hidden Agenda of Modernity (1990); Eric Voegelin, The New Science of Politics (1987 ed.); Michael Walzer, The Revolution of the Saints: A Study in the Origins of Radical Politics (1965) .

Some helpful sources focusing on postmodernism include the following: Zygmunt Bauman, Intimations of Postmodernity (1992) (hereafter Bauman, Intimations); Albert Borgmann, Crossing the Postmodern Divide (1992); Steven Connor, Postmodernist Culture (1989); David Harvey, The Condition of Postmodernity (1989); Robert Hollinger, Postmodernism and the Social Sciences (1994); Fredric Jameson, Postmodernism, or, The Cultural Logic of Late Capitalism (1991); Barbara Kruger, Remote Control: Power, Cultures, and the World of Appearances (1993); Hilary Lawson, Reflexivity: The Postmodern Predicament (1985); Vincent B. Leitch, Postmodernism: Local Effects, Global Flows (1996); Jean-Francois Lyotard, The Postmodern Condition: A Report on Knowledge (Geoff Bennington and Brian Massumi trans., 1984); Allan Megill, Prophets of Extremity (1985); Christopher Norris, What's Wrong with Postmodernism (1990); Thomas L. Pangle, The Ennobling of Democracy: The Challenge of the Postmodern Age (1992); Feminism/Postmodernism (Linda J. Nicholson ed., 1990); Roy Boyne and Ali Rattansi, *The Theory and Politics of Postmodernism: By Way of an Introduction*, in Postmodernism and Society 1 (Roy Boyne and Ali Rattansi eds., 1990); Stephen Crook, *The End of Radical Social Theory? Notes on Radicalism, Modernism and Postmodernism*, in Postmodernism and Society 46 (Roy Boyne and Ali Rattansi eds., 1990); Andreas Huyssen, *Mapping the Postmodern*, 33 New German Critique 5 (1984).

2. Plato developed his theory of Ideas in the *Republic* and the *Phaedo*. Plato, *The Republic*, in The Republic and Other Works 7, 169, 173 (Benjamin Jowett trans., 1973) (Anchor Books); Plato, *Phaedo*, in The Republic and Other Works 487, 505–12, 534–35 (Benjamin Jowett trans., 1973) (Anchor Books) (hereafter *Phaedo*); see Joseph Owens, A History of Ancient Western Philosophy (1959); David Ross, Plato's Theory of Ideas (1951).

3. Dupré, *supra* note 1, at 17; see Tarnas, *supra* note 1, at 17 ("a single fundamental order structured both nature and society"); Toulmin, *supra* note 1, at 67–68 (suggesting that the rational order of nature revealed and reinforced the rational order of human society).

4. Dupré, *supra* note 1, at 23 ("intrinsically," "both mind"); *Phaedo, supra* note 2, at 505, 508; see Plato, *Meno* (Benjamin Jowett trans., Liberal Arts Press 1949)

5. Robert M. Wallace, translator's Introduction, to Blumenberg, *supra* note 1, at xv ("the continual"); Löwith, *supra* note 1, at 4, 19 ("cyclic," "everything moves"); Thucydides, *The Peloponnesian War* 1.22 (Benjamin Jowett trans.), in 1 The Greek Historians 567, 576 (Francis R. B. Godolphin ed., 1942); see David Bolotin, *Thucydides*, in History of Political Philosophy 7, 7 (Leo Strauss and Joseph Cropsey eds., 3d ed., 1987); see David Ross, Aristotle 91 (5th ed., 1949) (relating Aristotle's rotatory concept of locomotion to cyclical

time). A cyclical view of history was perhaps most evident in the writings of the Stoics. For the Stoics (particularly the early Stoics), "there is an unending series of world-constructions and world-destructions. Moreover, each new world resembles its predecessor in all particulars." Frederick Copleston, 1 A History of Philosophy 389 (1946); see Greek and Roman Philosophy after Aristotle 92–93 (Jason L. Saunders ed., 1966) (with examples of Stoics).

6. Aristotle, *Nichomachean Ethics* 4.1–3 (I. Bywater trans.), in The Complete Works of Aristotle 1729–1867 (Jonathan Barnes ed., 1984); Aristotle, *The Politics,* 1.2; 3.7, 9, 13 (Carnes Lord trans., 1984). For a summary of Aristotle's political thought, see Carnes Lord, *Aristotle,* in History of Political Philosophy 118–54 (Leo Strauss and Joseph Cropsey eds., 3d ed., 1987).

7. Dupré, *supra* note 1, at 30; see Stephen M. Feldman, Please Don't Wish Me a Merry Christmas: A Critical History of the Separation of Church and State 10–27 (1997) (discussing the Christian distinction of the spiritual and the carnal); Tarnas, *supra* note 1, at 112 (on reason).

8. Quotations from *The City of God* are from volume 2, unless otherwise noted. Augustine, *City of God* 14.1, 28; 15.1 (Marcus Dods trans. and ed., 1948); R. A. Markus, *Marius Victorinus and Augustine,* in The Cambridge History of Later Greek and Early Medieval Philosophy 327, 412 (A. H. Armstrong ed., 1967) ("eschatological realities"); Augustine, *City of God,* 1. 35 ("[i]n truth"). For discussions of Augustine and his philosophical and political thought, see Etienne Gilson, The Christian Philosophy of Saint Augustine (L. E. M. Lynch trans., 1960); Etienne Gilson, History of Christian Philosophy in the Middle Ages 70–81 (1955) (hereafter Gilson, Middle Ages); Ernest L. Fortin, *St. Augustine,* in History of Political Philosophy 176 (Leo Strauss and Joseph Cropsey eds., 3d ed., 1987); R. A. Markus, *The Sacred and the Secular: From Augustine to Gregory the Great,* in Sacred and Secular 84 (1994).

9. On the general development of an eschatological view of history, see Blumenberg, *supra* note 1, at 27–51: Löwith, *supra* 1, at 1–19, 60–61; Voegelin, *supra* note 1, at 110–33; McKnight, *supra* note 1, at 59, 66. G. Edward White refers to this premodern conception of progress as reflecting a "prehistoricist sensibility." G. Edward White, The Marshall Court and Cultural Change 1815–1835, at 360 (1991).

10. See Etienne Gilson, The Christian Philosophy of St. Thomas Aquinas 16–17 (L. K. Shook trans., 1956) (discussing Thomas's conception of reason); Hamlyn, *supra* note 1, at 104 (referring to Thomas as the "great synthesizer"); Pocock, *supra* note 1, at 43 (arguing that the revival of Aristotelian thought reunited political history with eschatology); Walter Ullmann, A History of Political Thought: The Middle Ages 171, 175–76 (1965) (discussing Thomas's idea of the political); compare Gilson, Middle ages, *supra* note 8, at 382 (Augustinians objected to Thomas's incorporation of Aristotelian themes into Christian theology). Some of Thomas's most important works are the following: *On Kingship* (Gerald B. Phelan trans., 1982 ed.); *Summa Contra Gentiles: Providence* (book 3) (Vernon J. Bourke trans., 1956); *Summa Theologica* (Benziger, 1946, first complete American ed.); see Frederick Copleston, 2 A History of Philosophy 302–434 (1950); Brian Davies, The Thought of Thomas Aquinas (1992).

11. Niccolo Machiavelli, *Discourses on the First Ten Books of Titus Livius* (1516), at 3.43, in The Prince and the Discourses 99 (Christian E. Detmold trans., Modern Library ed. 1950) (hereafter Machiavelli, *Discourses*) ("Wise men say"); see 1.2; Pocock, *supra* note 1, at 400. Fortune stands for the random changes of the world that are, for the most part, be-

yond human control. Niccolo Machiavelli, *The Prince* (1513), at 7.25, in The Prince and the Discourses 2 (Luigi Ricci trans., Modern Library 1950) (hereafter Machiavelli, *Prince*). For a discussion of the breakdown of feudalism and the rise of nation-states, see Toulmin, *supra* note 1, at 89–97.

12. Machiavelli, *Discourses, supra* note 11, 1.2, 26; 3.41, 47; Machiavelli, *Prince, supra* note 11, at ch. 18; Skinner 1, *supra* note 1, at 183.

13. Martin Luther, *The Freedom of a Christian* (1520), in 31 Luther's Works 327, 345, 354, 356, 376 (Harold J. Grimm ed., 1957) (hereafter Luther, *Freedom*); see Martin Luther, *The Ninety-five Theses* (1517), in Martin Luther's Basic Theological Writings 21 (Timothy F. Lull ed., 1989) (criticizing the church's practice of selling indulgences); see Mitchell, *supra* note 1, at 20–24 (discussing Luther's attacks on Aristotle and Thomas); Skinner 2, *supra* note 1, at 8; Duncan B. Forrester, *Martin Luther and John Calvin*, in History of Political Philosophy 318, 321 (Leo Strauss and Joseph Cropsey eds., 3d ed., 1987) (discussing Luther's attacks on reason in religion). Luther did not suggest that each individual could idiosyncratically interpret Scripture, but rather that each person was free to receive its literal meaning.

14. John Calvin, *Institutes of the Christian Religion*, 4.20.2 (Ford Lewis Battles trans., John T. McNeill ed., 1960; first published 1536) (hereafter Calvin, *Institutes*). "The *Institutes* . . . were, as published in 1536, far from the extensive treatise into which they were to grow in Calvin's final edition of 1559; but they were already the most orderly and systematic popular presentation of doctrine and of the Christian life that the Reformation produced." Williston Walker, A History of the Christian Church 350 (3d ed., 1970). On the separation of church and state, see Calvin, *Institutes*, 4.10.5, 4.11.16; see Forrester, *supra* note 13, at 328–29. On Calvinist individualism, see Hill, *supra* note 23, at 278; Tarnas, *supra* note 1, at 239. Two excellent works on Calvin's political thought and the political implications of his theology are: Ralph C. Hancock, Calvin and the Foundations of Modern Politics (1989); Skinner 2, *supra* note 1.

15. For example, the French philosophes of the late Enlightenment, writing in the seventeenth century, argued that traditional societal arrangements and religion produced human misery. Hollinger, *supra* note 1, at 2, 7; Toulmin, *supra* note 1, at 141, 176.

16. See Theodore Dwight Bozeman, Protestants in an Age of Science 124 (1977) (arguing that the Reformation opened the possibility of "private judgment"); Dupré, *supra* note 1, at 120–44 (discussing the modernist concept of the self).

17. Marcel Gauchet, The Disenchantment of the World: A Political History of Religion 4 (Oscar Burge trans., 1997; published in French in 1985) (arguing that "Christianity proves to have been a religion for departing from religion"). Max Weber emphasized the relationship between the growing disenchantment of the western world and its increasing rationalization. Max Weber, *Science as a Vocation*, in From Max Weber: Essays in Sociology 129, 139 (H. H. Gerth and C. Wright Mills eds., 1946); see Stephen M. Feldman, *An Interpretation of Max Weber's Theory of Law: Metaphysics, Economics, and the Iron Cage of Constitutional Law*, 16 L. & Soc. Inquiry 205, 208 (1991).

18. See Hancock, *supra* note 14, at 98–99, 108–9, 133; Walker, *supra* note 14, at 355–56; 5 Encyclopaedia Judaica 67 (1971).

19. See Dupré, *supra* note 1, at 72 (on Francis Bacon advocating for the control of nature); Feldman, *supra* note 1, at 66–67 (discussing the development of the so-called Protestant work ethic); compare Thiele, *supra* note 1, at 198 (arguing that Weber's connection of Protestantism and capitalism is provocative, but that critics emphasize, first, that capitalism

somewhat developed before the Reformation and, second, that capitalism developed also in non-Protestant countries such as Italy); Walzer, *supra* note 1, at 304–7 (arguing that although Weber's thesis that Puritanism strongly contributed to the development of economic capitalism is questionable, the Puritans in fact were this-worldly activists and ascetics); Edmund S. Morgan, *The Puritan Ethic and the American Revolution*, 24 William & Mary Q. 3, 4–6 (1967) (supporting the idea of a Puritan ethic).

20. See Tarnas, *supra* note 1, at 225–26 (discussing the pre-Reformation scientific advances). For brief discussions of the scientific revolution of the sixteenth and seventeenth centuries, see Dupré, *supra* note 1, at 72–77; Tarnas, *supra* note 1, at 248–75; The Columbia History of the World 681–92 (John A. Garraty and Peter Gay eds., 1972); see, e.g., Francis Bacon, *Novum Organum* (1620), in The English Philosophers from Bacon to Mill 24–123 (Edwin A. Burtt ed., 1939).

21. McAllister, *supra* note 1, at 22–23; McKnight, *supra* note 1, at 9–15. While Karl Löwith and Eric Voegelin emphasize the significance of Christian eschatology in shaping the modernist idea of progress, Hans Blumenberg argues that the modern idea of progress was initially authentic, being based on genuine human advances, but then was misleadingly skewed by the application of Christian eschatology. In other words, some modernists made the mistake of taking a legitimate notion of human progress and extending it to fulfill a religious need. Compare Löwith, *supra* note 1, at 1–19, 60–61, 201–2 and Voegelin, *supra* note 1, at 110–12, 118–33 with Blumenberg, *supra* note 1, at 49.

22. Bauman, Modernity, *supra* note 1, at 65, 70, 73, 91–92, 113–14; White, *supra* note 9, at 6 ("historicist sensibility"); see Dorothy Ross, The Origins of American Social Science 3 (1991) (defining a historicist attitude). According to Stephen A. McKnight, "[s]ecularization results in independence and autonomy from God and the sacred. Sacralization transforms the secular realm to the point where it is indistinguishable from the sacred. Man becomes God, and society becomes an earthly paradise." Stephen A. McKnight, Sacralizing the Secular: The Renaissance Origins of Modernity 25 (1989).

23. Thomas Hobbes, Leviathan (C. B. Macpherson ed., 1968; first published 1651). For helpful discussions of Hobbes's writings, see Eldon Eisenach, Two Worlds of Liberalism: Religion and Politics in Hobbes, Locke, and Mill 13–71 (1981); Christopher Hill, Puritanism and Revolution 275–98 (1958); Mitchell, *supra* note 1, at 46–72; Perez Zagorin, A History of Political Thought in the English Revolution 164–88 (1954); Laurence Berns, *Thomas Hobbes*, in History of Political Philosophy 396 (Leo Strauss and Joseph Cropsey eds., 3d ed., 1987); C. B. Macpherson, introduction to Thomas Hobbes, Leviathan (C. B. Macpherson ed., 1968).

24. Hobbes, *supra* note 23, at 161, 183, 185–86; see Christopher Hill, The Century of Revolution, 1603–1714, at 181–82 (1961); Berns, *supra* note 23, at 407.

25. Hobbes, *supra* note 23, at 188, 227; see 223–27, 230; Berns, *supra* note 23, at 408; see also Hobbes, *supra* note 23, at 272, 375 (the commonwealth can dissolve if the sovereign fails to protect the subjects); see Hobbes, *supra* note 23, at 192, 199 (individuals cannot renounce their right to resist assault by force).

26. See Hill, *supra* note 23, at 277–78; Pocock, *supra* note 1, at 378; compare Walzer, *supra* note 1, at 1–6 (arguing that the Calvinists generated the idea that saints, citizens, or the people could remake the political order).

27. Hobbes wrote: "[i]t is impossible a Common-wealth should stand, where any other than the Soveraign, hath a power of giving greater rewards than Life; and of inflicting greater punishments, than Death." Hobbes, *supra* note 23, at 478; see 478–79; see also Eisenach, *supra* note 23, at 49, 57; Mitchell, *supra* note 1, at 47.

28. Hobbes, *supra* note 23, at 484, 515; see 442–45, 501, 525–26, 629; Mitchell, *supra* note 1, at 56–58. Although Calvinism influenced *Leviathan*, Hobbes himself was not a radical Puritan. Hill, *supra* note 23, at 284; Pocock, *supra* note 1, at 397.

29. Pocock, *supra* note 1, at 398; see Mitchell, *supra* note 1, at 53–58. From Hobbes's perpsective, Christianity had progressed in England from Roman Catholicism to Episcopacy to Presbyteries to congregations of the faithful. Hobbes, *supra* note 23, at 482, 710–11.

30. Zagorin, *supra* note 23, at 169. "Calvin's understanding of this [carnal] world reveals his profound affinities with the rationalistic materialism commonly associated with such authors as Hobbes and Locke." Hancock, *supra* note 14, at 20; see Feldman, *supra* note 1, at 98–116.

31. Hobbes, *supra* note 23, at 498–99; see 575, 627–715; Pocock, *supra* note 1, at 397–98.

32. Calvin, *Institutes, supra* note 14, at 1.6.2. According to Luther, once the Protestant faithful were freed from the traditions and works of Roman Catholicism, they could personally experience the primacy of "the most holy Word of God, the gospel of Christ." Luther, *Freedom, supra* note 13, at 345, 354, 356.

33. See Popkin, *supra* note 1, at 110 (arguing that modernist philosophy emerged as a quest for certainty in order to defend knowledge); see Dupré, *supra* note 1, at 27 (arguing that in the premodern world, the *kosmos* should not truly be understood as foundational because of the premodern metaphysical unity). My analysis of the modernist desire for epistemological foundations is influenced by Blumenberg's notion of "reoccupation": the notion that a concept from a later era tries to fulfill the function of a concept from an earlier era. Blumenberg *supra* note 1, at 49.

34. Dupré, *supra* note 1, at 87 ("into an epistemological"); René Descartes, *A Discourse on Method* (1637), in Philosophical Writings 21 (E. Anscombe and P. Geach ed. and trans., 1964, quoted in Thomas C. Grey, *Langdell's Orthodoxy*, 45 U. Pitt. L. Rev. 1, 18 n. 62 (1983) ("Those long chains"); see René Descartes, *Meditations* (1641) (John Veitch trans.), in The Rationalists 97, 112–27 (Anchor Books 1974) (hereafter Descartes, *Meditations*) (Descartes' *cogito*); Toulmin, *supra* note 1, at 81 (summarizing the Cartesian method).

35. Richard H. Popkin expressly ties the skepticism of early modernist philosophy to the religious skepticism of the Reformation period. Popkin, *supra* note 1, at 189–90. Popkin (42–87) and Stephen Toulmin (*supra* note 1, at 5–44) also emphasize that Descartes's skeptical method had philosophical roots in Renaissance humanism. On the emergence of individualism, see Tarnas, *supra* note 1, at 280 (arguing that Descartes provided "the prototypical declaration of the modern self"). It is worth noting that Descartes himself was not a Calvinist; he was Roman Catholic. Indeed, he claimed to accept the views of the Catholic Church "without question," Popkin, *supra* note 1, at 233, and he had a cardinal as a patron. Dupré, *supra* note 1, at 117. Nonetheless, the Protestant theological emphasis on the differentiation of the secular (or natural) and the spiritual had spread to Catholicism during the Counter-Reformation; 178. Furthermore, Descartes spent significant portions of his life in Protestant countries, at times apparently trying to avoid Catholic Church censorship. Toulmin, *supra* note 1, at 78.

36. Eric Voegelin, in particular, argued that the modernist belief that human knowledge could be liberating (or a type of salvation) was the secularization of gnosticism. Voegelin, *supra* note 1, at 124–33; see McAllister, *supra* note 1, at 21–23, 132; McKnight, *supra* note 1, at 57–61. A more detailed account of the rise of modernist philosophy would need to give greater attention to the Renaissance humanists, such as Michel de Montaigne. Popkin, *supra* note 1, at 42–87; Toulmin, *supra* note 1, at 5–44.

37. Benedict de Spinoza, *The Ethics* (1677) (R. H. M. Elwes trans.), in The Rationalists 179, 208–15 (Anchor Books 1974); see Popkin, *supra* note 1, at xviii, 229–48. Descartes claimed to prove the existence of God through rational arguments, but he then used God's existence to show that human knowledge in the secular realm extends beyond the *cogito ergo sum* (I think, therefore I am). Descartes, *Meditations, supra* note 34, at 128–43, 153–59 (proving God's existence). Popkin summarizes many of the critical reactions to Descartes's claim to objectively ground knowledge. Popkin, *supra* note 1, at 193–213.

38. See Bernstein, *supra* note 1, at 16–20 (explaining a "Cartesian Anxiety," arising from a tension between objectivism and relativism, as central to modernist philosophy); Jameson, *supra* note 1, at 11 (noting that the modernist era has been called the age of anxiety); McAllister, *supra* note 1, at 134 (emphasizing a quest for certainty).

39. John Locke, *An Essay Concerning Human Understanding* (1690), in The English Philosophers from Bacon to Mill 238, 248–49, 267 (Edwin A. Burtt ed., 1939). Locke defines primary qualities as "the bulk, figure, number, situation, and motion or rest" of external objects; 269.

40. Thiele, *supra* note 1, at 201 (quoting David Hume, A Treatise of Human Nature (1738–1740)); John Locke, The Second Treatise of Government 5–9, 48–49, 54–55, 65, 70–71, 75, 79–80, 123–24 (Liberal Arts Press 1952). On Locke's individualism, see Hamlyn, *supra* note 1, at 174; Borgmann, *supra* note 1, at 37–47. For a summary of Locke's political theory, see John Dunn, The Political Thought of John Locke (1969); Robert A. Goldwin, *John Locke*, in History of Political Philosophy 476 (Leo Strauss and Joseph Cropsey eds., 3d ed., 1987).

41. Locke, *supra* note 40, at 17–18, 21; see Mitchell, *supra* note 1, at 82–85. Douglas Hay calls Locke the apologist for the deification of property in the seventeenth century. Douglas Hay, *Property, Authority and the Criminal Law*, in Albion's Fatal Tree 18–19 (Douglas Hay et al. eds., 1975).

42. Adam Smith, The Wealth of Nations (1776), in Classics of Modern Political Theory 531, 532, 537–38, 545–47 (Steven M. Cahn ed., 1997); see also Adam Smith, The Wealth of Nations (1776), in The Essential Adam Smith 149, 241 (Robert L. Heilbroner ed., 1986) (including passage on societal progress); see Stephen Holmes, *The Secret History of Self-Interest*, in Beyond Self-Interest 267, 277–80 (Jane Mansbridge ed., 1990) (arguing that both Smith and Hume maintained that self-interest was not the only passion motivating humans).

43. David Hume, *An Enquiry Concerning Human Understanding* (1748), in The English Philosophers from Bacon to Mill 585, 598–607, 678–83 (Edwin A. Burtt ed., 1939); see Popkin, *supra* note 1, at 247–48 (arguing that Hume was the first religious and epistemological skeptic).

44. Immanuel Kant, *Critique of Pure Reason* (1781), in Kant Selections 1, 3–5, 14–27, 43–66 (Theodore M. Greene ed., 1929). On Kantian ethics, see Hamlyn, *supra* note 1, at 237; see Immanuel Kant, *Theory of Ethics*, in Kant Selections 268, 309 (Theodore M. Greene ed., 1929); taken from Kant's *The Fundamental Principles of the Metaphysic of Morals* (1785) and *The Critique of Practical Reason* (1788).

45. Friedrich Nietzsche, *The Gay Science* § 193 (1882), in The Portable Nietzsche 93, 96 (Walter Kaufmann ed., 1982); Friedrich Nietzsche, Beyond Good and Evil 12–13 (Walter Kaufmann trans., 1966, originally published in 1886) (hereafter Nietzsche, Beyond); see Walter Kaufmann, Nietzsche: Philosopher, Psychologist, Antichrist 103, 205 (4th ed., 1974) (explaining Nietzsche's criticism of Kant for assuming that synthetic a priori judg-

ments must exist); Lawson, *supra* note 1, at 40 (explaining Nietzsche's criticisms of Kant's transcendental arguments). Kant himself did not believe that he was grounding knowledge in the same way that earlier modernists, such as Descartes, had claimed to; rather, Kant sought to identify the limits of human understanding. Henry Aiken, The Age of Ideology 34–36 (1956); Hamlyn, *supra* note 1, at 218.

46. Romanticism "was rationalism's mirror-image." Toulmin, *supra* note 1, at 148; see Berlin, *supra* note 1, at 187–206; Tarnas, *supra* note 1, at 366–94; David A. Hollinger, *The Knower and the Artificer, with Postcript 1993*, in Modernist Impulses in the Human Sciences, 1870–1930, at 26 (Dorothy Ross ed., 1994). The fact that Nietzsche is usually characterized as a romantic underscores his ambiguous position within modernism. Hamlyn, *supra* note 1, at 264–65; Hollinger, *supra* note 1, at 8. Nietzsche's perpsectivism with regard to truth suggests a repudiation of modernism, see Nietzsche, Beyond, *supra* note 45, at 9–11, 46, but his concern about the lack of knowledge and values and his emphasis on an individualistic will to power suggest that he clung to modernism; see 136, 139, 203. This modernist understanding of Nietzsche is suggested by Walter Kaufmann. Kaufmann, *supra* note 45, at 122. On the use of the "methods of a discipline to criticize the discipline itself," see David Luban, *Legal Modernism*, 84 Mich. L. Rev. 1656, 1660 (1986).

47. Pierre Schlag, *Fish v. Zapp: The Case of the Relatively Autonomous Self*, 76 Geo. L. J. 37 (1987). The relatively autonomous self, according to Schlag, is "a constructed self that concedes that it is socially and rhetorically constituted yet maintains its own autonomy to decide just how autonomous it may or may not be." Pierre Schlag, *Normativity and the Politics of Form*, 139 U. Pa. L. Rev. 801, 895 n. 248 (1991).

48. Bauman, Modernity, *supra* note 1, at 13; see Max Horkheimer and Theodor W. Adorno, Dialectic of Enlightenment (John Cumming trans., 1972; 1st ed. 1944) (arguing that Enlightenment thought has led to disaster); McAllister, *supra* note 1, at 34–35 (emphasizing American shock in response to the Holocaust); Vivian Grosswald Curran, *Deconstruction, Structuralism, Antisemitism and the Law*, 36 B. C. L. Rev. 1, 2–3, 24–28 (1994) (arguing that deconstruction historically arose in the post-Holocaust rejection of the modernist faith in human progress); Avishai Margalit and Gabriel Motzkin, *The Uniqueness of the Holocaust*, 25 Phil. & Pub. Aff. 65, 80 (1996) (the Holocaust became a "moment of creation" for the postwar world).

49. See Dorothy Ross, *Modernism Reconsidered*, in Modernist Impulses in the Human Sciences, 1870–1930, at 1, 10 (Dorothy Ross ed., 1994).

50. Connor, *supra* note 1, at 188–89, 230–33.

51. Harvey, *supra* note 1, at 44 ("the most startling"); Richard Shusterman, *Postmodern Aestheticism: A New Moral Philosophy?* 5 Theory, Culture, & Soc'y 337, 351 (1988) ("old worship"); Kruger, *supra* note 1, at 7 ("Narrative has"); see David Held, Introduction to Critical Theory: Horkheimer to Habermas (1980) (on the Frankfurt School, which focused on the relation between the needs of capitalism and the production of culture); Kruger, *supra* note 1, at 70 (arguing that on television, "[t]hings are accepted at face value, at the surface of the screen").

52. Martin Heidegger, Being and Time 32, 65, 78–83, 169–72 (John Macquarrie and Edward Robinson trans., 1962; first published in German in 1927); see Lawson, *supra* note 1, at 58–89; George Steiner, Martin Heidegger 82–84 (1978); Stephen M. Feldman, *The New Metaphysics: The Interpretive Turn in Jurisprudence*, 76 Iowa L. Rev. 661, 675–81 (1991); Dagfinn Follesdal, *Husserl and Heidegger on the Role of Actions in the Constitution of the World*, in Essays in Honour of Jaakko Hintikka 365 (E. Saarinen, R. Hilpinen, I. Ni-

iniluoto, and M. Hintikka eds., 1979); Francis J. Mootz, *The Paranoid Style in Contemporary Legal Scholarship*, 31 Hous. L. Rev. 873, 884 n. 39 (1994). For a discussion of possible distinctions between the early and later Heidegger, see Lawson, *supra* note 1, at 79–85; Steiner, *supra*, at 3.

53. Gregory Leyh, introduction to Legal Hermeneutics: History, Theory, and Practice xi, xii (Gregory Leyh ed., 1992) (arguing that Gadamer explores the conditions of human understanding); see Diane Michelfelder and Richard Palmer, introduction to Dialogue and Deconstruction 1, 7–9 (Diane Michelfelder and Richard Palmer eds., 1989) (suggesting that Derrida is the supreme hermeneutician of the twentieth century and that Gadamer is the ultimate deconstructionist).

54. See, e.g., Raoul Berger, Government by Judiciary 45, 363–72 (1977).

55. Hans-Georg Gadamer, Truth and Method 89, 137, 140, 144, 159, 164–65, 462, 477–91 (Joel Weinsheimer and Donald Marshall trans.; 2d rev. ed., 1989; originally published in German in 1960) (hereafter Gadamer, Truth and Method). Some other important texts by Gadamer include the following: *"Destruktion" and Deconstruction*, in Dialogue and Deconstruction 102 (Diane Michelfelder and Richard Palmer eds., 1989) (hereafter Gadamer, *Deconstruction*); *On the Scope and Function of Hermeneutical Reflection* (1967), in Philosophical Hermeneutics 18 (D. Linge trans., 1976); *The Problem of Historical Consciousness*, in Interpretive Social Science—A Reader 146 (Paul Rabinow and William M. Sullivan eds., 1979) (hereafter Gadamer, *The Problem*); *The Universality of the Hermeneutical Problem*, in Josef Bleicher, Contemporary Hermeneutics 128 (1980) (hereafter Gadamer, *The Universality*). Helpful analyses of Gadamer's work are Georgia Warnke, Gadamer: Hermeneutics, Tradition, and Reason (1987); Joel Weinsheimer, Gadamer's Hermeneutics: A Reading of Truth and Method (1985); see also John D. Caputo, *Gadamer's Closet Essentialism: A Derridian Critique*, in Dialogue and Deconstruction 258 (Diane Michelfelder and Richard Palmer eds., 1989).

56. Gadamer, Truth and Method, *supra* note 55, at 282–84, 302, 306. For discussions of the concept of a text-analogue, see Clifford Geertz, *Deep Play: Notes on the Balinese Cockfight*, in The Interpretation of Cultures 412, 448–49 (1973); Paul Ricoeur, *The Model of the Text: Meaningful Action Considered as a Text*, in Interpretive Social Science—A Reader 73, 81 (Paul Rabinow and William M. Sullivan eds., 1979). Gadamer explicitly discusses the concept of "prejudices," *The Universality, supra* note 55, at 133, while Jürgen Habermas, in his early theory, developed the concept of human "interests," arguing that knowledge is possible only because of three "knowledge-constitutive interests"—an interest in prediction and control, an interest in understanding of meaning, and an interest in emancipation. See Jürgen Habermas, Knowledge and Human Interests (Jeremy Shapiro trans., 1971; first published in German in 1968).

57. Gadamer, Truth and Method, *supra* note 55, at 282, 293, 461–63; J. M. Balkin, *Understanding Legal Understanding: The Legal Subject and the Problem of Legal Coherence*, 103 Yale L. J. 105, 142, 167 (1993); see also J. M. Balkin, *Ideology as Cultural Software*, 16 Cardozo L. Rev. 1221, 1221–23 (1995) (acknowledging the drawbacks of the metaphor of cultural software).

58. Gadamer, *The Universality, supra* note 55, at 133.

59. Gadamer, Truth and Method, *supra* note 55, at 101–69, 267, 293–94, 332, 362–79.

60. *Id.* at 164–65, 281, 291, 462; Gadamer, *The Problem, supra* note, at 103, 146; Paul Rabinow and William M. Sullivan, *The Interpretive Turn: Emergence of An Approach*, in Interpretive Social Science—A Reader 1, 6–7 (Paul Rabinow and William M. Sullivan eds., 1979).

61. Gadamer, Truth and Method, *supra* note 55, at 293–94, 307–8, 340–41; see Stanley Fish, *Normal Circumstances, Literal Language, Direct Speech Acts, the Ordinary, the Everyday, the Obvious, What Goes without Saying, and Other Special Cases*, in Interpretive Social Science—A Reader 243, 256 (Paul Rabinow and William M. Sullivan eds., 1979) (arguing that we always encounter a text in a concrete context, and hence, the text always has a determinate meaning, though that meaning can change as the context changes). The emphasis on the unity of the hermeneutic act distinguishes Gadamerian hermeneutics from those followers of Wittgenstein who insist that understanding must be distinguished from interpretation. Understanding, according to these theorists, is unreflective, while interpretation always involves reflection. See, e.g., Dennis Patterson, *The Poverty of Interpretive Universalism: Toward the Reconstruction of Legal Theory*, 72 Tex. L. Rev. 1 (1993); Richard Shusterman, *Beneath Interpretation: Against Hermeneutic Holism*, 73 The Monist 181, 183, 195–99 (1990); James Tully, *Wittgenstein and Political Philosophy*, 17 Pol. Theory 172, 193–96 (1989). For a critique of this view, see Stephen M. Feldman, *The Politics of Postmodern Jurisprudence*, 95 Mich. L. Rev. 166, 177–82 (1996) (discussing the importance of understanding the hermeneutic act as a unified process) (hereafter Feldman, *The Politics*).

62. Some of Derrida's important works are as follows: Deconstruction in a Nutshell (John D. Caputo ed., 1997) (hereafter Derrida, Nutshell); Of Grammatology (Gayatri Chakravorty Spivak trans., 1976) (hereafter Derrida, Grammatology); Positions (Alan Bass trans., 1981) (hereafter Derrida, Positions); *Cogito and the History of Madness*, in Writing and Difference 31 (Alan Bass trans., 1978); *Deconstruction and the Other*, in Dialogues with Contemporary Continental Thinkers 107 (Richard Kearney ed., 1984) (hereafter Derrida, *Other*); Jacques Derrida, *Différance*, in Margins of Philosophy 3 (Alan Bass trans., 1982) (hereafter Derrida, *Différance*); *The Ends of Man*, in Margins of Philosophy 109 (Alan Bass trans., 1982); *Plato's Pharmacy*, in A Derrida Reader 112 (Peggy Kamuf ed., 1991) (hereafter Derrida, *Plato*); *Structure, Sign and Play in the Discourse of the Human Sciences*, in Writing and Difference 278 (Alan Bass trans., 1978) (hereafter Derrida, *Structure*); *Force of Law: The "Mystical Foundation of Authority*," 11 Cardozo L. Rev. 919 (1990) (hereafter Derrida, *Law*). For useful discussions of deconstruction, see Jonathan Culler, On Deconstruction (1982); Lawson, *supra* note 1, at 90–124; Christopher Norris, Derrida (1987); David Couzens Hoy, *Jacques Derrida*, in The Return of Grand Theory in the Human Sciences 41 (Quentin Skinner ed., 1985); Ronald K. L. Collins, *Outlaw Jurisprudence?* 76 Tex. L. Rev. 215 (1997). For discussions of the relation between Derrida and Gadamer, see Ernst Behler, Confrontations: Derrida, Heidegger, Nietzsche 137–57 (Steven Taubeneck trans., 1991); James S. Hans, *Hermeneutics, Play, Deconstruction*, 24 Philosophy Today 299 (1980); G. B. Madison, *Beyond Seriousness and Frivolity: A Gadamerian Response to Deconstruction*, in The Hermeneutics of Postmodernity 106 (1988).

63. Derrida, Grammatology, *supra* note 62, at 50, 73; see Derrida, Positions, *supra* note 62, at 20. Derrida and Gadamer use the term *play* in different ways. See Fred Dallmayr, *Hermeneutics and Deconstruction: Gadamer and Derrida in Dialogue*, in Dialogue and Deconstruction 75, 82 (Diane Michelfelder and Richard Palmer eds., 1989); Neal Oxenhandler, *The Man with Shoes of Wind: The Derrida-Gadamer Encounter*, in Dialogue and Deconstruction 265, 266 (Diane Michelfelder and Richard Palmer eds., 1989).

64. Derrida, Grammatology, *supra* note 62, at 48; Derrida, *Différance*, *supra* note 62, at 11; see Derrida, Positions, *supra* note 62, at 26–27; Derrida, *Other*, *supra* note 62, at 110 (calling *différance* a nonconcept).

65. Derrida, Grammatology, *supra* note 62, at 24, 70; Derrida, *Structure, supra* note 62, at 280–81, 285; see Bauman, Intimations, *supra* note 1, at 23.

66. Weinsheimer, *supra* note 55, at 9 (truth keeps happening); see 200 (the truth of a text exceeds each understanding); compare. Bauman, Intimations, *supra* note 1, at 31 (postmodern culture "is characterized by the overabundance of meanings"). On iterability, see Derrida, Nutshell, *supra* note 62, at 27–28; J. M. Balkin, *Deconstructive Practice and Legal Theory*, 96 Yale L. J. 743, 749, 779 (1987).

67. See Gadamer, Truth and Method, *supra* note 55, at 293–94; Hoy, *supra* note 62, at 54; Madison, *supra* note 62, at 113–15.

68. See Sanford Levinson, Constitutional Faith 17 (1988) (whenever a community rests upon an authoritative text, different modes of interpretation are likely to splinter that community); Richard Delgado, *Storytelling For Oppositionists and Others: A Plea for Narrative*, 87 Mich. L. Rev. 2411, 2414–15 (1989) (storytelling both builds and destroys community); James Risser, *The Two Faces of Socrates: Gadamer/Derrida*, in Dialogue and Deconstruction 176, 179–83 (Diane Michelfelder and Richard Palmer eds., 1989) (suggesting that Gadamer's philosophical hermeneutics has deconstructive potential).

69. Caputo, *supra* note 55, at 263 ("purchased by"); Collins, *supra* note 62, at 215 ("a move"). In suggesting that there is, in a sense, a conservation of power, I do not mean to imply that the total value or quantity of power always remains the same through all social and hermeneutic events. Rather, I am suggesting that every hermeneutic event is both constructive and destructive, though any particular event may be more one than the other. compare Stephen M. Feldman, *The Persistence of Power and the Struggle for Dialogic Standards in Postmodern Constitutional Jurisprudence: Michelman, Habermas, and Civic Republicanism*, 81 Geo. L. J. 2243, 2282–88 (1993) (discussing how not all traditions and communities are equally distortive and exclusive).

70. Derrida, Grammatology, *supra* note 62, at 62 ("no meaning would appear"); see Derrida, Other, *supra* note 62, at 118; Derrida, Grammatology, *supra* note 62, at 47; Norris, *supra* note 1, at 200 (discussing deconstruction and the conditions of human understanding); Richard J. Bernstein, *Incommensurability and Otherness Revisited*, in The New Constellation 57, 67–75 (1991) (comparing Levinas and Derrida on the Other).

71. Derrida suggests that he, like everybody else, engages in the practical activity of interpretation when he acknowledges that he always is "analyzing, judging, evaluating this or that discourse." Jacques Derrida, *Like the Sound of the Sea Deep within a Shell: Paul de Man's War*, 14 Critical Inquiry 590, 631 (Peggy Kamuf trans., 1988). Gadamer maintains that hermeneutics and deconstruction both try to continue Heidegger's effort to overcome metaphysics, though they do so along different paths. Gadamer, *Deconstruction, supra* note 55, at 109; see Fred Dallmayr, *Self and Other: Gadamer and the Hermeneutics of Difference*, 5 Yale J. L. & Human. 507, 515–16 (1993) (to Gadamer, deconstruction contains insights that are germane to hermeneutics).

72. Huyssen, *supra* note 1, at 8 ("the latest"); Kruger, *supra* note 1, at 3 ("To some"); see Marshall Berman, All That Is Solid Melts into Air 347–48 (1988 ed.) (arguing that modernity has not ended); Jameson, *supra* note 1, at 35–36 (viewing postmodernism as a cultural period associated with late capitalism); Harvey, *supra* note 1, at 49 (linking postmodernism and deconstruction); Mike Featherstone, *In Pursuit of the Postmodern: An Introduction*, 5 Theory, Culture, & Soc'y 195 (1988) (noting that efforts to develop a theory of the postmodern are open to criticism); Huyssen, *supra* note 1, at 36–46 (discussing the view that poststructuralism and postmodernism are different but related). For various attacks on

postmodernism, see Jürgen Habermas, The Philosophical Discourse of Modernity (Frederick Lawrence trans., 1987) (defending modernity from postmodern crisis); Stanley Rosen, The Ancients and the Moderns (1989). For an unusually fair-minded critique of postmodernism, see Pangle, *supra* note 1.

73. See Ludwig Wittgenstein, Philosophical Investigations 193–94 (G. E. M. Anscombe trans., 3d ed., 1958).

74. See Harvey, *supra* note 1, at 45–48 (linking postmodernism to different voice writing); Jameson, *supra* note 1, at 318; Anne Norton, *Response to Henry S. Kariel*, 18 Pol. Theory 273, 273 (1990) (arguing that feminism should be understood as a constitutive part of postmodernism). For examples of outgroup or different voice writers who accentuate the multiple potential meanings of texts, see Derrick Bell, And We Are Not Saved 22 (1987) (arguing that guarantees of racial equality get transformed into devices to perpetuate the racial status quo); Anthony E. Cook, *Beyond Critical Legal Studies: The Reconstructive Theology of Dr. Martin Luther King, Jr.*, 103 Harv. L. Rev. 985, 1015–21 (1990) (arguing that religion both legitimated and delegitimated authority for African-American slaves); Mari Matsuda, *Looking to the Bottom: Critical Legal Studies and Reparations*, 22 Harv. C. R.–C. L. L. Rev. 323, 333–35 (1987). See generally Stephen M. Feldman, *Whose Common Good? Racism in the Political Community*, 80 Geo. L. J. 1835, 1857–58 (1992).

75. Lyotard, *supra* note 1, at 60; see xxiv, 23–27, 60–66; Bauman, Intimations, *supra* note 1, at 21–23 (noting that postmodern intellectuals become interpreters); Harvey, *supra* note 1, at 44–48 (discussing postmodernist problems with meta-narratives).

76. Jameson, *supra* note 1, at 62; see Leitch, *supra* note 1, at 120; Douglas Kellner, *Postmodernism as Social Theory: Some Challenges and Problems*, 5 Theory, Culture, & Soc'y 239, 241 (1988) (discussing the postmodern subversion of academic disciplines).

77. See Connor, *supra* note 1, at 9–10, 18–19, 194 (discussing the paradoxes of postmodernism); Jameson, *supra* note 1, at 64–65, 68 (discussing the paradoxes of self-consciousness and language).

78. Michel Foucault, The History of Sexuality 93 (Robert Hurley trans., 1978) (hereafter Foucault, History of Sexuality); see Nancy Fraser, Unruly Practices: Power, Discourse, and Gender in Contemporary Social Theory 26 (1989). Other useful texts by Foucault include the following: Discipline and Punish (Alan Sheridan trans., 1977) (hereafter Foucault, Discipline and Punish); *Truth and Power*, in The Foucault Reader 51 (Paul Rabinow ed., 1984); *Two Lectures*, in Power/Knowledge 78 (1980) (hereafter Foucault, *Two Lectures*); *How Is Power Exercised?*, in Hubert L. Dreyfus and Paul Rabinow, Michel Foucault: Beyond Structuralism and Hermeneutics 216 (2d ed., 1983); *Why Study Power: The Question of the Subject*, in Hubert L. Dreyfus and Paul Rabinow, Michel Foucault: Beyond Structuralism and Hermeneutics 208 (2d ed., 1983) (hereafter Foucault, *Why Study Power*). For an outstanding synthesis of Foucault's work, see Hubert L. Dreyfus and Paul Rabinow, Michel Foucault: Beyond Structuralism and Hermeneutics (2d ed., 1983), and for an excellent collection of essays critiquing Foucault, see Foucault: A Critical Reader (David Couzens Hoy ed., 1986). Some other helpful sources on understanding the postmodern concept of power include the following: Pierre Bourdieu, In Other Words: Essays towards a Reflexive Sociology (Matthew Adamson trans., 1990); Pierre Bourdieu, Language and Symbolic Power (Gino Raymond and Matthew Adamson trans., 1991); Duncan Kennedy, Sexy Dressing Etc. (1993); Jana Sawicki, Disciplining Foucault: Feminism, Power, and the Body (1991); Thomas E. Wartenberg, The Forms of Power (1990); Pierre Bourdieu and Loïc Wacquant, *The Purpose of Reflexive Sociology*, in An Invitation to Reflexive Soci-

ology 61 (1992); Rethinking Power (Thomas E. Wartenberg ed., 1992); Sally Engle Merry, *Culture, Power, and the Discourse of Law*, 37 N. Y. L. Sch. L. Rev. 209 (1992).

79. In Austinian terms, utterances (or speech acts) are performatives because they have illocutionary and perlocutionary force. Illocutionary force arises from an act done in uttering—for example, a promise or a threat. Perlocutionary force arises when an utterance has an effect on others—for example, embarrassment or fright. See J. L. Austin, *Performative-Constative*, in The Philosophy of Language 13 (John Searle ed., 1971); John Searle, introduction to The Philosophy of Language 1 (John Searle ed., 1971).

80. Foucault, History of Sexuality, *supra* note 78, at 101 ("[d]iscourse"); Merry, *supra* note 78, at 217 ("distinct ways"); see Bourdieu, Language, *supra* note 78 (arguing that language is a means of communication and a medium of power); Foucault, *Two Lectures*, *supra* note 78, at 93 (arguing that relations of power cannot be established without discourse); Linda J. Nicholson, introduction to Feminism/Postmodernism 1, 11 (Linda J. Nicholson ed., 1990).

81. Gadamer, Truth and Method, *supra* note 55, at 384, 401, 403, 441, 443, 447, 457, 474; see Gadamer, *The Universality*, *supra* note 55, at 128, 139; see also Peter L. Berger and Thomas Luckmann, The Social Construction of Reality 34–46 (1967).

82. Wartenberg, *supra* note 78, at 165; see Peter L. Berger, Invitation to Sociology: A Humanistic Perspective 86–98 (1963) (emphasizing how social institutions pattern human conduct as if individuals were playing various roles); compare Stephen M. Feldman, *Diagnosing Power: Postmodernism in Legal Scholarship and Judicial Practice (With an Emphasis on the* Teague *Rule against New Rules in Habeas Corpus Cases)*, 88 Nw. U. L. Rev. 1046, 1071–72 (1994) (focusing on structural power in the context of habeas petitions); Douglas Hay, *Property, Authority and the Criminal Law*, in Albion's Fatal Tree 17, 44–45 (Douglas Hay et. al. eds., 1975) (in eighteenth-century England, the rule of law did not determine which criminal defendants were executed; more broadly, the rule of law did not control the exercise of power).

83. Derrida, Other, *supra* note 62, at 125; see Foucault, Discipline and Punish, *supra* note 78; Foucault, *Why Study Power*, *supra* note 78; Sawicki, *supra* note 78, at 63; see also Carol Gilligan, In a Different Voice (1982) (on the psychology of an ethic of care); Nel Noddings, Caring (1984) (on the philosophy of an ethic of care). Pierre Bourdieu argues that personal dispositions adjust to the logic of societal positions. Bourdieu, In Other, *supra* note 78, at 130; Bourdieu and Wacquant, *supra* note 78, at 74, 81.

84. Craig Haney, Curtis Banks, and Philip Zimbardo, *Interpersonal Dynamics in a Simulated Prison*, 1 International J. Criminology & Penology 69 (1973); see Stanley Milgram, Obedience to Authority: An Experimental View (1974) (psychology experiments suggesting that social roles produce inhumanity); see also Bauman, Modernity, *supra* note 1, at 152–67 (discussing implications of Milgram and Zimbardo's experiments).

85. Margaret A. Coulson and Carol Riddell, Approaching Sociology: A Critical Introduction 17–18, 39, 41, 46–47 (1970) (emphasizing that social roles or "positions" change); compare Karl Marx, *The Eighteenth Brumaire of Louis Bonaparte*, in The Marx-Engels Reader 594, 595 (Robert C. Tucker ed., 1978) ("[t]he tradition of all the dead generations weighs like a nightmare on the brain of the living").

86. Connor, *supra* note 1, at 5; see 5 (self-reflexivity is key to postmodernism); Crook, *supra* note 1, at 66–68 (reflexivity as a necessary feature of postfoundational radicalism).

87. Jean Baudrillard, *Game with Vestiges*, 5 On the Beach 19, 24 (1984); see Thiele, *supra* note 1, at 225–26 (discussing the postmodern form of irony); Huyssen, *supra* note 1,

at 25 (postmodernists used images and motifs from modern and postmodern cultures); see, e.g., Pierre Schlag, *The Problem of the Subject*, 69 Tex. L. Rev. 1627, 1649 (1991) (using changing styles to connote irony).

88. Richard J. Bernstein, *Foucault: Critique as a Philosophic Ethos*, in The New Constellation 142, 151 (1991) ("slippery slope"); Derrida, *Law*, supra note 62, at 945; see Derrida, *Other*, supra note 62, at 119–20 (denying that deconstruction is apolitical).

89. Leitch, *supra* note 1, at 3 (quoting Jacques Derrida, Specters of Marx 141 (1993)); compare Stephen K. White, Political Theory and Postmodernism 16 (1991) (arguing that deconstruction is political because it often exposes power where reason alone previously appeared).

90. Bauman, Intimations, *supra* note 1, at 50; see 54 (discussing the problem of structure); 201–3 (discussing the postmodern agent or subject); Robert N. Bellah, Richard Madsen, William M. Sullivan, Ann Swidler, and Steven M. Tipton, Habits of the Heart 6 (1985) (emphasizing the connection between individualism and culture); Lawrence M. Friedman, The Republic of Choice: Law, Authority, and Culture (1990).

91. Andreas Huyssen, who focuses on the use of term *postmodernism* rather than on postmodern themes, argues that a second stage of postmodernism emerged in the 1970s and 1980s. Huyssen, *supra* note 1, at 24–47.

92. See, e.g., Richard J. Bernstein, *An Allegory of Modernity/Postmodernity: Habermas and Derrida*, in The New Constellation 199 (1991).

93. Baudrillard, *supra* note 17, at 25.

94. Pangle, *supra* note 1, at 212, quoting Philip Roth, *N.Y. Times*, February 8, 1990, p.B1.

95. Don DeLillo, Mao II 157 (1991).

3. Premodern American Legal Thought

1. The following sources provide helpful historical accounts of American jurisprudence, the legal profession, legal education, and related matters for this time period. Edgar Bodenheimer, Jurisprudence (rev. ed., 1974); Lawrence Friedman, A History of American Law (2d ed., 1985); Grant Gilmore, The Ages of American Law (1977); Kermit L. Hall, The Magic Mirror (1989); James Herget, American Jurisprudence, 1870–1970: A History (1990); Morton J. Horwitz, The Transformation of American Law, 1780–1860 (1977) (hereafter Horwitz 1); James Willard Hurst, Law and the Conditions of Freedom in the Nineteenth-Century United States (1956); J. M. Kelly, A Short History of Western Legal Theory (1992); William P. LaPiana, Logic and Experience: The Origin of Modern American Legal Education (1994); Robert G. McCloskey, The American Supreme Court (1960); Perry Miller, The Life of the Mind in America (1965); Dorothy Ross, The Origins of American Social Science (1991); Bernard Schwartz, A History of the Supreme Court (1993); Robert Stevens, Law School: Legal Education in America from the 1850s to the 1980s (1983); G. Edward White, The Marshall Court and Cultural Change 1815–1835 (1991); Stephen M. Feldman, *From Premodern to Modern American Jurisprudence: The Onset of Positivism*, 50 Vand. L. Rev. 1387 (1997); Robert W. Gordon, *Legal Thought and Legal Practice in the Age of American Enterprise, 1870–1920*, in Professions and Professional Ideologies in America 70 (1983) (hereafter Gordon, *Enterprise*); Robert W. Gordon, *The Case For (and against) Harvard*, 93 Mich. L. Rev. 1231 (1995) (hereafter Gordon, *Harvard*); Thomas C. Grey, *Langdell's Orthodoxy*, 45 U. Pitt. L. Rev. 1 (1983) (hereafter Grey,

Langdell); M. H. Hoeflich, *Law and Geometry: Legal Science from Leibniz to Langdell*, 30 Am. J. Legal Hist. 95 (1986); Duncan Kennedy, *Toward an Historical Understanding of Legal Consciousness: The Case of Classical Legal Thought in America, 1850–1940*, 3 Research in Law & Sociology 3 (1980); William E. Nelson, *The Impact of the Antislavery Movement upon Styles of Judicial Reasoning in Nineteenth Century America*, 87 Harv. L. Rev. 513 (1974); H. Jefferson Powell, *Joseph Story's Commentaries on the Constitution: A Belated Review*, 94 Yale L. J. 1285 (1985); Ferenc M. Szasz, *Antebellum Appeals to the "Higher Law," 1830–1860*, 110 Essex Institute Hist. Collections 33 (1974); Robert Stevens, *Two Cheers for 1870: The American Law School*, 5 Persp. Am. Hist. 405 (1971). Deserving special mention as a contemporary account of the American scene is Alexis de Tocqueville, Democracy in America (Henry Reeve text, revised by Francis Bowen, edited by Phillips Bradley ed., Vintage Books 1990 first published in 2 volumes in French in 1835 and 1840). An especially helpful account of English legal history, with ramifications for American jurisprudence, is P. S. Atiyah, The Rise and Fall of Freedom of Contract (1979).

2. The Declaration of Independence, in 2 Great Issues in American History 70 (Richard Hofstadter ed., 1958); see Benjamin F. Wright, American Interpretations of Natural Law 10, 96–99 (1931); see also Charles G. Haines, The Revival of Natural Law Concepts (1958; first published in 1930).

3. James Wilson, The Works of James Wilson 124 (1967; first published in 1804); see Miller, *supra* note 1, at 164–65; compare Howard Horwitz, By the Law of Nature: Form and Value in Nineteenth-Century America vii (1991) (emphasizing that nature served as the ground of value during much of the nineteenth century); Philip A. Hamburger, *Natural Rights, Natural Law, and American Constitutions*, 102 Yale L. J. 907 (1993) (discussing the conceptions of natural rights and natural law during the framers' generation). Wilson's Lectures on Law were delivered in 1790 but not published until after his death in 1804. Miller, *supra* note 1, at 141. For an excellent recent discussion of Wilson's political and legal philosophy, see Mark David Hall, The Political and Legal Philosophy of James Wilson, 1742–1798 (1997). Other leading works of late-eighteenth- and early-nineteenth-century American jurisprudence (including legal and political thought) that I discuss in this section include the following: Nathaniel Chipman, Sketches of the Principles of Government (1793) (hereafter Chipman, Sketches); Nathaniel Chipman, Principles of Government; A Treatise on Free Institutions (1833) (hereafter Chipman, Principles); John Dickinson, The Letters of Fabius (1797) (first published in defense of the proposed Constitution in a Delaware newspaper in 1788); James Gould, A Treatise on the Principles of Pleading in Civil Actions (2d ed., 1836); Francis Hilliard, The Elements of Law (1835; reprint, 1972); David Hoffman, A Course of Legal Study (1817) (hereafter Hoffman, 1817); David Hoffman, A Course of Legal Study (2d ed., 1846) (hereafter Hoffman, 1846); Charles Jared Ingersoll, A View of the Rights and Wrongs, Power and Policy, of the United States of America (1808); James Kent, Commentaries on American Law (5th ed., 1844; first ed. published 1826–1830); Joseph Story, Commentaries on the Constitution of the United States (1987; reprint of Story's own 1833 one-volume abridgment of the original three-volume 1833 ed.) (hereafter Story, Constitution); Joseph Story, Commentaries on Equity Jurisprudence as Administered in England and America (first ed., 2 vols., 1836) (hereafter Story, Equity); Joseph Story, Miscellaneous Writings (1972; reprint of 1852 ed., William W. Story ed.) (hereafter Story, Miscellaneous); Zephaniah Swift, A System of the Laws of the State of Connecticut (1795) (a second volume was published in 1796; all citations are to the first or 1795 volume); St. George Tucker, Blackstone's Commentaries: With Notes of Refer-

ence to the Constitution and Laws, of the Federal Government of the United States; and of the Commonwealth of Virginia (1803) (4 books in 5 volumes; citations by book number); Jesse Root, *The Origin of Government and Laws in Connecticut* (1798), in The Legal Mind in America 31 (Perry Miller ed., 1962); The Federalist (Clinton Rossiter ed., 1961); see also Perry Miller, The Legal Mind in America (1962) (hereafter Miller, Legal Mind); The Federal and State Constitutions, Colonial Charters, and other Organic Laws of the United States (Ben Perley Poore ed., 2d ed., 1924; reprint, 1972; 2 vols.) (hereafter 1 Poore and 2 Poore).

Some helpful secondary sources are the following: Steven M. Cahn, Classics of Modern Political Theory (Steven M. Cahn ed., 1997); Roger Cotterrell, The Politics of Jurisprudence (1989).

4. William Blackstone, Commentaries on the Laws of England (1st ed., 4 vols., 1765–1769) see Miller, *supra* note 1, at 164–65 (discussing the influence of Blackstone's natural law orientation in America); Dennis R. Nolan, *Sir William Blackstone and the New American Republic: A Study of Intellectual Impact,* 51 N.Y.U. L. Rev. 731 (1976) (on Blackstone's influence in America).

5. Nathaniel Chipman, *Sketches of the Principles of Government* (1793), in The Legal Mind in America 19, 29 (Perry Miller ed., 1962) (emphasis added); see Miller, *supra* note 1, at 134; Nolan, *supra* note 4, at 761–67; see, e.g., Wilson, *supra* note 3, at 100, 614–16.

6. See, e.g., Story, Miscellaneous, *supra* note 3, at 74–75 (celebrating Blackstone). For one American edition of Blackstone, see William Blackstone, Commentaries on the Laws of England (1832, William E. Dean, Printer and Publisher, New York); see Anthony J. Sebok, *Misunderstanding Positivism,* 93 Mich. L. Rev. 2054, 2086–87 (1995) (discussing the influence of Blackstone on the nineteenth-century American treatise tradition).

7. 1 Blackstone, *supra* note 4, at 41–43; 2 Blackstone, *supra* note 4, at 2 ("rational science"); see Nolan, *supra* note 4, at 735, 760–61.

8. 2 Blackstone, *supra* note 4, at 9; see 2–9. Sometimes Blackstone wrote of both God's revealed law and law discoverable through reason as the law of nature. Other times he suggested that revealed law is, in effect, a higher form of natural law. See 1 Blackstone, *supra* note 4, at 40–44.

9. See, e.g., Root, *supra* note 3, at 34 (arguing that the common law of Connecticut was not the common law of England); see Horwitz 1, *supra* note 1, at 4–7; Miller, *supra* note 1, at 129; Perry Miller, introduction to The Legal Mind in America 15, 17 (Perry Miller ed., 1962); Stephen N. Subrin, *How Equity Conquered Common Law: The Federal Rules of Civil Procedure in Historical Perspective,* 135 U. Penn. L. Rev. 909, 928 (1987). For a contemporary discussion of whether the new nation should adopt the English common law, see Chipman, *supra* note 5.

10. Root, *supra* note 3, at 35–36; see Douglas T. Miller, The Birth of Modern America 1820–1850, at 117–25 (1970) (hereafter D. Miller); White, *supra* note 1, at 18–20; Gordon, *Enterprise, supra* note 1, at 83–89; see Gordon S. Wood, The Radicalism of the American Revolution (1991) (hereafter Wood, Radicalism) (emphasizing the spread of democracy).

11. The Great Awakening: Documents on the Revival of Religion, 1740–1745, at xii (Richard L. Bushman ed., 1969); see Miller, *supra* note 1, at 164–65, 206. See generally Edmund S. Morgan, *The Puritan Ethic and the American Revolution,* 24 William & Mary Q. 3 (1967).

12. Robert T. Handy, A Christian America 19 (2d ed., 1984) ("Christian civilization"); Winthrop S. Hudson and John Corrigan, Religion in America 82 (5th ed., 1992) ("great

unifying force"; quoting L. J. Trinterud, The Forming of an American Tradition 197 [1949]); see Sydney E. Ahlstrom, A Religious History of the American People 170–76, 292–94 (1972); Hudson and Corrigan, *supra*, at 18–19, 45–46, 75, 83, 111; see also Theodore Dwight Bozeman, Protestants in an Age of Science 45–48 (1977) (discussing the repudiation of religious skepticism in nineteenth-century America); Stephen M. Feldman, Please Don't Wish Me a Merry Christmas: A Critical History of the Separation of Church and State 119–74 (1997) (discussing the development of the institutions of church and state in colonies); Stephan Thernstrom, 1 A History of the American People 114–20 (2d ed., 1989) (discussing the Great Awakening). Other helpful books on American religion include the following: Jon Butler, Awash in a Sea of Faith: Christianizing the American People (1990); Nathan O. Hatch, The Democratization of American Christianity (1989); Martin E. Marty, Protestantism in the United States: Righteous Empire (2d ed., 1986).

13. Chipman, Sketches, *supra* note 3, at 115; 1 Swift, *supra* note 3, at 7; Hilliard, *supra* note 3, at iv–v, 8–9; see 1 Kent, *supra* note 3, at 2 (discussing natural jurisprudence and divine revelation); 1 Kent, *supra* note 3, at 470 (discussing natural justice); 2 Kent, *supra* note 3, at 1, 11–13 (discussing natural rights); 2 Kent, *supra* note 3, at 477 (mentioning universal justice). For discussions of the broad natural rights of property, security, and liberty, see Chipman, Principles, *supra* note 3, at 55–56; Hilliard, *supra* note 3, at 9; 2 Kent, *supra* note 3, at 1.

14. See, e.g., Hilliard, *supra* note 3, at iv; Hoffman, 1846, *supra* note 3, at 23; Story, Miscellaneous, *supra* note 3, at 69–71, 73, 79; Swift, *supra* note 3, at 3–4, 39.

15. Story, Miscellaneous, *supra* note 3, at 203; see, e.g., Hoffman, 1817, *supra* note 3, at iv; Hoffman, 1846 ed., *supra* note 3, at 20, 22, 36; 1 Kent, *supra* note 3, at v, 47, 475, 478, 505, 510; Wilson, *supra* note 3, at 356; see Bozeman, *supra* note 12, at 23–30.

16. Bozeman, *supra* note 12, at 60; see 3–10, 44–45, 56, 62–63; LaPiana, *supra* note 1, at 29. Bozeman acknowledges that competing views of science also existed at this time. See Bozeman, *supra* note 12, at 75, 86–96.

17. Wilson, *supra* note 3, at 356.

18. Theophilus Parsons, preface to The Law of Contracts (1857); see Theophilus Parsons, preface to The Law of Contracts xiv–xvi, 1st ed. (6th ed., 1873); see, e.g., Kent, *supra* note 3. In Story's *Commentaries on Equity Jurisprudence*, a rough approximation based on the included *Index to Cases Cited* suggests that Story cited over 3,100 cases in the first volume (which was 637 pages) and over 4,300 cases in the second volume (which was 748 pages). See 1 Story, Equity, *supra* note 3, at xi–xliii; 2 Story, Equity, *supra* note 3, at vii–li.

19. Kent, *supra* note 3, at 492–509 (on contracts); 3 Kent, *supra* note 3, at 401–48 (on property).

20. Hoffman, 1846, *supra* note 3, at 25, quoting William Jones, Essay on Bailment[s] ("a mere," "[i]f law"); David Hoffman, *A Lecture, Introductory to a Course of Lectures* (1823), in The Legal Mind in America 83, 85 (Perry Miller ed., 1962) ("must have"); see Miller, *supra* note 1, at 117–21.

21. David Ross, Plato's Theory of Ideas 225 (1951); see also Joseph Owens, A History of Ancient Western Philosophy (1959). Plato developed his theory of Ideas in *The Republic* and the *Phaedo*. See Plato, *The Republic*, in The Republic and Other Works 7 (Benjamin Jowett trans., 1973; Anchor Books) (hereafter *Republic*); Plato, *Phaedo*, in The Republic and Other Works 487 (Benjamin Jowett trans., 1973; Anchor Books) (hereafter *Phaedo*).

22. *Phaedo*, *supra* note 21, at 534; see *Republic*, *supra* note 21, at 169, 173; *Phaedo*, *supra* note 21, at 505–12, 534–35; see also Owens, *supra* note 21, at 197–229; Ross, *supra* note 21, at

225–45. See generally David Ross, Aristotle 158 (5th ed., 1949) (discussing the possibility of interpreting Plato's theory of Ideas in some other manner).

23. Hilliard, *supra* note 3, at v (emphasis omitted); *Swift v. Tyson*, 41 US (16 Pet.) 1, 18 (1842) (opinion of Story, J.), overruled by *Erie R. Co. v. Tompkins*, 304 US 64 (1938).

24. Szasz, *supra* note 1, at 35 n. 6 ("Medieval thinkers"); Miller, *supra* note 1, at 165–66 ("a quite baffling"); Hilliard, *supra* note 3, at vi; see Dickinson, *supra* note 3, at 15–16 n.* (arguing in 1791 that "[e]very civil right has for its foundation some natural right pre-existing in the individual"); compare Hamburger, *supra* note 3, at 908 (arguing that early Americans "relatively precisely defined" natural law and natural rights). For Supreme Court cases that assumed a consistency between natural law and constitutional provisions, see *Terrett v. Taylor*, 13 US (9 Cranch) 43, 50, 52 (1815) (Story, J., majority opinion); *Fletcher v. Peck*, 10 US (6 Cranch) 87, 139 (1810) (Marshall, C. J., majority opinion).

25. Story, Miscellaneous, *supra* note 3, at 702–3; see Chipman, Sketches, *supra* note 3, at 15, 116–18 (arguing that constitutional laws rights should reflect natural law and rights).

26. Story, Miscellaneous, *supra* note 3, at 702–4.

27. See John J. Cound et al., Civil Procedure (2d ed., 1974) 317, 329–33 (discussing common law writs and forms of action); Fleming James, Jr., and Geoffrey C. Hazard, Jr., Civil Procedure 8–12 (2d ed., 1977).

28. 3 Blackstone, *supra* note 4, at 115, 153–57.

29. *Id.* at 123.

30. Hoffman, 1846, *supra* note 3, at 289; Hilliard, *supra* note 3, at 240–44. Hoffman emphasized the importance of understanding pleading for understanding the law in general. Hoffman, 1846, *supra* note 3, at 348–56; see G. Edward White, Tort Law in America: An Intellectual History 9 (1980) (the writ system served as "a surrogate for doctrinal categories"). On the Litchfield Law School, see Advertisement for the Litchfield Law School, Janurary 1, 1828, in Dennis R. Nolan, Readings in the History of the American Legal Profession 204 (1980); Samuel H. Fisher, The Litchfield Law School 1775–1833, at 1–11, in Dennis R. Nolan, Readings in the History of the American Legal Profession 205 (1980).

31. Gould, *supra* note 3, at vi–viii; see 14–15; see LaPiana, *supra* note 1, at 42–44 (discussing the importance of pleading to antebellum legal science). Two treatises on pleading that were originally published in England were especially popular among practicing American lawyers: Joseph Chitty and Thomas Chitty, A Treatise on the Parties to Actions and on Pleading (8th American ed., 3 vol., 1840) (this American ed. is based on the 6th London ed.); Henry John Stephen, A Treatise on the Principles of Pleading in Civil Actions (8th American ed., 1856) (probably from the 1834 London ed.). As was common with American versions of English treatises, the American editions contained the exact text of the English edition plus additional footnotes for American readers and, in Stephen's *Treatise*, special appendices. Stephen has models of the various writs and explanations of when each writ was appropriate. Henry John Stephen, A Treatise on the Principles of Pleading in Civil Actions 8–21 (London, 1824). He also devotes considerable space to the use of pleading to produce a single material issue to be decided in a case; 144–347.

32. Wood, Radicalism, *supra* note 10, at 19, quoting Jonathan Edwards, quoted in Fiering, Jonathan Edward's Moral Thought and Its British Context 131. Helpful sources on the Revolutionary, framing, and early national years include the following: Joyce Appleby, Capitalism and a New Social Order: The Republican Vision of the 1790s (1984); Bernard Bailyn, The Ideological Origins of the American Revolution (1967); Samuel H. Beer, To Make a Nation: The Rediscovery of American Federalism (1993); Stanley Elkins and Eric

McKitrick, The Age of Federalism (1993); Henry F. May, The Enlightenment in America (1976); Forrest McDonald, Novus Ordo Seclorum (1985); Edmund S. Morgan, Inventing the People: The Rise of Popular Sovereignty in England and America (1988); Jennifer Nedelsky, Private Property and the Limits of American Constitutionalism (1990); Thomas L. Pangle, The Spirit of Modern Republicanism (1988); J. G. A. Pocock, The Machiavellian Moment (1975); Jack N. Rakove, Original Meanings: Politics and Ideas in the Making of the Constitution (1996); John Phillip Reid, Constitutional History of the American Revolution (abridged ed., 1995); Ellis Sandoz, A Government of Laws: Political Theory, Religion, and the American Founding (1990); James Roger Sharp, American Politics in the Early Republic (1993); Herbert J. Storing, What the Anti-Federalists Were For (1981); Morton White, The Philosophy of the American Revolution (1978) (hereafter White, Revolution); Morton White, Philosophy, The Federalist, and the Constitution (1987) (hereafter White, Constitution); Gordon S. Wood, The Creation of the American Republic, 1776–1787 (1969) (hereafter Wood, Creation); Wood, Radicalism, *supra* note 10; Martin S. Flaherty, *History "Lite" in Modern American Constitutionalism*, 95 Colum. L. Rev. 523 (1995); Stow Persons, *The Cyclical Theory of History in Eighteenth Century America*, 6 Am. Q. 147 (1954); Dorothy Ross, *The Liberal Tradition Revisited and the Republican Tradition Addressed*, in New Directions in American Intellectual History 116 (John Higham and Paul K. Conkin eds., 1979).

33. The Declaration of Independence (1776), in 2 Great Issues in American History 70, 72–74 (Richard Hofstadter ed., 1958); see Reid, *supra* note 32 (emphasizing the merit of the American Revolutionaries' constitutional arguments). For discussions of the importance of the Opposition or Country Ideology in America, see Bailyn, *supra* note 32, at v–xii, 19; Pocock, *supra* note 32, at 406–8, 462–548; Wood, Radicalism, *supra* note 10, at 174–75, 205–10; Flaherty, *supra* note 32, at 540–42; Ross, *supra* note 32, at 117.

34. Virginia Bill of Rights (1776), in 2 Poore, *supra* note 3, at 1908–9; see Constitution of Pennsylvania (1776); in 2 Poore, *supra* note 3, at 1540–42; see Pocock, *supra* note 32, at 462 (arguing that the American Revolution and Constitution should be understood as the "last act of Civic Renaissance"); Rakove, *supra* note 32, at 290–91 (noting that state constitutions generally protected life, liberty, property, and freedom of conscience); compare Bailyn, *supra* note 32, at 23–36 (discussing various sources that Revolutionary generation relied on); Pangle, *supra* note 32, at 43–47, 124–27 (emphasizing that framing of Constitution was Lockean as well as civic republican).

35. Virginia Bill of Rights (1776), in 2 Poore, *supra* note 3, at 1908, 1908; see Constitution of New York (1777), in 2 Poore, *supra* note 3, at 1328, 1332; Morgan, *supra* note 32; Thomas L. Pangle, The Ennobling of Democracy: The Challenge of the Postmodern Age 99–101 (1992) (discussing different conceptions of a republic); Wood, Radicalism, *supra* note 10, at 5–8, 11, 19, 63, 169–87, 232–33, 266, 271; see, e.g., Aristotle, *The Politics* 3.7 (Carnes Lord trans., 1984) (discussing mixed governments).

36. Appleby, *supra* note 32, at 8–9 ("there were two orders"); Wood, Radicalism, *supra* note 10, at 27 (including quotations from Washington and Adams and similar quotations from others); see White, Revolution, *supra* note 32, at 258 (arguing that Revolutionary leaders did not believe that all could equally see self-evident truths); Leslie Paul Thiele, Thinking Politics: Perspectives in Ancient, Modern, and Postmodern Political Theory 87 (1997) (on the number of voters for ratification). James Harrington was an important civic republican theorist who assumed that the gentry should rule over ordinary people. James

Harrington, The Commonwealth of Oceana (1656), in The Commonwealth of Oceana and A System of Politics 1, 33, 100–101 (J. G. A. Pocock ed., 1992).

37. Letter from John Jay to George Washington (June 27, 1786), in 2 Great Issues in American History 80, 81 (Richard Hofstadter ed., 1958); see Pocock, *supra* note 32, at 516–17; Wood, Radicalism, *supra* note 10, at 229–30, 245–54.

38. The Federalist no. 17, at 120 (Alexander Hamilton) (Clinton Rossiter ed., 1961); The Federalist no. 57, at 351 (James Madison) (Clinton Rossiter ed., 1961); The Federalist no. 71, at 432 (Alexander Hamilton) (Clinton Rossiter ed., 1961); see The Federalist no. 6, at 54 (Alexander Hamilton) (Clinton Rossiter ed., 1961) (factions occur because "men are ambitious, vindictive, and rapacious"); see also Dickinson, *supra* note 3, at 57 (in defending the proposed Constitution, concerned that "folly or wickedness" can undermine the "public good"). On the importance of deliberation, see Beer, 270–75 (arguing that Madison believed in "government by discussion"); Storing, *supra* note 32, at 3 (arguing that the framers believed they were deliberating about the common good); see also The Federalist no. 37, at 231 (James Madison) (Clinton Rossiter ed., 1961) (suggesting the same).

39. Records of the Federal Convention of 1787, at 125 (Max Farrand ed., 1966, reprint of 1937 rev. ed.), quoted in Sandoz, *supra* note 32, at 22. For a discussion of the framers' view of human psychology, see White, Constitution, *supra* note 32, at 88–99. For a discussion of the differing views of the Federalists and anti-Federalists with regard to rule by elites, see Storing, *supra* note 32, at 17, 43–45; Wood, Creation, *supra* note 32, at 483–99; see, e.g., *Speech Delivered by Melancton Smith at the Convention of New York on the Adoption of the Federal Constitution* (June 21, 1788), in The Anti-Federalist 340–41 (Herbert J. Storing ed., 1985) (an anti-Federalist lamenting that the proposed Constitution would lead to the election of a "natural aristocracy" as government officials).

40. The Federalist no. 57, at 350 (James Madison) (Clinton Rossiter ed., 1961); see The Federalist no. 10 (James Madison) (Clinton Rossiter ed., 1961); The Federalist no. 51, at 322 (James Madison) (Clinton Rossiter ed., 1961) ("Ambition must be made to counteract ambition."); Pocock, *supra* note 32, at 462–552; White, Constitution, *supra* note 32, at 132–48. For Publius's emphasis on the public or common good, see The Federalist no. 1, at 33–35 (Alexander Hamilton) (Clinton Rossiter ed., 1961); The Federalist no. 10 (James Madison) (Clinton Rossiter ed., 1961). A faction was characterized as any group, whether a minority or a majority, that opposed the public good. The Federalist no. 10, at 78 (James Madison) (Clinton Rossiter ed., 1961).

41. U.S. Const. pmbl.; see The Federalist no. 39, at 241 (James Madison) (Clinton Rossiter ed., 1961); Harrington, *supra* note 36, at 64–243; Wood, Creation, *supra* note 32, at 24 (on the Americans' Revolutionary-era conception of liberty); compare Louis Hartz, The Liberal Tradition in America 59–62 (1955) (placing enormous emphasis on the Lockean impulses of the framers in seeking to limit governmental power).

42. Persons, *supra* note 32, at 154; quoting John Adams, Discourses on Davila, in VI Works 232–34, 239; see 155–57 (discussing Jefferson); see also D. Miller, *supra* note 10, at 35–36; Morgan, *supra* note 11, at 6–7, 17–19.

43. Persons, *supra* note 32, at 152–53; quoting David Tappan, A Discourse, Delivered to the Religious Society in Brattle-Street, Boston 18–19 (April 5, 1798); Morgan, *supra* note 11, at 17; quoting Benjamin Franklin at the Second Continental Congress, July 6, 1775, in 1 Letters of Members of the Continental Congress 156 (E. C. Burnett ed., 1921–1936)).

44. Constitution of Pennsylvania (1776), in 2 Poore, *supra* note 3, at 1540, 1540.

45. Swift, *supra* note 3, at 4–5; Dickinson, *supra* note 3, at 68; see Chipman, Sketches, *supra* note 3, at 285 (governmental officials should makes laws to produce human action that is consistent with the laws of nature); Ross, *supra* note 1, at 23.

46. 1 Tucker, *supra* note 3, at vii; see 9 (appendix). Wilson wrote: "[o]n the publick mind, one great truth can never be too deeply impressed—that the weight of the government of the United States, and of each state composing the union, rests on the shoulders of the people." Wilson, *supra* note 3, at 73.

47. Chipman, Sketches, *supra* note 3, at 56–57, 117, 291–92; Swift, *supra* note 3, at 35; 1 Tucker, *supra* note 3, at xvii, 28 (appendix).

48. 1 Tucker, *supra* note 3, at 30 (appendix). Swift argued that his own systematization of the laws of Connecticut would help preserve republican government. Swift, *supra* note 3, at 4–5.

49. Swift, *supra* note 3, at 20, 29. Swift wrote: "The people are possessed of all the power, that can be safely lodged in their hands. The republics of Athens and Rome, have demonstrated the danger of trusting the supreme power in large popular assemblies. The rights of electing the legislature and the supreme executive, may safely be vested in them in their collective capacity, and this will be an eternal barrier to despotism." (28) See also Chipman, Sketches, *supra* note 3, at 114, 251–53 (drawing on the history of ancient republics); Dickinson, *supra* note 3, at 55–56 (a framer drawing on ancient history to defend the proposed Constitution); 1 Tucker, *supra* note 3, at xvii–xviii (expressing concern that "men of talents and virtue are not always" elected).

50. Chipman, Sketches, *supra* note 3, at 282–83; see 33 (on progress or improvement); Swift, *supra* note 3, at 21 (on the progressive improvement of government). James Wilson combined the premodern metaphorical comparison of societies and organisms with an idea of progress. Wilson, *supra* note 3, at 84.

51. Chipman, Sketches, *supra* note 3, at 292 ("perpetual"); Wilson, *supra* note 3, at 73; Miller, Legal Mind, *supra* note 3, at 21; compare Hall, *supra* note 3, at 107–9 (discussing Wilson's populism). See generally Hall, *supra* note 3, at 40 (arguing that although Wilson talked of human happiness, he was not a utilitarian; rather happiness was the "natural result of following God's benevolent laws").

52. Jeremy Bentham, *An Introduction to the Principles of Morals and Legislation* (1789), in The English Philosophers from Bacon to Mill 791, 792 (Edwin A. Burtt ed., 1939). "If there is one thing which the modern world owes to Bentham, it is the belief that the social order can be manipulated by the mere act of legislation." Atiyah, *supra* note 1, at 326. Of course, as revealed by the French Revolution, with its *Declaration of the Rights of Man and of the Citizen*, many Europeans still believed in natural rights. The Declaration of the Rights of Man and of the Citizen (1789), in Classics of Modern Political Theory 663 (Steven M. Cahn ed., 1997) see Haines, *supra* note 2, at 65–68 (describing general decline in natural law thinking in early-nineteenth-century Europe); Herget, *supra* note 1, at 8 (emphasizing that Kant and Rousseau, writing in the latter eighteenth century, were the last great European natural rights theorists). Dorothy Ross notes that "Europeans in the early nineteenth century began to apprehend time in a historicist [or modernist] mode," while Americans did not do so until later in the century. Ross, *supra* note 32, at 121.

53. 1 Tocqueville, *supra* note 1, at 98–105 (explaining individualism and how it is "of democratic origin"); see Morgan, *supra* note 32, at 288–306 (on equality and sovereignty); Wood, Radicalism, *supra* note 10, at 5–8, 11, 19, 63, 169–87, 215–18, 232–33, 266, 271; Edmund S. Morgan, *The Second American Revolution*, New York Review of Books, June 25,

1992, at 23–25 review of Wood, Radicalism, *supra* note 10); compare Appleby, *supra* note 32, at 14–15, 23, 95–96 (discussing the changing ideas concerning the individual, society, and virtue); Pocock, *supra* note 32, at 464–65, 522–23 (discussing the importance of Adam Smith to the ideology of self-interest in contravention to civic republican ideas).

54. Hatch, *supra* note 12, at 3; Articles of Religion of the Reformed Episcopal Church in America (1875), in 3 The Creeds of Christendom 814, 818 (Philip Schaff ed., 3d ed., 1877); see Feldman, *supra* note 12, at 178–83; Hudson and Corrigan, *supra* note 12, at 129–30; Stow Persons, *Evolution and Theology in America*, in Evolutionary Thought in America 422, 422–24 (Stow Persons ed., 1956). On African Americans in the Second Great Awakening, see Butler, *supra* note 12, at 129–63; Hatch, *supra* note 12, at 102-13.

55. See U.S. Const. art. II, § 8, cl. 3; Nedelsky, *supra* note 32, at 1–3 (the framers were primarily concerned with protecting private property from the tyranny of the majority). Shays' Rebellion was named after Daniel Shays, a former militia captain and one of the leaders of the insurrection. In 1785 and 1786, a commercial depression struck Massachusetts, leading to foreclosures on many tracts of land. Town meetings led to demands for legislative action to protect the vulnerable landowners, but no legislative relief was granted. Finally, in the autumn of 1786, Shays led a rebellion in central and western Massachusetts, breaking up meetings at courts and threatening the armory at Springfield. In the end, the insurrection was suppressed, but the state legislature enacted many of the reforms and protections sought by the protestors. See Shays' Rebellion (1786), in 1 Documents of American History 126 (Henry Steele Commager ed., 3d ed., 1947); Thernstrom, *supra* note 12, at 196–98; Wood, Creation, *supra* note 32, at 410–13.

56. Ingersoll, *supra* note 3, at 6; see 2 Tocqueville, *supra* note 1, at 156 (almost all Americans "are engaged in productive industry").

57. 2 Tocqueville, *supra* note 1, at 157; see D. Miller, *supra* note 10, at 28–30, 126–27, 292, 297; 1 Thernstrom, *supra* note 12, at 224–30, 236–38, 344–49; Wood, Radicalism, *supra* note 10, at at 308–47.

58. Wood, Radicalism, *supra* note 10, at 337, 340; Thernstrom, *supra* note 12, at 251–53; see Adam Smith, The Wealth of Nations (1776), in Classics of Modern Political Theory 531, 532, 537–38, 545–47 (Steven M. Cahn ed., 1997); see also Adam Smith, The Wealth of Nations (1776), in The Essential Adam Smith 149, 241 (Robert L. Heilbroner ed., 1986) (including passage on societal progress).

59. Elkins and McKitrick, *supra* note 32, at 77 (on the multiple interpretations of the Federalist-Republican conflict); see Appleby, *supra* note 32, at 58–59, 74.

60. Elkins and McKitrick, *supra* note 32, at 691; Sharp, *supra* note 32, at 12–13, 278.

61. Richard Hofstadter, Anti-Intellectualism in American Life 145 (1962) ("sages, scientists"); Appleby, *supra* note 32, at 3 ("hierarchical values"); see Elkins and McKitrick, *supra* note 32, at 750–51.

62. Hofstadter, *supra* note 61, at 154–55; 1 Tocqueville, *supra* note 1, at 5, 240; see White, *supra* note 1, at 57, 61 (arguing that republicanism was recast to emphasize union); Wood, Radicalism, *supra* note 10, at 302–5 (starting in the Jacksonian era, any ordinary man could hold office); see, e.g., Story, Constitution, *supra* note 3, at 717–19 (emphasizing the idea of union). Tocqueville observed that in America the "principle of the sovereignty of the people" was central. 1 Tocqueville, *supra* note 1, at 55.

63. See Elkins and McKitrick, *supra* note 32, at 263–66; D. Miller, *supra* note 10, at 156–57; Sharp, *supra* note 32, at 285; 1 Thernstrom, *supra* note 12, at 324–27; White, *supra* note 1, at 55; Wood, Radicalism, *supra* note 10, at 294; Howard Zinn, A People's History of

the United States 95 (1980). The three states that did not by 1825 extend the franchise to all white males were Rhode Island, Virginia, and Louisiana.

64. See Appleby, *supra* note 32, at 27; Lawrence M. Friedman, The Republic of Choice: Law, Authority, and Culture 51–60 (1990); Wood, Radicalism, *supra* note 10, at 5–8, 11, 19, 63, 169–87, 232–33, 266, 271.

65. See Robert M. Cover, Justice Accused: Antislavery and the Judicial Process (1975); White, *supra* note 1, at 674–740; see, e.g., *The Antelope*, 23 US (10 Wheat.) 66 (1825); *State v. Post*, 20 N.J.L. 368 (1845).

66. See Cound, *supra* note 27, at 362–65; Horwitz 1, *supra* note 1, at 17–20, 257–58; James, *supra* note 27, at 18–19; Miller, *supra* note 1, at 239–65; Subrin, *supra* note 9, at 932–39; An Act to Simplify and Abridge the Practice, Pleadings, and Proceedings of the Courts of this State, 1848 N.Y. Laws 379, §§ 118, 120. By 1897, twenty-seven states had adopted the Field Code and additional states had pleading systems that closely resembled the Code. Subrin, *supra* note 9, at 939.

67. Horwitz 1, *supra* note 1, at xvi ("[E]mergent entrepreneurial"); see 101; James M. McPherson, Battle Cry of Freedom: The Civil War Era 7, 24–25 (1988) (emphasizing emerging class conflicts); D. Miller, *supra* note 10, at 117, 124–25; 1 Thernstrom, *supra* note 12, at 252–53; White, *supra* note 1, at 26, 38 (discussing how American society was equal in some ways and unequal in others).

68. Sharp, *supra* note 32, at 12–13 ("dangerously"); Wood, Radicalism, *supra* note 10, at 325 ("umpire"); see May, *supra* note 32, at 288; Nedelsky, *supra* note 32, at 188–89 (focusing on the Marshall Court's establishment of judicial power to combat perceived democratic excesses); Sharp, *supra* note 32, at 2, 7–10, 91, 281–83; 1 Tocqueville, *supra* note 1, at 102, 272–75; H. Jefferson Powell, *The Original Understanding of Original Intent*, 98 Harv. L. Rev. 885, 924–25 (1985) (discussing the Alien and Sedition Acts).

69. 2 Tocqueville, *supra* note 1, at 6; Ahlstrom, *supra* note 12, at 149 ("glorious kingdom"; quotation from Urian Oakes, New England Pleaded With 49 [1673]); Dorothy Ross, *Modernist Social Science in the Land of the New/Old*, in Modernist Impulses in the Human Sciences, 1870–1930, at 171, 174 (Dorothy Ross ed., 1994) ("on a millennial"); see John Winthrop, *A Modell of Christian Charity* (1630), in 1 The Puritans 195, 199 (Perry Miller and Thomas H. Johnson eds., 1963).

70. Hoffman, 1846, *supra* note 3, at 65; *People v. Ruggles*, 8 Johns. R. 290 (N.Y. 1811), in 5 The Founders' Constitution 101, 101 (Philip B. Kurland and Ralph Lerner eds., 1987). Hoffman's second edition was not actually published until 1846. Hoffman, 1846, *supra* note 3, at i–iii. For discussions of additional cases invoking Christianity in the name of the common law, see Morton Borden, Jews, Turks, and Infidels 100, 111–25 (1984); Feldman, *supra* note 12, at 187–89; Miller, *supra* note 1, at 192–95; compare Miller, *supra* note 1, at 195–96 (some jurists denied that Christianity was part of the common law); Stuart Banner, *When Christianity Was Part of the Common Law*, 16 L. & Hist. Rev. 27 (1998) (questioning the significance of nineteenth-century declarations that Christianity was part of the common law).

71. Elkins and McKitrick, *supra* note 32, at 323 ("Paine did more"); Thomas Paine, Age of Reason 6 (1942; first published 1794); see Thomas Paine, *Common Sense* (1776), in Common Sense and Other Political Writings 3 (Nelson F. Adkins ed., 1953); see also Elkins and McKitrick, *supra* note 32, at 308–11, 329; Sharp, *supra* note 32, at 69–76; Sean Wilentz, *The Air around Tom Paine*, New Republic, April 24, 1995, at 34, 35. Compare Chipman, Sketches, *supra* note 3, at 106–7 with Chipman, Principles, *supra* note 3, at 62–65.

72. 1 Tucker, *supra* note 3, at 8. Chipman wrote: "[t]he experience, which we have already had, is sufficient to found a confidence, not only in the efficiency of the federal government; but in the coincidence of its principles, with the laws of civil and social nature, and the present state of manners and knowledge." Chipman, Sketches, *supra* note 3, at 280.

73. D. Miller, *supra* note 10, at 21 (quoting Kent); see Arthur Alphonse Ekirch, Jr., The Idea of Progress in America, 1815–1860 (1969, reprint of 1944 ed.) (stressing the significance of geographical expansion and technological advancement to the early-nineteenth-century American idea of progress); McPherson, *supra* note 67, at 3–6; White, *supra* note 1, at 374, 671; Edward S. Corwin, *The Impact of the Idea of Evolution on the American Political and Constitutional Tradition*, in Evolutionary Thought in America 182, 184 (Stow Persons ed., 1956); Persons, *supra* note 32, at 158–63.

74. White, *supra* note 1, at 374 ("a repository"); Powell, *supra* note 1, at 1310; quoting Letter from Joseph Story to James Kent (October 27, 1832), in 2 Joseph Story, Life and Letters of Joseph Story 109 (William Story ed., Boston 1851) ("with a sincere"); Story, Constitution, *supra* note 3, at 1–2. The "new vocabulary of progress and improvement did not so much replace as overlay the older vocabulary of virtue and corruption." Jean V. Matthews, Toward a New Society: American Thought and Culture, 1800–1830, at 137 (1991).

75. 1 Kent, *supra* note 3, at 479; Story, Miscellaneous, *supra* note 3, at 508, 526.

76. 2 Tocqueville, *supra* note 1, at 37, 42; Story, Miscellaneous, *supra* note 3, at 478; see Hilliard, *supra* note 3, at viii (asserting that, today, "all knowledge is held to be practical"). "Americans expected of education what they expected of religion, that it 'be practical and pay dividends.'" Hofstadter, *supra* note 61, at 299; quoting Henry Steele Commager, The American Mind 10 (1950).

77. 1 Kent, *supra* note 3, at 477; Hilliard, *supra* note 3, at vi; see Story, Miscellaneous, *supra* note 3, at 275 (discussing Mansfield's role with regard to the commercial law of Britain). For additional celebrations of Mansfield's greatness, see Hilliard, *supra* note 3, at 8; 1 Kent, *supra* note 3, at 477.

78. Hurst, *supra* note 1, at 21; see Horwitz 1, *supra* note 1, at 99–102, 211–52; White, *supra* note 1, at 51; Nelson, *supra* note 1, at 520; compare 1 Tocqueville, *supra* note 1, at 252 (democracy generates tremendous "energy" among the people, who "produce wonders").

79. *Dartmouth College v. Woodward*, 17 US (4 Wheat.) 518, 624–28 (1819); see White, *supra* note 1, at 612–28. The granting of a few select and exclusive corporate charters or franchises to facilitate long-term development was somewhat common in the late eighteenth and early nineteenth centuries, but during the early decades of the nineteenth century, states started granting hundreds of charters, thus sparking more economic competition. See D. Miller, *supra* note 10, at 25, 28 (giving examples of exclusive charters); Wood, Radicalism, *supra* note 10, at 308–15.

80. *Charles River Bridge v. Warren Bridge Comp.*, 36 US (11 Pet.) 420, 547–48 (1837); Hurst, *supra* note 1, at 28.

81. Story, Miscellaneous, *supra* note 3, at 69; 2 Kent, *supra* note 3, at 319; see 2 Kent, *supra* note 3, at 318–19.

82. *Norway Plains Co. v. Boston & Maine R.R. Co.*, 67 Mass. 263, 267 (1854); Grey, *Langdell, supra* note 1, at 8–9 n. 27. Perry Miller cautions that the freedom of judges during this period to instrumentally shape the law should not be overstated. See Miller *supra* note 1, at 128, 234–35.

83. Hilliard, *supra* note 3, at 3.

84. Chipman, Sketches, *supra* note 3, at 51—52; Chipman, Principles, *supra* note 3, at 36. The notion of a moral sense was a form of moral intuitionism especially popular with English and Scottish philosophers of the eighteenth century. *See* Wood, Radicalism, *supra* note 10, at 239–40; The Oxford Companion to Philosophy 597, 815 (Ted Honderich ed., 1995); A Dictionary of Philosophy 238 (Antony Flew ed., rev. 2d ed., 1979).

85. Chipman, Principles, *supra* note 3, at 71; see Chipman, Sketches, *supra* note 3, at 64–69 (on property rights). Benjamin Wright described the later Chipman as attempting to blend Blackstone with Bentham. Wright, *supra* note 2, at 243–51. As early as 1817, David Hoffman was recommending and extensively discussing Bentham in his *Course of Legal Study*. Hoffman, 1817, *supra* note 3, at 36, 218–19, 226–29.

86. Chipman, Principles, *supra* note 3, at 74, 168. Further revealing his belief that natural law and utilitarianism were consistent, the later Chipman wrote "that the right of property originates in natural principles, is confirmed by them, and finally sanctioned by the principle of utility, the general interest, which is the great end of all the laws of nature"; 71. Tellingly, in 1793, Chipman grounded property rights in natural law with no reference to utility at all. Chipman, Sketches, *supra* note 3, at 64–69.

87. Chipman, Principles, *supra* note 3, at 299–301; Chipman, Sketches, *supra* note 3, at 292. Compare Chipman, Principles, *supra* note 3, at 298–302 (on governmental corruption) with Chipman, Sketches, *supra* note 3, at 281–92 (same).

88. Story, Miscellaneous, *supra* note 3, at 69, 533, 535; Story, Constitution, *supra* note 3, at 501.

89. Story, Miscellaneous, *supra* note 3, at 526; see *Swift v. Tyson*, 41 US (16 Pet.) 1, 19–20 (1842), overruled by *Erie R. Co. v. Tompkins*, 304 US 64 (1938); see also Gilmore, *supra* note 1, at 30–36; Horwitz 1, *supra* note 1, at 245–52.

90. White, *supra* note 1, at 360; Story, Miscellaneous, *supra* note 3, at 70, 524; see Story, Miscellaneous, *supra* note 3, at 214–15, 224. With regard to common law pleading, Story not only wrote a treatise on pleading, A Selection of Pleadings in Civil Actions, Subsequent to the Declaration. With Occasional Annotations on the Law of Pleading (Salem, 1805; reprint , Buffalo, 1980), he also linked an understanding of pleading with an understanding of principles. *See* Story, Miscellaneous, *supra* note 3, at 82–85.

4. *Modern American Legal Thought*

1. Helpful accounts of the Civil War and Reconstruction include the following: William R. Brock, Conflict and Transformation: The United States, 1844–1877 (1973); Bruce Catton, The Civil War (1960); Eric Foner, Reconstruction, 1863–1877 (1988); James M. McPherson, Battle Cry of Freedom: The Civil War Era (1988); Allan Nevins, 1 Ordeal of the Union: Fruits of Manifest Destiny, 1847–1852 (1947); Peter J. Parish, The American Civil War (1975); Arthur Bestor, *The American Civil War as a Constitutional Crisis*, 69 Am. Hist. Rev. 327 (1964); Robert J. Kaczorowski, *Revolutionary Constitutionalism in the Era of the Civil War and Reconstruction*, 61 N. Y. U. L. Rev. 863 (1986). Helpful historical accounts of the late nineteenth and early and late twentieth centuries include the following: Godfrey Hodgson, America in Our Time (1976); Richard Hofstadter, The Age of Reform (1955); William E. Leuchtenberg, Franklin D. Roosevelt and the New Deal (1963); James T. Patterson, Grand Expectations: The United States, 1945–1974 (1996); Stephan Thernstrom, A History of the American People (2d ed., 1989); Robert H. Wiebe, The Search for Order, 1877–1920 (1967); Howard Zinn, A People's History of the United States (1980).

2. Parish, *supra* note 1, at 13; Foner, *supra* note 1, at 460; see Catton, *supra* note 1, at 263; McPherson, *supra* note 1, at viii; Bestor, *supra* note 1, at 327; see also Paul D. Carrington, *Hail! Langdell!* 20 Law & Soc. Inquiry 691, 702 (1995).

3. Wiebe, *supra* note 1, at xiii ("island communities"); Arthur Hertzberg, The Jews in America 152 (1989) ("the largest wave"); Gordon S. Wood, *Faux Populism*, New Republic, October 23, 1995, at 39, 41; review of Robert H. Wiebe, Self-Rule: A Cultural History of American Democracy (1995); Foner, *supra* note 1, at 23; *see* Hofstadter, *supra* note 1, at 23–93; Howard M. Sachar, A History of the Jews in America 283–304 (1992) (an overview of the assault on open immigration); 2 Thernstrom, *supra* note 1, at 433–58, 551–60; Wiebe, *supra* note 1, at xiii–xiv, 17–27, 65, 84–90; Zinn, *supra* note 1, at 247–49. Members of the old-stock Protestant gentry class were often called "mugwump" during the Gilded Age because of their "efforts to replace corrupt politicians with the disinterested leadership of the 'best men,' namely themselves. Faced with the specter of class conflict, they both feared for their established position and welcomed their opportunity for leadership" (Dorothy Ross, The Origins of American Social Science 61 [1991]). Robert Wiebe emphasizes the development of distinct social classes as central to the evolution of American democracy. Robert H. Wiebe, Self-Rule: A Cultural History of American Democracy 115–16 (1995).

4. Some helpful sources on intellectual developments during the nineteenth and twentieth centuries, including the development of American universities, include the following: Theodore Dwight Bozeman, Protestants in an Age of Science (1977); John G. Gunnell, The Descent of Political Theory (1993); George M. Marsden, The Soul of the American University: From Protestant Establishment to Established Nonbelief (1994); Peter Novick, That Noble Dream: The "Objectivity Question" and the American Historical Profession (1988); Edward A. Purcell, Jr., The Crisis of Democratic Theory (1973); Dorothy Ross, The Origins of American Social Science (1991); Morton White, Social Thought in America (1976); Laurence R. Veysey, The Emergence of the American University (1965); Edward S. Corwin, *The Impact of the Idea of Evolution on the American Political and Constitutional Tradition*, in Evolutionary Thought in America 182 (Stow Persons ed., 1956); Stow Persons, *Evolution and Theology in America*, in Evolutionary Thought in America 422 (Stow Persons ed., 1956); Robert Scoon, *The Rise and Impact of Evolutionary Ideas*, in Evolutionary Thought in America 4 (Stow Persons ed., 1956).

5. Charles Darwin, The Origin of Species (1859); see Bozeman, *supra* note 4, at 164, 168–69; Persons, *supra* note 4, at 425–26.

6. Corwin, *supra* note 4, at 185; Scoon, *supra* note 4, at 19; see Bozeman, *supra* note 4, at 164–69; Richard Hofstadter, Anti-Intellectualism in American Life 117–18 (1962) (emphasizing mass culture); Marsden, *supra* note 4, at 155–58; Ross, *supra* note 4, at 54–57; Persons, *supra* note 4, at 425–26; see Stephen M. Feldman, Please Don't Wish Me a Merry Christmas: A Critical History of the Separation of Church and State 191 (1997) (on Protestant culture in America in late nineteenth century); see also Martin E. Marty, Protestantism in the United States: Righteous Empire 67–68 (2d ed., 1986) (suggesting that the spread and success of Protestantism in some spheres helped secularize other spheres). As a reaction against the growing secularism, some Protestants turned to a more fundamentalist biblicism during this period. Bozeman, *supra* note 4, at 172; see also John Dewey, *The Influence of Darwinism on Philosophy* (1910), in The Philosophy of John Dewey 31, 32 (John J. McDermott ed., 1981).

7. G. Edward White, The Marshall Court and Cultural Change 1815–1835, at 6 (1991) ("historicist sensibility"); Ross, *supra* note 4, at 58 ("historical upheaval;" "sense

that"); Dorothy Ross, *Modernist Social Science in the Land of the New/Old*, in Modernist
Impulses in the Human Sciences, 1870–1930, at 171, 177 (Dorothy Ross ed., 1994) ("radical
discontinuity").

8. The following sources provide helpful historical accounts of American jurispru-
dence, the legal profession, legal education, and related matters. Jerold S. Auerbach, Un-
equal Justice: Lawyers and Social Change in Modern America (1976); Edgar Bodenheimer,
Jurisprudence (rev. ed., 1974); Edward S. Corwin, The "Higher Law" Background of
American Constitutional Law (1955; reprint of Edward S. Corwin, *The "Higher Law"
Background of American Constitutional Law*, 42 Harv. L. Rev. 149 [1928–1929]); Neil
Duxbury, Patterns of American Jurisprudence (1995); Lawrence Friedman, A History of
American Law (2d ed., 1985); Grant Gilmore, The Ages of American Law (1977); Charles
G. Haines, The Revival of Natural Law Concepts (1958; first published in 1930); Kermit L.
Hall, The Magic Mirror (1989); James Herget, American Jurisprudence, 1870–1970: A His-
tory (1990); Morton J. Horwitz, The Transformation of American Law, 1780–1860 (1977)
(hereafter Horwitz 1); Morton J. Horwitz, The Transformation of American Law
1870–1960 (1992) (hereafter Horwitz 2); N. E. H. Hull, Roscoe Pound and Karl Llewellyn:
Searching for an American Jurisprudence (1997); Laura Kalman, The Strange Career of
Legal Liberalism (1996); J. M. Kelly, A Short History of Western Legal Theory (1992);
William P. LaPiana, Logic and Experience: The Origin of Modern American Legal Educa-
tion (1994); Robert G. McCloskey, The American Supreme Court (1960); Perry Miller,
The Life of the Mind in America (1965); Gary Minda, Postmodern Legal Movements
(1995); John Henry Schlegel, American Legal Realism and Empirical Social Science (1995);
Bernard Schwartz, A History of the Supreme Court (1993); Robert Stevens, Law School:
Legal Education in America from the 1850s to the 1980s (1983); White, *supra* note 7; Robert
H. Wiebe, Self-Rule: A Cultural History of American Democracy (1995) (hereafter
Wiebe, Self-Rule); Benjamin F. Wright, American Interpretations of Natural Law (1931);
W. Burlette Carter, *Reconstructing Langdell*, 32 Ga. L. Rev. 1 (1997); Anthony Chase, *The
Birth of the Modern Law School*, 23 Am. J. Legal Hist. 329 (1979); Stephen M. Feldman,
*From Modernism to Postmodernism in American Legal Thought: The Significance of the War-
ren Court*, in The Warren Court: A Retrospective 324 (Bernard Schwartz ed., 1996); Robert
W. Gordon, *Legal Thought and Legal Practice in the Age of American Enterprise, 1870–1920*,
in Professions and Professional Ideologies in America 70 (1983) (hereafter Gordon, *Enter-
prise*); Robert W. Gordon, *The Case for (and against) Harvard*, 93 Mich. L. Rev. 1231 (1995)
(hereafter Gordon, *Harvard*); Thomas C. Grey, *Holmes and Legal Pragmatism*, 41 Stan. L.
Rev. 787 (1989) (hereafter Grey, *Holmes*); Thomas C. Grey, *Langdell's Orthodoxy*, 45 U.
Pitt. L. Rev. 1 (1983) (hereafter Grey, *Langdell*); Thomas C. Grey, *Modern American Legal
Thought*, 106 Yale L. J. 493 (1996); review of Neil Duxbury, Patterns of American Ju-
risprudence (1995) (hereafter Grey, *Modern*); M. H. Hoeflich, *Law and Geometry: Legal
Science from Leibniz to Langdell*, 30 Am. J. Legal Hist. 95 (1986); Morton J. Horwitz, *Fore-
word: The Constitution of Change: Legal Fundamentality without Fundamentalism*, 107 Harv.
L. Rev. 30 (1993) (hereafter Horwitz, *Foreword*); Duncan Kennedy, *Toward an Historical
Understanding of Legal Consciousness: The Case of Classical Legal Thought in America,
1850–1940*, 3 Research in Law & Sociology 3 (1980); Eben Moglen, *Holmes's Legacy and
the New Constitutional History*, 108 Harv. L. Rev. 2027 (1995); review of Owen M. Fiss, 8
History of the Supreme Court of the United States: Troubled Beginnings of the Modern
State, 1888–1910 (1993); William E. Nelson, *The Impact of the Antislavery Movement upon
Styles of Judicial Reasoning in Nineteenth Century America*, 87 Harv. L. Rev. 513 (1974);

Gary Peller, *The Metaphysics of American Law,* 73 Calif. L. Rev. 1151 (1985) (hereafter Peller, *Metaphysics*); Gary Peller, *Neutral Principles in the 1950s,* 21 U. Mich. J. L. Ref. 561 (1988) (hereafter Peller, *Neutral Principles*); Stephen A. Siegel, *Historism in Late Nineteenth-Century Constitutional Thought,* 1990 Wis. L. Rev. 1431; Joseph William Singer, *Legal Realism Now,* 76 Cal. L. Rev. 465 (1988); Marcia Speziale, *Langdell's Concept of Law as Science: The Beginning of Anti-Formalism in American Legal Theory,* 5 Vt. L. Rev. 1 (1980); Robert Stevens, *Two Cheers for 1870: The American Law School,* 5 Persp. Am. His t. 405 (1971).

9. Miller, *supra* note 8, at 206. Some important primary sources and collections of primary sources relating to the slavery crisis include the following: John C. Calhoun, *A Disquisition on Government,* in 1 The Works of John C. Calhoun 1 (1851) (hereafter Calhoun, *Disquisition*); John C. Calhoun, *Speech On the Reception of Abolition Petitions, Delivered in the Senate* (February 6, 1837), in 2 The Works of John C. Calhoun 625 (1851) (hereafter Calhoun, *Speech*); George Fitzhugh, Cannibals All! (1857; reprint, 1960) (hereafter Fitzhugh, Cannibals); George Fitzhugh, *Sociology for the South* (1854), in Slavery Defended: The Views of the Old South 34 (Eric L. McKitrick ed., 1963) (hereafter Fitzhugh, *Sociology*); Samuel Seabury, American Slavery Distinguished from the Slavery of English Theorists and Justified by the Law of Nature (2d ed., 1861; reprint, 1969); Cotton is King and Pro-Slavery Arguments (E. N. Elliott, ed.; Augusta: Pritchard, Abbot and Loomis, 1860); The Pro-Slavery Argument: as Maintained by the Most Distinguished Writers of the Southern States (Charleston: Walker, Richards, 1852); Abolitionism: Disrupter of the Democratic System or Agent of Progress? (Bernard A. Weisberger ed., 1963); Agitation for Freedom: The Abolitionist Movement (Donald G. Mathews ed., 1972); Slavery Defended: The Views of the Old South (Eric L. McKitrick ed., 1963). Some helpful secondary sources include the following: Robert M. Cover, Justice Accused: Antislavery and the Judicial Process (1975); James Brewer Stewart, Holy Warriors: The Abolitionists and American Slavery (1976); Larry E. Tise, Proslavery: A History of the Defense of Slavery in America, 1701–1840 (1987); William M. Wiecek, The Sources of Antislavery Constitutionalism in America, 1760–1848 (1977); Bertram Wyatt-Brown, Yankee Saints and Southern Sinners (1985); Arthur Bestor, *State Sovereignty and Slavery: A Reinterpretation of Proslavery Constitutional Doctrine, 1846–1860,* 54 Ill. St. Hist. Soc'y J. 117 (1961); William E. Nelson, *The Impact of the Antislavery Movement upon Styles of Judicial Reasoning in Nineteenth Century America,* 87 Harv. L. Rev. 513 (1974); Ferenc M. Szasz, *Antebellum Appeals to the "Higher Law," 1830–1860,* 110 Essex Institute Hist. Collections 33 (1974); Frederick E. Welfle, *The Higher Law Controversy,* 21 Mid-America 185 (1939); Antislavery (Paul Finkelman ed., 1989); Proslavery Thought, Ideology, and Politics (Paul Finkelman ed., 1989).

10. Wright, *supra* note 8, at 228–29; see Cover, *supra* note 9, at 33; Parish, *supra* note 1, at 28–31; Paul Finkelman, introduction to Proslavery Thought, Ideology, and Politics xi (Paul Finkelman ed., 1989); compare Jack N. Rakove, Original Meanings: Politics and Ideas in the Making of the Constitution 72–74 (1996) (on slavery at the Constitutional Convention); Garrett Ward Sheldon, The Political Philosophy of Thomas Jefferson 129–40 (1991) (discussing Jefferson's views and actions regarding slavery); Gordon S. Wood, The Radicalism of the American Revolution 186–87 (1991) (emphasizing Revolutionary ideology as motivating the antislavery movement).

11. Thomas R. Dew, *Review of the Debate in the Virginia Legislature* (1832), in Slavery Defended: The Views of the Old South 20, 27 (Eric L. McKitrick ed., 1963); Szasz, *supra*

note 9, at 45; quoting Garrison, quoted in Walter M. Merrill, Against Wind and Tide: A Biography of William Lloyd Garrison 205 (1963). For examples of immediatist arguments, see William Lloyd Garrison, *An Address Delivered Before the Old Colony Anti-Slavery Society* (July 4, 1839), reprinted in Agitation for Freedom: The Abolitionist Movement 26 (Donald G. Mathews ed., 1972); Wendell Phillips, *The Philosophy of the Abolition Movement* (speech delivered 1853, published 1863), in Agitation for Freedom: The Abolitionist Movement 35 (Donald G. Mathews ed., 1972). For an example of a Northerner's gradualist argument, see Horace Mann, *Address to the Boston Young Men's Colonization Society* (March 13, 1833), in Abolitionism: Disrupter of the Democratic System or Agent of Progress? 13 (Bernard A. Weisberger ed., 1963). See generally McPherson, *supra* note 9, at 8 (emphasizing the country's geographical growth as exacerbating slavery crisis); Parish, *supra* note 1, at 28–31 (discussing factors that led Southerners to develop increasingly elaborate and aggressive defenses of slavery); Tise, *supra* note 9 (arguing that Northerners were more responsible than Southerners for proslavery arguments); Nelson, *supra* note 9, at 525 (arguing that the antislavery movement was revived when legal instrumentalism was strong during the 1830s).

12. Szasz, *supra* note 9, at 46 (quoting Seward, Congressional Globe, 1850, 1st session, 31st Congress, XXII, part 1, 263–69); see Welfle, *supra* note 9, at 185–87.

13. See Haines, *supra* note 8, at 21–27; 52–53; Wright, *supra* note 8, at 4–12, 211–25, 229–39; Szasz, *supra* note 9, at 33, 37 (emphasizing the emergence of distinct Northern and Southern versions of higher law); see also Wiecek, *supra* note 9, at 138, 186, 259–61.

14. Wright, *supra* note 8, at 212. For another example of an immediatist argument invoking natural rights and the Declaration of Independence, see William Lloyd Garrison, *To the Public* (1831), in Agitation for Freedom: The Abolitionist Movement 23, 24 (Donald G. Mathews ed., 1972); see also Lydia Maria Child, *Colonization Society and Anti-Slavery Society* (1833), in Abolitionism: Disrupter of the Democratic System or Agent of Progress? 20, 27 (Bernard A. Weisberger ed., 1963) (arguing that slavery violates "the laws of God").

15. Charles Sumner, *Freedom National, Slavery Sectional* (August 26, 1852), in Abolitionism: Disrupter of the Democratic System or Agent of Progress? 48, 49 (Bernard A. Weisberger ed., 1963); Charles Sumner, *The Party of Freedom: Its Necessity and Practicability* (September 15, 1852), in Abolitionism: Disrupter of the Democratic System or Agent of Progress? 45, 47 (Bernard A. Weisberger ed., 1963). In a similar vein, William Hosmer wrote in 1852: "[e]very man has a natural right to himself—his own body and mind, with their various faculties and powers." Welfle, *supra* note 9, at 197; quoting William Hosmer, The Higher Law 89 (1852); see James Brewer Stewart, *The Aims and Impact of Garrisonian Abolitionism, 1840–1860,* in Antislavery 413 (Paul Finkelman ed., 1989) (arguing that Garrisonian antislavery arguments were eventually absorbed and used by other antislavery advocates).

16. Calhoun, *Disquisition, supra* note 9, at 54–57; Calhoun, *Speech, supra* note 9, at 630–31; see Wright, *supra* note 8, at 233–34, 272–74.

17. Theodore Dwight Weld, *American Slavery as It Is: Testimony of a Thousand Witnesses* (1839), in Agitation for Freedom: The Abolitionist Movement 54, 56 (Donald G. Mathews ed., 1972).

18. Albert Taylor Bledsoe, *Liberty and Slavery: or, Slavery in the Light of Moral and Political Philosophy,* in Cotton is King and Pro-Slavery Arguments 271, 273 (E. N. Elliott, ed.; Augusta: Pritchard, Abbot and Loomis, 1860; reprint, 1968); see James Henry Hammond,

Hammond's Letters on Slavery (January 28, 1845), in The Pro-Slavery Argument: As Maintained by the Most Distinguished Writers of the Southern States 99, 109–11 (Charleston: Walker, Richards, 1852).

19. Fitzhugh, Cannibals, *supra* note 9, at 5, 15–19, 71, 235; Fitzhugh, *Sociology, supra* note 9, at 44–48; see Nevins, *supra* note 1, at 198–202; Wright, *supra* note 8, at 238–39. William Harper, in a similar vein, expressly criticized the Declaration of Independence and argued that free laborers were worse off than slaves. William Harper, *Slavery in the Light of Social Ethics,* in Cotton is King and Pro-Slavery Arguments 547, 553, 569 (E. N. Elliott, ed.; Augusta: Pritchard, Abbot and Loomis, 1860; reprint, 1968); see George Frederick Holmes, *Review of Uncle Tom's Cabin* (1852), in Slavery Defended: The Views of the Old South 99, 108–9 (Eric L. McKitrick ed., 1963). On Fitzhugh's reputation, as being well known but extreme, see Drew Gilpin Faust, *A Southern Stewardship: The Intellectual and the Proslavery Argument,* in Proslavery Thought, Ideology, and Politics 129, 141–42 (Paul Finkelman ed., 1989); Robert A. Garson, *Proslavery as Political Theory: The Examples of John C. Calhoun and George Fitzhugh,* in Proslavery Thought, Ideology, and Politics 177, 180, 185 (Paul Finkelman ed., 1989); Richard Hofstadter, *John C. Calhoun: The Marx of the Master Class,* in Proslavery Thought, Ideology, and Politics 225, 247 (Paul Finkelman ed., 1989).

20. Bestor, *supra* note 9, at 179; quoting Corner-Stone Speech, March 21, 1861, in Henry Cleveland, Alexander H. Stephens, in Public and Private: With Letters and Speeches 721 (Philadelphia, 1866).

21. William Gilmore Simms, *The Morals of Slavery* (1837), in The Pro-Slavery Argument: As Maintained by the Most Distinguished Writers of the Southern States 175, 258 (Charleston: Walker, Richards, 1852) ("The democracy which they [the founding fathers] asserted not only recognized, but insisted upon inequalities"); see Nevins, *supra* note 1, at 156; Ross, *supra* note 4, at 30–31; 1 Thernstrom, *supra* note 1, at 385; Tise, *supra* note 9, at 43–57, 110–11. Tise notes that the earliest published American proslavery tract, written in 1701, argued that slavery fit the natural order of society. Tise, *supra* note 9, at 16–18. Tise adds that proslavery thought was "part and parcel of mainline American social thought." Larry E. Tise, *The Interregional Appeal of Proslavery Thought: An Ideological Profile of the Antebellum American Clergy,* in Proslavery Thought, Ideology, and Politics 454, 458 (Paul Finkelman ed., 1989).

22. See Richard Hofstadter, Social Darwinism in American Thought, 1860–1915 (1944); Novick, *supra* note 4, at 74–76; see, e.g., William Graham Sumner, *The Absurd Effort to Make the World Over* (1894), in 3 Great Issues in American History 84 (1982). To be sure, some jurisprudential scholars may have repudiated the natural law argument for slavery solely because it was right or just to do so. My point, though, is that if the South had won the Civil War, the rightness or justice of the Northern antislavery view would have mattered little during the postbellum period. Finally, the idea of a naturally segregated if not ordered society, of course, reemerged in the Supreme Court's constitutional jurisprudence with the Court's articulation of the separate-but-equal doctrine in *Plessy v. Ferguson. Plessy v. Ferguson,* 163 US 537 (1896).

23. Parish, *supra* note 1, at 27; Moglen, *supra* note 8, at 2045; see LaPiana, *supra* note 8, at 75–76; Wright, *supra* note 8, at 276, 293, 298–99; Szasz, *supra* note 9, at 47; Welfle, *supra* note 9, at 204.

24. Abraham Lincoln, *Gettysburg Address* (November 19, 1863), in Witness to America 764, 765 (Henry Steele Commager and Allan Nevins eds., 1949); see Wright, *supra* note 8, at 175–76, 180; Bestor, *supra* note 1, at 346–47.

It is worth noting that in a study of the law of slavery, Robert Cover characterized the early nineteenth century as positivistic. See Cover, *supra* note 9. To me, by focusing so strongly on the slavery controversy in the courts, Cover failed to account for the strong natural law strains of nineteenth-century legal thought. Moreover, Cover did not adequately distinguish between nineteenth-century arguments based on natural rights and arguments based on natural law. Compare White, *supra* note 7, at 129 n. 190 (criticizing Cover's characterization of early-nineteenth-century legal thought as positivist); Anthony J. Sebok, *Misunderstanding Positivism*, 93 Mich. L. Rev. 2054, 2081 n. 112 (1995) (criticizing Cover's characterization of late-nineteenth-century formalism as natural law oriented). Yet, while I disagree with Cover's ultimate characterization of the early nineteenth century, I believe that the slavery debates and, eventually, the Civil War strongly contributed to the transition from natural law to positivism in American jurisprudence (as discussed in the text). Moreover, I agree with Cover insofar as he suggested that, in America, the sovereignty of the people often was held out as above the natural law.

25. John Austin, The Province of Jurisprudence Determined 29, 157–58 (Wilfrid E. Rumble ed., 1995; 1st ed., 1832); see 285; LaPiana, *supra* note 8, at 76–78, 116–18; Wilfrid E. Rumble, introduction to Austin, *supra*, at vii–xxiv; Sebok, *supra* note 24, at 2056–57, 2062–64, 2086–87.

26. See Bruce A. Ackerman, Reconstructing American Law (1984) (discussing the transition of the American legal landscape in the twentieth century so that legislation dominated over the common law); Robert W. Gordon, *American Law through English Eyes: A Century of Nightmares and Noble Dreams*, 84 Geo. L. J. 2215, 2218 (1996) (discussing "the main job of modern jurisprudence").

27. See Ross, *supra* note 4, at 61, 318 (discussing the academic desire for control); Marsden, *supra* note 4, at 187; Veysey, *supra* note 4, at 2–17 (distinguishing old antebellum colleges from postbellum new universities); Friedrich Nietzsche, *The Gay Science* at § 125, in The Portable Nietzsche 93, 95 (Walter Kaufmann ed., 1982) (asserting that "God is dead").

28. Marsden, *supra* note 4, at 187; Novick, *supra* note 4, at 16 ("the central norm"); White, *supra* note 4 (focusing on the rejection of formalism in early twentieth century). On the significance of scientific authoritativeness, see Novick, *supra* note 4, at 31; Ross, *supra* note 4, at 62. The American university builders of the late nineteenth century initially drew upon the German university as a model for the developing American universities. Marsden, *supra* note 4, at 88; Veysey, *supra* note 4, at 2, 16–17, 439.

29. See LaPiana, *supra* note 8, at 7–28 (discussing Eliot and Langdell); Marsden, *supra* note 4, at 186–89 (focusing on Eliot); Chase, *supra* note 8, at 332–46 (arguing that all Harvard departments underwent similar reforms around 1870 and after). On professionalization in law as well as other fields, see Richard L. Abel, American Lawyers (1989); Magali Sarfatti Larson, The Rise of Professionalism: A Sociological Analysis (1977); see also Gunnell, *supra* note 4, at 42–45 (discussing professionalization in social sciences); Novick, *supra* note 4, at 47–60 (emphasizing professionalization in the discipline of history). Although Eliot chose Langdell, the faculty still had to vote Langdell in as dean, but no other faculty member was interested. Carter, *supra* note 8, at 14–16; Speziale, *supra* note 8, at 6–11. Max Weber emphasized the connection between the establishment of university law schools and the formal rationalization of law. See Stephen M. Feldman, *An Interpretation of Max Weber's Theory of Law: Metaphysics, Economics, and the Iron Cage of Constitutional Law*, 16 L. & Soc. Inquiry 205, 224–25, 230–32 (1991); see also George Ritzer, *Professional-*

ization, Bureaucratization and Rationalization: The Views of Max Weber, 53 Social Forces 4 (1975) (discussing the Weberian connection of professionalization and rationalization).

I expressly refer to the Langdellian law professors as men because no women were in the legal academy during the heyday of Langdellianism. The struggle for women to become lawyers (not law professors) only began in the 1860s and 1870s. By the early twentieth century, women could join the bar in almost every state. But even when women could become lawyers, many law schools did not admit them to study. In 1870, a total of 1,611 students were attending thirty-one law schools. Of those students, four were women, though not all four were allowed to graduate. By 1890, there were seven thousand students in all, including 135 women. Still, well into the twentieth century many law schools were not admitting women. For example, Columbia admitted its first woman student only in 1929. D. Kelly Weisberg, *Barred from the Bar: Women and Legal Education in the United States 1870–1890,* 28 J. Legal Educ. 485 (1977). The first woman law professors in any school of law were Ellen Spencer Mussy and Emma Gillett, who founded in 1898 their own law school, the Washington College of Law. Washington, however, was not accepted for membership in the Association of American Law Schools (AALS) (which was founded in 1900) until 1947, and shortly afterward the school became affiliated with American University. "The first woman law professor appointed to a tenure-track position in an American Bar Association (ABA)-approved, AALS-member school was Barbara Nachtrieb Armstrong," who was given a tenure-track appointment as an instructor in law and social economics in 1922 at the University of California, Berkeley. By the end of World War II, only three women had "held tenure or tenure-track appointments in member schools." Soia Mentschikoff first began teaching at Harvard in 1947, before Harvard admitted women as students! Herma Hill Kay, *The Future of Women Law Professors,* 77 Iowa L. Rev. 5 (1991); see Donna Fossum, *Women Law Professors,* 1980 Am. B. Found. Res. J. 903.

30. When more intellectual mugwumps found state and national governments to be less amenable to their claims of authority than the colleges, they led the emergence of the new universities. Ross, *supra* note 4, at 62–63. Thomas C. Grey places the Langdellians within this mugwump class. Grey, Langdell, *supra* note 8, at 35. I rely largely on the following works by C. C. Langdell: Cases on Contracts (2d ed., 1879) (hereafter Langdell, Casebook); Summary of the Law of Contracts (2d ed., 1880) (hereafter Langdell, Summary); *Preface to the First Edition,* in Cases on Contracts (2d ed., 1879) (hereafter Langdell, *Preface*); *Teaching Law as a Science,* 21 Am. L. Rev. 123 (1887) (hereafter Langdell, *Teaching*); *Classification of Rights and Wrongs,* 13 Harv. L. Rev. 537 (1900); *Classification of Rights and Wrongs (Part II),* 13 Harv. L. Rev. 659 (1900) (hereafter Langdell, *Classification*); *Mutual Promises as a Consideration for Each Other,* 14 Harv. L. Rev. 496 (1901) (hereafter Langdell, *Mutual*); *Dominant Opinions in England during the Nineteenth Century in Relation to Legislation as Illustrated by English Legislation, or the Absence of it, During That Period,* 19 Harv. L. Rev. 151 (1906) (hereafter Langdell, *Dominant*). I also rely on Joseph Beale, 1 A Treatise on the Conflict of Laws (1916); Samuel Williston, The Law of Contracts (1920); William A. Keener, preface, to A Selection of Cases on the Law of Quasi-Contracts iii (1888) (hereafter Keener, preface); William A. Keener, *Methods of Legal Education (Part II),* 1 Yale L.J. 143 (1892) (hereafter Keener, *Methods*). For a collection of recent essays on Langdell, see *Colloquy on Langdell,* 20 Law & Soc. Inquiry 691 (1995).

I disagree with Thomas C. Grey insofar as he implicitly suggests that Langdellian legal science is premodern. In his otherwise excellent study of Langdell, Grey refers to Langdellian legal science as the "classical orthodoxy" that serves as "the indispensable foil" for "modern legal thought." Grey, *Langdell, supra* note 8, at 3. I agree that Langdellian legal science serves as a foil for much of what follows in American jurisprudence, but it is not classical in the sense of being premodern. Hence, despite serving as a foil, Langdellian legal science is also modern, and it therefore shares much in common with the other forms of modernist jurisprudence that followed it. LaPiana, *supra* note 8, at 59, 187 n. 11 (questioning whether Langdell's writing on contract law should be called classical or orthodox). Previously, I too have used the term *classical orthodoxy.* See, e.g., Feldman, *supra* note 8, at 329. While the term usefully underscores the importance of Langdellian legal science to American jurisprudence—as the standard or long dominant approach to law—I now believe that the word *classical* can be misleading (as it suggests premodern). In a more recent article, Grey himself characterizes Langdellian legal science as modern. See Grey, *Modern, supra* note 8, at 494.

31. Langdell, *Preface, supra* note 30, at viii–ix; Langdell, *Dominant, supra* note 30, at 151; Langdell, *Classification, supra* note 30, at 542; Beale, *supra* note 30, at 143; see Beale, *supra* note 30, at 149–50 (arguing that the common law progresses); LaPiana, *supra* note 8, at 122–31, 136 (discussing other Langdellian positivists and evidence of Langdell's positivism); Grey, *Langdell, supra* note 8, at 28–29 and n. 99 (discussing the Langdellians' rejection of natural law and acceptance of an idea of legal development).

32. Langdell, *Teaching, supra* note 30, at 124 ("ultimate sources"); Langdell, *Preface, supra* note 30, at ix ("original sources"); see Beale, *supra* note 30, at 148–49 (arguing that common law judges discover and do not make the law); Keener, *Methods, supra* note 30, at 144 (integrating legal science with the case method of teaching); Langdell, *Teaching, supra* note 30, at 124–25 (on the qualifications of law professors for teaching law in universities). On antebellum legal education and the initial hostility encountered by Langdell, see LaPiana, *supra* note 8, at 29–54 (describing antebellum legal education); Charles Warren, History of the Harvard Law School 372–74 (1970; reprint of 1908 ed.).

33. Langdell, *Preface, supra* note 30, at viii–ix; Stephen Toulmin, Cosmopolis: The Hidden Agenda of Modernity 33 (1990); see Beale, *supra* note 30, at 135 (law "is not a mere collection of arbitrary rules, but a body of scientific principle"); Beale, *supra* note 30, at 148–49 (explaining that many cases are wrongly decided and therefore not truly law); see also Friedman, *supra* note 8, at 617–18; Grey, *Langdell, supra* note 8, at 16–20.

34. Langdell, Summary, *supra* note 30, at 15, 18–21. After this assertion, Langdell continued his discussion of justice: "but, assuming it to be relevant, it may be turned against those who use it without losing any of its strength"; 21. He then argued that deeming an acceptance to be effective upon dispatch would lead to greater injustice. Because of this more practical argument, Thomas Grey has suggested that Langdell's initial response—that a focus on justice was irrelevant—was "an intentional jurisprudential flourish." Grey, *Langdell, supra* note 8, at 4 n. 11. I believe that Langdell's express language suggests that Grey has overstated this point. First, when deeming justice to be irrelevant, Langdell declared that this was the "true answer." Second, when beginning his discussion of justice and practical concerns, Langdell suggested that he was offering these thoughts merely as an "even if" type of argument: even if you do not accept my first argument (which is the true answer), you might be convinced by this additional argument. Hence, Langdell initiated his discussion of justice by saying, "but, assuming it to be relevant." Langdell, Summary, *supra* note 30, at 21. Langdell structured his discussion of the revocation of an offer for a unilateral contract in a similar fashion; 3–4.

35. William A. Keener, *The Inductive Method in Legal Education,* 17 Am. Bar Assoc. Rpts. 473, 484 (1894); quoted in LaPiana, *supra* note 8, at 135.

36. James Barr Ames, *Novation,* 6 Harv. L. Rev. 184, 192 (1892); see Langdell, Summary, *supra* note 30; Williston, *supra* note 30; see, e.g., Joseph Beale, A Selection of Cases and Other Authorities Upon Criminal Law (1894); William A. Keener, A Selection of Cases on the Law of Contracts (1898); William A. Keener, A Selection of Cases on the Law of Quasi-Contracts (1888); Joseph Beale, *Gratuitous Undertakings,* 5 Harv. L. Rev. 222, 230 (1891). On the importance of the repudiation of the common law forms of action, see LaPiana, *supra* note 8, at 4, 58, 104.

37. Grey, *Langdell, supra* note 8, at 21.

38. David Ross, Aristotle 157 (5th ed. 1949); see Joseph Owens, A History of Ancient Western Philosophy (1959).

39. Ross, *supra* note 38, at 158; see Aristotle, *Metaphysics,* in Aristotle 65, 77–78 (Philip Wheelwright trans.; Odyssey Press 1951) (hereafter Aristotle, *Metaphysics*); Aristotle, *Natural Science,* in Aristotle 3, 17–18, 23 (Philip Wheelwright trans.; Odyssey Press 1951); Aristotle, *Psychology* (*De Anima*), in Aristotle 115, 120–21 (Philip Wheelwright trans.; Odyssey Press 1951) (hereafter Aristotle, *Psychology*); compare Aristotle, *Nichomachean Ethics* (I. Bywater trans.), in The Complete Works of Aristotle 1729 (J. Barnes ed., 1984) (hereafter Aristotle, *Ethics*) (rejecting Plato's theory of Ideas or Forms). Another important related work by Aristotle is *Zoology,* in Aristotle 105 (Philip Wheelwright trans.; Odyssey Press 1951) (hereafter Aristotle, *Zoology*).

40. Owens, *supra* note 38, at 303; quoting Aristotle; see Aristotle, *Metaphysics, supra* note 39, at 67–104; Aristotle, *Zoology, supra* note 39, at 107–13; see also D. W. Hamlyn, A History of Western Philosophy 60–62, 66–71 (1987); Ross, *supra* note 38, at 24, 54–55.

41. Keener, *Methods, supra* note 30, at 144 (emphasis added); see Keener, preface, *supra* note 30, at iii–iv. Beale argued that the principles of the "Common Law" truly existed but only insofar as they "came into existence" by their acceptance as the positive law (or "common law") of particular jurisdictions. See Beale, *supra* note 30, at 138–39, 144.

42. Keener, *Methods, supra* note 30, at 144 (emphasis added); see Gilmore, *supra* note 8, at 58–59 (on the West National Reporter System).

43. Compare Andrei Marmor, *No Easy Cases?* in Wittgenstein and Legal Theory 189, 193 (Dennis M. Patterson ed., 1992) (rule-rule relations can be logical, but rule-world relations cannot be).

44. Aristotle, *Ethics 1, supra* note 39 (discussing the *telos,* or natural end, of human life); see Louis Dupré, Passage to Modernity 17–18, 26–28 (1993).

45. Miller, *supra* note 8, at 156; quoting James Gould, *The Law School at Litchfield,* United States Law Journal (1822); see Hoeflich, *supra* note 8 (discussing the idea of legal science in antebellum and postbellum periods). For an example of a Langdellian treatise filled with citations in footnotes, see Williston, *supra* note 30.

46. Dorothy Ross, *The Liberal Tradition Revisited and the Republican Tradition Addressed,* in New Directions in American Intellectual History 116, 125 (John Higham and Paul K. Conkin eds., 1979); see Sebok, *supra* note 24, at 2081–83 (criticizing commentators who have considered Langdell a natural law theorist).

47. See Grey, *Modern, supra* note 8, at 494 (on hybrid form of scholarship); Pierre Schlag, *The Problem of the Subject,* 69 Tex. L. Rev. 1627, 1633–62 (1991) (on Langdell and the social construction of the self).

48. See Gordon, *supra* note 8, at 88–89; Peller, *Neutral Principles, supra* note 8, at 576; Gunnell, *supra* note 4, at 45 (emphasizing the overlap of universities and business interests).

49. *Lochner v. New York,* 198 US 45, 57, 64 (1905); Duxbury, *supra* note 8, at 3 (linking Langdellian formalism with Lochnerian formalism); Singer, *supra* note 8, at 478–79 (connecting Langdellian legal science with the protection of contractual freedom). Some other Lochnerian cases include: *Bailey v. Drexel Furniture Co.* (Child Labor Tax Case), 259 US 20 (1922); *Hammer v. Dagenhart* (Child Labor Case), 247 US 251 (1918); *Allgeyer v. Louisiana,* 165 US 578 (1897); *Chicago, Milwaukee & St. Paul Railway v. Minnesota* (Minnesota Rate Case), 134 US 418 (1890).

50. Kaczorowski, *supra* note 1, at 924; see Derrick Bell, Race, Racism, and American Law (2d ed., 1980) (detailing the African-American struggle for protection of rights); Foner, *supra* note 1, at 228–80 (discussing the various Republican positions on rights and federal power).

51. Thomas M. Cooley, A Treatise on the Constitutional Limitations Which Rest Upon the Legislative Power of the States of the American Union (Da Capo Press 1972; reprint of first ed., 1868) (hereafter Cooley, Constitutional Limitations); Thomas M. Cooley, A Treatise on the Law of Torts or the Wrongs which Arise Independent of Contract (1880) (hereafter Cooley, Torts); Christopher G. Tiedeman, A Treatise on the Limitations of Police Power in the United States (Da Capo Press 1971; reprint of first ed., 1886) (hereafter Tiedeman, Limitations); Christopher G. Tiedeman, The Unwritten Constitution of the United States (1974, photo. reprint of first ed., 1890) (hereafter Tiedeman, Unwritten); see LaPiana, *supra* note 8, at 136–37; Gordon, *Harvard, supra* note 8, at 1254; Grey, *Modern, supra* note 8, at 496–97. James Barr Ames and Joseph Beale, Langdell's disciples, threatened to withdraw their support for the new law school at the University of Chicago because Chicago intended to include courses related to political science in the law school curriculum. LaPiana, *supra* note 8, at 129–30; Grey, *Langdell, supra* note 8, at 34–35.

52. Tiedeman, Limitations, *supra* note 51, at 1, 7; see 10–11. Cooley's *Constitutional Limitations* even less clearly articulated a theory of natural rights. See, e.g., Cooley, Constitutional Limitations, *supra* note 51, at 35–36 (one of Cooley's strongest statements regarding natural rights).

53. Siegel, *supra* note 8, at 1517; quoting Tiedeman, Annual Address: The Doctrine of Natural Rights in its Bearing Upon American Constitutional Law, in Report of the Seventh Annual Meeting of the Missouri Bar Association 97, 111 (1887); see at 1437, 1489–91, 1515–18, 1542–43; see, e.g., Cooley, Constitutional Limitations, *supra* note 51, at 21–25 (emphasizing the historical development of the common law). In *Unwritten Constitution,* Tiedeman wrote:

> Technically, this criticism of the Roman doctrine *jus naturale* is sound; for there can be no legal right which is not recognized or created by the sovereign power of the state. The commands of the sovereign are always law, and hence legally right, it matters not how many so-called natural rights are thereby violated. But the error of the Austinites, in this case, as in the general question of the origin and development of law, lies in failing to take note of the fact that popular notions of rights, however wrong they may be from a scientific standpoint, do become incorporated into, and exert an influence upon, the development of the actual law. (*Supra* note 51, at 71–72)

See generally Owen M. Fiss, 8 History of the Supreme Court of the United States: Troubled Beginnings of the Modern State, 1888–1910, at 389–90 (1993) (discussing the *Lochner* era conception of liberty as an individual's possession).

54. Cooley, Constitutional Limitations, *supra* note 51, at 393; see Grey, *Modern, supra* note 8, at 496–97 (discussing laissez-faire constitutionalism); Siegel, *supra* note 8, at 1452–53 (same). Tiedeman expressly declared that he aimed to support *"laissez-faire* doctrine, which denies to government the power to do more than to provide for the public order and personal security." Tiedeman, Limitations, *supra* note 51, at vi.

55. See *Adair v. United States*, 208 US 161, 173 (1908) (citing Cooley, Torts, *supra* note 51); Siegel, *supra* note 8, at 1487 (presenting the common historical link between Cooley and Lochnerian decisions). For Supreme Court citations of Cooley's *Constitutional Limitations* related to the laissez-faire proposition, see *Hammer v. Dagenhart*, 247 US 251, 274 (1918); *Citizens' Saving & Loan Ass'n v. City of Topeka*, 87 US 655, 663 and n. 4 (1874). A Westlaw computer search for the word *Allgeyer*, revealed that the Supreme Court cited the *Allgeyer* case, decided in 1897, at least forty-nine times before the Court repudiated the *Lochnerian* approach in 1937. See *Allgeyer v. Louisiana*, 165 US 578 (1897). For one example of a chain-cite of laissez-faire decisions, see *Adkins v. Children's Hospital of the District of Columbia*, 261 US 525, 545 (1923).

56. *The Slaughterhouse Cases*, 83 US (16 Wall.) 36, 96–97 (1873) (Field, J., dissenting); *Allgeyer v. Louisiana*, 165 US 578, 589 (1897) (quoting *Butchers' Union Co. v. Crescent City Co.*, 111 US 746, 762 (1883) (Bradley, J., concurring)); see *The Slaughterhouse Cases*, 83 US (16 Wall.) at 114–16 (Bradley, J., dissenting); *Butchers' Union Co. v. Crescent City Co.*, 111 US 746, 754–57 (1883) (Field, J., concurring); 762 (Bradley, J., concurring). In *Frisbie v. United States*, decided in 1895, the Court had mentioned that "the inalienable rights of the citizen" include "the liberty of contract," but the Court there upheld the disputed governmental action. *Frisbie v. United States*, 157 US 160, 165 (1895). In *Loan Association v. Topeka*, the Court struck down a city tax law without referring to the Constitution. The Court did write, however, that there "are limitations on [governmental] power which grow out of the essential nature of all free governments." *Loan Association v. Topeka*, 87 US (20 Wall.) 655, 663 (1874). In *Adair v. United States*, the Court emphasized "fundamental rights" but did not suggest that they were natural rights. Instead, it declared that Congress's power under the commerce clause could not "be exerted in violation of any fundamental right secured by other provisions of the Constitution." *Adair v. United States*, 208 US 161, 180 (1908). In *Coppage v. Kansas*, the Court referred to liberty and property as "coexistent human rights." *Coppage v. Kansas*, 236 US 1, 17 (1915).

57. See Wright, *supra* note 8, at 298–99 (arguing that the *Lochner* Court implicitly relied on natural rights). For examples of scholars writing for and against *Lochner* during the *Lochner* era itself, see Arthur W. Machen, *Corporate Personality*, 24 Harv. L. Rev. 253, 261–62 (1911) (supporting laissez-faire constitutionalism by arguing that corporations are natural entities); Haines, *supra* note 8, at 172–95 (criticizing natural rights reasoning of *Lochner* Court). For disagreements among more recent scholars regarding whether natural rights reasoning was explicit or even implicit in some of the Supreme Court's substantive due process cases from the late nineteenth century, compare Moglen, *supra* note 8, at 2032–33 (arguing that Supreme Court used natural rights reasoning) and Nelson, *supra* note 8, at 552–57 (same) with Horwitz 2, *supra* note 8, at 156–59 (arguing that Progressives in the early twentieth century mistakenly characterized the late-nineteenth-century Supreme Court as following natural rights) and Robert W. Gordon, *The Elusive Transfor-*

mation, 6 Yale J.L. & Human. 137, 154 (1994) (reviewing Horwitz 2, *supra* note 8) (agreeing with Horwitz on this point).

58. Karen Orren, Belated Feudalism: Labor, the Law, and Liberal Development in the United States 111–17 (1991); see Erwin Chemerinsky, Constitutional Law: Principles and Policies 482 (1997).

59. Herget, *supra* note 8, at 120–21 ("partisan," "speeches"); James Coolidge Carter, Law: Its Origin, Growth, and Function 83, 209–10 (1907); see Friedrich Carl von Savigny, Of the Vocation of Our Age for Legislation and Jurisprudence (Abram Hayward trans., 1831; first published in German in 1814), in The Great Legal Philosophers 290, 290 (Clarence Morris ed., 1959); see also Bodenheimer, *supra* note 8, at 70–83; Horwitz 2, *supra* note 8, at 117–21 (discussing Carter's opposition to codification).

60. Langdell, *Dominant, supra* note 30, at 153, 166–67 (praising a book by Dicey on English legislation during the nineteenth century); see LaPiana, *supra* note 8, at 124. On Carter's opposition to legislation, see Carter, *supra* note 59, at 204–40; Herget, *supra* note 8, at 120–30.

61. On the relative insignificance of the historical school, see Herget, *supra* note 8, at 22 (the historical school "played not a dominant but a main supporting role in American legal philosophy"); compare Duxbury, *supra* note 8, at 34 (noting that Holmes drew on the historical jurisprudence of Maine and Savigny, but otherwise failing to discuss the historical school); Horwitz 2, *supra* note 8, at 121 (describing Carter as "pedestrian").

62. Oliver Wendell Holmes, Jr., *Natural Law,* 32 Harv. L. Rev. 40 (1918), in The Essential Holmes 180, 181 (Richard A. Posner ed., 1992) ("naïve"); Oliver Wendell Holmes, Jr., review of Frederick Pollock, *Law and Command,* The Law Magazine and Review 189 (1872), 6 Am. L. Rev. 723 (1872), in Justice Oliver Wendell Holmes: His Book Notices and Uncollected Letters and Papers 21, 22 (1973) ("sovereignty is a form"); see also Oliver Wendell Holmes, Jr., *Codes, and the Arrangement of Law,* 5 Am. L. Rev. 1, 4–5 (1870) (hereafter Holmes, *Codes*) (arguing that who has sovereign power is a question of fact). Later in his career, Holmes clearly and sharply separated the study of law from morality. See Oliver Wendell Holmes, Jr., *The Path of the Law,* 10 Harv. L. Rev. 457, 459–62 (1897) (hereafter Holmes, *Path*). For comparisons between Langdell and Holmes, see Duxbury, *supra* note 8, at 46 and n. 147 (discussing commentators who have considered Holmes as a pure anti-formalist and thus opposed to Langdell); LaPiana, *supra* note 8, at 169 (emphasizing similarities between Langdell and Holmes).

63. Oliver Wendell Holmes, Jr., The Common Law 35–36, 51, 77–78, 111 (Dover ed., 1991; first ed., 1881). Holmes himself believed that his generation was the first without premodern faith. See G. Edward White, Justice Oliver Wendell Holmes: Law and the Inner Self 37 (1993).

64. See, e.g., Oliver Wendell Holmes, Jr., review of A. V. Dicey, A Treatise on the Rules for the Selection of the Parties to an Action (1870), 5 Am. L. Rev. 534 (1871) (hereafter Holmes, Dicey); Oliver Wendell Holmes, Jr., review of C. C. Langdell, Summary of Contracts (1880), 14 Am. L. Rev. 233 (1880), in Mark D. Howe, Justice Oliver Wendell Holmes, The Proving Years 156 (1963) (hereafter Holmes, Langdell). Holmes, also like Langdell, recognized the significance of the transition from the common law forms of action to code pleading in the classification of the law. See Holmes, *Codes, supra* note 62, at 13; Holmes, Dicey, *supra,* at 535; see also White, *supra* note 63, at 117.

65. Holmes, *Codes, supra* note 62, at 4; Holmes, *supra* note 63, at 35; see Grey, *Holmes, supra* note 8, at 819 (emphasizing Holmes's pragmatism). Nicholas St. John Green, who

was somewhat Holmesian in his jurisprudence, initially taught at Harvard under Langdell but left in protest against the overly theoretical approach of the Langdellians. He went on to help start the law school at Boston University. See LaPiana, *supra* note 8, at 110–22; see, e.g., Nicholas St. John Green, *Slander and Libel*, 6 Am. L. Rev. 593 (1872); review of John Townsend, A Treatise on the Wrongs Called Slander and Libel, and On the Remedy by Civil Action for Those Wrongs (1872).

66. Holmes, *supra* note 63, at 1; Holmes, Langdell, *supra* note 64, at 156; see Minda, *supra* note 8, at 16 (arguing that the modern era in jurisprudence bloomed with Holmes); Grey, *Holmes*, *supra* note 8, at 796–98 (discussing the importance of a historicist attitude in Holmes's jurisprudence).

67. Holmes, *supra* note 63, at 305. Langdell had argued, based on his syllogistic proof, that acceptance should be effective only upon receipt; practical considerations and justice were beside the point. Whenever Langdell did discuss such pragmatic concerns, he carefully circumscribed their importance, explaining that they were not principles that could legitimately ground judicial decisions. In stark contrast to Langdell's argument, Holmes asserted that convenience alone could be determinative. Holmes then, as an ancillary matter, added a logical argument in favor of deeming an acceptance effective upon dispatch, specifically criticizing Langdell's syllogistic reasoning; see 305–7. On Holmes recommending conscious judicial law making, see 36; Holmes, *Path*, *supra* note 62, at 467.

68. Holmes, *supra* note 63, at 36 ("The truth is"); Oliver Wendell Holmes, Jr., *Law in Science and Science in Law*, 12 Harv. L. Rev. 443 (1899), in The Essential Holmes 185, 198 (Richard A. Posner ed., 1992) ("I believe that").

69. Holmes, *Path*, *supra* note 62, at 457–61; see, e.g., Jerome Frank, *Mr. Justice Holmes and Non-Euclidean Legal Thinking*, 17 Cornell L. Q. 568 (1932) (emphasizing Holmes's role in the turning away from Langdellian jurisprudence).

70. Roscoe Pound, *Mechanical Jurisprudence*, 8 Colum. L. Rev. 605, 605–9 (1908) (hereafter Pound, *Mechanical*); see also Benjamin Cardozo, The Nature of the Judicial Process (1921); Roscoe Pound, *The Scope and Purpose of Sociological Jurisprudence*, 25 Harv. L. Rev. 489 (1912); Roscoe Pound, *The Theory of Judicial Decision*, 36 Harv. L. Rev. 940 (1923). For excellent discussions of sociological jurisprudence, see Hull, *supra* note 8; G. Edward White, *From Sociological Jurisprudence to Realism: Jurisprudence and Social Change in Early Twentieth-Century America*, in Patterns of American Legal Thought 99 (1978).

71. See Roscoe Pound, *Liberty of Contract*, 18 Yale L. J. 454, 455, 464–68 (1909) (attacking laissez-faire constitutionalism as being based on natural rights) (hereafter Pound, *Liberty*). On Progressivism in general, see Hofstadter, *supra* note 1, at 176–82; Weibe, *supra* note 1, at 164–95.

72. Extended discussions of realism include the following: Laura Kalman, Legal Realism at Yale, 1927–1960 (1986) (hereafter Kalman, Legal Realism); Schlegel, *supra* note 8; William Twining, Karl Llewellyn and the Realist Movement (1973). For a compilation of various lists of realists, see Hull, *supra* note 8, at 343–46.

73. Fred Rodell, *Goodbye to Law Reviews*, 23 Va. L. Rev. 38, 38 (1936); see Stephen M. Feldman, *Diagnosing Power: Postmodernism in Legal Scholarship and Judicial Practice (With an Emphasis on the Teague Rule against New Rules in Habeas Corpus Cases)*, 88 Nw. U. L. Rev. 1046, 1090–91 (1994); John Henry Schlegel, *Langdell's Legacy or, The Case of the Empty Envelope*, 36 Stan. L. Rev. 1517, 1529–30 (1984), review of Robert S. Stevens, Law School: Legal Education in America From the 1850s to the 1980s (1983).

74. Laura Kalman, *Bleak House*, 84 Geo. L. J. 2245, 2245 (1996); quoting Schlegel, *supra* note 8, at 8, paraphrasing a Dewey lecture; Walter Wheeler Cook, The Logical and Legal Basis of the Conflict of Laws 4 (1942) (the "experimental" method); see Purcell, *supra* note 4, at 3–73 (on the emergence of scientific naturalism); Schlegel, *supra* note 8, at 57–61.

75. Laura Kalman, Abe Fortas: A Biography 23 (1990); Leuchtenberg, *supra* note 1, at 333 ("to make the industrial system"); see Hofstadter, *supra* note 1, at 316–17; Leuchtenberg, *supra* note 1, at 338–39, 344 (comparing Progressivism with New Deal); see, e.g., Thomas Reed Powell, *The Judiciality of Minimum Wage Legislation*, 37 Harv. L. Rev. 545, 554–56 (1924) (arguing from a realist perspective that freedom of contract was a right invented by *Lochner* Court justices; freedom of contract was not part of the Constitution). I am not suggesting that realist jurisprudence should be equated with the New Deal, but rather that many realists became New Dealers, even working for the Roosevelt Administration. See Duxbury, *supra* note 8, at 153–54; Grey, *Modern*, *supra* note 8, at 501–2. Obviously the realist jurisprudence resonated strongly with New Deal politics and thus facilitated the movement of many realists into New Deal political positions. See, e.g., Kalman, *supra* note 8, at 17.

76. Felix Cohen, *Transcendental Nonsense and the Functional Approach*, 35 Colum. L. Rev. 809 (1935), in The Legal Conscience 33, 34–37 (1960).

77. Karl Llewellyn, The Bramble Bush 12 (1930) (emphasis omitted) (hereafter Llewellyn, Bramble Bush). The final sentence in the quoted passage eventually became the center of controversy, and Llewellyn retracted it in a subsequent edition of the book; Karl Llewellyn, The Bramble Bush 8–9 (1951); see Karl N. Llewellyn, *On Reading and Using the Newer Jurisprudence*, 40 Colum. L. Rev. 581, 603 (1940) (expressing "open penance" for suggesting in *The Bramble Bush* that law was whatever officials did, however arbitrary it might be).

78. Joseph Hutcheson, *The Judgment Intuitive: The Function of the "Hunch" in Judicial Decision*, 14 Cornell L. Q. 274, 278, 286–87 (1929); Rodell, *supra* note 73, at 38; Kalman, *supra* note 8, at 46; quoting Fortas, from Kalman's interview with Fortas's clerk, John Griffiths; see Karl Llewellyn, *Some Realism about Realism—Responding to Dean Pound*, 44 Harv. L. Rev. 1222, 1238–41 (1931); Max Radin, *The Theory of Judicial Decision Or: How Judges Think*, 11 A. B. A. J. 357 (1925). For historical information on the Restatement movement, see Grant Gilmore, The Death of Contract 58–65 (1974); H. Goodrich and P. Wolkin, The Story of the American Law Institute 1923–1961 (1961); J. Honnold, The Life of the Law 144–80 (1964); see, e.g., Restatement of Contracts (1932). For realist criticisms of the Restatement movement, see Cohen, *supra* note 76, at 59; Walter Wheeler Cook, *Scientific Method and the Law*, 13 A. B. A. J. 303, 307 (June 1927).

79. Robert L. Hale, *Coercion and Distribution in a Supposedly Non-coercive State*, 38 Pol. Sci. Q. 470, 470 (1923); see Robert L. Hale, *Force and the State: A Comparison of "Political" and "Economic" Compulsion*, 35 Colum. L. Rev. 149, 149, 168, 198–201 (1935). The sociological jurisprudent Morris R. Cohen made a similar argument. Morris R. Cohen, *The Basis of Contract*, 46 Harv. L. Rev. 553, 585–87 (1933).

80. *Lochner v. New York*, 198 US 45, 74–76 (1905) (Holmes, J., dissenting); see White, Holmes, *supra* note 63, at 364–65 (discussing the significance of Holmes's dissent).

81. Jerome Frank, *Mr. Justice Holmes and Non-Euclidean Legal Thinking*, 17 Cornell L. Q. 568, 571, 580 (1932); see Jerome Frank, Law and the Modern Mind (1930); see also Donald H. Gjerdingen, *The Future of Legal Scholarship and the Search for a Modern Theory of*

Law, 35 Buffalo L. Rev. 381, 395–96 (1986); Peller, Metaphysics, *supra* note 8, at 1154, 1239–41, 1260–61.

82. Walter Wheeler Cook, *Legal Logic*, 31 Colum. L. Rev. 368 (1931); Ross, *supra* note 4, at 311 ("quantitative methods"); Novick, *supra* note 4, at 141; see William O. Douglas and Dorothy S. Thomas, *The Business Failures Project—2. An Analysis of Methods of Investigation*, 40 Yale L. J. 1034, 1036 (1931); Underhill Moore and Gilbert Sussman, *Legal and Institutional Methods Applied to the Debiting of Direct Discounts—3. The Connecticut Studies*, 40 Yale L. J. 752 (1931); see, e.g., William O. Douglas, *Some Functional Aspects of Bankruptcy*, 41 Yale L. J. 329 (1932). On the importance of the social sciences, see Purcell, *supra* note 4, at 3–94; Schlegel, *supra* note 8; see, e.g., Jerome Frank, *Why Not a Clinical Lawyer-School?*, 81 U. Penn. L. Rev. 907, 921–22 (1933) (recommending the integration of social sciences into law schools).

83. Grey, *Holmes*, *supra* note 8, at 802 ("the practical need"); William O. Douglas, *Wage Earner Bankruptcies—State v. Federal Control*, 42 Yale L. J. 591, 593 (1933); Kalman, *Fortas*, *supra* note 75, at 28; quoting Fortas; see Cook, *supra* note 78 (realist emphasizing a pragmatic type of empiricism); William James, *Pragmatism's Conception of Truth*, in Pragmatism: The Classic Writings 227 (H. Thayer ed., 1982); see also Ross, *supra* note 4, at 311–13 (noting how social scientists sought control to counter their awareness of rapid historical change).

84. Llewellyn, *Bramble Bush*, *supra* note 77, at 12 ("concrete instance"); Cohen, *supra* note 76, at 839–40; see Felix Cohen, Ethical Systems and Legal Ideals 62–63, 237 (1933); Llewellyn, *supra* note 78, at 1237. For a discussion of how Cohen applied this method in writing his *Handbook of Federal Indian Law*, published in 1941, see Stephen M. Feldman, *Felix S. Cohen and His Jurisprudence: Reflections on Federal Indian Law*, 35 Buffalo L. Rev. 479 (1986). The sociological jurisprudents first began using the term *social engineering*. See, e.g., Pound, *Mechanical*, *supra* note 70, at 609.

85. Gunnell, *supra* note 4, at 105; Purcell, *supra* note 4, at 40–42, 69–73; Ross, *supra* note 4, at 314–15.

86. Schlegel, *supra* note 8, at 230; quoting Douglas in Douglas to Hutchins, 4/7/34, Robert Maynard Hutchins Papers, University of Chicago; see Gunnell, *supra* note 4, at 105, 122–23, 127–45; Purcell, *supra* note 4, at 96, 112–14, 138; Schlegel, *supra* note 8, at 2, 20, 211, 230 (on the demise of realism); Singer, *supra* note 8, at 468; G. Edward White, *From Realism to Critical Legal Studies: A Truncated Intellectual History*, in Intervention and Detachment 274, 278 (1994) (hereafter White, *From Realism*).

87. *Harper v. Virginia Board of Elections*, 383 US 663 (1966) (poll taxes); *Reynolds v. Sims*, 377 US 533 (1964) (one person, one vote); *Gomillion v. Lightfoot*, 364 US 339 (1960) (racial gerrymandering); Voting Rights Act of 1965, 79 Stat. 437, 42 U.S.C. §§ 1973 et seq.; Civil Rights Act of 1964, 78 Stat. 241, 42 U.S.C. §§ 1971, 1975(a)–(d), 2000(a)–2000(h)(4); see Purcell, *supra* note 4, at 5 (nineteenth-century "Americans were unconcerned with elaborate theoretical justifications" of democracy); Wiebe, *Self-Rule*, *supra* note 8, at 55 (noting that as "late as 1841, the publishing firm of Harper and Brothers claimed that no American book on democracy existed"); Morton J. Horwitz, *Foreword: The Constitution of Change: Legal Fundamentality without Fundamentalism*, 107 Harv. L. Rev. 30, 56–57 (1993) (on the emerging importance of democracy) (hereafter Horwitz, *Foreword*). But see Barry Friedman, *The History of the Countermajoritarian Difficulty, pt. 1, The Road to Judicial Supremacy*, 73 N. Y. U. L. Rev. 333, 385 (1998) (citing George Sidney Camp, Democracy (1841), and suggesting that Camp published the first American treatise on democracy in

1841). Congress previously had enacted the Civil Rights Acts of 1957 and 1960, both of which included inadequate sections on voting rights. See Derrick Bell, Race, Racism, and American Law 145–46 (2d ed., 1980).

88. Clarence Dykstra, *The Quest for Responsibility*, 33 Am. Pol. Sci. Rev. 1, 11, 22 (1939); see Novick, *supra* note 4, at 281 (on the intellectual and material mobilization of America).

89. John Dewey, Freedom and Culture 134, 175 (1939). Dewey used the term *culture* in a broad sense so that it would include economic and other social institutions; See 6–12; see also Robert Brooks, *Reflections on the "World Revolution" of 1940*, 35 Am. Pol. Sci. Rev. 1 (1941).

90. See Purcell, *supra* note 4, at 235–66; Jane Mansbridge, *The Rise and Fall of Self-Interest in the Explanation of Political Life*, in Beyond Self-Interest 8–9 (Jane Mansbridge ed., 1990); compare Daniel Bell, The Cultural Contradictions of Capitalism 23–24 (1978) (on the shift of economic principles into politics); Joseph A. Schumpeter, Capitalism, Socialism, and Democracy 242 (3d ed., 1950) (emphasizing that democracy is a means for arriving at decisions).

91. Robert Dahl, A Preface to Democratic Theory 6 (1956); see, e.g., V. O. Key, Politics, Parties, and Pressure Groups (4th ed., 1958; first published in 1942) (emphasizing politics as the exercise of power, and discussing the role played by pressure groups in that exercise of power); David B. Truman, The Governmental Process (1951) (an extensive study of the functioning and influence of political interest groups); see also Purcell, *supra* note 4, at 254–72, 283.

92. Dahl, *supra* note 91, at 143; Purcell, *supra* note 4, at 253; see Gunnell, *supra* note 4, at 241; Purcell, *supra* note 4, at 231, 235–66; see, e.g., Louis Hartz, The Liberal Tradition in America 14–20, 58–59, 85–86, 134 (1955) (emphasizing American moral unanimity); Richard Hofstadter, The American Political Tradition and the Men Who Made It (1948).

93. Hodgson, *supra* note 1, at 137 ("age of bland"); Patterson, *supra* note 1, at 344 ("the dramatic expansion"); Novick, *supra* note 4, at 325 ("a climate"); Patterson, *supra* note 1, at 82 ("immeasurably stronger"); John Kenneth Galbraith, The Affluent Society (1958); Patterson, *supra* note 1, at 61 ("quarter century"; quoting Daniel Yankelovich, The New Morality 166 (1974)); Hodgson, *supra* note 1, at 12 ("that the businessman"). On the importance of television, see Hodgson, *supra* note 1, at 134–52; 2 Thernstrom, *supra* note 1, at 812–13.

94. Eugene V. Rostow, *The Democratic Character of Judicial Review*, 66 Harv. L. Rev. 193 (1952); see Harold D. Lasswell and Myres S. McDougal, *Legal Education and Public Policy: Professional Training in the Public Interest*, 52 Yale L. J. 203, 206, 217 (1943) (legal education should be training for policy making to help achieve democratic values); Lon L. Fuller, *Reason and Fiat in Case Law*, 59 Harv. L. Rev. 376, 395 (1946) (emphasizing a "spirit of compromise and tolerance without which democratic society is impossible") (hereafter Fuller, *Reason and Fiat*). For criticisms of the realists, see Walter B. Kennedy, *Functional Nonsense and the Transcendental Approach*, 5 Ford. L. Rev. 272 (1936) (criticizing Felix Cohen's realism); Francis Lucey, *Natural Law and American Legal Realism*, 30 Geo. L. J. 493 (1942) (condemning realists from a natural law perspective); see also Henry M. Hart, Jr., *Holmes' Positivism—An Addendum*, 64 Harv. L. Rev. 929, 934 (1951) (criticizes the behaviorism and positivism of Holmes and the legal realists for rejecting the power of ideas or reason to change conduct) (hereafter Hart, *Holmes' Positivism*); Louis L. Jaffe, *Foreword: The Supreme Court, 1950 Term*, 65 Harv. L. Rev. 107 (1951) (criticizes realists for believing that the Supreme Court's work focused on politics and not law). On the survival of

realism in the years after World War II, see Laura Kalman's discussion of Yale, Legal Realism, *supra* note 72, at 145–87; see, e.g., Robert L. Hale, *Bargaining, Duress, and Economic Liberty,* 43 Colum. L. Rev. 603 (1943) (an example of a post-1940 realist article). On homogeneity among law professors, see Richard A. Posner, *The Decline of Law as an Autonomous Discipline: 1962–1987,* 100 Harv. L. Rev. 761, 765–66 (1987) (emphasizing the lack of ideological strife among law professors in late 1950s and early 1960s). On the small number of women in the legal academy in the years after World War II, see Fossum, *supra* note 29; Kay, *supra* note 29. During the 1940s and 1950s, some Jews, such as Herbert Wechsler, entered the legal academy, though during this time, most such Jews tended to avoid overt displays of their Jewish identity and heritage. See Leonard Dinnerstein, Antisemitism in America 87–88 (1994) (discussing widespread discrimination against Jews in the academy).

95. Lon L. Fuller, The Morality of Law 155 (rev. ed., 1969); see Lon L. Fuller, The Law in Quest of Itself 45–59, 109–10, 122–23 (1940); see also John Dickinson, *Legal Rules: Their Place in the Process of Decision,* 79 U. Pa. L. Rev. 833 (1931); Fuller, *Reason and Fiat, supra* note 94, at 378–79, 395. For an early attack on rule-skepticism, see Morris Cohen, *The Place of Logic in the Law,* 29 Harv. L. Rev. 622 (1915), in Law and the Social Order 165 (1933). For discussions of legal process, see Neil Duxbury, *Faith in Reason: The Process Tradition in American Jurisprudence,* 15 Cardozo L. Rev. 601, 622–32 (1993); William N. Eskridge, Jr., and Philip P. Frickey, *The Making of The Legal Process,* 107 Harv. L. Rev. 2031 (1994); Peller, *Neutral Principles, supra* note 8; G. Edward White, *The Evolution of Reasoned Elaboration: Jurisprudential Criticism and Social Change,* in Patterns of American Legal Thought 136 (1978). Fuller elaborated his early ideas in the context of a dispute with H. L. A. Hart, a British analytic jurisprudent. See H. L. A. Hart, The Concept of Law (1961); H. L. A. Hart, *Positivism and the Separation of Law and Morals,* 71 Harv. L. Rev. 593 (1958); Lon Fuller, *Positivism and Fidelity to Law—A Reply to Professor Hart,* 71 Harv. L. Rev. 630 (1958).

96. Hart, *Holmes' Positivism, supra* note 94, at 936 n. 21 ("principle of institutional settlement"); Henry Hart, Jr., and Albert Sacks, The Legal Process: Basic Problems in the Making and Application of Law 4 (tentative ed., 1958) (hereafter Hart and Sacks, tentative ed.); Henry Hart, Jr., *The Power of Congress to Limit the Jurisdiction of Federal Courts: An Exercise in Dialectic,* 66 Harv. L. Rev. 1362, 1365 (1953) (on essential functions thesis); see Hart and Sacks, tentative ed., at iii, 3, 366–68, 662. Hart and Sacks were already working on the Legal Process course materials by 1954. In addition, they and other professors had been developing related courses (for example, courses on legislation) for more than a decade, and Hart and Sacks drew on those related course materials. See Eskridge and Frickey, *supra* note 95, at 2033–45. Hart and Sacks's *Legal Process* casebook was finally published in 1994. Henry Hart, Jr., and Albert Sacks, The Legal Process: Basic Problems in the Making and Application of Law (William N. Eskridge and Philip P. Frickey eds., 1994) (hereafter Hart and Sacks, 1994).

97. Henry M. Hart, Jr., and Herbert Wechsler, preface to The Federal Courts and the Federal System (1953); compare Grey, *Modern, supra* note 8, at 504 (emphasizing legal process theorists' fondness for administrative law and federal courts).

98. Hart and Sacks, tentative ed., *supra* note 96, at 164–67; Hart and Sacks, 1994, *supra* note 96, at 147; see Peller, *Neutral Principles, supra* note 8, at 571, 592–97, 600, 603; White, *From Realism, supra* note 86, at 281.

99. Hartz, *supra* note 92, at 156; Hart and Sacks, 1994 *supra* note 96, at 148; Louis

Henkin, *Foreword: On Drawing Lines,* 82 Harv. L. Rev. 63, 63 (1968); see Hartz, *supra* note 92, at 59–62 (on individualism); Kalman, *supra* note 8, at 32–33 (describing how Frankfurter and Sacks exchanged letters after Sacks had criticized the Court's use of per curiam opinions); Richard H. Fallon, Jr., *Reflections on the Hart and Wechsler Paradigm,* 47 Vand. L. Rev. 953, 962 (1994); Peller, *Neutral Principles, supra* note 8, at 568–72; Mark Tushnet and Timothy Lynch, *The Project of the Harvard "Forewords": A Social and Intellectual Inquiry,* 11 Const. Commentary 463 (1994–1995) (a history of the Harvard *Forewords*). For an example of a Justice Frankfurter opinion that expressly discussed the scholarly proposals of the legal process writers, see *Textile Workers Union v. Lincoln Mills,* 353 US 448, 473–74 (1957) (Frankfurter, J., dissenting) (discussing the theory of protective jurisdiction).

100. See G. Edward White, *Judicial Activism and the Identity of the Legal Profession,* in Intervention and Detachment 222, 234 (1994) (hereafter White, *Judicial Activism*).

101. Jerome A. Chanes, *Antisemitism and Jewish Security in America Today: Interpreting the Data. Why Can't Jews Take "Yes" for an Answer?* in Antisemitism in America Today 3, 24 (Jerome A. Chanes ed., 1995); Benjamin Ginsberg, The Fatal Embrace: Jews and the State 141 (1993) (by 1960, the news media declared overt antisemitic expressions to be extremist and un-American). On European émigrés' perceptions of American antisemitism in the 1930s, see Martin Jay, The Dialectical Imagination: A History of the Frankfurt School and the Institute of Social Research, 1923–1950, at 34 (1973); Gunnar Myrdal, An American Dilemma 53, 1186 n. 4 (1944).

102. On the civil rights movement in general, see David J. Garrow, Bearing the Cross: Martin Luther King, Jr., and the Southern Christian Leadership Conference (1986); Robert Weisbrot, Freedom Bound: A History of America's Civil Rights Movement (1990); see Hodgson, *supra* note 1, at 149 (linking television and the civil rights movement); Patterson, *supra* note 1, at 480 (same); see also Novick, *supra* note 4, at 348–60 (on the development of a postwar anti-racist consensus). On antisemitism in the postwar period, see Dinnerstein, *supra* note 94, at 162–66.

103. *United States v. Carolene Products,* 304 US 144, 152 n. 4 (1938); *West Coast Hotel Co. v. Parrish,* 300 US 379 (1937) (the transformed Court showing judicial restraint). For discussions of the split on the Court, see Horwitz 2, *supra* note 8, at 252; Richard Kluger, Simple Justice 240–41, 582–84 (1975); Schwartz, *supra* note 8, at 253–55, 269–76; Bernard Schwartz, Super Chief 32, 40–48 (1983). For discussions about footnote 4—which was written by Stone's clerk, Louis Lusky—as the origin of the preferred freedoms dispute, see Horwitz 2, *supra* note 8, at 252; Schwartz, *supra* note 8, at 281; Alpheus Thomas Mason, *The Core of Free Government, 1938–1940: Mr. Justice Stone and "Preferred Freedoms,"* 65 Yale L. J. 597 (1956); see also Joseph Tussman and Jacobus tenBroek, *The Equal Protection of the Laws,* 37 Cal. L. Rev. 341 (1949) (emphasizing the emergence of Supreme Court decisions on equal rights). Various justices and scholars debated whether the preferred freedoms doctrine was consistent or inconsistent with Holmes's *Lochner* dissent. See Horwitz, *Foreword,, supra* note 87, at 81; Mason, *supra,* at 602. G. Edward White recently has argued that the preferred freedoms doctrine was historically rooted in earlier First Amendment cases. G. Edward White, *The First Amendment Comes of Age: The Emergence of Free Speech in Twentieth-Century America,* 95 Mich. L. Rev. 299, 327–30 (1996). The flag salute cases were *West Virginia State Board of Education v. Barnette,* 319 US 624 (1943), overruling *Minersville v. Gobitis,* 310 US 586 (1940); see Mason, *supra,* at 622 (on the surge in religious bigotry); Richard Primus, Note, *A Brooding Omnipresence: Totalitarianism in Postwar Constitutional Thought,* 106 Yale L. J. 423, 437–38 (1996) (attributing the Supreme Court's

overruling of *Gobitis* to a desire to separate America symbolically from Nazi Germany). I do not mean to suggest that the Court's decision alone caused the outbreaks of bigotry and violence.

104. *Brown v. Board of Education*, 347 US 483 (1954). Richard Kluger and Bernard Schwartz had portrayed Frankfurter in the more heroic role, while Mark Tushnet and Katya Lezin have argued that his role was more modest. Kluger, *supra* note 103, at 599; Schwartz, *supra* note 8, at 286–88; Schwartz, Super Chief, *supra* note 103, at 76–81; Mark Tushnet and Katya Lezin, *What Really Happened in Brown v. Board of Education*, 91 Colum. L. Rev. 1867 (1991); see Kalman, *supra* note 8, at 28–34.

105. *Brown*, 347 US at 495–96; *Brown v. Board of Education*, 349 US 294 (1955) (*Brown II*); *Plessy v. Ferguson*, 163 US 537 (1896); Schwartz, Super Chief, *supra* note 103, at 88–93; Tushnet and Lezin, *supra* note 104, at 1878; see Derrick A. Bell, *Brown v. Board of Education and the Interest-Convergence Dilemma*, 93 Harv. L. Rev. 518 (1980); see also Mary L. Dudziak, *Desegregation as a Cold War Imperative*, 41 Stan. L. Rev. 61 (1988); compare Kluger, *supra* note 103, at 710 (the Supreme Court acted as the conscience of the nation by enforcing American principles, by granting "simple justice"). On the role of the NAACP, see Mark Tushnet, Segregated Schools and Legal Strategy: The NAACP's Campaign Against Segregated Education, 1925–1950 (1987); Jerome M. Culp, Jr., *Toward a Black Legal Scholarship: Race and Original Understandings*, 1991 Duke L. J. 39, 55 and n. 42 (arguing that the NAACP had a more consistent legal strategy than acknowledged by Tushnet).

106. *Brown*, 347 US at 492–95.

107. See Kalman, *supra* note 8, at 5–6 (emphasizing eventual importance of *Brown* for legal scholarship); Minda, *supra* note 8, at 39 (same); Peller, *Neutral Principles*, *supra* note 8, at 592 (early legal process did not focus on judicial review). The course materials, *The Legal Process: Basic Problems in the Making and Application of Law*, did not even mention *Brown*. See Eskridge and Frickey, *supra* note 95, at 2050.

108. Albert M. Sacks, *Foreword: The Supreme Court, 1953 Term*, 68 Harv. L. Rev. 96, 96–99 (1954); Robert Braucher, *Foreword: The Supreme Court, 1954 Term*, 69 Harv. L. Rev. 120, 120 (1955).

109. Alexander M. Bickel and Harry H. Wellington, *Legislative Purpose and the Judicial Process: The Lincoln Mills Case*, 71 Harv. L. Rev. 1, 6 (1957); Ernest J. Brown, *Foreword: Process of Law*, 72 Harv. L. Rev. 77 (1958); Henry M. Hart, Jr., *Foreword: The Time Chart of the Justices*, 73 Harv. L. Rev. 84, 94–101 (1959).

110. Herbert Wechsler, *Toward Neutral Principles of Constitutional Law*, 73 Harv. L. Rev. 1, 15–16, 31–34 (1959).

111. Wechsler, *supra* note 110, at 32; see Kalman, *supra* note 8, at 27 (arguing that the *Brown* opinion seemed "self-consciously realist"); G. Edward White, *Earl Warren as Jurist*, 67 Va. L. Rev. 461, 462–73 (1981) (on Warren's lack of concern for legal process demands) (hereafter White, *Earl Warren*). Other prominent criticisms of *Brown* included the following: Raoul Berger, Government by Judiciary 243–45 (1977) (Warren ignored the true history of the adoption of the Fourteenth Amendment); Alexander Bickel, The Supreme Court and the Idea of Progress 37 and n.* (1978; 1st ed., 1970) (hereafter Bickel, Idea of Progress) (*Brown* was headed toward historical obsolescence); Learned Hand, The Bill of Rights 54–55 (1958) (criticizes the *Brown* Court for acting similar to the *Lochner* Court).

112. Louis H. Pollak, *Racial Discrimination and Judicial Integrity: A Reply to Professor Wechsler*, 108 U. Pa. L. Rev. 1 (1959); Charles L. Black, Jr., *The Lawfulness of the Segregation Decisions*, 69 Yale L. J. 421 (1960).

113. Moses Lasky, *Observing Appellate Opinions from Below the Bench*, 49 Cal. L. Rev. 831, 832–34 (1961); Addison Mueller and Murray L. Schwartz, *The Principle of Neutral Principles*, 7 U. C. L. A. L. Rev. 571, 577–78, 586 (1960).

114. Karl Llewellyn, The Common Law Tradition 3 (1960) (Llewellyn here actually refers to lawyers in general and not just legal scholars); Ronald Dworkin, Taking Rights Seriously (1978); John Rawls, A Theory of Justice (1971); Frank I. Michelman, *Foreword: On Protecting the Poor through the Fourteenth Amendment*, 83 Harv. L. Rev. 7, 9, 14–15 (1969); The Impact of Supreme Court Decisions (Theodore L. Becker ed., 1969) (containing gap studies). On the relation of Dworkin to legal process, see Duxbury, *supra* note 8, at 295; Vincent A. Wellman, *Dworkin and the Legal Process Tradition: The Legacy of Hart and Sacks*, 29 Ariz. L. Rev. 413 (1987). Michelman, writing in 1969, cited the articles by Rawls that preceded the 1971 publication of *A Theory of Justice*. Michelman, *supra*, at 15 n. 20; see Charles Reich, *The New Property*, 73 Yale L. J. 733 (1964) (arguing, similarly to Michelman, to protect right to governmental largesse); see also Kalman, *supra* note 8, at 62–68 (on the use of Rawls). On the development of the law and society movement, see Duxbury, *supra* note 8, at 440–45; Kalman, *supra* note 8, at 49. See generally Novick, *supra* note 4, at 457–58 (emphasizing the lack of "overarching interpretation" in the history profession in the 1960s).

115. Ronald Coase, *The Problem of Social Cost*, 3 J. L. & Econ. 1 (1960); see James R. Hackney, Jr., *Law and Neoclassical Economics: Science, Politics, and the Reconfiguration of American Tort Law Theory*, 15 Law & Hist. Rev. 275 (1997) (a historical account of the emergence of the law and economics movement).

116. Richard Posner, Economic Analysis of Law (1st ed., 1973); see A. Mitchell Polinsky, An Introduction to Law and Economics (1983) (a summary of the early law and economics movement).

117. Richard A. Posner, *Volume One of The Journal of Legal Studies—An Afterword*, 1 J. Legal Stud. 437, 437 (1972). For a discussion of public choice theory, see Daniel A. Farber and Philip P. Frickey, Law and Public Choice (1991).

118. See, e.g., Alan David Freeman, *Legitimizing Racial Discrimination through Antidiscrimination Law: A Critical Review of Supreme Court Doctrine*, 62 Minn. L. Rev. 1049 (1978); Peter Gabel, *Intention and Structure in Contractual Conditions: Outline of a Method for Critical Legal Theory*, 61 Minn. L. Rev. 601 (1977); Duncan Kennedy, *Form and Substance in Private Law Adjudication*, 89 Harv. L. Rev. 1685 (1976). For a leading collection of CLS essays, see The Politics of Law (David Kairys ed., 1982). For a summary of critical legal studies by one of its leading practitioners, see Mark Kelman, A Guide to Critical Legal Studies (1987). On the "haves" winning, see Marc Galanter, *Why the "Haves" Come Out Ahead*, 9 L. & Soc'y Rev. 95 (1974). On the need for total transformation, see Roberto Mangabeira Unger, Knowledge and Politics (1975) (rejecting a partial critique of liberalism); Duncan Kennedy, *How the Law School Fails: A Polemic*, 1 Yale Rev. L. & Soc. Action 71, 80 (1970) (written when Kennedy was still a law student).

119. Duncan Kennedy, *The Structure of Blackstone's Commentaries*, 28 Buff. L. Rev. 205, 211–12 (1979).

120. Robert Gordon, *New Developments in Legal Theory*, in The Politics of Law 281, 288 (David Kairys ed., 1982); Gerald Frug, *The City as a Legal Concept*, 93 Harv. L. Rev. 1057 (1980); Frances E. Olsen, *The Family and the Market: A Study of Ideology and Legal Reform*, 96 Harv. L. Rev. 1497 (1983).

121. Kennedy, *supra* note 119, at 213; compare Joan C. Williams, *Critical Legal Studies:*

The Death of Transcendence and the Rise of the New Langdells, 62 N. Y. U. L. Rev. 429 (1987) (arguing that the crits remained trapped in traditional—or modernist—metaphysics by being either structuralists or irrationalists).

122. Peter Gabel and Duncan Kennedy, *Roll over Beethoven,* 36 Stan. L. Rev. 1, 18 (1984) ("it must be utterly"); Paul Brest, *The Fundamental Rights Controversy: The Essential Contradictions of Normative Constitutional Scholarship,* 90 Yale L. J. 1063 (1981); Mark Tushnet, *Darkness on the Edge of Town: The Contributions of John Hart Ely to Constitutional Theory,* 89 Yale L. J. 1037 (1980); see Paul D. Carrington, *Of Law and the River,* 34 J. Legal Educ. 222 (1984); compare Kalman, *supra* note 8, at 125 (suggesting that the *Roll over Beethoven* dialogue marked an important shift in critical scholarship). For biographical background on the CLS movement from a leading crit, see Gordon, *supra* note 120, at 282–83. For an example of Tushnet's more recent scholarship, see Mark V. Tushnet, Making Civil Rights Law: Thurgood Marshall and the Supreme Court, 1936–1961 (1994).

123. Richard A. Wasserstrom, The Judicial Decision 25–28 (1961). For examples of attacks on the Warren Court, see Alexander M. Bickel, The Least Dangerous Branch 82–83 (2d ed., 1986; 1st ed., 1962) (hereafter Bickel, Least Dangerous); Gerald Gunther, *The Subtle Vices of the "Passive Virtues"—A Comment on Principle and Expediency in Judicial Review,* 64 Colum. L. Rev. 1, 4–5 (1964) (applauding Bickel's condemnation of supporters of the Warren Court).

124. Bickel, Least Dangerous, *supra* note 123, at 16; see 20, 24–25, 27, 225–26; Bickel, Idea of Progress, *supra* note 111, at 37 and n.*. For a historical account of the idea of the countermajoritarian difficulty, see Barry Friedman, *The History of the Countermajoritarian Difficulty, pt. 1, The Road to Judicial Supremacy,* 73 N. Y. U. L. Rev. 333 (1998).

125. Bickel, Least Dangerous, *supra* note 123, at 58.

126. Id. at 111–98; Alexander M. Bickel, *Foreword: The Passive Virtues,* 75 Harv. L. Rev. 40 (1961).

127. Gunther, *supra* note 123, at 13, 15, 17; see Bickel, Idea of Progress, *supra* note 111, at 99, 165; Alexander Bickel, The Morality of Consent 24–25 (1975); compare J. Skelly Wright, *Professor Bickel, The Scholarly Tradition, and the Supreme Court,* 84 Harv. L. Rev. 769 (1971) (criticizing Bickel's transition); see also Minda, *supra* note 8, at 44 (noting Bickel's repudiation of the idea of neutral principles).

The exact parameters of the legal process concept of "neutral principles" were never precisely defined. See Duxbury, *supra* note 8, at 276–77 and nn. 481, 484 (noting that Wechsler was criticized for not adequately defining the concept of neutral principles). In particular, neutral principles, at times, seemed to connote an abstract type of neutrality. From this perspective, a neutral principle was a value that somehow did not substantively favor various competing political positions—so courts, by relying on such a neutral principle, could therefore pronounce judgments without intruding into the sphere of legislative decision making. Most often, the legal process scholars appeared to discuss neutral principles in this abstract sense. At other points, though, the concept of neutral principles appeared to connote no more than broad acceptance throughout American society, or in Robert Gordon's words, "'neutral' by virtue of resting upon broad political consensus." Robert W. Gordon, *American Law through English Eyes: A Century of Nightmares and Noble Dreams,* 84 Geo. L. J. 2215, 2216 (1996). This notion of neutral principles was less abstract and more pragmatic, but in the end, both conceptions of neutral principles became problematic. Under the first and more abstract conception, the idea of neutral principles collapsed as a matter of logic. No principle can exist that has meaning and can be applied in concrete cases and that nonetheless does not favor any particular political position. Under the second and more pragmatic conception, the embittered splintering of American society in the 1960s, to be discussed in chapter 5, would belie the possibility of achieving the necessary broad political consensus on any serious issues.

128. John H. Ely, Democracy and Distrust 1–104 (1980). The roots of representation-reinforcement theory can be traced back to John Marshall. *McCulloch v. Maryland*, 17 US (4 Wheat.) 316 (1819); see also Jesse Choper, Judicial Review and the National Political Process 2, 127–28 (1980); Robert G. McCloskey, *Foreword: The Reapportionment Case*, 76 Harv. L. Rev. 54, 72–74 (1962).

129. Ely, *supra* note 128, at 101, 117; see 105–79.

130. Paul Brest, *The Substance of Process*, 42 Ohio St. L. J. 131, 142 (1981); see Richard D. Parker, *The Past of Constitutional Theory—And Its Future*, 42 Ohio St. L. J. 223, 234–35 (1981).

5. Postmodern American Legal Thought

1. Useful sources on American history, including jurisprudential and legal history, that I cite in this chapter include the following: David J. Garrow, Liberty and Sexuality: The Right to Privacy and the Making of *Roe v. Wade* (1994); Godfrey Hodgson, America in Our Time (1976); Richard Hofstadter, Anti-Intellectualism in American Life (1962); Laura Kalman, The Strange Career of Legal Liberalism (1996); Gary Minda, Postmodern Legal Movements (1995); Peter Novick, That Noble Dream: The "Objectivity Question" and the American Historical Profession (1988); James T. Patterson, Grand Expectations: The United States, 1945–1974 (1996); Bernard Schwartz, A History of the Supreme Court (1993); Stephan Thernstrom, A History of the American People (2d ed., 1989); Howard Zinn, A People's History of the United States (1980); Thomas Bender, *Politics, Intellect, and the American University, 1945–1995*, 126 Daedalus 1 (1997).

2. Hodgson, *supra* note 1, at 16 ("a fool's paradise"); Patterson, *supra* note 1, at 451–52 ("grand expectations," "[p]eople talked confidently"); Hodgson, *supra* note 1, at 492 ("tore consensus").

3. For historical information on Vietnam, see Gabriel Kolko, Anatomy of a War: Vietnam, The United States, and the Modern Historical Experience (1994); Patterson, *supra* note 1, at 593–636; Thernstrom, *supra* note 1, at 844–56; Zinn, *supra* note 1, at 460–92.

4. David Halberstam, The Best and the Brightest (1972); Zinn, *supra* note 1, at 538; quoting Culver.

5. Martin Luther King, Jr., *Pilgrimage to Nonviolence* (1960), in A Testament of Hope: The Essential Writings of Martin Luther King, Jr., 35, 36 (James M. Washington ed., 1986); Martin Luther King, Jr., *An Address before the National Press Club* (1962), in A Testament of Hope: The Essential Writings of Martin Luther King, Jr., 99, 103 (James M. Washington ed., 1986). For a brief summary of King's views, see Stephen M. Feldman, *Whose Common Good? Racism in the Political Community*, 80 Geo. L. J. 1835, 1866–76 (1992).

6. Hodgson, *supra* note 1, at 189; Martin Luther King, Jr., *I Have A Dream* (1963), in A Testament of Hope: The Essential Writings of Martin Luther King, Jr., 217–20 (James M. Washington ed., 1986); Malcolm X, *The Ballot or the Bullet*, in Malcolm X Speaks 23, 26 (George Breitman ed., 1965) (Cleveland, April 3, 1964); Hodgson, *supra* note 1, at 200 (quoting Malcolm X) ("the farce"); Hodgson, *supra* note 1, at 179 ("from a protest"). For

historical studies of the civil rights movement, see David J. Garrow, Bearing the Cross: Martin Luther King, Jr., and the Southern Christian Leadership Conference (1986); Robert Weisbrot, Freedom Bound: A History of America's Civil Rights Movement (1990); see also Zinn, *supra* note 1, at 440–59. For a discussion of the Kennedy Administration's role in the March, see Garrow, *supra*, at 265–86; Hodgson, *supra* note 1, at 157, 196–97; Patterson, *supra* note 1, at 482–83; Zinn, *supra* note 1, at 448–49. On the relation between King and Malcolm X, see James H. Cone, Martin and Malcolm and America (1991). On the emergence of the Black Power movement, see Garrow, *supra*, at 481–525; Weisbrot, *supra*, at 196–221.

7. Hodgson, *supra* note 1, at 15; see Robert Wuthnow, The Restructuring of American Religion 269–70 (1988); Bender, *supra* note 1, at 22 (loss of faith in elite institutions, including universities).

8. Patterson, *supra* note 1, at 453 ("dominated American"); see Hodgson, *supra* note 1, at 365, 492; Minda, *supra* note 1, at 66; Novick, *supra* note 1, at 415; Patterson, *supra* note 1, at 452–53; see also Mark Tushnet and Katya Lezin, *What Really Happened in Brown v. Board of Education*, 91 Colum. L. Rev. 1867, 1867 (1991) (on rights-consciousness).

9. *Engel v. Vitale*, 370 US 421, 422, 430 (1962) (quoting the prayer); Naomi W. Cohen, Jews in Christian America: The Pursuit of Religious Equality 168 (1992) (quoting the letters).

10. *Engel*, 370 US at 425–26, 430–31; *Engel v. Vitale*, The New Republic, July 9, 1962, in Religious Liberty in the Supreme Court 142 (Terry Eastland ed., 1993) ("savage"); Cohen, *supra* note 9, at 171 ("had betrayed"); *In the Name of Freedom*, Wall Street Journal, June 27, 1962, in Eastland, *supra*, at 138 ("[p]oor kids"); see Cohen, *supra* note 9, at 171–77, 211; Stephen M. Feldman, Please Don't Wish Me a Merry Christmas: A Critical History of the Separation of Church and State 190–91, 222, 234 (1997) (discussing various proposals to add a Christian amendment to the Constitution) (hereafter Feldman, Please Don't). Howard M. Sachar writes: "[i]n 1962 alone, a group of Southern and Republican congressmen sponsored forty-nine separate constitutional amendments to permit school prayer." Howard M. Sachar, A History of the Jews in America 796 (1992).

11. *Griswold v. Connecticut*, 381 US 479 (1965); see Garrow, *supra* note 1, at 1–269.

12. *Poe v. Ullman*, 367 US 497, 508 (1961); see Garrow, *supra* note 1, at 196–269. In 1962, Justices White and Goldberg had replaced Frankfurter and Whittaker; 224. Mark Tushnet suggests that the true (liberal) Warren Court existed only after this transition in personnel. Mark Tushnet, *The Warren Court as History: An Interpretation*, in The Warren Court in Historical and Political Perspective 1, 4–6 (Mark Tushnet ed., 1993) (hereafter Tushnet, *Warren Court*).

13. *Griswold*, 381 US at 482; see Garrow, *supra* note 1, at 246 (Brennan's letter).

14. *Griswold*, 381 US at 484 (citations omitted); see 482–83.

15. *Id.* at 485–86.

16. Hence, Justices Clark, Goldberg, Brennan, and Chief Justice Warren joined Douglas to create the majority opinion. See *Griswold*, 381 US at 479–531; Garrow, *supra* note 1, at 248–52 (discussing the accumulation of five votes to create a majority opinion); see also Garrow, *supra* note 1, at 240–41 (discussing concerns about abortion).

17. *Griswold*, 381 US at 520–21 (Black, J., dissenting); see 511–18 (Black, J., dissenting); 527–31 (Stewart, J., dissenting). Only Justice White's concurring opinion did not expressly react to the institutional critique of *Lochner*. Goldberg reasoned that the Fourteenth Amendment protects fundamental personal rights, but he wrote circumspectly about the

relevance of the Ninth Amendment to the Court's holding; 493 (Goldberg, J., concurring; quoting *Snyder v. Massachusetts,* 291 US 97, 105 (1934). Justice Harlan most clearly accepted a substantive due process approach, closely resembling *Lochner,* but he stressed that the Court was nonetheless constrained in constitutional adjudication. *Griswold,* 381 US at 501 (Harlan, J., concurring).

18. Paul G. Kauper, *Penumbras, Peripheries, Emanations, Things Fundamental and Things Forgotten: The Griswold Case,* 64 Mich. L. Rev. 235 (1965); Hyman Gross, *The Concept of Privacy,* 42 N. Y. U. L. Rev. 34, 40–46 (1967); Raoul Berger, Government by Judiciary 265 (1977); Thomas I. Emerson, *Nine Justices in Search of a Doctrine,* 64 Mich. L. Rev. 219, 234 (1965). In fact, Paul Kauper supported the conclusion in *Griswold,* and suggested that the Court should have more openly admitted that it was a substantive due process/fundamental rights case. Kauper, *supra,* at 253–54; see Robert G. Dixon, Jr., *The* Griswold *Penumbra: Constitutional Charter for an Expanded Law of Privacy?* 64 Mich. L. Rev. 197 (1965) (supports the result but criticizes the reasoning in *Griswold*).

19. Robert H. Bork, *Neutral Principles and Some First Amendment Problems,* 47 Ind. L. J. 1, 1, 4, 7–9, 17, 22–23 (1971); see Garrow, *supra* note 1, at 263–65.

20. *Roe v. Wade,* 410 US 113 (1973); Garrow, *supra* note 1, at 521–22, 537–38, 547–59; see also Kalman, *supra* note 1, at 7 (*Roe* was a "defining case" for a generation of scholars); Schwartz, *supra* note 1, at 337–61 (discussing *Roe*). *Roe* was decided with a companion case that challenged the constitutionality of the Georgia state anti-abortion laws. *Doe v. Bolton,* 410 US 179 (1973).

21. Garrow, *supra* note 1, at 580–86.

22. *Roe,* 410 US at 116–17; quoting *Lochner v. New York,* 198 US 45, 76 (1905) (Holmes, J., dissenting).

23. *Roe,* 410 US at 129–47.

24. *Id.* at 152–53.

25. *Id.* at 154–55, 162–64.

26. *Id.* at 167–68 (Stewart, J., concurring); 212 n. 4 (Douglas, J., concurring); 174 (Rehnquist, J., dissenting); 221–22 (White, J., dissenting).

27. John Hart Ely, *The Wages of Crying Wolf: A Comment on Roe v. Wade,* 82 Yale L. J. 920, 927, 933–35, 939–40 (1973). David Garrow calls Ely's article "[f]ar and away the most important critique" of *Roe.* Garrow, *supra* note 1, at 609.

28. Robert Bork, The Tempting of America 112 (1990); Archibald Cox, The Role of the Supreme Court in American Government 114 (1976). For additional criticisms of *Roe,* see Richard A. Epstein, *Substantive Due Process by Any Other Name: The Abortion Cases,* 1973 Sup. Ct. Rev. 159; Gerald Gunther, *Some Reflections on the Judicial Role: Distinctions, Roots, and Prospects,* 1979 Wash. U. L. Rev. 817. For discussions of the reactions to *Roe,* see Garrow, *supra* note 1, at 605–17; Kalman, *supra* note 1, at 58–59.

29. Sylvia Law, *Rethinking Sex and the Constitution,* 132 U. Penn. L. Rev. 955 (1984). Some others who criticized the *Roe* opinion but attempted to defend the result include the following: Ruth Bader Ginsburg, *Some Thoughts on Autonomy and Equality in Relation to Roe v. Wade,* 63 N. C. L. Rev. 375 (1985); Philip B. Heymann and Douglas E. Barzelay, *The Forest and the Trees: Roe v. Wade and Its Critics,* 53 B. U. L. Rev. 765 (1973); Laurence H. Tribe, *Structural Due Process,* 10 Harv. C. R.–C. L. L. Rev. 269 (1975). For other interesting defenses of substantive constitutional rights, see Michael J. Perry, The Constitution, the Courts, and Human Rights (1982) (emphasizes moral philosophy and sees judicial review as an opportunity for the moral development of the nation); Thomas C. Grey, *Eros,*

Civilization and the Burger Court, 43 Law & Contemp. Probs. 83, 84–85 (1980) (the best defense of *Griswold* was based on tradition); Thomas C. Grey, *Origins of the Unwritten Constitution: Revolutionary Thought*, 30 Stan. L. Rev. 843 (1978) (relying on natural law).

30. Archibald Cox, *Foreword: Constitutional Adjudication and the Promotion of Human Rights*, 80 Harv. L. Rev. 91, 94, 98 (1966); Arthur Allen Leff, *Unspeakable Ethics, Unnatural Law*, 1979 Duke L. J. 1129, 1232 (emphasis in original); Roberto M. Unger, *The Critical Legal Studies Movement*, 96 Harv. L. Rev. 561, 675 (1983); see Gary Minda, *Jurisprudence at Century's End*, 43 J. Legal Educ. 27, 58 (1993) (growing sentiment that we are at the end of an era in jurisprudence); John Henry Schlegel, *American Legal Realism and Empirical Social Science: From the Yale Experience*, 28 Buff. L. Rev. 459, 462 (1979) ("post-Realist legal theory has about run its course headlong into a dead end").

31. John Hart Ely, Democracy and Distrust 1 (1980); see Thomas C. Grey, *Do We Have an Unwritten Constitution?* 27 Stan. L. Rev. 703, 705–6 (1975) (contrasting interpretivism and noninterpretivism); Paul Brest, *The Misconceived Quest for the Original Understanding*, 60 B. U. L. Rev. 204 (1980) (using the terms originalism and nonoriginalism). For an example of an interpretivist, see Berger, *supra* note 18, at 45, 363–72. For an example of a natural law argument, see Thomas C. Grey, *Origins of the Unwritten Constitution: Revolutionary Thought*, 30 Stan. L. Rev. 843 (1978). For a summary of various noninterpretivist positions, see Ely, *supra*, at 43–72.

32. Ely, *supra* note 31, at 50; see 1–73. For criticisms of Ely's theory, see Paul Brest, *The Substance of Process*, 42 Ohio St. L. J. 131 (1981); Richard D. Parker, *The Past of Constitutional Theory—and Its Future*, 42 Ohio St. L. J. 223 (1981).

33. Paul Brest, *The Fundamental Rights Controversy: The Essential Contradictions of Normative Constitutional Scholarship*, 90 Yale L. J. 1063 (1981); Paul Brest, *The Misconceived Quest for the Original Understanding*, 60 B. U. L. Rev. 204 (1980); Thomas C. Grey, *The Constitution as Scripture*, 37 Stan. L. Rev. 1, 1 (1984); see also Ronald Dworkin, *Law's Empire* 359–60 (1986); Larry Simon, *The Authority of the Constitution and its Meaning: A Preface to a Theory of Constitutional Interpretation*, 58 S. Cal. L. Rev. 603, 619–22 (1985); Richard H. Weisberg, *Text into Theory: A Literary Approach to the Constitution*, 20 Ga. L. Rev. 939, 940–41 (1986).

34. James Boyd White, The Legal Imagination: Studies in the Nature of Legal Thought and Expression (1973) (a textbook for law students containing excerpts from English literature as well as law); James Boyd White, When Words Lose Their Meaning (1984); see Kalman, *supra* note 1, at 60–61; Minda, *supra* note 1, at 68, 149–50.

35. Novick, *supra* note 1, at 574; see Kalman, *supra* note 1, at 60–61; Thomas C. Grey, *Modern American Legal Thought*, 106 Yale L. J. 493, 505 (1996).

36. Bender, *supra* note 1, at 26 ("This intergenerational"); Kalman, *supra* note 1, at 99; quoting Clifford Geertz, *Blurred Genres: The Refiguration of Social Thought*, in Local Knowledge: Further Essays in Interpretive Anthropology 20 (1983); see Kalman, *supra* note 1, at 101–12 (emphasizing Geertz's influence, especially through his speech at a 1981 Yale conference on legal scholarship); Novick, *supra* note 1, at 577–92 (on the widespread breakdown of disciplinary boundaries in the 1980s).

37. Thomas S. Kuhn, The Structure of Scientific Revolutions 113 (2d ed., 1970); see Novick, *supra* note 1, at 537 (on scientific objectivity providing a foundation or ideal for work in other fields).

38. Kuhn, *supra* note 37, at 111; see 162–73.

39. Novick, *supra* note 1, at 524; Robert M. Cover, *Foreword: Nomos and Narrative*, 97

Harv. L. Rev. 4, 9, 6 and n. 10 (1983); Suzanna Sherry, *Civic Virtue and the Feminine Voice in Constitutional Adjudication*, 72 Va. L. Rev. 543, 543 (1986); see Kalman, *supra* note 1, at 99; Novick, *supra* note 1, at 532–35 (arguing that Kuhn intended to support and not undermine the work of natural scientists); Paul Rabinow and William M. Sullivan, *The Interpretive Turn: Emergence of An Approach*, in Interpretive Social Science—A Reader 1 (Paul Rabinow and William M. Sullivan eds., 1979) (on the interpretive turn in general).

40. See, e.g., Owen M. Fiss, *Objectivity and Interpretation*, 34 Stan. L. Rev. 739 (1982) (relying on Stanley Fish to develop views on law and interpretation); Sanford Levinson, *Law as Literature*, 60 Tex. L. Rev. 373 (1982) (same). But see Stanley Fish, *Fish v. Fiss*, 36 Stan. L. Rev. 1325 (1984) (criticizing how Fiss had interpreted Fish's works); Stanley Fish, *Interpretation and the Pluralist Vision*, 60 Tex. L. Rev. 495 (1982) (criticizing how Levinson had interpreted Fish's works). Legal scholars (other than myself) who have relied extensively on Gadamer's philosophical hermeneutics include J. M. Balkin, *Understanding Legal Understanding: The Legal Subject and the Problem of Legal Coherence*, 103 Yale L. J. 105 (1993); William N. Eskridge, Jr., *Gadamer/Statutory Interpretation*, 90 Colum. L. Rev. 609 (1990); Francis J. Mootz, *The Ontological Basis of Legal Hermeneutics: A Proposed Model of Inquiry Based on the Work of Gadamer, Habermas, and Ricoeur*, 68 B. U. L. Rev. 523 (1988); see Stephen M. Feldman, *The New Metaphysics: The Interpretive Turn in Jurisprudence*, 76 Iowa L. Rev. 661 (1991); see also David Couzens Hoy, *Interpreting the Law: Hermeneutical and Poststructuralist Perspectives*, 58 S. Cal. L. Rev. 135 (1985) (a nonlegal scholar discussing Gadamer in a jurisprudential context). For a controversial use of Rorty, see Joseph William Singer, *The Player and the Cards: Nihilism and Legal Theory*, 94 Yale L. J. 1 (1984), which was criticized in John Stick, *Can Nihilism Be Pragmatic?* 100 Harv. L. Rev. 332 (1986).

Some other works by Fish that I cite and discuss include the following: Stanley Fish, *Introduction: Going Down the Anti-Formalist Road*, in Doing What Comes Naturally 1 (1989) (hereafter Fish, *Anti-Formalist Road*); preface, to Doing What Comes Naturally ix (1989) (hereafter Fish, preface); *Still Wrong after All These Years*, in Doing What Comes Naturally 356 (1989) (hereafter Fish, *Still Wrong*); *Dennis Martinez and the Uses of Theory*, 96 Yale L. J. 1773 (1987) (hereafter Fish, *Dennis Martinez*); *Change*, 86 South Atlantic Quarterly 423 (1987) (hereafter Fish, *Change*); *Working on the Chain Gang: Interpretation in the Law and in Literary Criticism*, in The Politics of Interpretation 271 (W. Mitchell ed., 1983) (hereafter Fish, *Chain Gang*); *Introduction, or How I Stopped Worrying and Learned to Love Interpretation*, in Is There a Text in This Class? 1 (1980) (hereafter Fish, *Stopped Worrying*); *Is There a Text in This Class?*, in Is There a Text in This Class? 303 (1980) (hereafter Fish, *Is There*); *Normal Circumstances, Literal Language, Direct Speech Acts, the Ordinary, the Everyday, the Obvious, What Goes without Saying, and Other Special Cases*, in Interpretive Social Science—A Reader 243 (Paul Rabinow and William M. Sullivan eds., 1979) (hereafter Fish, *Normal Circumstances*).

41. On reader-response theory and Fish's transitions, see Jonathan Culler, On Deconstruction 64–78 (1982).

42. Fish, *Anti-Formalist Road*, *supra* note 40, at 4.

43. Fish, *Change*, *supra* note 40, at 423–24 ("assumed distinctions"); Fish, *Dennis Martinez*, *supra* note 40, at 1795 ("there has never").

44. Fish, *Stopped Worrying*, *supra* note 40, at 13–14 ("at once enable"); Fish, *Dennis Martinez*, *supra* note 40, at 1795 ("already-in-place"); Fish, *Dennis Martinez*, *supra* note 40, at 1790 ("know how," "a sense"); Fish, *Still Wrong*, *supra* note 40, at 360 ("The very ability"); see Fish, *Chain Gang*, *supra* note 40, at 273; Fish, *Dennis Martinez*, *supra* note 40, at 1788.

45. Fish, *Normal Circumstances, supra* note 40, at 249; see Fish, *Is There, supra* note 40, at 307–10.

46. Fish, *Dennis Martinez, supra* note 40, at 1779; see 1797 (any theory "is entirely irrelevant to the practice it purports to critique and reform"); Fish, preface, *supra* note 40, at ix (same).

47. Dennis Patterson, introduction into Postmodernism and Law xi, xii, xiv (Dennis Patterson ed., 1994); see Dennis Patterson, Law and Truth (1996); Dennis Patterson, *Postmodernism/Feminism/Law,* 77 Cornell L. Rev. 254 (1992). Of course, not everybody agrees with Patterson's interpretation of Quine or Wittgenstein. See, e.g., Brian Leiter, *Why Quine Is Not a Postmodernist,* 50 S. M. U. L. Rev. 1739 (1997) (criticizing Patterson's understanding of Quine). I have criticized Patterson's conception of interpretivism from a Gadamerian perspective. Stephen M. Feldman, *The Politics of Postmodern Jurisprudence,* 95 Mich. L. Rev. 166, 169–85 (1996). For examples of other jurisprudents who invoke analytical philosophy as support for their postmodern inclinations, see Anthony D'Amato, *Pragmatic Indeterminacy,* 85 Nw. U. L. Rev. 148 (1990); Anthony D'Amato, *Aspects of Deconstruction: The "Easy Case" of the Under-aged President,* 84 Nw. U. L. Rev. 250 (1989); Margaret J. Radin, *Reconsidering the Rule of Law,* 69 B. U. L. Rev. 781 (1989).

48. Richard Delgado and Jean Stefancic, *Why Do We Tell the Same Stories? Law Reform, Critical Librarianship, and the Triple Helix Dilemma,* 42 Stan. L. Rev. 207, 208 (1989) ("devices function") (hereafter Delgado and Stefancic, *Stories*); Jean Stefancic and Richard Delgado, *Outsider Jurisprudence and the Electronic Revolution: Will Technology Help or Hinder the Cause of Law Reform?* 52 Ohio St. L. J. 847, 854 (1991) ("[f]ree text") (hereafter Stefancic and Delgado, *Outsider*). Delgado and Stefancic suggest that computer-assisted legal research promises "only a partial solution" to the problems generated by traditional research methods. Delgado and Stefancic, *Stories, supra,* at 209, see Stefancic and Delgado, *Outsider, supra,* at 855–57 (detailing some of the drawbacks and limitations of computer-assisted research).

49. George P. Landow, Hypertext 2.0, at 88–89 (rev. ed., 1997); see Delgado and Stefancic, *Stories, supra* note 48, at 215 (on the number of cases published by West).

50. Steven Johnson, Interface Culture 238–39 (1997).

51. Posner, *supra* note 1, at 766, 769. Compare Gerald N. Rosenberg, The Hollow Hope: Can Courts Bring about Social Change? 110–56 (1991) (*Brown* impeded the civil rights movement by inflaming Southern racists, who were able to delay political changes) and Michael J. Klarman, Brown, *Racial Change, and the Civil Rights Movement,* 80 Va. L. Rev. 7 (1994) (*Brown* indirectly aided the civil rights movement by generating violent Southern resistance, which in turn aroused apathetic Northern whites to support political change) with Richard Kluger, Simple Justice 758–61 (1975) (although *Brown* alone did not change America, it was a central element in social change).

52. Kalman, *supra* note 1, at 61 ("[o]ver 135,000"); Donna Fossum, *Women Law Professors,* 1980 Am. B. Found. Res. J. 903, 914 ("the number"); see Fossum, *supra,* at 905–6 (giving statistics on number of women law faculty); Grey, Modern, *supra* note 35, at 505; see also Bender, *supra* note 1, at 4–5, 28–29 (discussing changing demographics since World War II in university professoriates in general).

53. Richard Delgado, *Shadowboxing: An Essay on Power,* 77 Cornell L. Rev. 813, 818 (1992) (using the term *outsider jurisprudence*); see, e.g., Derrick Bell, And We Are Not Saved 251–54 (1987) (critical race scholar suggesting the possibility that the Constitution and American society can be transformed to eliminate economic oppression); Anthony E.

Cook, *Beyond Critical Legal Studies: The Reconstructive Theology of Dr. Martin Luther King, Jr.*, 103 Harv. L. Rev. 985, 1015–21 (1990) (religion both legitimated and delegitimated authority for African-American slaves). But compare Bell, *supra*, at 22 (guarantees of racial equality get transformed into devices to perpetuate the racial status quo).

54. Patricia J. Williams, *Alchemical Notes: Reconstructed Ideals from Deconstructed Rights*, 22 Harv. C. R.–C. L. L. Rev. 401, 410–11 (1987); see Alvin Kernan, *Change in the Humanities and Higher Education*, in What's Happened to the Humanities? 3, 5–6 (Alvin Kernan ed., 1997) (emphasizing a "paradigm shift in higher education" due to changes in university demographics).

55. William N. Eskridge, Jr., *Gaylegal Narratives*, 46 Stan. L. Rev. 607, 607–8 (1994); see Bell, *supra* note 53 (using storytelling); Richard Delgado, *Storytelling for Oppositionists and Others: A Plea For Narrative*, 87 Mich. L. Rev. 2411 (1989); see also Patricia J. Williams, The Alchemy of Race and Rights (1991); Kathy Abrams, *Hearing the Call of Stories*, 79 Cal. L. Rev. 971 (1991); Marc A. Fajer, *Can Two Real Men Eat Quiche Together? Storytelling, Gender-Role Sterotypes, and Legal Protection for Lesbians and Gay Men*, 46 U. Miami L. Rev. 511 (1992). Delgado's series of *Rodrigo Chronicles*, which largely follow the fictitious conversations between a law professor and student, are prototypical examples of storytelling. See, e.g., Richard Delgado, *Rodrigo's Sixth Chronicle: Intersections, Essences, and the Dilemma of Social Reform*, 68 N. Y. U. L. Rev. 639 (1993). For examples of lesbian legal theory, see Ruthann Robson, Lesbian (Out)Law: Survival under the Rule of Law (1992); Patricia A. Cain, *Litigating for Lesbian and Gay Rights: A Legal History*, 79 Va. L. Rev. 1551 (1993).

56. Martha Minow, *Incomplete Correspondence: An Unsent Letter to Mary Joe Frug*, 105 Harv. L. Rev. 1096, 1104 (1992). On liberal feminism, see Sylvia Law, *Rethinking Sex and the Constitution*, 132 U. Penn. L. Rev. 955 (1984); Wendy W. Williams, *Equality's Riddle: Pregnancy and the Equal Treatment/Special Treatment Debate*, N. Y. U. Rev. of L. & Social Change 325 (1984–1985). On cultural feminism, see Lynne N. Henderson, *Legality and Empathy*, 85 Mich. L. Rev. 1574 (1987); Martha Minow, *Foreword: Justice Engendered*, 101 Harv. L. Rev. 10 (1987); Suzanna Sherry, *Civic Virtue and the Feminine Voice in Constitutional Adjudication*, 72 Va. L. Rev. 543 (1986); Robin West, *The Difference in Women's Hedonic Lives: A Phenomenological Critique of Feminist Legal Theory*, 3 Wis. Women's L. J. 81 (1987); Robin West, *Jurisprudence and Gender*, 55 U. Chi. L. Rev. 1 (1988); see Carol Gilligan, In a Different Voice (1982); Nell Noddings, Caring (1984). On radical feminism, see Catharine A. MacKinnon, Feminism Unmodified (1987). For summaries of feminism, see Minda, *supra* note 1, at 128–48 (providing an excellent summary of four types of feminism and recognizing early feminists as modernists); Patricia A. Cain, *Feminism and the Limits of Equality*, 24 Ga. L. Rev. 803 (1990) (same); Linda Lacey, *Introducing Feminist Jurisprudence: An Analysis of Oklahoma's Seduction Statute*, 25 Tulsa L. J. 775, 784–93 (1990) (providing an excellent summary of the first three types of feminism).

57. Angela P. Harris, *Race and Essentialism in Feminist Legal Theory*, 42 Stan. L. Rev. 581, 585 (1990); see Audre Lorde, Sister Outsider 110–13 (Quality Paperback Book Club 1993; first published 1984) (emphasizing how white feminists ignore the differences of African-American, lesbian, and poor women); Nancy Fraser and Linda Nicholson, *Social Criticism without Philosophy: An Encounter between Feminism and Postmodernism*, 5 Theory, Culture, & Soc'y 373, 381–90 (1988) (on essentialism and reductionism in early feminism in general); Harris, *supra*, at 585–602 (criticizing white feminists for their essentialist conceptions of women).

58. Christine Di Stefano, *Dilemmas of Difference: Feminism, Modernity, and Postmodernism*, in Feminism/Postmodernism 63, 75 (Linda J. Nicholson ed., 1990) ("white, privileged"); Charles R. Lawrence, *The Id, the Ego, and Equal Protection: Reckoning with Unconscious Racism*, 39 Stan. L. Rev. 317 (1987); see Pierre Schlag, *Normative and Nowhere to Go*, 43 Stan. L. Rev. 167 (1990) (postmodern critique of normative legal scholarship); Robin West, *Feminism, Critical Social Theory and Law*, 1989 U. Chi. Legal F. 59 (a leading feminist criticizing postmodern, including Foucauldian, approaches). Christine Di Stefano, a feminist political theorist, explicitly asked the following: "[w]hy is it, just at the moment in Western history when previously silenced populations have begun to speak for themselves and on behalf of their subjectivities, that the concept of the subject and the possibility of discovering/creating a liberating 'truth' become supsect?" Di Stefano, *supra*, at 75; see Rita Felski, The Gender of Modernity 208 (1995) (on the tension between members of outgroups and other intellectuals inclined toward postmodernism). Early critical race theorists accentuated their normativity. See Mari Matsuda, *Looking to the Bottom: Critical Legal Studies and Reparations*, 22 Harv. C. R.–C. L. L. Rev. 323 (1987); Kimberle Crenshaw, *Race, Reform, and Retrenchment: Transformation and Legitimation in Antidiscrimination Law*, 101 Harv. L. Rev. 1331 (1988).

59. Joan C. Williams, *Dissolving the Sameness/Difference Debate: A Post-Modern Path Beyond Essentialism in Feminist and Critical Race Theory*, 1991 Duke L. J. 296, 299–308; Mary Joe Frug, *A Postmodern Feminist Legal Manifesto (An Unfinished Draft)*, 105 Harv. L. Rev. 1045, 1046 (1992); Drucilla Cornell, Beyond Accommodation 4, 150 (1991).

60. Cormac McCarthy, All the Pretty Horses 239 (1992).

61. Some postmodern jurisprudential works (or works about postmodernism) that I cite in this section include the following: Drucilla Cornell, Beyond Accommodation (1991); Drucilla Cornell, The Philosophy of the Limit (1992) (hereafter Cornell, Limit); Stanley Fish, Doing What Comes Naturally (1989); Douglas E. Litowitz, Postmodern Philosophy and Law (1997); Gregory S. Alexander, *Takings and the Post-Modern Dialectic of Property*, 9 Const. Comment. 259 (1992); Marie Ashe, *Mind's Opportunity: Birthing a Poststructuralist Feminist Jurisprudence* (1987), in Legal Studies as Cultural Studies 85 (Jerry Leonard ed., 1995); Larry Catá Backer, *The Many Faces of Hegemony: Patriarchy and Welfare as a Woman's Issue*, 92 Nw. U. L. Rev. 327 (1997); J. M. Balkin, *Tradition, Betrayal, and the Politics of Deconstruction*, 11 Cardozo L. Rev. 1613 (1990) (hereafter Balkin, *Tradition*); J. M. Balkin, *Transcendental Deconstruction, Transcendent Justice*, 92 Mich. L. Rev. 1131 (1994) (hereafter Balkin, *Transcendental*); J. M. Balkin, *What Is a Postmodern Constitutionalism?* 90 Mich. L. Rev. 1966 (1992) (hereafter Balkin, *Postmodern Constitutionalism*); J. M. Balkin, *Understanding Legal Understanding: The Legal Subject and the Problem of Legal Coherence*, 103 Yale L. J. 105 (1993) (hereafter Balkin, *Understanding*); J. M. Balkin, *Deconstructive Practice and Legal Theory*, 96 Yale L. J. 743 (1987) (hereafter Balkin, *Deconstructive*); James Boyle, *Is Subjectivity Possible? The Post-Modern Subject in Legal Theory*, 62 U. Colo. L. Rev. 489 (1991); Anthony D'Amato, *Aspects of Deconstruction: The "Easy Case" of the Under-aged President*, 84 Nw. U. L. Rev. 250 (1989); Richard Delgado, *Storytelling for Oppositionists and Others: A Plea for Narrative*, 87 Mich. L. Rev. 2411 (1989); Richard Delgado and Jean Stefancic, *Images of the Outsider in American Law and Culture: Can Free Expression Remedy Systemic Social Ills?* 77 Cornell L. Rev. 1258 (1992) (hereafter Delgado and Stefancic, *Images*); Jacques Derrida, *Force of Law: The "Mystical Foundation of Authority,"* 11 Cardozo L. Rev. 919 (1990); William N. Eskridge, Jr., *Gadamer/Statutory Interpretation*, 90 Colum. L. Rev. 609 (1990); Patricia Ewick and Susan S. Silbey, *Conformity, Contestation,*

and Resistance: An Account of Legal Consciousness, 26 New Eng. L. Rev. 731 (1992); Stephen M. Feldman, *Playing with the Pieces: Postmodernism in the Lawyer's Toolbox,* 85 Va. L. Rev. 151 (1999) (hereafter Feldman, *Playing*); Stephen M. Feldman, *The Politics of Postmodern Jurisprudence,* 95 Mich. L. Rev. 166 (1996) (hereafter Feldman, *The Politics*); Stephen M. Feldman, *Diagnosing Power: Postmodernism in Legal Scholarship and Judicial Practice (With an Emphasis on the Teague Rule against New Rules in Habeas Corpus Cases),* 88 Nw. U. L. Rev. 1046 (1994) (hereafter Feldman, *Diagnosing Power*); William L. F. Felstiner and Austin Sarat, *Enactments of Power: Negotiating Reality and Responsibility in Lawyer-Client Interactions,* 77 Cornell L. Rev. 1447 (1992); Angela P. Harris, *Race and Essentialism in Feminist Legal Theory,* 42 Stan. L. Rev. 581 (1990); Tracy E. Higgins, *"By Reason of Their Sex": Feminist Theory, Postmodernism, and Justice,* 80 Cornell L. Rev. 1536 (1995); Sanford Levinson and J. M. Balkin, *Law, Music, and Other Performing Arts,* 139 U. Pa. L. Rev. 1597 (1991); Robert Justin Lipkin, *Can American Constitutional Law Be Postmodern?* 42 Buff. L. Rev. 317 (1994); Francis J. Mootz, *The Ontological Basis of Legal Hermeneutics: A Proposed Model of Inquiry Based on the Work of Gadamer, Habermas, and Ricoeur,* 68 B. U. L. Rev. 523 (1988); Francis J. Mootz, *Postmodern Constitutionalism as Materialism,* 91 Mich. L. Rev. 515 (1992); Francis J. Mootz, *Is the Rule of Law Possible in a Postmodern World?* 68 Wash. L. Rev. 249 (1993) (hereafter Mootz, *Rule of Law*); Francis J. Mootz, *The Paranoid Style in Contemporary Legal Scholarship,* 31 Hous. L. Rev. 873 (1994) (hereafter Mootz, *Paranoid Style*); Dennis M. Patterson, *Postmodernism/Feminism/Law,* 77 Cornell L. Rev. 254 (1992) (hereafter Patterson, *Postmodernism*); Dennis Patterson, *The Poverty of Interpretive Universalism: Toward the Reconstruction of Legal Theory,* 72 Tex. L. Rev. 1 (1993) (hereafter Patterson, *The Poverty*); Dennis M. Patterson, *Law's Pragmatism: Law as Practice and Narrative,* 76 Va. L. Rev. 937 (1990) (hereafter Patterson, *Law's Pragmatism*); john a. powell, *The Multiple Self: Exploring between and beyond Modernity and Postmodernity,* 81 Minn. L. Rev. 1481 (1997); Margaret J. Radin and Frank Michelman, *Pragmatist and Poststructuralist Critical Legal Practice,* 139 U. Pa. L. Rev. 1019 (1991); Peter C. Schanck, *Understanding Postmodern Thought and Its Implications for Statutory Interpretation,* 65 S. Cal. L. Rev. 2505, 2508–09 (1992); Pierre Schlag, *Law and Phrenology,* 110 Harv. L. Rev. 877 (1997) (hereafter Schlag, *Phrenology*); Pierre Schlag, *Law as the Continuation of God by Other Means,* 85 Calif. L. Rev. 427 (1997) (hereafter Schlag, *God*); Pierre Schlag, *Hiding the Ball,* 71 N. Y. U. L. Rev. 1681 (1996) (hereafter Schlag, *Hiding*); Pierre Schlag, *Clerks in the Maze,* 91 Mich. L. Rev. 2053 (1993) (hereafter Schlag, *Clerks*); Pierre Schlag, *Writing for Judges,* 63 U. Colo. L. Rev. 419 (1992) (hereafter Schlag, *Writing*); Pierre Schlag, *The Problem of the Subject,* 69 Tex. L. Rev. 1627 (1991) (hereafter Schlag, *The Problem*); Pierre Schlag, *Normativity and the Politics of Form,* 139 U. Pa. L. Rev. 801 (1991) (hereafter Schlag, *Normativity*); Pierre Schlag, *Normative and Nowhere to Go,* 43 Stan. L. Rev. 167 (1990) (hereafter Schlag, *Nowhere*); Pierre Schlag, *"Le Hors De Texte—C'est Moi": The Politics of Form and the Domestication of Deconstruction,* 11 Cardozo L. Rev. 1631 (1990) (hereafter Schlag, *Form*); Pierre Schlag, *Fish v. Zapp: The Case of the Relatively Autonomous Self,* 76 Geo. L. J. 37 (1987) (hereafter Schlag, *Fish v. Zapp*); Susan Silbey, *Making a Place for Cultural Analyses of Law,* 17 Law & Soc. Inquiry 39 (1992); Anthony D. Taibi, *Banking, Finance, and Community Economic Empowerment: Structural Economic Theory, Procedural Civil Rights, and Substantive Racial Justice,* 107 Harv. L. Rev. 1463 (1994); Kendall Thomas, *Beyond the Privacy Principle,* 92 Colum. L. Rev. 1431 (1992); Joan C. Williams, *Rorty, Radicalism, Romanticism: The Politics of the Gaze,* 1992 Wis. L.

Rev. 131; Steven L. Winter, *Indeterminacy and Incommensurability in Constitutional Law,* 78 Calif. L. Rev. 1441 (1990).

62. Feldman, *Diagnosing Power, supra* note 61, at 1096 (introducing the concept of postmodern policing).

63. Litowitz, *supra* note 61, at 4–5 ("a deep distrust"); Higgins, *supra* note 61, at 1537 ("'[w]oman' is").

64. D'Amato, *supra* note 61, at 252, 254; see Martha Minow and Elizabeth Spelman, *In Context,* 63 S. Cal. L. Rev. 1597 (1990) (emphasizing how a focus on context can be used to critique the positions of others).

65. Schlag, *Hiding, supra* note 61, at 1684, 1687.

66. Schlag, *Phrenology, supra* note 61, at 900, 908.

67. Rosenfeld, *supra* note 61, at 1212.

68. Harris, *supra* note 61, at 585 ("gender essentialism," "in order to privilege"); Ashe, *supra* note 61, at 116 ("throws into question"); Feldman, *The Politics, supra* note 61, at 200 ("deconjustice"); Backer, *supra* note 61, at 369; Balkin, *Deconstructive, supra* note 61, at 763 ("to remember," "[d]econstruction is not"); see Cornell, Limit, *supra* note 61, at 62, 81–82 (emphasizing deconstruction as central to an ethics that focuses on "a nonviolent relationship to the Other"); Derrida, *supra* note 61, at 945 (declaring that "[d]econstruction is justice,"); Feldman, *The Politics, supra* note 61, at 197–201 (emphasizing the connection between deconstruction and justice).

69. Balkin, *Deconstructive, supra* note 61, at 762 ("unregulated market," "our social vision"); Amartya K. Sen, *Rational Fools: A Critique of the Behavioral Foundations of Economic Theory,* in Beyond Self-Interest 25, 35, 37 (Jane J. Mansbridge ed., 1990) ("a social moron," "[T]he assumption").

70. Balkin, *Deconstructive, supra* note 61, at 763; see Stephen M. Feldman, *Whose Common Good? Racism in the Political Community,* 80 Geo. L. J. 1835, 1844–49 (1992) (criticizing the view of individuals as motivated solely by self-interest).

71. Ashe, *supra* note 61, at 116 ("forces us"); Alexander, *supra* note 61, at 260–62; see also Delgado and Stefancic, *supra* note 61, at 1280–81 (questioning the traditional marketplace of ideas theory of freedom of speech); Thomas, *supra* note 61, at 1435 (challenging the "limitations of [right of] privacy rhetoric as a conceptual resource for discussing the constitutional issues" arising from the criminalization of homosexual conduct).

72. Felstiner and Sarat, *supra* note 61, at 1447–58.

73. Delgado and Stefancic, *Images, supra* note 61, at 1278–79; see Charles R. Lawrence, *The Id, the Ego, and Equal Protection: Reckoning with Unconscious Racism,* 39 Stan. L. Rev. 317, 330 (1987); see Backer, *supra* note 61, at 371 (arguing that a culture of "Biblical foundationalism" prevents Americans from even imagining the systemic changes needed to prevent poverty).

74. Balkin, *Postmodern Constitutionalism, supra* note 61, at 1978, 1981. For a collection of essays that view law from the perspective of cultural study, see Legal Studies as Cultural Studies (Jerry Leonard ed., 1995); see also Ewick and Silbey, *supra* note 61; Sally Engle Merry, *Culture, Power, and the Discourse of Law,* 37 N. Y. L. Sch. L. Rev. 209 (1992).

75. On the general importance of hypertext, see George P. Landow, Hypertext 2.0 (rev. ed., 1997). On the development of professions, see Richard L. Abel, American Lawyers (1989); Magali Sarfatti Larson, The Rise of Professionalism: A Sociological Analysis (1977). For one of the more useful critiques of interdisciplinary scholarship in the

field of constitutional law, see Martin S. Flaherty, *History "Lite" in Modern American Constitutionalism,* 95 Colum. L. Rev. 523 (1995); compare Stephen M. Feldman, *Intellectual History in Detail,* 26 Reviews in Amn. Hist., 737 (1998) (commenting on the criticism of interdisciplinary work). Some historians have written approvingly of interdisciplinary scholarship. Kalman, *supra* note 1, at 9, 169; G. Edward White, *Reflections on the "Republican Revival": Interdisciplinary Scholarship in the Legal Academy,* 6 Yale J. L. & Human. 1 (1994).

76. Schanck, *supra* note 61, at 2514; see 2574.

77. Richard Delgado, *Words That Wound: A Tort Action for Racial Insults, Epithets, and Name-calling,* 17 Harv. C. R.–C. L. L. Rev. 133 (1982); Delgado and Stefancic, *Images, supra* note 61, at 1278–81.

78. Felstiner and Sarat, *supra* note 61, at 1454 ("a 'thing'"); Thomas, *supra* note 61, at 1478 ("we speak"); Feldman, *Please Don't, supra* note 10, at 6; quoting Nancy Fraser, Unruly Practices: Power, Discourse, and Gender in Contemporary Social Theory 26 (1989) ("that 'power is'"); Felstiner and Sarat, *supra* note 61, at 1457 ("[Power] is not like"); see, e.g., Higgins, *supra* note 61, at 1569–70. For some discussions and citations of Foucault in legal studies, see Marie Ashe, *Inventing Choreographies: Feminism and Deconstruction,* 90 Colum. L. Rev. 1123, 1128 (1990); Backer, *supra* note 61, at 374; Thomas, *supra* note 61, at 1478–79; Steven L. Winter, *The "Power" Thing,* 82 Va. L. Rev. 721, 794–806 (1996).

79. Felstiner and Sarat, *supra* note 61, at 1458 ("[p]ower has many"); Patterson, *Postmodernism, supra* note 61, at 274 ("[a]ll understanding"); Balkin, *Deconstructive, supra* note 61, at 760; quoting Jacques Derrida, Of Grammatology 158–59 (Gayatri Chakravorty Spivak trans., 1976 ("[t]here is"); Levinson and Balkin, *supra* note 61, at 1613 ("exceptional," "legal act"); Higgins, *supra* note 61, at 1585 ("[P]ostmodernism emphasizes"); see Schlag, *Form, supra* note 61.

80. Schanck, *supra* note 61, at 2508–9.

81. Stephen M. Feldman, *The New Metaphysics: The Interpretive Turn in Jurisprudence,* 76 Iowa L. Rev. 661, 693 (1991). Mootz argues that philosophical hermeneutics accounts not only for the understanding of legal texts but also for the rule of law. Mootz, *Rule of Law, supra* note 61; see Eskridge, *supra* note 61, at 632–33 (exploring the ramifications of Gadamerian hermeneutics for statutory interpretation).

82. Patterson, *The Poverty, supra* note 61, at 21–22, 55.

83. Patterson, *Law's Pragmatism, supra* note 61, at 940 ("interpretive enterprise," "law is an activity"); Dennis Patterson, *Conscience and the Constitution,* 93 Colum. L. Rev. 270, 289 (1993) ("[a] claim"); Dennis Patterson, Law and Truth 169 (1996) ("special language"); Dennis Patterson, *Wittgenstein and Constitutional Theory,* 72 Tex. L. Rev. 1837, 1838 (1994) ("rules," "game"); Philip Bobbitt, Constitutional Interpretation 12–13, 22 (1991) ("modalities of argument," "historical"); see Philip Bobbitt, Constitutional Fate (1982). Bobbitt approvingly cites Wittgenstein; 182–83. Other postmodernists turn to some type of postmodern pragmatism, often inspired by the philosophical writings of Richard Rorty. See Lipkin, *supra* note 61, at 337.

84. J. M. Balkin & Sanford Levinson, *Constitutional Grammar,* 72 Tex. L. Rev. 1771, 1803 (1994) ("to preserve"); Patterson, *The Poverty, supra* note 61, at 56 ("the accurate"); Feldman, *The Politics, supra* note 61, at 183 ("uncritical acceptance"). "Like Bobbitt, Patterson esteems the status quo." Steven L. Winter, *One Size Fits All,* 72 Tex. L. Rev. 1857, 1867 (1994).

85. Feldman, *Please Don't, supra* note 370, at 265 ("language simultaneously"); Fel-

stiner and Sarat, *supra* note 61, at 1449 ("While people work"); see Feldman, Please Don't, *supra* note 370, at 265–70; Anthony V. Alfieri, *Stances,* 77 Cornell L. Rev. 1233, 1251–52 (1992); Anthony V. Alfieri, *Practicing Community,* 107 Harv. L. Rev. 1747, 1758–59 (1994), review of Gerald P. Lopez, Rebellious Lawyering: One Chicano's Vision of Progressive Law Practice (1992); Naomi R. Cahn, *Inconsistent Stories,* 81 Geo. L. J. 2475, 2507 (1993).

86. Thomas, *supra* note 61, at 1467; quoting Claudia Card, *Rape as a Terrorist Institution,* in Violence, Terrorism, and Justice 297–98 (R. G. Frey and Christopher W. Morris eds., 1991) ("Homophobic violence"); Thomas, *supra* note 61, at 1490 n. 203; quoting Charles L. Black, *The Lawfulness of the Segregation Decisions,* 69 Yale L. J. 421, 425 (1960) ("The combined force"); see Backer, *supra* 61, at 373 (arguing that welfare generates social normalization rather than relieving poverty).

87. See Feldman, Please Don't, *supra* note 370, at 266–67, 270; Felstiner and Sarat, *supra* note 61, at 1448–49; Silbey, *supra* note 61, at 41–42.

88. Richard Delgado, *Campus Antiracism Rules: Constitutional Narratives in Collision,* 85 Nw. U. L. Rev. 343 (1991); see Delgado and Stefancic, *Images, supra* note 61, at 1278–81; Angela Harris, *Foreword: The Jurisprudence of Reconstruction,* 82 Calif. L. Rev. 741, 743 (1994) (emphasizing that racism is part of "the deep structure of American law and culture"); Mari Matsuda, *Public Response to Racist Speech: Considering the Victim's Story,* 87 Mich. L. Rev. 2320, 2357–63 (1989) (emphasizing racism as structural component of American society that affects how speech works); Taibi, *supra* note 61, at 1469 (a sophisticated analysis of underinvestment in nonwhite communities that stresses the need for structural change).

89. Schlag, *Normativity, supra* note 91, at 895.

90. Balkin, *Understanding, supra* note 61, at 108. On racial realism, see Derrick Bell, *Racial Realism,* 24 Conn. L. Rev. 363 (1992); Delgado and Stefancic, *supra* note 61, at 1289–91.

91. powell, *supra* note 61, at 1483 ("self as a site"); Boyle, *supra* note 61, at 521 ("the determinants"); powell, *supra* note 61, at 1511 ("[t]he theory"); see Harris, *supra* note 61, at 608 (multiplicitous self); powell, *supra* note 61, at 1511 (intersectional self).

92. Ewick and Silbey, *supra* note 61, at 741–42. For examples of postmodern legal writers attempting to maintain a critical political stance, see Taibi, *supra* note 61; Thomas, *supra* note 61; Note, *Patriarchy Is Such a Drag: The Strategic Possibilities of a Postmodern Account of Gender,* 108 Harv. L. Rev. 1973 (1995).

93. See Paul Campos, *That Obscure Object of Desire: Hermeneutics and the Autonomous Legal Text,* 77 Minn. L. Rev. 1065, 1094–95 (1993) (refusing to make a normative recommendation for how to interpret legal texts); Thomas, *supra* note 61, at 1436 ("I harbor no illusions that the theoretical argument elaborated in these pages will find doctrinal expression in the constitutional jurisprudence of the current Supreme Court"); Schlag, *Nowhere, supra* note 61 (criticizing the normative quality of modernist scholarship); Winter, *supra* note 61, at 1496 (arguing that prescriptions for normative improvements mistakenly "presuppose the relatively autonomous subject, magically capable of transcending her own limitations with a single, rationalist bound"). For examples of individuals who are more modernist than postmodernist but who nevertheless are influenced by postmodern culture to the extent that they are doing scholarship about scholarship, see Kenneth Lasson, *Scholarship Amok: Excesses in the Pursuit of Truth and Tenure,* 103 Harv. L. Rev. 926 (1990); Richard A. Posner, *The Decline of Law as an Autonomous Discipline: 1962–1987,* 100 Harv. L. Rev. 761 (1987); Edward L. Rubin, *The Practice and Discourse of Legal Scholarship,* 86 Mich. L. Rev. 1835 (1988).

94. Schlag, *The Problem, supra* note 61, at 1629, 1700–1701; see Schlag, *Phrenology, supra* note 61; Schlag, *Nowhere, supra* note 61.

95. Schlag, *Clerks, supra* note 61, at 2060–61; see Schlag, *God, supra* note 61, at 427–28. For a postmodern critique of Schlag's argument, see Mootz, *Paranoid Style, supra* note 61. "Each law professor is quite aware of the plasticity of law, and yet writes about law as if it is determinate." Anthony D'Amato, *Pragmatic Indeterminacy,* 85 Nw. U. L. Rev. 148, 164 (1990).

96. Pierre Schlag, *This Could Be Your Culture—Junk Speech in a Time of Decadence,* 109 Harv. L. Rev. 1801, 1807 (1996). On judges not caring about legal scholarship, see Schlag, *Writing, supra* note 61, at 421; Schlag, *Normativity, supra* note 61, at 871–72; Winter, *supra* note 61, at 1452–53; compare Sanford Levinson, *The Audience for Constitutional Meta-Theory (Or, Why, and to Whom, Do I Write the Things I Do?),* 63 U. Colo. L. Rev. 389, 405 n. 28 (1992) (an empirical study shows that the Supreme Court was less likely to cite law review articles in 1986 than twenty years earlier).

97. Schlag, *The Problem, supra* note 61, at 1739, 1743; Schlag, *Normativity, supra* note 61, at 909; Schlag, *Nowhere, supra* note 61, at 185–86.

98. Stanley Fish, *How Come You Do Me Like You Do? A Response to Dennis Patterson,* 72 Tex. L. Rev. 57, 57–59 (1993); Schlag, *Fish v. Zapp, supra* note 61; Mootz, *Paranoid Style, supra* note 61, at 879. Fish was responding to an earlier criticism of his work by Patterson. See Patterson, *The Poverty, supra* note 61. For examples of postmodernists who display a type of postmodern normativeness, see Anthony V. Alfieri, *Practicing Community,* 107 Harv. L. Rev. 1747 (1994); Higgins, *supra* note 61; Taibi, *supra* note 61; Thomas, *supra* note 61.

99. Feldman, *Playing, supra* note 61, at 178; see Balkin, *Tradition, supra* note 61, at 1625–30; compare Zygmunt Bauman, Intimations of Postmodernity 21–22 (1992) (arguing that one of the best ways to understand the movement from modernity to postmodernity is in the transition of the role of intellectuals from legislators to interpreters); Jacques Derrida, Of Grammatology 24 (Gayatri Chakravorty Spivak trans., 1976) (deconstructionists cannot escape the modernist metaphysics of presence). On the structural roles of postmodern (and modern) legal scholars, see Feldman, *Diagnosing Power, supra* note 61, at 1088–98; Kenneth Lasson, *Scholarship Amok: Excesses in the Pursuit of Truth and Tenure,* 103 Harv. L. Rev. 926, 949 (1990).

100. Balkin, *Tradition, supra* note 61, at 1627 ("has a particular"); Feldman, *Playing, supra* note 61, at 179 (on deconstructive implosion); see Balkin, *Tradition, supra* note 61, at 1627 (arguing that although deconstruction could go on and on forever, "we always do stop").

101. Feldman, *Playing, supra* note 61; see Minda, *supra* note 1, at 248 (discussing a "postmodern temperament"). Jean Baudrillard writes: "[a]ll that remains to be done is to play with the pieces. Playing with the pieces—that is post-modern." Jean Baudrillard, *Game with Vestiges,* 5 On the Beach 19, 24 (1984).

102. On pastiche, see Levinson and Balkin, *supra* note 61, at 1639.

103. Balkin, *Tradition, supra* note 61, at 1620; Schlag, *The Problem, supra* note 61, at 1649. For Schlag's juxtaposition of Dworkin and L.A. Law, see Schlag, *Normativity, supra* note 61, at 864–65; see Ronald Dworkin, Law's Empire (1986); see also Feldman, *Diagnosing Power, supra* note 61, at 1105 (concluding the article with a Stephen Sondheim stanza). Less often, postmodern legal scholars evoke a second form of postmodern irony stressing how texts cannot be controlled because of their iterability—their repeatability in different

contexts. In an article on deconstruction and law, Charles M. Yablon analyzes a blank form for a summons in a civil action, "set forth in Form 1 of the Appendix of Forms as issued pursuant to Rule 4 of the Federal Rules of Civil Procedure." Yablon stresses how this summons is, in some contexts, "a routine legal form," while in other contexts, it is "an instrument of power and pain." Charles M. Yablon, *Forms,* 11 Cardozo L. Rev. 1349, 1349, 1352–53 (1990).

104. Balkin, *Transcendental, supra* note 61, at 1141; Feldman, *The Politics, supra* note 61, at 199 ("[W]henever we"); Derrida, *supra* note 61, at 945.

105. Eskridge, *supra* note 55, at 608; see Schlag, *The Problem, supra* note 61, at 1739, 1743.

106. *Roe v. Wade,* 410 US 113, 116 (1973); *Planned Parenthood v. Casey,* 505 US 833, 849 (1992).

107. *Casey,* 505 US at 864; see 864–69.

108. *Texas v. Johnson,* 491 US 397, 422 (1989) (Rehnquist, C.J., dissenting); see Stephen M. Feldman, *Republican Revival/Interpretive Turn,* 1992 Wis. L. Rev. 679, 725–31 (discussing the flag desecration dispute and cases). The decision in *Johnson* led to national calls for the prohibition of flag desecration pursuant to either a constitutional amendment or a federal statute that would pass constitutional muster. In October 1989 Congress enacted a statute, The Flag Protection Act, Pub. L. No. 101–131, 103 Stat. 777 (1989), which the Court eventually held to be unconstitutional. *United States v. Eichman,* 496 US 310 (1990).

109. *Johnson,* 491 US at 423–25 (Rehnquist, C. J., dissenting). Rehnquist has used unusual or bizarre references or quotations in other cases. See, e.g., *Church of Scientology of California v. Internal Revenue Service,* 484 US 9, 17–18 (1987) (referring to Sir Arthur Conan Doyle's "dog that didn't bark").

110. *Smith v. Goguen,* 415 US 566, 602 (1974) (Rehnquist, J., dissenting). Goguen had been convicted for violating the Massachusetts law when he "wore a small cloth version of the United States flag sewn to the seat of his trousers"; 568.

111. *County of Sacramento v. Lewis,* 118 S.Ct. 1708, 1716–17 (1998).

112. *Lewis,* 118 S.Ct. at 1724 (Scalia, J., concurring) (paraphrasing Cole Porter, "You're the Top" (1934), in The Complete Lyrics of Cole Porter 169 (Robert Kimball ed., 1983); see *Lewis,* 118 S.Ct. at 1723–24 (Scalia, J., concurring); *Washington v. Glucksberg,* 117 S.Ct. 2258 (1997). In a footnote in *Lewis,* Scalia added: "[F]or those unfamiliar with classical music, I note that the exemplars of excellence in the text are borrowed from Cole Porter's 'You're the Top,' copyright 1934." At 1724 n. 1 (Scalia, J., concurring). For other unusual passages from Scalia, see *Clinton v. City of New York,* 118 S.Ct. 2091, 2117 (1998) (Scalia, J., concurring and dissenting) (referring to "the Mahatma Ghandi [*sic*] of all impounders"); *United States v. Virginia,* 518 US 515, 601–3 (1996) (Scalia, J., dissenting) (providing a lengthy quotation from the Virginia Military Institute's *Code of a Gentleman*).

113. *James B. Beam Distilling Co. v. Georgia,* 111 S.Ct. 2439, 2450–51 (1991) (Scalia, J., concurring in the judgment) (citations omitted, emphases added and omitted). This case involved the retroactive application of a rule of constitutional law in the context of a state tax refund. For an extensive discussion of the manifestation of postmodernism in the opinions of Rehnquist and Scalia, in the context of a series of cases focusing on habeas corpus, see Feldman, *Diagnosing Power, supra* note 61, at 1052–84, 1098–1104.

114. *Planned Parenthood v. Casey,* 505 US 833, 993–94 (1992) (Scalia, J., concurring and dissenting). The idea of tattered remnants of modernist beliefs is a paraphrase from Louis

Michael Seidman and Mark V. Tushnet, Remnants of Belief 23 (1996). In terms of Scalia's point that the Court can call a holding whatever it wants to, Scalia's dissent in *United States v. Virginia* made a similar point in several places. For example, he refers to the Court's equal protection standards—rational basis, intermediate scrutiny, and strict scrutiny—as "made-up tests." 518 US 515, 570 (1996) (Scalia, J., dissenting). He added: "[t]hese tests are no more scientific than their names suggest, and a further element of randomness is added by the fact that it is largely up to us which test will be applied in each case"; 567. Plus, he argued that, with regard to the intermediate scrutiny test, the justices "essentially apply it when it seems like a good idea to load the dice"; 568.

With regard to the justices' reliance on their clerks, see Mary Ann Glendon, A Nation under Lawyers 146–48 (1994); Bernard Schwartz, Decision: How the Supreme Court Decides Cases 48–55, 256–62 (1996); Mark V. Tushnet, *A Republican Chief Justice*, 88 Mich. L. Rev. 1326, 1327 (1990). In the words of Jack Balkin, the Court applies in this postmodern era "quasi-industrial methods to the administration of justice." *Postmodern Constitutionalism*, supra note 61, at 1983. Rehnquist has admitted that his clerks write the first draft of almost all opinions issued in his name; *supra*, 52. According to Mary Ann Glendon, only Scalia and Stevens supposedly take a "leading role" in writing opinions; *supra*, 146. Bernard Schwartz adds that, contrary to the usual belief that oral argument substantively matters, "the principal purpose of the argument before the Justices is a public-relations one"; *supra*, 16.

115. Stephen M. Feldman, *From Modernism to Postmodernism in American Legal Thought: The Significance of the Warren Court*, in The Warren Court: A Retrospective 324, 352–53 (Bernard Schwartz ed., 1996); see, e.g., Jay P. Moran, *Postmodernism's Misguided Place in Legal Scholarship: Chaos Theory, Deconstruction, and Some Insights from Thomas Pynchon's Fiction*, 6 S. Cal. Interdisciplinary L. Forum 155, 159 (1997) (arguing to reject postmodernism and "return to traditional and cohesive legal principles"). "From the standpoint of modernism, postmodernism is just another ideology—another claim to totalizing discourse. But from its own perspective postmodernism cannot be such a discourse because it is not merely a set of beliefs, but also a cultural environment in which beliefs occur." Balkin, *Postmodern Constitutionalism*, supra note 61, at 1976.

6. Conclusion

1. See, e.g., Stephen M. Feldman, *Felix S. Cohen and His Jurisprudence: Reflections on Federal Indian Law*, 35 Buff. L. Rev. 479 (1986) (discussing the influence of Felix Cohen's realism on the development of American Indian law); Pierre Schlag, *Law and Phrenology*, 110 Harv. L. Rev. 877 (1997) (discussing Langdellian legal science from a postmodern perspective).

2. For examples of modernist legal scholars who castigate postmodernism, see Arthur Austin, A Primer on Deconstruction's *"Rhapsody of Word-Plays"* 71 N.C. L. Rev. 201 (1992); Steven Lubet, *Is Legal Theory Good for Anything?* 1997 U. Ill. L. Rev. 193; Suzanna Sherry, *The Sleep of Reason*, 84 Geo. L. J. 453 (1996). On the ambiguity of the border between modernism and postmodernism, see Anthony Giddens, The Consequences of Modernity 45-53 (1990) (talking of the radicalization of modernity instead of a transition to postmodernity); Richard J. Bernstein, *An Allegory of Modernity/Postmodernity: Habermas and Derrida*, in The New Constellation 199 (1991).

3. I first heard the metaphor of the lawyer's toolbox from my professor in contract law,

Jon Jacobson, who often referred to promissory estoppel as an essential tool in the contract lawyer's toolbox. Compare Pierre Schlag, *Normativity and the Politics of Form,* 139 U. Pa. L. Rev. 801, 803, 860 (1991) (characterizing legal doctrine as a tool, especially for trial lawyers, used to coerce others).

4. Steven D. Smith, Foreordained Failure: The Quest for a Constitutional Principle of Religious Freedom 6 (1995).

5. *Id.* at 63; see 55–118.

6. *Id.* at 68.

7. *Id.* at 61, 126; see viii; see also Stephen M. Feldman, *Principle, History, and Power: The Limits of the First Amendment Religion Clauses,* 81 Iowa L. Rev. 833 (1996) (focusing on the importance of Smith's conclusions in the specific context of religion clause jurisprudence).

8. Cass Sunstein is another outstanding modernist scholar who uses postmodern insights as tools in the construction of modernist arguments. See Stephen M. Feldman, *Playing With the Pieces: Postmodernism in the Lawyer's Toolbox,* 85 Va. L. Rev. 151 (1999); Stephen M. Feldman, *Exposing Sunstein's Naked Preferences,* 1989 Duke L. J. 1335; see, e.g., Cass R. Sunstein, The Partial Constitution (1993).

9. Robert M. Cover, *Foreword: Nomos and Narrative,* 97 Harv. L. Rev. 4 (1983) (discussing how courts, in effect, kill legal meaning); Leading Cases, Table II (A), 112 Harv. L. Rev. 372 (1998) (on the number of Supreme Court case dispositions).

10. For instance, Justice Scalia reasonably can be accused of inauthenticity or disingenuousness when one compares his statements regarding the flexibility of the Supreme Court, which I mentioned toward the end of chapter 5, with some of his claims to seek formalistic approaches that supposedly would diminish judicial discretion. See Eric J. Segall, *Justice Scalia, Critical Legal Studies, and the Rule of Law,* 62 Geo. Wash. L. Rev. 991 (1994) (emphasizing Scalia's advocacy of formalistic approaches).

11. Compare Robert Post, *Postmodern Temptations,* 4 Yale J. L. & Human. 391, 396 (1992) ("There is no postmodern law, although there are postmodern commentaries on law"). For examples of Supreme Court justices denigrating the legal academy, see *Romer v. Evans,* 517 US 620, 652–53 (1996) (Scalia, J., dissenting); *Seminole Tribe of Florida v. Florida,* 517 US 44, 68–69 (1996) (Rehnquist, J., majority opinion). J. M. Balkin argues that postmodern constitutionalism is characterized by this very gap between the legal academy and reactionary judges. J. M. Balkin, *What Is a Postmodern Constitutionalism?* 90 Mich. L. Rev. 1966, 1967 (1992).

12. Jonathan Culler, On Deconstruction 110 (1982); Madeleine Plasencia, *Who's Afraid of Humpty Dumpty: Deconstructionist References in Judicial Opinions,* 21 Seattle U. L. Rev. 215, 247 (1997); see Culler, *supra,* at 131–34, 280; Plasencia, *supra,* at 246–47; compare Robert M. Cover, *Violence and the Word,* 95 Yale L. J. 1601 (1986) (arguing that legal interpretation may lead to loss of freedom, property, and so forth).

13. Suck.: Worst-Case Scenarios in Media, Culture, Advertising, and the Internet 114 (Joey Anuff and Ana Marie Cox eds., 1997).

Index

Abernathy, Ralph, 139
abolitionism. *See* slavery
abortion. *See* Planned Parenthood v. Casey;
    Roe v. Wade
Adair v. United States, 235 nn.55–56
Adams, John, 59, 62, 68, 75
Adkins v. Children's Hospital of the District of
    Columbia, 235 n.55
Administrative Procedure Act, 157
African Americans, 67, 71, 101, 116, 123, 125,
    135, 139, 158; *see also* outsider jurisprudence
Alexander, Gregory S., 167
ALI. *See* American Law Institute
Alien and Sedition Acts, 72
Allgeyer v. Louisiana, 104, 234 n.49, 235
    nn.55–56
American Anti-Slavery Convention, 87
American Historical Association, 150
American Law Institute (ALI), 111
American legal realism. *See* realism
American Political Science Association, 116
American Protestantism, 51, 67, 72–73, 75,
    84–85; *see also* Great Awakening, First; Great
    Awakening, Second
American Revolution, 49–51, 58–59, 65–66
Ames, James Barr, 95–96, 234 n.51
antebellum legal education. *See* legal education;
    Litchfield Law School

Antelope (*The Antelope*), 222 n.65
anti-elitism, 69; *see also* elitism
anti-essentialism, 38, 159, 161, 163–65, 170–71,
    175, 192
anti-Federalists, 60
anti-foundationalism, 38, 153–54, 159, 161,
    163–65, 170–71, 175, 180, 183, 192
anti-intellectualism. *See* anti-elitism
Aquinas, St. Thomas, 14
Arendt, Hannah, 131
Aristotle, 12, 88, 96–99
Arnold, Thurman, 110
Articles of Confederation, 59, 63
Augustine, St., 13
Austin, John, 90–91, 106, 129

Backer, Larry Catá, 165
Bacon, Francis, 17, 56; and Baconian science,
    52–56
Bailey v. Drexel Furniture Co. (*Child Labor Tax
    Case*), 234 n.49
Balkin, J.M. (Jack), 31, 165, 168, 170, 174,
    180–81, 259–60 n.114, 261 n.11
Bankruptcy Act, 113
Baudrillard, Jean, 43, 46, 258 n.101
Bauman, Zygmunt, 18
Beale, Joseph, 93, 233 n.41, 234 n.51
Bell, Derrick, 159, 174

Bentham, Jeremy, 65–66, 70, 90; *see also* utilitarianism

Berger, Raoul, 144

Bickel, Alexander, 124, 126, 133–35

Black, Charles, 128

Black, Hugo, 124, 143

Black Power, 139

Blackmun, Harry, 144–47, 182

Blackstone, William, 50, 91; and forms of action, 56

blasphemy, 73

Bledsoe, Albert Taylor, 88

Blumenberg, Hans, 204 n.21, 205 n.33

Bobbitt, Philip, 172

Bork, Robert, 144, 148

Boston University Law School, 236–37 n.65

Boyle, James, 175

Bozeman, Theodore, 53

Bradley, Joseph P., 104

Braucher, Robert, 126

Brennan, William J., 142–43, 145

Brest, Paul, 132, 136, 150

Brown, Ernest, 126

Brown v. Board of Education, 8, 123–28, 133, 135–36, 147–49, 157–58, 243 n.104

Brown v. Board of Education (*Brown II*), 125, 243 n.105

Budweiser, 196–98

Burger, Warren, 144, 147

Burke, Edmund, 122

Butchers' Union Co. v. Crescent City Co., 104, 235 n.56

Butler, Pierce, 60

Calhoun, John C., 88–89

Calvin, John, 15–18, 21–23, 66–67, 203 n.14, 205 n.30; and Hobbes, Thomas, 20–21; *see also* predestination

Calvinism. *See* Calvin, John

Cardozo, Benjamin, 5, 109

Carmichael, Stokely, 139

Carrington, Paul D., 132–33

Carter, James Coolidge, 105–6

case method. *See* legal education

Chanes, Jerome A., 123

Charles River Bridge v. Warren Bridge Comp., 77–78, 223 n.80

Chicago, Milwaukee & St. Paul Railway v. Minnesota (*Minnesota Rate Case*), 234 n.49

Chipman, Nathaniel, 4–5, 50, 52, 63–65, 74, 80–81, 223 n.72, 224 nn.85–86

Christianity, 12–14, 21–22, 141; *see also* American Protestantism; Protestant Reformation

Church of Scientology of California v. Internal Revenue Service, 259 n.109

Citizens' Saving & Loan Ass'n v. City of Topeka, 235 n.55

civic republicanism, 66, 89; and Aristotle, 12, 88; and Machiavelli, 14–15, 58, 60; *see also* republican government

Civil Rights Acts, 101, 116, 123, 157, 239–40 n.87

civil rights movement, 29, 123, 137–40, 158–59; *see also* Brown v. Board of Education

Civil War, 6, 65, 74, 83, 85–86, 90–91, 102, 140, 188; *see also* slavery

Clark, Charles, 113

classical orthodoxy, 231–32 n.30; *see also* Langdellian legal science

Clinton v. City of New York, 259 n.112

Coase, Ronald, 129, 150

Coase Theorem. *See* law and economics

codification of common law, 70–71, 105–6; Massachusetts commission (with Joseph Story), 55–56

Cohen, Felix, 110–11, 114

Cohen, Morris, 238 n.79

Cold War, 116, 118, 123, 125, 138, 140

common law, 76–77, 81–82, 91; American acceptance of English common law, 50–51; and Christianity, 51, 73, 222 n.70; *see also* codification of common law; forms of action

computer-assisted legal research, 155–57, 162; *see also* computers

computers, 29; graphical user interface (GUI), 157, 162; hypertext, 156, 168; *see also* computer-assisted legal research

Confederate Constitution, 89

confidence, 137–38, 140; in legal academy, 157, 162; *see also* idea of progress

Connor, Steven, 42

consensus (social), 109, 117–19, 137–41; in legal academy, 157–58, 162

consensus theory. *See* consensus (social)

Constitution (American), 59–63, 75–76, 118, 149, 158–59; Christian amendment, 141; and liberty (contrasted with Revolutionary era), 61; and property, 67; ratification, 60; *see also*

Brown v. Board of Education; Griswold v.
   Connecticut; interpretive turn; Lochner v.
   New York; Planned Parenthood v. Casey;
   Roe v. Wade
contraceptives. *See* Griswold v. Connecticut
Cook, Walter Wheeler, 110, 113
Cooley, Thomas M., 102–6; and Supreme
   Court, 235 n.55
Coppage v. Kansas, 235 n.56
Cornell, Drucilla, 162
corner-stone speech, 89
correspondence theory of truth, 155
Corwin, Edward S., 85
countermajoritarian difficulty, 134–35
Country (Opposition) ideology. *See* republican
   government
County of Sacramento v. Lewis, 185, 259 n.111
Cover, Robert, 152, 230 n.24
Cox, Archibald, 148–49
critical legal studies (CLS), 129–33, 150, 176
critical race theory, 159–61, 174
cultural relativism. *See* ethical relativism
cultural studies, 39–40, 44–45, 193; *see also* postmodern legal thought
Culver, John C., 138
cyclical time. *See* premodernism; premodern
   legal thought

Dahl, Robert, 118
D'Amato, Anthony, 164
Dartmouth College v. Woodward, 77, 223 n.79
Darwin, Charles, 84–85
decentered self, 174–75
Declaration of Independence, 49, 58, 87–88,
   104
deconjustice, 165
deconstruction, 33–38, 193; and anything goes,
   195; deconstructive implosion, 180; and legal
   scholarship, 159, 164–67, 170, 172, 176,
   179–81, 193; *see also* deconjustice; Derrida,
   Jacques
Delgado, Richard, 155–56, 159, 167, 169, 174, 251
   n.48, 252 n.55
DeLillo, Don, 48
democracy, 68–70, 115–20, 123, 133–36; *see also*
   pluralist political theory; relativist theory of
   democracy
democratic theory. *See* democracy
Derrida, Jacques, 30, 33–38, 42–44, 167, 209

n.62, 210 n.71; and legal scholarship, 155, 165,
   194; *see also* deconstruction
Descartes, René, 22–24, 94, 205 n.35, 206 n.37
Dew, Thomas R., 87
Dewey, John, 110, 113, 117, 240 n.89
Dickinson, John, 63
different voice, 38–39, 159–60; *see also* outsider
   jurisprudence
Doe v. Bolton, 248 n.20
Douglas, William O., 113–15, 124, 142–44, 147
due process. *See* Fourteenth Amendment
Duke University, 153; Law School, 133
Durkheim, Emile, 131
Dworkin, Ronald, 128, 181
Dykstra, Clarence, 116–17

easy cases, 163–64
Edwards, Jonathan, 58
Eliot, Charles, 92–93
elitism, 58–61, 64, 68–69, 72, 89; *see also* anti-
   elitism
Ely, John Hart, 135–36, 147, 149–50, 248 n.27;
   see also representation-reinforcement theory
Emerson, Ralph Waldo, 184
Emerson, Thomas, 144
empiricism (second-stage modernism), 24–26
empiricist legal thought. *See* realism
Engel v. Vitale, 140–41, 247 n.9
equal protection. *See* Fourteenth Amendment
Erie R. Co. v. Tompkins, 217 n.23
eschatological time. *See* premodernism; premodern legal thought
Eskridge, William, 159–60, 182
ethical relativism, 115–17, 149–50
Euclidean geometry, 94
Ewick, Patricia, 175
expansion (geographical), 67, 75

Fajer, Marc A., 159
Federal Rules of Civil Procedure, 157
Federalists, 60, 68–69, 72, 74; *see also* Hamilton,
   Alexander; Madison, James
Felstiner, William L.F., 167, 170, 173
feminist jurisprudence, 159–63, 170, 175
Feuerbach, Ludwig, 131
Field Code, 70–71, 222 n.66
Field, David Dudley, 71
Field, Stephen J., 104
Fifteenth Amendment, 101, 116

Fifth Amendment, 142
First Amendment, 141–42, 184, 191
Fish, Stanley, 152–55, 163, 169, 171, 178
Fitzhugh, George, 89
flag desecration, 183–84
Flag Protection Act, 259 n.108
Fletcher v. Peck, 217 n.24
Foner, Eric, 83–84
footnote four. *See* United States v. Carolene
    Products
forms of action (common law writs), 56–
    57
Fortas, Abe, 110–11, 114
Foucault, Michel, 30, 40, 155, 167, 169–70
Fourteenth Amendment, 100–101, 104, 124–25,
    145–46, 185
Fourth Amendment, 142
framing. *See* Constitution (American)
Frank, Jerome, 110, 113
Frankfurter, Felix, 122, 124–25, 141, 242 n.99,
    243 n.104, 247 n.12
Franklin, Benjamin, 62
French philosophes, 203 n.15
Freudian psychology, 28
Frietchie, Barbara, 184
Frisbie v. United States, 235 n.56
Frug, Gerald E., 132
Frug, Mary Joe, 162
Fugitive Slave Act, 88
Fuller, Lon, 119–20
fundamental contradiction, 131–32

Gadamer, Hans-Georg, 30–38, 40–42, 208 n.56,
    209 n.62, 210 n.71; and legal scholarship,
    152–55, 167, 171, 250 n.40; *see also* philosophi-
    cal hermeneutics
Garrison, William Lloyd, 86; *see also* slavery
gay and lesbian studies, 159, 161, 173
Geertz, Clifford, 151
Gilded Age. *See* industrialization
Gilligan, Carol, 160
Glendon, Mary Ann, 4
Goldberg, Arthur J., 143–44
Gomillion v. Lightfoot, 239 n.87
Gordon, Robert W., 131
Gould, James, 57, 99
graphical user interface (GUI). *See* computers
Great Awakening, First, 51, 66; *see also* Ameri-
    can Protestantism

Great Awakening, Second, 66, 69, 72–73, 84; *see
    also* American Protestantism
Green, Nicholas St. John, 236–37 n.65
Grey, Thomas, 78, 96, 150, 231–32 n.30, 232
    n.34
Griswold v. Connecticut, 141–49, 162, 247 n.11,
    247–48 nn.16–18
Gross, Hyman, 144
Gunther, Gerald, 134

Habermas, Jürgen, 131, 208 n.56
Hale, Robert, 112
Hamilton, Alexander, 60, 68
Hammer v. Dagenhart (*Child Labor Case*), 234
    n.49, 235 n.55
Harlan, John M., 143
Harper v. Virginia Board of Elections, 239 n.87
Harrington, James, 61, 67, 218 n.36
Harris, Angela P., 161
Hart, Henry, Jr., 5, 120–22, 127; *see also* legal
    process
Hart, H.L.A., 129
Hartz, Louis, 122
Harvard Law Review, 120, 122, 126, 149
Harvard University, 92, 119; Law School, 92
Harvey, David, 29
Hatch, Nathan, 66
hate speech, 169, 174
Heidegger, Martin, 30, 33, 131, 167
Higgins, Tracy E., 170
Hilliard, Francis, 52, 54–55, 57, 76–77, 79
historical school of jurisprudence, 105–6
historicism, 19; 84–85, 91–93, 99–100, 106, 113–14
Hitler, Adolph, 123
Hobbes, Thomas, 19–21, 25, 204 n.27, 205 n.29
Hodgson, Godfrey, 139
Hoffman, David, 52–54, 56, 73, 92
Hofstadter, Richard, 69
Holmes, Oliver Wendell, Jr., 5, 106–9, 112, 114,
    145, 236–37 nn.62–69; and mailbox rule, 237
    n.67
Holocaust, 28, 123
Horwitz, Morton, 71
House Un-American Activities Committee, 118
humanities, job shortage in, 150
Hume, David, 24–26
Husserl, Edmund, 131
Hutcheson, Joseph, 111
hypertext. *See* computers

idea of progress, 10, 13–14, 17–19, 25, 28–29, 93, 106, 112–15, 121–22, 129, 132, 174; and periodization of progress or history, 17–18; and premodern legal thought, 74–82; *see also* individualism

ideas, history of. *See* intellectual history

immigration, 71, 83–84; *see also* population

individualism, 16, 23–26, 28, 66–67, 70, 72, 100, 113–15, 121–22, 129, 161, 167, 176–78; *see also* idea of progress; modernism; social construction of the self

Industrial Revolution. *See* industrialization

industrialization, 67–68, 83–84

Ingersoll, Charles Jared, 67

instrumentalism. *See* premodern legal thought

intellectual history, the movement of ideas, 5–8, 189; *see also* idea of progress; meta-narratives

interdisciplinary legal scholarship, 4–5, 92, 128–31, 109–10, 113–14, 150–53, 155, 162, 166–68

interdisciplinary scholarship, 39–40, 255–56 n.75; *see also* interdisciplinary legal scholarship

interpretive turn, 150–55, 162–63, 171–72; *see also* law and literature

interpretivism, 149–50

Jackson, Robert H., 124

Jacksonian Democrats, 70

James B. Beam Distilling Co. v. Georgia, 185–86, 259 n.113

James, William, 113

Jameson, Fredric, 40

Jay, John, 42, 60

Jefferson, Thomas, 49, 62, 68–70, 75

Jeffersonian Republicans, 68–70, 72, 74

Jews, 84, 123, 141, as law professors, 241 n.94

Jim Crow laws, 123, 125, 158–59, 174

Joachim of Flora, 18

Johns Hopkins University, 151; Institute of Law at Johns Hopkins University, 110

Johnson, Steven, 157

Journal of Legal Studies, 130

jurisprudence, compared to legal thought, 4–5

Kalman, Laura, 110, 152

Kant, Immanuel, 26–27, 117, 206–7 n.45

Kauper, Paul, 144

Keener, William A., 95, 97–98

Kelly, Alfred, 144

Kennedy, Anthony, 182

Kennedy, Duncan, 131–32

Kennedy, John F., 137, 140

Kennedy, Robert F., 137

Kent, James, 5, 52–53, 73, 75–76

Key, Francis Scott, 184

King, Martin Luther, Jr., 137, 139

kosmos, 11, 13

Kruger, Barbara, 37

Kuhn, Thomas, 151–52, 154, 167, 171

Lacan, Jacques, 155, 167

laissez-faire constitutionalism, 100–105, 109–10, 112, 120, 124

laissez-faire economic theory, 166; *see also* Smith, Adam

Landow, George P., 156

Langdellian legal science, 92–101, 106–11, 122, 176, 231 n.30; and Aristotle's philosophy, 96–99; and constitutional law, 101–2; and Descartes, 94; *see also* classical orthodoxy; Langdell, Christopher Columbus

Langdell, Christopher Columbus, 92–96, 106–8, 181; and legislation, 106; and mailbox rule, 94–95, 232 n.34, 237 n.67; selection as dean, 230 n.29; *see also* Langdellian legal science

Lasky, Moses, 128

late crisis (fourth-stage modernism), 26–28

late crisis legal thought, 126–36, 148–49; events leading to late crisis, 123–26

law and economics, 129–31

law and literature, 150; *see also* interpretive turn

Law and Society Association, 129, 189

Law, Sylvia, 148, 160

Lawrence, Charles R., 161

Leff, Arthur Allen, 149

legal education, 92, 164; case method (of teaching), 93–94, 97–98; demographic transformation of academy, 158, 162; job boom, 151; and professionalization of law professors, 92, 168, 177–78; *see* antebellum legal education; Litchfield Law School

legal process, 119–23, 130, 143–44, 148; and Brown v. Board of Education, 126–28, 133–36, 158, 243 n.107; course materials, 241 n.96, 243 n.107; events leading to legal process, 115–19; and Frankfurter, Felix, 242 n.99;

legal process, (*continued*)
 neutral principles, 127–28, 134–35, 245 n.127;
 passive virtues, 134, 142; reasoned elabora-
 tion, 121, 127
legal science. *See* Langdellian legal science; premodern legal thought
legal thought, compared to jurisprudence, 4–5
Levinson, Sanford, 170
Lévi-Strauss, Claude, 131
liberty, 61
Lincoln, Abraham, 83, 90
linguistic power. *See* power
Litchfield Law School, 50, 57
Litowitz, Douglas E., 163
Llewellyn, Karl, 5, 111, 128; and Bramble Bush
 controversy, 238 n.77
Loan Association v. Topeka, 235 n.56
Lochnerian jurisprudence. *See* Lochner v. New
 York
Lochner v. New York, 8, 100–101, 103–5, 110,
 112, 114, 120, 124, 142–45, 147, 234 n.49; *see
 also* laissez-faire constitutionalism
Locke, John, 24–25, 49, 52, 58, 61, 67, 88, 122,
 206 nn.39–41
loss of confidence. *See* confidence
loss of consensus. *See* consensus (social)
Louisiana Purchase, 67
Löwith, Karl, 12, 204 n.21
Luther, Martin, 15, 21, 203 n.13

Machiavelli, Niccolo, 14–15, 58
MacKinnon, Catharine A., 160–61
Madison, James, 60–61, 69–70
mailbox rule. *See* Holmes, Oliver Wendell, Jr.;
 Langdell, Christopher Columbus
Maine, Henry, 105
Malcolm X, 139
Manifest Destiny, 67
Mansfield, Lord, 76, 78
Marsden, George, 92
Marshall, John, 246 n.128
Marshall, Leon, 110
Marshall, Thurgood, 145
Marx, Karl, 131
Massachusetts Bay Puritans, 73
McCarthy, Cormac, 162
McCarthy, Joseph, 118
McCulloch v. Maryland, 246 n.128
mechanical jurisprudence, 109

Merleau-Ponty, Maurice, 131
meta-narratives, 6
meta-scholarship, 176, 196, 198
Mexican War, 67
Michelman, Frank, 129
Miller, Perry, 65, 86
Minersville v. Gobitis, 242 n.103
Minow, Martha, 160
modern legal thought, 3–4, 7–10, 83–136,
 163–65, 176–78, 188–92; secularization,
 84–85, 91–92; *see also* historicism; Langdellian legal science; modernism; realism
modernism, 3, 8–9, 15–28; anxiety, 24, 195; and
 the periodization of history or progress, 18;
 see also empiricism; individualism; late crisis;
 modern legal thought; rationalism; transcen-
 dentalism
Monroe, James, 69, 75
Montaigne, Michel de, 205 n.36
Montesquieu, 64
Moore, Underhill, 110, 113
Mootz, Francis J., 170, 178
Mueller, Addison, 128
mugwumps, 84, 225 n.3, 231 n.30

NAACP (National Association for the Advancement of Colored People), 125
National Organization for Women (NOW),
 140
National Reporter System, 98
Native Americans, 63, 71
natural law, 49–52, 54–56, 65, 70, 72–74, 93, 96,
 99, 106, 148, 150, 188–89; American impreci-
 sion, 55; natural rights after Civil War, 101–5;
 and slavery, 86–90; split from natural rights,
 86–90
natural rights. *See* natural law
Nazism, 115, 117, 123
neutral principles. *See* legal process
New Deal, 4, 110, 112, 114, 124; *see also* realism
Nietzsche, Friedrich, 27, 167, 207 n.46
Nineteenth Amendment, 116
Ninth Amendment, 142, 146
Nixon, Richard, 138, 140, 144
noninterpretivism, 149–50
nonoriginalism. *See* noninterpretivism
Norway Plains Co. v. Boston & Maine R.R.
 Co., 223 n.82
Novick, Peter, 150, 152

O'Connor, Sandra Day, 182

Oliphant, Herman, 110

Olsen, Frances E., 132

Opposition (Country) ideology. *See* republican government

originalism. *See* interpretivism

Orren, Karen, 105

Other. *See* deconstruction; outsider jurisprudence

outsider jurisprudence, 158–63, 167–68, 173–75, 178–79, 181–82; tensions with postmodern scholarship, 160–61, 182

Paine, Thomas, 73–74

paradoxes. *See* postmodernism; postmodern legal thought

Parish, Peter, J., 83, 90

Parks, Rosa, 139

Parsons, Theophilus, 53

passive virtues. *See* legal process

pastiche, 180, 185

Patterson, Dennis, 155, 170–72, 178, 251 n.47

Patterson, James T., 137

Pennsylvania Constitution of 1776, 62–63

People v. Ruggles, 73, 222 n.70

phenomenology, 28

Phillips, Wendell, 86; *see also* slavery

philosophes, 203 n.15

philosophical hermeneutics, 30–38, 40–41; and legal scholarship, 153, 170–71, 256 n.81; *see also* Gadamer, Hans-Georg

Planned Parenthood v. Casey, 182–83, 259 n.106

Plato, 11–12, 54–56, 78–82, 96, 201 n.2

playing with the pieces, 43, 46, 180, 185–86, 195

Plessy v. Ferguson, 125, 229 n.22, 243 n.105

pluralist political theory, 117–18, 133, 149–50

Poe v. Ullman, 141–42, 247 n.12

political parties, 70, 72

Pollak, Louis, 128

popular sovereignty, 59–60, 66–71, 74, 89–90, 106; *see also* suffrage

population (of United States), 67, 75; *see also* immigration

Porter, Cole, 185

positivism (legal), 90–91, 93–94, 96–99, 106, 109

Posner, Richard, 130, 157

postmodern interpretivism. *See* interpretive turn

postmodern legal thought, 3–4, 7–10, 132, 137–87, 189–98; cultural studies, 167–68, 193; emergence of postmodern legal thought, 137–62; influencing modernist scholars, 190–92; irony, 180–81, 185, 258–59 n.103; paradoxes, 169; and politics, 181–86, 191–92, 195–96; second-stage postmodern legal thought, 192–98; self-reflexivity, 176–80, 183, 185; and Supreme Court, 182–86, 193–96; themes (eight) of postmodern legal thought, 162–87; *see also* anti-essentialism; anti-foundationalism; computer-assisted legal research; interdisciplinary legal scholarship; interpretive turn; outsider jurisprudence; pastiche; playing with the pieces; postmodernism; power; social construction of the self

postmodern policing, 163, 172

postmodernism, 3, 8–9, 28–48; and communication technology, 29, 155–57; and human freedom (or liberation), 47; irony, 43, 46; and meta-narratives, 6, 29, 39–40; paradoxes, 40; and politics, 43–44; postmodern subject (or self), 44–45, 193; second-stage postmodernism, 45–48; self-reflexivity, 42–43; themes (eight) of postmodernism, 38–45; *see also* anti-essentialism; anti-foundationalism; cultural studies; interdisciplinary scholarship; postmodern legal thought; pastiche; playing with the pieces; power; social construction of the self

Pound, Roscoe, 109–10

powell, john a., 175

Powell, Lewis F., 144

power, 40, 169–70, 190–91; and language, 40–41, 170–74; social structures, 41, 167, 173–75, 186, 193, 198

pragmatism (philosophical), 113–14

predestination, 66–67

preferred freedoms, 124, 242 n.103

premodern legal thought, 3–4, 7–8, 10, 49–82, 188–89; cyclical time, 61–65, 69; early American treatises, 53; eschatological time, 75; first-stage premodern legal thought, 57–65; and hierarchical social order, 58; instrumentalism, 76–82, 94; legal science, 50, 52–57; and Plato's philosophy, 54–56, 78–82, 96, 98; second-stage premodern legal thought, 74–82; *see also* Bacon, Francis; elitism; forms of action; natural law; premodernism; republican government premodernism, 3, 8–9, 11–15; cyclical time, 11–12; eschatological time, 11–15; *see also* premodern legal thought

professionalization of law professors. *See* legal education

progress. *See* idea of progress

Progressivism, 109–10, 112, 124

property, 67, 167; transformation of concept, 77–78

Protestant Reformation, 15–18, 22–23; *see also* American Protestantism; Calvin, John; Luther, Martin

public choice theory, 130

Purcell, Edward, 118

Quine, Willard van Orman, 155

racial realism, 174

railroads, 67, 84

rationalism (first-stage modernism), 22–24

rationalist legal thought. *See* Langdellian legal science

Rawls, John, 129, 150

reader-response theory, 153

realism, 108–15, 150; after World War II, 119–20, 122–23, 129, 133, 240–41 n.94; criticisms of realism, 240 n.94; and New Deal, 238 n.75; *see also* Llewellyn, Karl

reasoned elaboration. *See* legal process

Reconstruction, 101, 116, 140

Reeve, Tapping, 57

Reformed Episcopal Articles of Religion, 66–67

Rehnquist, William H., 42, 144, 147, 182–86, 195, 259–60 n.114

relativist theory of democracy, 117–19, 122; *see also* consensus (social); pluralist political theory

representation-reinforcement theory, 135-36, 147, 150, 246 n.128

republican government, 12, 58–65, 72, 116; and Opposition (Country) ideology, 58; *see also* civic republicanism; elitism; popular sovereignty; premodern legal thought

Republicans. *See* Jeffersonian Republicans

Restatments, 111–12

Revolution. *See* American Revolution

Reynolds v. Sims, 239 n.87

right of privacy. *See* Griswold v. Connecticut; Planned Parenthood v. Casey; Roe v. Wade

Rodell, Fred, 109

Roe v. Wade, 8, 141, 144–49, 162, 182–83, 248 n.20, 259 n.106

Roosevelt, Franklin, 110

Root, Jesse, 51

Rorty, Richard, 152, 167, 250 n.40, 256 n.83

Rosenfeld, Michel, 165

Ross, David, 54, 96

Ross, Dorothy, 99

Rostow, Eugene V., 119

Roth, Philip, 47

Sacks, Albert, 120–22, 126–27; *see also* legal process

Sarat, Austin, 167, 170, 173

Sartre, Jean-Paul, 131

Savigny, Friedrich Carl von, 105–6

Scalia, Antonin, 185–86, 195, 261 n.10

Schanck, Peter, 169

Schlag, Pierre, 164–65, 174, 176–78, 180–81

Schwartz, Murray L., 128

Scientific Revolution, 17–18

self-reflexivity. *See* postmodernism; postmodern legal thought

Sen, Amartya, 166

Seward, William H., 87

Shaw, Lemuel, 78–79

Shays' Rebellion, 67, 221 n.55

Sherry, Suzanna, 152

Shuttlesworth, Fred, 139

Silbey, Susan S., 175

Slaughterhouse Cases (*The Slaughterhouse Cases*), 104, 235 n.56

slavery, 71, 86–90, 158–59, 174

Smith, Adam, 25, 66, 68, 100

Smith, Steven D., 190–92, 198

Smith v. Goguen, 184, 259 n.110

social construction of the self, 41–42, 174–78

social Darwinism, 90

social engineering, 114–15, 239 n.84

social sciences, 109–10, 113–14; job shortage in, 150

sociological jurisprudence, 108–9, 112, 239 n.84

Souter, David, 182, 185

Southern Christian Leadership Conference (SCLC), 139

Spinoza, Benedictus, 23

Stanford Law School, 132
State v. Post, 222 n.65
Stefancic, Jean, 155–56, 167, 169, 174, 251
    n.48
Stephens, Alexander H., 89
Stewart, Potter, 143
Stoics, 202 n.5
Stone, Harlan F., 124
Story, Joseph, 5, 50, 52, 54–55, 75–76, 78, 81–82,
    224 n.90
storytelling, 159–60
structuralism, 28; *see also* power
Student Nonviolent Coordinating Committee
    (SNCC), 139
suffrage, 69–71, 116; voting as irrational, 166
Sumner, Charles, 88
Sunstein, Cass, 261 n.8
Supreme Court, in relation to legal scholars,
    194; *see also* Cooley, Thomas M.; postmodern
    legal thought
Swift, Zephaniah, 52, 63–64, 220 nn.48–49
Swift v. Tyson, 81, 217 n.23

Taney, Roger, 77
Tappan, David, 62
television, 29, 44, 118, 123, 168, 180–81
Terrett v. Taylor, 217 n.24
Texas v. Johnson, 183–84, 259 n.108; *see also*
    Flag Protection Act
text-analogue, 208 n.56
Textile Workers Union v. Lincoln Mills, 242
    n.99
Third Amendment, 142
Thomas, Kendall, 169, 173
Thucydides, 12
Tiedeman, Christoper G., 102–6, 234 n.53, 235
    n.54
Tocqueville, Alexis de, 4, 66, 68–69, 72, 76
toolbox, lawyer's, 190–91
totalitarianism, 115–17
Toulmin, Stephen, 94
transcendental legal thought. *See* legal process
transcendental nonsense, 111
transcendentalism (third-stage modernism),
    26
Tucker, St. George, 52, 63, 74
Tushnet, Mark V., 132, 145
Twenty-fourth Amendment, 116
Twenty-sixth Amendment, 116

Unger, Roberto, 149
United States v. Carolene Products, 124, 242
    n.103
United States v. Eichman, 259 n.108
United States v. Virginia, 259 n.112, 259–60
    n.114
universities, 91–93
University of Chicago Law School, 234
    n.51
University of Michigan, 150
utilitarianism, 65, 76–82

Van Buren, Martin, 70
Vietnam War, 130, 132, 137–38
Vinson, Fred M., 125
Virginia Bill of Rights, 58–59
Voegelin, Eric, 204 n.21, 205 n.36
voting. *See* suffrage
Voting Rights Act of 1965, 116, 239 n.87
War of 1812, 67–68
Warren Court, 126–29, 133, 141, 144, 149; *see
    also* Warren, Earl
Warren, Earl, 125–26, 127, 141, 143, 147; *see also*
    Warren Court
Washington, George, 59–60, 68
Washington v. Glucksberg, 185, 259 n.112
Wasserstrom, Richard, 133
Watergate Affair, 138, 158
Weber, Max, 3, 131, 203 nn.17, 19, 230 n.29
Wechsler, Herbert, 121, 127–28, 134
Weld, Theodore Dwight, 88
Wellington, Harry, 126
West Coast Hotel Co. v. Parrish, 242 n.103
West Publishing Company, 98, 155–56
West, Robin, 160
West Virginia State Board of Education v. Bar-
    nette, 242 n.103
White, Byron R., 143, 147
White, G. Edward, 81
White, James Boyd, 150
Whittier, John Greenleaf, 184
Williams, Joan, 162
Williams, Patricia J., 159
Williams, Wendy, 160
Williston, Samuel, 95
Wilson, James, 4–5, 49, 52–53, 65, 214 n.3, 220
    n.46, 220 n.50
Wittgenstein, Ludwig, 155, 167, 170–72
women, 67, 71, 145–48, 158; as lawyers and law

women (*continued*)
  professors, 231 n.29, 241 n.94; suffrage, 116;
  women's movement, 29, 140, 158; *see
  also* feminist jurisprudence; outsider
  jurisprudence
Wonderbread, 196–98

Wood, Gordon, 59, 68, 84
World War II, 6, 116–19, 122–24
Wythe, George, 50

Yale Law School, 147
Yntema, Hessel, 110